MOM, DAD, AND THE NEWFOUNDLAND RENAISSANCE

MOM, DAD, AND THE NEWFOUNDLAND RENAISSANCE

E.G. HYNES

BREAKWATER BOOKS LIMITED
www.breakwaterbooks.com
P O Box 2188 · St. John's · NL · Canada · A1C 6E6

CERTIFIED CANADIAN PUBLISHER

LIBRARY AND ARCHIVES CANADA CATALOGUING IN PUBLICATION
Mom, Dad, and the Newfoundland Renaissance / E.G. Hynes.
Hynes, E.G., author.
Canadiana (print) 20260219002 | Canadiana (ebook) 20260219045
ISBN 9781778530982 (softcover) | 9781778530999 (epub)
LCSH: Arts, Canadian—Newfoundland and Labrador—20th century.
LCSH: Newfoundland and Labrador—Intellectual life—20th century.
LCSH: Newfoundland and Labrador—Social life and customs—20th century.
LCGFT Novels.
LCC FC2169 .H96 2026 | DDC 709.71809/04—dc23

DESIGN Ian Sullivan Cant

COVER IMAGE Manfred Buchheit

AUTHOR PHOTO Susan Doupee

THE PUBLISHER GRATEFULLY ACKNOWLEDGES THE SUPPORT OF
The Canada Council for the Arts; The Government of Canada through the Department of Heritage; and The Government of Newfoundland and Labrador through the Department of Tourism, Culture, Arts and Recreation

Canada Council for the Arts | Conseil des arts du Canada
Canada
Newfoundland Labrador

PRINTED AND BOUND IN CANADA
Breakwater Books is committed to choosing papers and materials for our books that help to protect our environment. To this end, this book is made of certified and other controlled material.

FSC www.fsc.org MIX Paper | Supporting responsible forestry FSC® C103567

For those who came before me,
for Ron and Jane,
and for the artists.

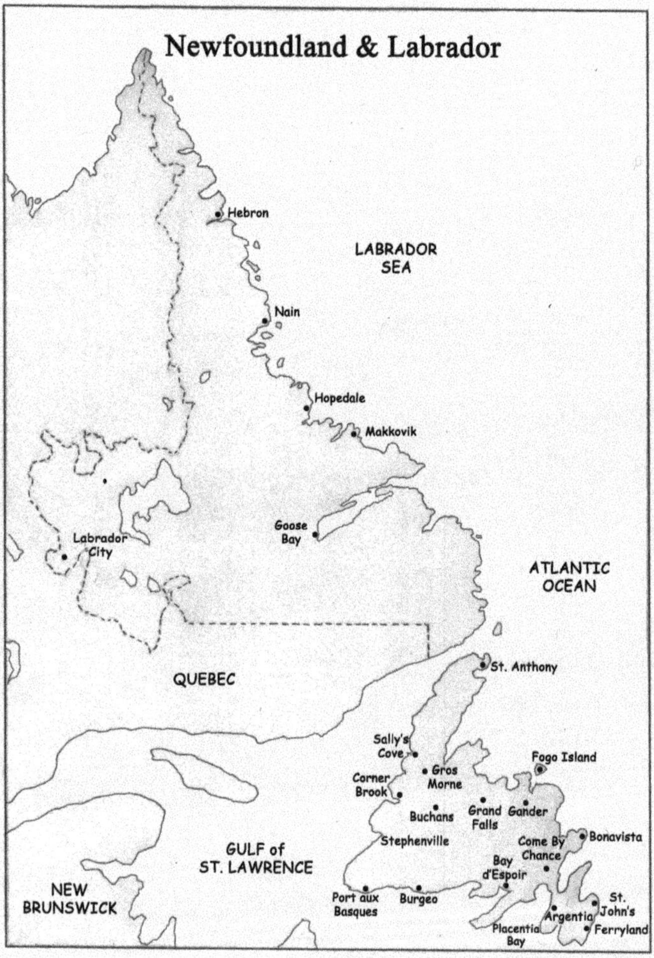

Map of Newfoundland and Labrador.[1]

1 Map by E.G. Hynes, 2023–2024.

Table of Contents

Preface

"For whatsoever from one place doth fall
is with the tyde unto another brought:
For there is nothing lost that may be found, if sought."

– Edmund Spenser, *The Faerie Queene* (1590)

Burial

Dad's funeral was hardly worthy of the name. There was nothing funereal about it. It was more than a celebration of his life. It was a *show.* Funerals are usually awful, gut-wrenching, no matter who the departed was or what they meant to you. The brightest flowers cannot obscure the washed-out and anguished faces trying to assimilate loss. Instead, Dad's funeral was simply beautiful, even joyful, and that warmed my heart even as it continued to sink in grief. The send-off that his family and friends gave him would have touched him to his core and puffed him up in equal measure: An honour guard of gorgeous Newfoundland dogs with tartan bandanas around their necks stood sentinel by each of the church doors, seemingly smiling at the people filing into the vestibule; fifteen hundred people filled the Basilica to its very capacity—any more would have been in violation of the fire regulations. The friends who rose to eulogize him were all such brilliant writers, raconteurs, and comedians, that the laughter flowed as easily as the tears among the congregation as we listened. Some of Newfoundland's most gifted musicians, Dad's friends and bandmates, played his most widely beloved songs, and dozens rose to dance with one another in the aisles when they played "St. John's Waltz." The impression that we were all in attendance at a grand and final concert rather than a funeral remained throughout the following reception at the Delta Hotel in downtown St. John's, where musician after musician took the stage to perform a song or two from the Ron Hynes catalogue. More than one person remarked to me that it was like "the show of the year," that "everybody was here," and they couldn't believe that Dad wasn't just about to stroll into the room from a side door, carrying his guitar, ready to get up onstage and play "Sonny's Dream" to finish the night.

Nearly two years later, during the summer of 2017, I went home to St. John's again—this time to scatter Dad's ashes. This was quite a production to arrange since the old man has four daughters, none of whom live in the same city. Consequently, finding a time when we could all get home at the same time took a while. Lily still wasn't quite ready to say goodbye to Dad. So, on a warm, bright August day, Rebecca and I picked up Lori, and the three of us set off up the Southern Shore in my little rented sedan, searching for the town of Long Beach.

Aunt Evelyn had suggested that Dad might appreciate being laid to rest by the river where, as a boy, he used to play with his siblings, cousins, and friends during the summers. The problem was one of access. Long Beach had been resettled some sixty years previously; while I consulted several maps, none identified with any real precision where the original site was located. Neither could I discern any road on any modern map that might lead us there. However, I was able to identify the river in question, which runs through the former town site and all the way south, where it flows into the Atlantic about halfway between the town of Portugal Cove South and the Cape Race Lighthouse. Using this exceedingly rough geography, the three of us embarked on a journey that I will never forget.

The drive south from St. John's was as beautiful and idyllic as it usually is in August, with those rolling emerald-green hills and those lovely brightly painted saltbox houses. The Great Beast, the deep blue Atlantic, reared up again and again to the east, its surface appearing deceptively calm. The three of us chatted as I drove, with Rebecca on moose-watch, singing along with the radio a bit. We drove by Dad's family home in Ferryland along the way and I raised a hand, smiling wistfully, as we passed. We drove through Aquaforte, Fermeuse, Renews, and Cappahayden. Then the ocean on our left disappeared, the radio signal chittered a little before collapsing into static, and we were into the barrens. Our sunny day turned suddenly cloudy and chill, a fitting accompaniment to the rough, boggy landscape that is nonetheless magnificent in its own stark and bleak way. Here we fell silent.

Then, the rocky, marshy ground became gently sloping green hills once more, and the fog rolled in as we entered Portugal Cove South.

As we drove through the town, I mentally consulted my rough geography once again. Long Beach would have to be east of here, but only one road was even vaguely situated in that direction. Unfortunately, this road was not really a road at all but an uneven path little more than a single car's width across, heavily laden with jagged, football-sized rocks. I eased forward apprehensively and gingerly over the first fifteen feet or so of loose, rocky ground, but it was clear that this particular car would have none of it. I had a brief moment of panic at my own stupidity for thinking this might be feasible. Even if we'd had ATVs, getting down that road would have been a tall order. Amidst thoughts of flat tires and broken axles, I was acutely aware that I was in a rental. My tolerance for risk fully exhausted, I reversed and retreated as carefully as I could.

Having made it back to the blissfully smooth pavement once more, we got out of the car and tried to get our bearings. The houses were clustered in little groups around the narrow winding road. A woman who was playing with her dogs behind the house nearest to us straightened as she heard the car doors close and waved us over. "Hello there!" We asked if she knew how to get to Long Beach. Without missing a beat, she asked without really asking: "You're Hyneses, aren't ya?" Anyone less used to the minuscule degrees of separation between Newfoundlanders might have been dumbfounded, but we simply smiled and replied in the affirmative. She directed us southward, through the scattered tangle of cheerful homes, their bright colours vivid even through the wreaths of fog. We came upon what was evidently the only passable road running east from Portugal Cove South, a narrow but thankfully much smoother gravel path that followed the shoreline along the southeastern tip of the Avalon Peninsula. I believed we had now gone too far south, but I thought that if we could find the river, then we might be able to follow it north towards the town site.

We drove slowly and carefully along the path, going no faster than a crawl as the fog thickened into a voluminous gluey curtain that prevented us from seeing more than nine or ten feet ahead of the car. We had gone only a short distance when a shadowy figure appeared out of the mist, sitting on the right side of the road, low to the ground, its head cocked to one side, growing more distinct as we approached.

"Is that a dog?" I asked, pushing up my glasses and squinting.

"No, I don't think so," Rebecca answered. "The shape . . . and it's red. It's a fox!"

As we drove slowly toward him, the fox watched us steadily. He did not shift nervously or back away at our approach; he just maintained his curious appraisal. As we passed, we noticed that he was missing his left rear leg. Poor little fella, I thought.

"He's still watching us," said Lori, craning her neck to look out the rear window. "Stop the car. Let's see what he does."

As soon as I hit the brakes, the fox jumped to his feet without hesitation and trotted down the road toward the car. He reared up on his remaining hind leg, pressed his front paws rather brazenly against the passenger side window and peered in at us.

"Aww! He must be hungry." Rebecca began to rifle through one of the lunch bags we'd packed that morning. With no more lunchmeat left to share, she pulled a carrot stick out of a Ziploc bag, rolled down the window an inch or two, and tossed the carrot out. The fox went after it with a will and then promptly hustled back toward the passenger side window and sat down once again to watch us, awaiting developments.

"How neat is this?" I mused. "I wonder what it means."

"It's Dad!" Lori exclaimed, and the three of us had a good laugh at the notion that the vast unknowable workings of the universe might have returned Ron Hynes to his beloved island home in the form of a three-legged fox. I'm always the first to scoff at such things—notions of spirits, magic, or the realms of the invisible. Yet, as we waved goodbye to our little friend and drove slowly away, I couldn't help but think of what I'd observed of the fox's stance when he first appeared out of the fog. Expectant. Attentive. As if he'd been waiting for us.

When we finally came upon the river, we pulled over and hopped out of the car in triumph. But as we approached and followed the river north with our eyes, my heart sank. I looked at Rebecca and her face wore a similar expression of defeat. There was no way we were going to be able to hike upriver toward Long Beach. The amount of twisted, thorny growth obstructing our path made the task virtually impossible. The riverbank before us would have to do. We comforted ourselves with the knowledge that we had, at least, found the river and that it was an undoubtedly beautiful and peaceful spot. We returned to the car briefly. Rebecca and I collected our ukuleles from the backseat and each of us retrieved a small vial containing some of Dad's ashes.

We sat down on the bank with him. Rebecca and I played some of his songs and we all sang together, though I can no longer remember which ones we played. We talked to him, told him we loved him, and each said our own silent goodbyes. Then, together, we released him into the river and watched as his ashes travelled south under the little bridge, headed for the vast and endless Atlantic.

We drove back to St. John's, each of us a little less talkative than we'd been on the drive up the shore. As we approached Renews, the radio mercifully sputtered to life again and provided some welcome distraction. Many of the specific events and circumstances surrounding Dad's passing are shadowy and amorphous to me now, as painful experiences usually become over time, but I remember that day fairly well. In spite of the sadness, I remember feeling something akin to what I'd felt on the day of his funeral; a profound appreciation simply for the beauty of being in Newfoundland. I thought of the lovely woman we'd met in Portugal Cove South, that perfect stranger who had called us by name. I thought of our odd and charming meeting with the three-legged fox, his total lack of skittishness. Even though my brain automatically intruded to suggest that the poor animal was probably inured to human contact because an animal rescue or compassionate local had taken him in and nursed him back to health at some point, something inside me nonetheless drew comfort from the notion that Dad was somehow looking lovingly at us through the fox's eager and curious eyes. I remembered the sight of his ashes receding south with the river's current towards the sea where, in the fullness of time, he might return again and again to rocky shores.

Exiles

Surely I'm romanticizing and, as a result, I can positively *feel* some of my fellow Newfoundlanders collectively rolling their eyes. I've encountered this attitude more than once, and I can quite easily understand it. Some Newfoundlanders and Labradorians dislike the mystification of the province in the public imagination, with its implications for the stereotyping and commodification of the region's culture, people, and natural environment. "Tell me how romantic this place is once you've lived through just one full winter here," I can hear some of them saying, "or once you've had to live low-income or unemployed here, like so many of us have had to." Some have made the argument that the emphasis on an idyllic outport culture, so essential to the tourism industry, has had the effect of glossing over the experiences of poverty and hardship of generations.[2] Intellectually, I know there are many arguments against the mystification or romanticization of life in Newfoundland that I cannot dispute, but I must honestly admit that nonetheless, for me, there has always been something quite magical about the place. My perspective is, of course, distorted and ill-formed because while I was born in St. John's, I did not grow up in Newfoundland. Neither have I lived there for any significant length of time since moving to Toronto with my mother and my sister Rebecca at just three years old, a fact that any bayman worth his salt would have instantly deduced had he seen me frigging around trying to find Long Beach.

In his essay, "Coming Home: Nostalgia and Tourism in Newfoundland," sociologist James Overton quite aptly described the experience of exiles like my sister and I—Newfoundlanders who grew up "away"—as one which makes of the province a kind of utopia, aided by the romantic nostalgia of their parents and fellow exiles from home. Indeed, I lived in Toronto for most of my life but, among ourselves, Mom, Rebecca, and I only ever referred to Newfoundland as "home." Historian Sean Cadigan's discussions of the nostalgia cultivated in exile communities rang true for me as well, particularly the appearance of Toronto bars and taverns owned or overwhelmingly patronized by Newfoundlanders. In such venues, folk singers like Harry Hibbs stoked a rosy nostalgia and a longing for home with traditional music and storytelling. I grew up in the Danforth/Riverdale area of Toronto and, while I never went to the recently shuttered Olde Eton House, a well-known haunt for expat Newfoundlanders just west of Jones and Danforth, I do recall the ever-present inference that when visiting this bar, one might find any number of homesick Newfoundlanders alternately tapping their feet to a rendition of "Heave Away" or openly weeping at "Tickle Cove Pond." Overton's description of the interactions between

2 James Overton, *Making a World of Difference: Essays on Tourism, Culture and Development in Newfoundland* (St. John's: Institute of Social and Economic Research, 1996): 105, 107; Susan Newhook, "Six Degrees of Film, Social, and Cultural History: The Fogo Island Film Project of 1967 and 'Newfoundland Renaissance,'" *Acadiensis* 39, no. 2 (Summer/Autumn, 2010): 59.

diaspora Newfoundlanders was also very familiar to me; whenever anyone Mom had known from Newfoundland was in town, they usually did not fail to visit, if not crash on our couch. One of Mom's best friends and fellow actor from Newfoundland, Barry Greene, shared a house with us during our first few years in Toronto. Up on the mainland, one got the sense that every Newfoundlander's house was a satellite beacon for visiting Newfoundlanders and fellow exiles.[3] The three of us went "home" every year to visit family, sometimes twice per year—two weeks at Christmas, two weeks in the summer.

The fact that Newfoundland was always the holiday destination for me most likely has everything to do with how I view the place. Yet still, even though my every inclination tends towards skepticism, Newfoundland remains for me a place in which I am never quite convinced that magic, spirits, or the realms of the invisible aren't real. I could be anywhere else on the planet and be satisfied in my conviction that the world, that the universe, is just as it seems. But when I'm in Newfoundland, the part of me that still has faith invariably stirs.

Widening the Circle

Following our odd journey to Portugal Cove South, I returned to my job teaching American history at a local high school in Los Angeles, where I'd been living since the spring of 2015. It was a job I absolutely *loved.* I had only had the opportunity to teach one full-year history course in my career prior to that, despite the fact that history is my greatest area of interest, education, and expertise. Before I completed my first year in the new job, I decided to pursue a master's degree in history as well. It took me nearly four years to complete, studying part-time and, for the most part, teaching full-time. And then, in March of 2020, just before I was about to begin work on my thesis, we all went home.

With all my graduate courses completed and no more teaching duties to attend to for the foreseeable future, I was thrown back on

---

3 James Overton, "Coming Home: Nostalgia and Tourism in Newfoundland," *Acadiensis* 14, no. 1 (Autumn 1984): 85–88; Sean Cadigan, *Newfoundland and Labrador: A History* (Toronto: University of Toronto Press, 2009): 251.

myself a bit. I had been working ten-to-fourteen-hour days for so long by that point that it felt a little like coming off one of those moving airport walkways at full stride. I also sustained a pretty serious back injury, which kept me bedridden for the summer and fall of 2020. Predictably, with no job to go to, unable to get out of bed, and with the pandemic raging outside, all of my concentration fell upon my thesis. Most of my graduate coursework had centred on the early modern Atlantic region, particularly seventeenth-, eighteenth-, and early nineteenth-century North America. I decided to base my thesis on colonial Newfoundland. The region was, I noted, paradoxically made conspicuous by its absence from early modern histories of North America despite Newfoundland's pivotal strategic, military, and economic importance in the contemporary Atlantic basin.

At the bottom of all of this, what was truly conspicuous was Dad's absence in my daily consciousness. I tend to put things away for a while after grief. I had even avoided listening to Dad's music in the years since his passing, but I don't suppose I had really buried him after all. I spent a year and a half reading extensively about the Newfoundland I didn't have the opportunity to grow up in and wrote what I hoped would be an interesting contribution to the greater body of work about early modern Newfoundland. I don't recall thinking much about Dad throughout that process, but I now realize that on some level, I must have been circling around him. He had been there all the time, at the bottom of a pile of work, waiting for his moment to reappear. My initial research was quite closely concentrated on Ferryland, his hometown. I do wonder at the fact that I chose such a thesis topic when Newfoundland was not even a footnote in any of the texts I'd read or the graduate courses I'd taken towards my degree.

Once I received my master's, I allowed the research I'd been doing on my thesis to take on a different focus. I'd already read Jerry Bannister's "The Politics of Cultural Memory," which examines how nationalism has influenced the writing of Newfoundland history and how cultural memory has been shaped and presented in Newfoundland and Labrador since the early 1970s. I had promptly fallen down a rabbit hole of footnotes, leading to a fairly broad historical discourse with personal significance for me that went far beyond simple heritage, one which described a historic cultural and artistic movement in which my own parents, Ron Hynes and Jane Dingle, had participated.

If ever there were an ideal post-graduate project for a fledgling historian, this was probably it. I drew up a working bibliography and enlisted my mother's assistance in gathering contact details for an oral history project.

Mom did not disappoint and, with her help, I managed to collect sixteen interviews with seventeen members of the arts community who were active predominantly in the theatre and music scenes of Newfoundland and Labrador during the late 1960s and 1970s. I have made every effort to treat these oral history narratives and their narrators with the respect and consideration they are owed. In terms of the interviews I collected personally, I have presented quotes from them verbatim as often as possible, only minimally editing or altering text in order for it to flow more smoothly and naturally in a literary sense. Almost no one, after all, speaks exactly in a manner conducive to easy reading. I have also avoided using any quote or section of any interview out of context. In other words, I have tried to be conservative about quoting a narrator on anything that did not represent a larger theme in the broader scope of their interview.

Discovery

During the spring of 2022, I finally listened to Dad's debut album, *Discovery*, for the first time, an experience that was beyond cathartic. When I heard "Ode to Long Beach," I flashed immediately to the summer of 2017 and my journey up the Southern Shore to scatter Dad's ashes with my sisters. It was one of those moments where the significance of something you did long ago finally becomes clear. I wept abruptly and noisily, which I'd thought I was done doing. At the same time, I couldn't help but smile at the incredible gift of being able to hear the voice of my now-departed father at just twenty-one years of age, a full decade before I was even thought of. I have since learned that my grandmother, Mary Ellen O'Neill Hynes, was in fact born at Long Beach. No wonder Aunt Evelyn had suggested it for Ron's final resting place. Hearing the song's lyrics, I had the first real sense of the scars that resettlement had left upon him, his family, and his community:

Old Long Beach Town, it has passed to the ages
Faded in shadows of mystical grey
Empty and bare like a book without pages
Ghost of an echo of children at play[4]

I also had a fuller sense of how little I actually knew about him, or about the dramatic changes that had taken place in Newfoundland following Confederation with Canada. Despite the implied centrality of such things to one's identity, both my father and my birthplace have remained rather mysterious to me for most of my life. Listening to Dad's debut album reinforced one thing I already knew: Songwriting was the primary medium through which he expressed himself. He didn't do the long analytical discussion or personal revelation—not with his kids anyway.

"I always felt like Ron and I were friends," singer and songwriter Mary Barry told me when I visited her during the summer of 2022, ". . . but Ron didn't 'do' friendship. Do you get my drift?'"[5] I did indeed get Mary's drift. Dad was kind, funny, loving, and he did have many lifelong friends, but he was always hard to get close to. He rarely talked about his family or his past. It seemed to me that the deepest, most personal, and most eloquent part of him spoke only in his art.

I recall my sister Rebecca once telling me about an opinion piece on Dad's work she had read a few years previously in some Newfoundland publication or other, something like "Ron Hynes is holding up the sky." The author waxed enthusiastic, she said, as if Ron were single-handedly holding the line for Newfoundland's cultural memory. I was in my late teens, when dads in general are still terminally uncool, and I was almost certainly just angry with him at the time, but I admit that in that moment, I sighed and rolled my eyes: "Gimme a break!" You will see, dear reader, that I have since arrived at a somewhat different perspective on the importance of a robust and well-supported artistic and cultural community, and I admit that to a certain extent, I'm prepared to eat my words—with no salt. And Dad was not alone, but just one of numerous artists whose work has also helped articulate the experiences and the cultural memory of the province's people.

---

4 Ron Hynes, "Ode to Long Beach," track 10 on *Discovery* (Audat, 1972), LP.
5 Mary Barry, interview by author, St. John's, August 15, 2022.

Dad's commitment to his art and to the people of Newfoundland and Labrador was undeniable and remained the great work of his life to the very end. Chris Brookes, co-founder and long-time artistic director of the Mummers Troupe, recalled seeing Ron play for the last time just three days before he passed away.

> There was a house concert, a tiny house concert out in Torbay somewhere. There must have been no more than twenty people there. The cancer had gotten Ron's voice and it was all cracking up, but he sang! By Christ, he did! He was determined.[6]

I was not at all surprised to hear that Dad was still actively and regularly performing pretty much right up until the day he died. Nor was I surprised to hear that at the hour of his death, all of the lights went out in downtown St. John's, plunging every bar into darkness and every amplifier and microphone into silence. His lifelong commitment to his music resulted in a wonderfully rich and prolific career. He won the love of his fellow Newfoundlanders by telling their stories, as well as the love of many of his fellow artists for his mentorship and the atmosphere of collaboration he helped to cultivate within the arts community. The story of the Newfoundland "renaissance,"[7] or the arts and culture movement that accompanied great changes in the decades following Confederation with Canada, also encompasses my family's origin story. My parents were among the artists who together tried to build an arts industry where there was little support, education, or infrastructure. Their art reflected many of the nationalist and anti-colonial critiques whose expression had become louder in recent years.

Against this backdrop, Mom and Dad found one another. They came together, they loved, they birthed two children, then they parted. By the time I was born, in 1982, the renaissance, an artistic movement that helped define a modern regional identity, seemed to be mostly over. I spent most of my young life ignorant of the fact that I was born into an aftermath, that there was a vast tapestry of life lived before my own advent that I had yet to fathom. Of course, I never thought of such

---

6 Chris Brookes, interview by author, Seattle/St. John's, July 23, 2022.

7 A term that is still avidly debated and criticized as a potential misnomer or for giving the arts and culture movement it describes a rather colonial tinge.

things—I just missed my Dad. I wondered why we weren't together, why we couldn't be together more often, why I didn't even really know him. How do you get to know a person you only see twice a year?

While such discussions are perhaps only suitable for a therapist, I was nonetheless forced to confront my family's fragmentation as part and parcel of this project. I listened to a great many stories about my parents, as individuals and as partners, from some of their closest friends and colleagues. Having done so and likewise having examined many of my own memories, I now recognize the influences behind everything they went on to do separately as artists, as people, and as Newfoundlanders. My enormous pride in the respective parts they played as pioneers in an artistic and cultural movement provides some salve to the sting of loss. True, it is a loss I cannot actually remember but it's also one I cannot recall ever living without. Revolution, as Chris Brookes once so aptly observed, can be made with less than perfect people.[8] And I would venture to add that families can too.

Growing up in a state of constant separation from Dad didn't afford much opportunity to forge familial bonds. As a result, I rarely felt closer to him or prouder of him than when he was up onstage, doing what he absolutely did best. In that vein, I have approached this project with a primary view towards what Mom, Dad, and their fellow artists did, what they created, and what they experienced as a group and as individuals during the period often referred to as the "Newfoundland renaissance." Between the mid-1960s and the early 1980s, Newfoundlanders and Labradorians began to explore, showcase, and celebrate art and culture of regional significance, blending heritage, nationalism, and a spirit of rebellion against political, economic, and cultural colonialism from Britain, the United States, and Canada. I have tried to emphasize the centrality of artists in the movement's development, especially as it pertains to the origin of a distinctly regional artistic style and ethos. Although Dad is gone, I'm lucky enough to still have my mother, actress Jane Dingle, and doubly lucky that she loves to tell stories. It is primarily to her and to the other sixteen members of the Newfoundland arts community whom I interviewed for this book that I owe my greatest debt of gratitude. I felt Dad's absence keenly throughout the course of

8 Chris Brookes, *A Public Nuisance: A History of the Mummers Troupe* (St. John's: Institute of Social and Economic Research, 1988): 174.

these interviews as did many of the narrators I spoke to, but I remain deeply appreciative that they were willing to speak for Ron, bringing him to life again if only in my mind's eye. They also brought to life a very exciting time and reaffirmed my conviction that one of the most significant talents Newfoundlanders possess is storytelling. And interestingly, despite the fairly common resistance to romanticization in the Newfoundland attitude, most of the narrators I spoke to did not fail to paint the Newfoundland of that time in a rather magical light.

"The years I spent in Newfoundland were truly the best years of my life," remarked actress Shifra Zisman.

> In the seventies, it was the most amazing place. It was bursting with the arts, any art, whether it was theatre, dance, music, it was just exploding. It was so *alive*. I don't have another word for it. You would go to Duckworth Street and just the bars, the music . . . it was really happening there.[9]

"I was so happy to be a part of it," musician, songwriter, and former lead singer of Figgy Duff Pamela Morgan told me.

> I had so much pride and joy in Newfoundland and so much love for the people. I spent a lot of time [travelling] in those early years learning songs from old people. And you don't just learn songs, you learn about their way of life, their history, their values.[10]

Many more artists besides Morgan began to visit the outports during the late 1960s and 1970s and to tour their original work there. While these efforts were sometimes gruelling with little funding and few paved roads, it was nonetheless an amazing experience according to actor, writer, and director Andy Jones. "We got to see Newfoundland in an incredible way," he remembered. As the provincial arts scene swelled and its artists gained confidence, they then began to speak to an audience of fellow Canadians beyond Newfoundland and Labrador. "It feels like we just laughed," Andy remembered of his early work and tours

9 Shifra Zisman, interview by author, Seattle/Toronto, August 4, 2022.
10 Pamela Morgan, interview by author, St. John's, August 3, 2022.

with the comedy troupe CODCO. "We just laughed ourselves to death and made fun of the whole world."[11] I'm honoured to have been given the opportunity to share with you some of the wonderful stories that were so generously shared with me, as well as the narrators' insights and experiences pioneering a new artistic sensibility and cultural landscape. It is primarily with their stories and oral narratives that I have constructed and curated this history.[12]

Laying Ron Hynes to rest was a long, complex, and painful process, one which is in many ways still incomplete, but this book has been an important part of that process for me. Despite the rather personal nature of this preface, I want to clarify that this book is not a memoir. Nor is it, strictly speaking, biographical. It is fair to say that it has journalistic overtones, but these considerations have not prevented me from sharing some personal or sentimental details about myself, my parents, or the narrators who contributed to this study. For one, the perspectives, life experiences, and emotional responses of narrators assist in painting a fuller picture of the world they inhabited. Moreover, it's difficult not to sentimentalize a bit when writing about your parents—particularly your departed father—and using as your guide and inspiration the words of some of the dearest friends and compatriots of their youth. Attempting to maintain the appearance of a dry and detached academic would be an exercise in denial under such circumstances. Above all, I intended this text to be a work of social history, of the "bottom-up" sort. I have attempted to analyze and synthesize what has previously been written about the period often referred to as the Newfoundland renaissance, a pivotal artistic and cultural movement in which both of my parents, among numerous others, played key roles. In addition, by offering my own framework and interpretation of the cultural developments in mid-twentieth-century Newfoundland, I hope to make at least a small contribution to the considerable body of work already completed on this fascinating era.

Completed March 2023.

---

11 Andy Jones, interview by author, St. John's, August 8, 2022.

12 Oral History Interviews Project 1 (OHI1): see Appendix 1.

INTRODUCTION

"Go forward. Keep finding ways to build and hold on.
Change and cherish. Figure a way."
– Donna Butt (2022)

"We Lived Here Then and We're Living Here Still"

Donna Butt's image jittered a little on my laptop screen, but her voice came through just as clear as a bell. With my webcam carefully positioned to disguise what a horrid mess my office actually was at the time, I listened avidly as she recalled the Mummers Troupe's 1976 play, *What's That Got to Do With the Price of Fish?*, a searing indictment of Canada's handling of the provincial fishing industry. As Donna spoke, the notion of Newfoundland art as a vehicle for political and social commentary, as well as an assertion of identity and pride, grew stronger.

> We created it collectively and we toured it across the country. We were all terribly idealistic, completely Newfoundland nationalists. The whole story was about what had been done to us, mostly what Canada had done to us. Ron wrote three or four songs for that show, but the one that I love, and have had people perform here since, now that we're in Trinity and we're doing shows here, is "Back Home on the Island." The words, the images . . .
>
> > *The tired nights 'round the warm wood stove, and*
> > *that old Sou'wester, how she really drove,*

Into every harbour and every cove, like the devil outside your door . . .

Nobody can deny what a great songwriter he is . . . was. Luckily, his voice will be heard for a long, long time if you live here. So, at the end of *What's That Got to Do With the Price of Fish?*, Rick Boland and I were onstage together and the show ended with us talking about our grandparents and who they were, that they were working people . . .

Back home on the island, people are watching the sun go down,

On what used to be a mighty good fishing ground; It'll never be the same again,

'Cause all the trawlers came and they picked it clean, and what was left of the pickings was a little too lean,

Now Lukey's old boat is a just a pale shade of green, and she's laying up on the sand . . .

We talked about them and what kind of people they were, what kind of place this was, that it had honour and dignity. We were very emotional about it. So there we were, Rick and I onstage, having poured our hearts out about where we were from, our own stories, and those of our grandparents, with Ron singing "Back Home on the Island."

We lived here then and we're living here still, and we're watching that ocean roll . . .

That's a connection, for me, to a time and maybe a certain innocence, of youth, of pride . . . I always loved that song.[13]

13 Donna Butt, interview by author, Seattle/Trinity, NL, December 20, 2022; Ron Hynes, "Back Home on the Island," 1976.

Origins and Context of the Cultural Movement

Since the 1970s, an appreciable though not extensive amount of writing and scholarly work has been completed on what Sandra Gwyn dubbed the Newfoundland renaissance in her 1976 article in *Saturday Night* magazine. Virtually every writer or scholar who has tackled the cultural movement refers to this article and understandably so. Its publication represents a particular moment when the political, economic, and social developments of the previous few decades appeared to coalesce into a new regional artistic and cultural sensibility, one inseparable from a burgeoning nationalist ethos. Gwyn discussed the varied and notably original profusion of theatre, visual art, literature, and film being created across the province at the time of the article's writing and the veritable explosion of up-and-coming artists among a population comparable to Hamilton or Winnipeg. They were producing "some of the freshest, brashest, most compelling art in the country," she wrote, and likened it to the artistic movement that preceded the Quiet Revolution in Quebec. Gwyn observed that like their Quebec counterparts, Newfoundland artists drew their inspiration from their folk tradition and that their art represented similar attempts "both to celebrate the past and to build a democratic future." What distinguished Newfoundland artists and cultural nationalists in Gwyn's eyes however, was how much closer to "the nerve ends of their own story" Newfoundlanders were.

> Their equivalent to the Plains of Abraham—Confederation—happened in their own lifetime. Confederation, resettlement, federal funds that have created a social as well as an economic dependency, the decline of the fishery, the decay of the old outport way of life, are the sources of their inspiration and their sense of urgency.[14]

Gwyn referred to the decline of the fishing industry, the adversarial attitude of government and business toward unions and workers, and the terrible after-effects of resettlement strategies that had followed

14 Sandra Gwyn, "The Newfoundland Renaissance," *Saturday Night* 91, no. 2 (1976), reprinted in *The Newfoundland Quarterly* 103, no. 3 (Winter 2010/11): 41–2, 53.

Confederation. She praised the artists who were pioneering a new arts industry, as well as speaking out through their art about life in the province and the province's place in Canada. The dark houses and empty windows in the paintings of Christopher Pratt, Gwyn noted, reflected the desolation of abandoned and resettled towns. The Mummers Troupe's latest play, *I.W.A.: The Newfoundland Loggers' Strike of 1959*, channelled the still-simmering resentment of loggers and their families toward Premier Joey Smallwood for his handling of the 1959 loggers' strike and his decision to decertify their union. The sketch-comedy theatre of CODCO addressed the inferior position of Newfoundland within the Canadian federation and defanged the Newfie joke, making the mainlanders who had always mocked Newfoundlanders the butt of the joke instead.[15] Gwyn's article was published roughly halfway through the most active period in the cultural movement and, therefore, did not establish any temporal beginning. However, the article represented broader recognition that meaningful change was already underway. The 1970s was arguably the most significant period of artistic and cultural development in Newfoundland, but while it is true that many such developments came to fruition during that decade, they were rooted in the political, economic, institutional, and cultural developments of the earlier twentieth century.

Most of those who have written about the Newfoundland renaissance are more or less in agreement about the movement's overall origin, influences, and progression. In general, regional scholars have emphasized the political and economic developments of the first half of the twentieth century as key to understanding the rise of a deeply nationalist cultural movement by the late 1960s and 1970s. Between 1900 and 1949, Newfoundland's polity evolved from a self-governing British Dominion to an undemocratic Commission of Government conceived by elites during a time of financial crisis, and thence to a Canadian province. These events proceeded with no cession of land from the province's Indigenous nations, no consultation with their band councils, or even consideration of their rights in the context of Confederation.

Such dramatic shifts in such a short period of time seem enough to give any group of people historical whiplash and nearly an entire generation had to pass before Newfoundlanders and Labradorians

15 Gwyn, 40–3, 47–8, 51.

as a group began to find the means to fully articulate who they once were, what they had lost, what they had become, and what they could yet be.[16] The efforts of Newfoundland and Labrador's first premier, Joseph R. Smallwood, to industrialize, modernize, and improve quality of life in the province had effects ranging across a full spectrum. Some were amazingly positive, such as the establishment of Memorial University of Newfoundland (MUN) as a fully accredited institution and dynamo of regional development. Others, like the efforts to industrialize the province, were uneven and often disappointing in their conception and/or implementation. Still others, like resettlement, proved difficult for communities to adjust to at best and disastrous for entire communities at worst, obliterating a way of life established over centuries in hundreds of outport towns.[17] After nearly two decades within the Canadian fold, Newfoundland and Labrador was still one of the poorest regions in the country with the highest unemployment rate—a figure that had continued to rise steadily since the early 1960s.[18] These struggles exacerbated a distinct sense of social and cultural inferiority that had long existed within the wider context of the Canadian federation, a stereotype that cast Newfoundlanders in the role of unenlightened, even unintelligent rustics, which they often couldn't help but internalize. The explosion of cultural activity and art in the province during the 1970s was in many ways a rejection of that cultural denigration, an assertion of dignity, worth, uniqueness,

---

16 James Overton, "A Newfoundland Culture?" *Journal of Canadian Studies* 23, nos. 1 & 2 (Spring/Summer 1988): 7, 9; Shane O'Dea, "Culture and Country: The Role of the Arts and Heritage in the Nationalist Revival in Newfoundland," *Newfoundland Studies* 19, no. 2 (2003): 379–80, 382; Jerry Bannister, "The Politics of Cultural Memory: Themes in the History of Newfoundland and Labrador in Canada, 1972–2003," Royal Commission on Renewing and Strengthening Our Place in Canada (March 2003): 129; Mekaela Gulliver, "Preserving the Best: Newfoundland's Cultural Movement, 1965–1983" (unpublished PhD thesis, Memorial University of Newfoundland, 2014): 5–6, 284–86; Bernice Hillier, "Confederation anniversary is no cause to celebrate, says Mi'kmaw elder," *CBC News*, April 1, 2024. https://www.cbc.ca/news/canada/newfoundland-labrador/mi-kmaq-confederation-anniversary-newfoundland-1.7158585; David MacKenzie, "The Indian Act and the Aboriginal Peoples of Newfoundland at the Time of Confederation," *Newfoundland and Labrador Studies* 25, no. 2 (2010): 161–181.

17 Jeff Webb, "The Rise and Fall of Memorial University's Extension Service, 1959–1991," *Newfoundland and Labrador Studies* 29, no. 1 (Spring 2014): 84–85; Harry H. Hiller, "Dependence and independence: Emergent nationalism in Newfoundland," *Ethnic and Racial Studies* 10, no. 3 (1987): 262; S.J.R. Noel, *Politics in Newfoundland* (University of Toronto Press, 1971), 262; Peter Neary, *The Political Economy of Newfoundland* (Toronto: Copp Clark, 1973), 226–27, 230.

18 Hiller, 260; Historical Statistics of Newfoundland and Labrador, Volume II (3), Newfoundland Statistics Agency (July 1981): 49.

talent, and potential.[19] Significant academic consensus exists regarding the notion that political, economic, social, and institutional factors helped set the stage for the development of Newfoundland's mid-twentieth-century cultural movement. But what about the role of individuals or small groups?

The Artists

While it was not until the 1970s that a distinct regional style of Newfoundland art and culture began to become more formalized, two different artistic traditions emerged on the island during the preceding century and more, both of which were propelled by individuals and small communities of artists. One tradition was town-based and the other outport-based. The distinctions between the two traditions strongly reflect one of the island's long-standing social divides: urban vs. rural or "townies" vs. "baymen" as they say in Newfoundland. Because this division stems from unequal access to wealth, merchant capital, communication, mobility advantages, and political and social influence, the obvious class implications served to politicize the art produced in both traditions by the 1970s.

The beginning of the "town" tradition dates to the early 1820s in St. John's. Over more than a century of development, it retained a thoroughly colonial and bourgeois character. Virtually the entire theatrical repertoire presented was drawn from the British tradition, although by the early- to mid-twentieth century, American plays began to be performed locally as well. Performers were frequently professional actors or experienced amateur community theatre groups from Britain, but even if they were locals, they delivered their lines using English accents. The mode of interaction between performers and audience was highly prescribed and traditional. This was the kind of theatre in which spectators dressed in their very best and kept as quiet and as still as possible during the performance. Performers would never acknowledge the spectators and a firm physical and psychic distance was imposed between those onstage and those in the audience. This thoroughly conventional theatre

19 O'Dea, "Culture and Country," 380, 382.

model was rarely if ever featured in most outports until well into the twentieth century. The outport tradition of artistic and cultural expression was almost opposed to the town tradition.[20]

The outport tradition was far less formal. Full-length plays were rarely if ever staged in outports and large-scale entertainments more often took on the appearance of a free-form variety show or musical/theatrical review. Local community leaders might organize concerts or "times" (a Newfoundland term that usually suggests some combination of musical performance, dancing, and general carrying on). Unlike the town tradition where the art was highly stylized with clear and privileged demarcation lines drawn between audience and performers, the outport tradition emphasized an "all-hands" attitude where anyone with a particular talent might be recruited for the show. Sometimes they might even be spontaneously pulled from the audience during the actual performance: "Sing us a song!" Isolation and low population density were the defining characteristics of rural outport communities, which resulted in extraordinarily close-knit and familiar relations between community members. Virtually everyone performing in or attending an outport concert would have known each other, so it was expected that performers and audience members might address each other directly and openly at times during the performance. Performers might make good-natured fun of local personalities outright and audience members might respond with saucy but equally good-natured retorts. These concerts might include skits, instrumental performances, singing, dance, or dramatic recitations, and were often guided by a host or presenter. Both the town and outport traditions represent efforts by small groups of individuals to build and/or maintain a repertoire of local art forms, all of which survived to become politicized and laden with signifiers of political affiliation and social class by the 1970s.[21]

---

20 Michael Devine, "Necessary Evils: Strangers, Outsiders, and Outports in Newfoundland Drama," (unpublished PhD thesis, University of Toronto, 2006), 76–77; David Ferry, "The Development of Professional Theatre in St. John's, 1967–1982: A Personal Perspective" (revised extracts from a presentation delivered at the conference, "Shifting Tides: Atlantic Canadian Theatre Yesterday, Today, and Tomorrow"), 26 March 2004, 144; Bernice Morgan, "The Culture of Place," *Newfoundland Studies* 19, no. 2 (2003): 374–75.

21 Devine, 76, 82–88, 90; Alan Filewod, "The Mummers Troupe, the Canada Council, and the Production of Theatre History," *Theatre Research in Canada* 19, no. 1 (Fall 1998): 3–34. Accessed April 1, 2023. https://journals.lib.unb.ca/index.php/tric/article/view/7116/8175.

For theatre artists, touring the outports at the time was an amazing experience and most of the narrators I interviewed spoke fondly and enthusiastically about those early tours despite the hardships of the road and the tight budgets. "People were not expecting us," Andy Jones remembered.

> A lot of these tiny towns had never seen a theatre company before. My favourite line from one of the bookers was: "Oh, you came! They came! They're here!" In other words, no publicity, nothing. They didn't think we were actually going to come and do a play. "Oh, you came!"[22]

Touring the outports could only have reinforced the notion of a vast gulf between the "town" tradition of theatre and the rural tradition of the community concert, which many outport Newfoundlanders were used to attending. Audience behaviour and reactions to the performances were as different as one can imagine from the typical middle-class theatregoers in St. John's. It was positively vaudevillian, my mother, Jane, recalled. "People would be eating in the front row, eating sandwiches, talking to each other, talking to the actors. They were so relaxed! I thought: 'My God, they're shouting out stuff!'"[23] In response to the action they saw unfolding on the stage, audience members sometimes yelled out injunctions to the actors or speculated loudly: "You'd better get out of there now!" or "What's she gon' do now, I wonder?"

> When we did *The Doctor in Spite of Himself*, Kevin Noble played the doctor and I played the nurse. In the play, they're attracted to each other and there's this big chemistry going on onstage. It had been choreographed so that the two people are on opposite sides of the stage and come toward each other in slow motion. One night, Kevin and I were going through this scene. We came close together until we were almost touching. At that moment, the old skipper who was sitting there smoking his pipe in the front row yelled out: "My son, what's wrong wit' ya? I'd be aboard 'er by now!"

---

22 Jones, interview.

23 Jane Dingle, interview by author, St. John's, August 23, 2022.

> Sure, the place went up then. Everyone was laughing. And Kevin started to shake with laughter. He was sweating under the lights and he started to shake and I could see the drops falling. We didn't break, but nearly.[24]

Jane Dingle and Kevin Noble, *The Doctor in Spite of Himself.*[25]

***

Social history is interested in the experiences, roles, and impacts of various individuals and small groups on larger movements and events. Indeed, some writers and commentators have given credit to particular individuals for helping to catalyze Newfoundland's cultural movement. In his editorial foreword to the 1973 anthology of Newfoundland literature *Baffles of Wind and Tide*, Clyde Rose, co-founder of Breakwater Books, partly credited Canadian writer Farley Mowat with helping to launch a regional literary movement. Mowat, who was an Ontario native,

24 Dingle, interview.
25 Photo by Paul Dingle.

had fallen in love with Newfoundland, moved to Burgeo, and become one of the province's most devoted allies and promoters by the 1960s, during which time he wrote several works about Newfoundland. "He taught us," Rose wrote, "that we were worth writing about."[26]

In his essay "Sparking a Cultural Revolution," James Overton examined the contributions of Farley Mowat, Newfoundland writer Harold Horwood, and Premier Joseph Smallwood to the emergence of the Newfoundland renaissance with clear acknowledgement of the weaknesses of the "great man" approach to history—the sort of narrative that lionizes a few elites and tends to obscure either the institutional or grassroots nature of movements. Overton asks the reader to temporarily suspend their distrust of the "great man" framework long enough to fairly examine the contributions of these three figures, which are admittedly considerable. In establishing Memorial University of Newfoundland with a particular vision and mandate, Smallwood created the basic institutional framework and policy conditions in which the cultural movement germinated. Horwood and Mowat both made impressive literary contributions to the cultural life of the province, spurring other local aspiring writers to continue developing a Newfoundland literary tradition, and both attempted to use their influence for Newfoundland's development and betterment in multiple ways. These three individuals did indeed play important roles in initiating and contributing to the flowering of the cultural movement during the later 1970s, but as Overton observes, the cultural fires "were already smouldering" during the mid-1960s when Horwood and Mowat pitched their nationalist arts manifesto and their ideas for a historical reclamation project to Smallwood.[27]

The faculty, staff, and students from the Folklore department at MUN were similarly inspired and were already collecting oral histories in the outports. Aspiring young visual artists, writers, actors, and musicians, some working with MUN Extension and some conducting research independently, began to undertake similar visits to outports to collect oral histories and examples of Newfoundland folk music, art,

---

26 Clyde Rose (ed.), *Baffles of Wind and Tide* (Portugal Cove, Newfoundland: Breakwater Books, 1973), xi.

27 James Overton, "Sparking a Cultural Revolution: Joey Smallwood, Farley Mowat, Harold Horwood and Newfoundland's Cultural Renaissance," *Newfoundland Studies* 16, no. 2 (2000): 169–72, 187–88, 197–99.

and theatre traditions. Resident artists who had lived all of their lives in the outports began to receive invitations to perform or showcase their talents around the province. Encouraged by the well-funded institution of Memorial University, which was staffed by multitalented and often extraordinarily progressive individuals,[28] numerous young aspiring artists together pioneered a new artistic and cultural sensibility, one which clearly hearkened back to the heritage of settler Newfoundlanders but which was also imbued with elements of the 1960s counterculture and of concurrent decolonization, independence and nationalist movements elsewhere in the Atlantic world.

The Newfoundland Renaissance and the Atlantic Perspective

In his seminal work, *Atlantic History: Concept and Contours,* Bernard Bailyn partly credited historical geographer D.W. Meinig with helping to articulate a crystallized social history perspective on the early modern Atlantic basin. The Atlantic world, he wrote, was a stage on which a "vast interaction" played out, one that involved far more than the simple advent of Europeans to North America. It was a sharp, dramatic and frequently violent interaction, not between an "old" and "new" world, but between "two old worlds," which permanently and irrevocably altered both "and integrated them into a single New World." The entire Atlantic basin felt the impact of this collision of cultures: Europeans, Africans, and Indigenous North and South Americans.[29] Bailyn observed that a social history approach was particularly crucial to articulating the Atlantic perspective because traditional frameworks such as predominantly imperial or institutional ones tend to underemphasize the human element and often to the detriment of a richer,

28 Anita Best, interview by author, Seattle/St. John's, December 4, 2022; Edythe Goodridge, interview by Cathryn Boak, "Pathways" (1984), video, 30:12, Memorial University of Newfoundland Educational Television Centre. http://collections.mun.ca/cdm/ref/collection/extension/id/8710ai:collections.mun.ca:extension/871; Webb, "The Rise and Fall of Memorial University's Extension Service," 99.

29 Bernard Bailyn, *Atlantic History: Concept and Contours* (e-book version) (Cambridge: Harvard University Press, 2005) 454–462.

fuller historical perspective.[30] A framework that emphasizes the impetus for change and development as initiated by ordinary individuals and small groups reveals a much more nuanced picture of historical process than one that primarily emphasizes broad shifts in large economic, political, or institutional bodies. It is for this reason that I chose to ground this book within Bailyn's conception of the Atlantic perspective. This should not suggest, however, that I discount or ignore the considerable influence that elites, governments, or institutions had on the development of the 1960s and 1970s cultural movement in Newfoundland and Labrador.

The Atlantic framework provides us with a significantly nuanced mental picture of the shape of international interactions in the Atlantic basin since the beginning of the Age of Sail. Historically, the Atlantic has been seen as a barrier to be conquered before international and cross-cultural interactions could take place. Instead, the Atlantic perspective views the ocean as a highway between regions and peoples, a surprisingly accessible medium through which people, goods, and ideas moved far more easily during the Age of Sail than one might suppose, making this exceptionally broad and diverse world seem much smaller. For most of modern history, as Bailyn observes, the Atlantic basin was primarily a conduit for exploration, trade, conquest, and slavery. The economic fruits of Indigenous dispossession and genocide, of slavery and slavery-dependent economic activities, permeated all societies situated around the early modern Atlantic.[31] In recent decades, historians have begun to write more frequently of a "Black Atlantic" as well as a "Red Atlantic," amplifying the historical voices of people of African and Indigenous North and South American descent. These efforts have resulted in diverse historical perspectives that challenge the Eurocentricity of the early modern Atlantic history field, which has traditionally treated Black and Indigenous communities as rather passive historical actors or as token-esque footnotes in larger histories. These developments heighten the many close connections as well as differential experiences between different groups of Atlantic peoples. While different peoples may have experienced broad historical shifts differently, many responded to them in similar ways. By embracing

30 Bailyn, locations 342–50, 392–402.

31 Bailyn, locations 760–68.

and incorporating into their own practice some of the ideas and art forms of their neighbours, Atlantic peoples demonstrated how truly interconnected the Atlantic basin is and has always been.

By the mid-twentieth century, with the advance of mobility and communications technologies, people, goods, and ideas were travelling faster than ever. Across the post–World War II Atlantic basin, decolonization, independence, and ethnic and regional nationalist movements were popping up everywhere. Many of these movements were artist-led as cultural pride began to find expression in visual art, music, drama, literature, and film. Just as the art produced by young Newfoundlanders during the 1970s was in some ways a resurrection of regional forms in clear protest against more rigid, stylized, and colonial art forms of predominantly British and American origin, similar movements were underway across the Atlantic world, including, paradoxically, *within* those enormous colonial entities. Functioning either as forms of protest against injustice or as accompaniment to liberation or nationalist movements, forms of regional artistic expression were flourishing around the various Atlantic peripheries from Europe to Africa, in South America, the Caribbean, and North America. Often these artistic movements could not be divorced from the political goals of their adherents or the social reforms they championed. These were movements that hearkened back to one's heritage, established a sense of group solidarity, sought justice and social change, and encouraged authenticity and truth in art above glamour, spectacle, escapism, or refinement.

During the late 1960s and 1970s, Newfoundland artists sought to reconnect with their cultural roots and produce art of regional significance. Because this process began against the backdrop of massive international social change and concurrent ethnic and cultural nationalist movements elsewhere in the Atlantic region, clear reflections of burgeoning social change were finding their way into many examples of artistic expression and practice in Newfoundland. Bands like Figgy Duff, Red Island, and the Wonderful Grand Band blended the traditional music of Newfoundland settlers with current folk, rock, and jazz influences then emerging from the British Isles and the United States. Some of these artistic influences emerged from the context of ethnic, nationalist, or liberation movements underway within the Atlantic basin such as the Northern Ireland conflict and the American civil rights movement. Literature and drama written by settler Newfoundlanders began to reflect a greater consciousness of the province's Indigenous peoples, the issues facing them, and the advocacy they were then undertaking on their own behalf. With the advent of an international movement for Indigenous rights, plays like the Mummers Troupe's *Weather Permitting* began to help shine a light on groups of Indigenous Newfoundlanders and Labradorians who had been largely forgotten by many of the province's settler contingent for decades. As the women's movement progressed across the international stage, books, plays, and artistic practice in the province began to reflect a nascent feminism and intimations of a sexual revolution already underway. Plays like *Stars in the Sky Morning* helped centre the voices of women in the arts, in Newfoundland history, and in the province generally. Finally, the Newfoundland artistic and cultural aesthetic couldn't help but be influenced by the heavy international tide of decolonization and increasingly clearer calls for social and economic justice. World War II had been over for less than thirty years and the new imperialist system seemed to be as much an economic as a political one. As a consequence, Newfoundland art in the 1970s featured heavy indictments of both colonialism and capitalism, as well as a deeply pro-labour stance.

This book aims to emphasize the heavily people-powered nature of cultural developments in Newfoundland and Labrador during the late 1960s and 1970s. While it is true that federal and provincial agencies and institutions did play important roles in fostering and funding the arts in the province at key times during the 1960s and 1970s, this assistance was invariably offered within a piecework structure and was often given to facilitate short-term economic development goals, particularly around tourism, leaving broader provincial arts policy significantly underdeveloped. The most notable exception is Memorial University, particularly the MUN Extension program. MUN was probably the most important institutional source of support for artistic and cultural workers during this period, although the Canadian Broadcasting Corporation (CBC) should also be acknowledged as a major employer and incubator of local talent at the time. This is precisely why a fuller historical analysis of the cultural movement requires a shift in focus from institutions to the artists themselves—because many of the artists that pioneered new modes of seeing, of creating and performing during the cultural movement, did so with far less institutional or financial support than one might suppose.

Many Voices

The Newfoundland renaissance, if it can be termed such, was a massive collective effort that required the concerted action of innumerable individuals, too many to name. In light of this, perhaps the best approach to documenting the history of the 1970s arts movement is one that emphasizes the *numerous* voices—as many as possible—that helped to define, clarify, and celebrate Newfoundland culture and identity at a time when both seemed to be at risk of erasure. At the same time, documentary research must also surely be an important facet of such a project. Policy papers, government statistics, news reports, and magazine articles are very important for a historian who hopes to deal in facts. Yet, such sources cannot always speak sufficiently to the feelings and motivations of the broader population of a movement, or of the diversity of perspectives among them. They can speak with only limited eloquence or precision regarding how individuals formed their particular views on the world, or how those views translated into action. Oral history is, perhaps, better suited to such a purpose.

Of course, this is not to say that oral history does not have its limitations in terms of reliability, or in terms of what questions it may conclusively answer for the historian. Oral histories are necessarily subjective, biased, and vulnerable to corruption and errors based on either the accuracy of the narrator's memory, or on how much of the truth they are personally willing to tell. Traditionally, historians have been exhorted to "return to the documents" in order to give their work the best evidentiary support possible and such orthodoxy is still sound advice for most scholars. However, as pieces of evidence, one could argue that documents and oral history narratives may sometimes share similar potential weaknesses. Like oral narratives, documents are created by individuals and as such, often have the creator's subjectivities, biases, omissions and errors—intentional or unintentional—baked right in. What's more, one can ask an oral history narrator to elaborate on something they have said. They can request an additional, more thorough interview. A document, on the other hand, simply says what it says and it is up to the scholar to work out the most informed interpretation they can with whatever resources and information they have at their disposal.

The history field as it currently exists is a relatively young discipline. Only in the twentieth century did historians begin to develop the kinds of investigative and interpretive methodologies and habits of mind that helped add legitimacy to the profession. This discipline was needed to curb the fanciful editorializing and the tendency toward broad generalization, in the absence of evidence, that many more historians tended to engage in a century and more ago. Yet, humanity's narrative extends far further back than a mere century. Over the millennia of human history, stories have been passed down to us by our ancestors, often for thousands of years before being written. Oral history remains important in virtually every global culture.

With these perspectives in mind, I approached this study with a tri-faceted focus on previously published academic analysis, documents from the period, and fifty-four oral history interviews representing a total of thirty-nine respondents.[32] As for the first type of source, I have relied primarily on the work of historians Peter Neary, S.J.R. Noel and Sean Cadigan for my analysis of the region's political and economic history. Furthermore, considerable analysis on the Newfoundland cultural movement has been completed by scholars working in the fields of history, sociology, politics, economics, and the arts and this study has benefited immensely from their work, particularly that of James Overton, Jerry Bannister, Jeff Webb, and Alan Filewod. The unpublished doctoral dissertations of Michael Devine and Mekaela Gulliver were also invaluable and represent some of the most recent and thorough works in this subject area.

A good deal of analysis on arts policy and the position of the arts in Newfoundland's cultural and economic life was written around the turn of this century, but little examination of the late 1960s and 1970s arts and culture movement has been undertaken in the years since. To date, as Overton observed, there has been no comprehensive study of

32 Please note, I have only quoted in this volume from interviews I conducted personally. Because I had no formal agreement with a sizeable proportion of the narrators who contributed to either the STAGE Project or the Reid Theatre History Project, I have not quoted directly from those interviews in this study without express permission. Rather, I have largely used the interviews from these two studies as references to track how widespread certain experiences and perspectives were among practising artists and cultural workers of the time. In a few instances, these interviews also helped confirm various historical details and chronology. While a few dozen respondents is an admittedly small sample size for any research project, especially considering the inordinately heavy presence of artists and contributors to the provincial cultural movement, the similarities among perspectives and experiences across a range of these interviews is meaningful and sometimes striking (see Appendices 2, 3, 5, and 6).

the overall movement.[33] This book represents, among other goals, my attempt to analyze and synthesize existing historical perspectives as well as offer my own. However, I cannot claim that the focus of this study is at all comprehensive in terms of its coverage. Almost all of the interviews I collected were with actors and musicians—although as I shall illustrate, these artists were and are far more multidisciplinary in terms of their practice throughout their careers. Because the theatre and music scenes were the primary milieu through which my parents moved during the renaissance period, most of the oral history collection I personally undertook was with their fellow actors and musicians. The majority of this study's focus is therefore on the development of Newfoundland theatre and music, although other areas of artistic and cultural development will be touched upon periodically.

Relevant documents I have examined include census data, policy papers, business directories, maps, newspapers, and magazine articles. The memoirs of Chris Brookes and Dudley Cox helped me delve more deeply, more personally, and more minutely into the world they wrote about. Yet finally, it is often in the art itself that the artist, whose voice I want to amplify above all, actually speaks. I have therefore also looked to the creative developments of that time, particularly in music and theatre, to help articulate the artists' perspectives and experiences.

We have already observed that an oral history narrator's contribution could be compromised by memory problems, but these may not be limited to simple forgetfulness or the decline of memory over time. Rather, a more pertinent concern in this case might be the shaping that occurs within memories over time, especially if the narrator has told the story many times in a particular context or with particular associations or connotations. Many of the narrators I spoke to have shared their experiences in multiple interviews and almost certainly many more times under less formal circumstances. The human memory has limitations and how a person perceives an historical event, especially years later, may not represent anything approaching a complete understanding of the event. Another potential weakness is the bias of the historian themselves; I am writing a history in which I am locating my own parents—enough said. In reviewing my research process during the course of writing this text, I will admit that my own preconceived

33 Overton, "Sparking a Cultural Revolution," 167.

ideas about what I was likely to discover in my interviews fairly leapt out at me from my initial research notes. I have therefore taken careful account of how my own bias might have altered the shape of the interviews I conducted, or how it might have influenced my interpretation of the narrators' responses at the time. I tried to keep these methodological issues in mind throughout the analysis phase of this study.

Embarking on an oral history project, the issue foremost in my mind was that of ethics, especially as it pertains to the potentially problematic intersection of personal narrative and commercial publication. Personal narratives are the sum of one's life experiences, one's thoughts, beliefs, and emotions. What else can a person claim to own with more legitimacy? And therefore, with all the implications for capitalist commodification of people's stories and identities, how can one ethically use another's personal narrative in a commercial publication?

While I remain somewhat conflicted on this issue, I tried to address it by reserving copyright of each interview to the narrator and allowing ample opportunity to request redactions. One narrator rather sheepishly asked me if I could just edit out all the times they said "f--k," which honestly made me sad because it was every other sentence, and hilarious. However, the incidence of redaction requests throughout the course of this project was actually much less common than I thought it would be. The vast majority of such requests pertained to deeply personal information that neither added nor detracted from the broader scope or overall themes of any one interview. Every stage of this project was characterized by an "opt-in" philosophy, which I felt helped begin to reconcile the ethical conundrum that exists where oral history and commercial publication intersect.

Chapter One
1949–1966

"The prayer to which we say 'Amen'
is written with a poisoned pen."
- Ron Hynes, "The Final Breath" (1992)

The Great War, a Crippling Debt, and a Quiet Coup

The rise of a cultural nationalist movement in Newfoundland during the late 1960s and 1970s had a great deal to do with the political climate that unfolded with the advent of Confederation with Canada in 1948–49. Andy Jones, undoubtedly one of the most active and prolific artists to emerge during the renaissance, illustrates how he perceived this profound change as a member of his generation.

> We were very steeped in Newfoundland politics. Our parents had voted on Confederation and those debates were still on the go. I had relatives who never spoke to each other . . . well, they spoke but they were very cool to each other because of Confederation. Catholics were supposed to be anti-Confederate and my father actually was pro-Confederate. In fact, he ran for the National Convention. My uncle was Sir Albert Walsh.[34] He signed the Terms of Confederation

34 First Lieutenant-Governor of the province of Newfoundland and Labrador and later chief justice, Walsh also officiated at Smallwood's swearing-in ceremony as the province's first premier (Neary, *The Political Economy of Newfoundland, 1929–1972*, 171–72).

> and he was a Catholic and pro-Confederate. I love this story and I've told it—in fact, I've even used the line in a play. When he did that, Catholics were quite upset with him. Judge Fox, who was a leading Catholic layman . . . His wife wrote him [Walsh] a telegram that day saying: "Ride on traitor—you have earned your spurs."[35]

The acrimony between those in favour of responsible government[36] and those in favour of Confederation rings clear here and it is obviously loaded with baggage from long-standing religious divides in Newfoundland. However, other differences such as social class and place of residence played roles in the decision-making process of voters as well. While there was significantly mixed response to the 1948 referendum across classes as well as religious and regional differences, in general, those from higher population centres, particularly the Avalon Peninsula, tended to lean more towards responsible government, as did many of this eastern region's Roman Catholics. The Protestant middle and upper classes concentrated on the Avalon Peninsula also tended to lean more toward responsible government. Meanwhile, the working class and Newfoundlanders from rural areas beyond the more populous Avalon tended to lean more toward Confederation.[37]

Hostility and both official and unofficial discrimination against Catholics—a majority of whom were Irish rather than English—had a long history in Newfoundland dating back to the first significant waves of Irish immigration during the mid-eighteenth century. While religious turmoil was no longer the order of the day in the twentieth century, sectarianism remained an effective and ever-present force in

35 Jones, interview.

36 I use the term "responsible government" here rather than "independence" because independence as it is typically understood in the colonial Atlantic context was not actually on the ballot in 1948. As a Dominion of the British Empire, Newfoundland was not, strictly speaking, independent to begin with. Foreign affairs were controlled by the British Parliament, in which Newfoundland had no representation, and there was always an appointed imperial governor with the powers of "reservation" signing off on the decisions of Newfoundland's House of Assembly (Jeff A. Webb, "Confederation, Conspiracy and Choice: A Discussion," *Newfoundland Studies* 14, no. 2 [1998]: 179–81, 187).

37 Noel, 259–60; Mark Graesser, "Who voted for Confederation? An analysis of voting patterns in the 1948 National Referendum" (presented to the Newfoundland Historical Society Symposium "Encounters with the Wolf," March 20, 1999); Peter Neary, *The Political Economy of Newfoundland, 1929–1972*, 105–106; Webb, "Confederation, Conspiracy and Choice: A Discussion," 176–77.

Newfoundland politics. A significant concern for Catholics was that Newfoundland's denominational school system might be threatened by union with Canada.[38]

Some have argued that a greater weight of fearful indecision rested upon those in the outports than those in more prosperous or urban areas. The middle and upper classes, the merchants, business owners, office-holders and educated professionals likely felt more secure in choosing responsible government than their working-class brethren and poorer, rural counterparts. If Newfoundland returned to responsible government, those with the most resources would undoubtedly have become the nation's power brokers, since they would be best placed to take control of the region's destiny. But among the working class and those in many rural areas, the memories of the lean interwar years and the Great Depression were still fresh and the security offered by Canada's social safety net would be a guarantee that they and their families would never again be at risk of starving when the fishery next suffered a downturn or when the next international economic crisis should befall them.[39] St. John's had a fairly consistent history of appropriating the lion's share of relief funds during hard times by offering the rationalization that outport communities were better equipped for self-sufficiency to begin with. This was a questionable notion when one considers the vast inequities in political influence and access to capital or resources held by urban and rural populations, respectively. At this time, half of the country's labour force was still engaged in the fishery and most rural fish producers continued to exist in the merchant stranglehold of a "truck" credit system in which merchants advanced supplies annually to fishermen in exchange for virtually their entire catch. In a rural economy where cash rarely changed hands, the phrase "hard times" could often seem an understatement. In the end, in the latter of two referenda, the outcome was painfully close: just fifty-two per cent of Newfoundland voters elected to join Canada rather than return to responsible government as a British Dominion.[40]

The razor-thin margin of the 1948 referendum's outcome made the decision to join Canada contentious and controversial for many people

38 Neary, *The Political Economy of Newfoundland, 1929–1972*, 12–13; Noel, 21, 267–68.

39 Noel, 259–60; Neary, *The Political Economy of Newfoundland, 1929–1972*, 105–106, 140–41.

40 Peter Neary, *Newfoundland in the North Atlantic World, 1929–1949* (Montreal: McGill-Queen's University Press, 1988): 9–10; Noel, 259.

in the province in the decades to come and, over time, a fundamental disconnect emerged between the general academic perspective on Confederation and the perspective of many in the broader provincial public. The manner in which the loss of nationhood and Newfoundland's subsequent absorption into Canada occurred created fertile conditions for the growth of conspiracy theories. Members of the academic community working in the Newfoundland history space in recent decades have roundly and repeatedly challenged the notion that Newfoundland's Confederation with Canada was illegitimate.[41] Meanwhile, some nationalist commentators and independence-minded Newfoundland scholars have continued to posit that the referendum might have been rigged in one or more ways, a notion that has been amplified in public discourse in the decades since Confederation.[42] This suspicion was explored in literature and art as well, notably in the 1993 feature film *Secret Nation*, written by Ed Riche and directed by Michael Jones.

Ron had a great albeit small role in the film, which starred Cathy Jones as Frieda Vokey, a plucky graduate student investigating the conditions under which Newfoundland had joined Canada. Ron played the role of Daniel Maddox, a scummy academic in possession of a confidential collection of historical documents Frieda surreptitiously reads and pilfers after sleeping with him. I was told by production staff who worked on the film that Ron's bare backside was photographed several times during the course of filming that particular scene and I am grateful beyond measure to Michael Jones that no such shot made it into the final cut of the film.[43] Still, it's amusing to know that Dad's behind is preserved on film somewhere—for posterity you might say. Besides his "brief" role, Ron also wrote a song for the production called "The Final Breath," which won a Genie Award from the Academy of Canadian Cinema & Television for best original song. Its refrain speaks

41 Raymond B. Blake, *Canadians at Last: Canada Integrates Newfoundland as a Province* (Toronto: University of Toronto Press, 1994); Neary, *Newfoundland in the North Atlantic World, 1929–1949*; Webb, "Confederation, Conspiracy and Choice: A Discussion".

42 Phillip McCann, "British Policy and Confederation," *Newfoundland Studies* 14, no. 2 (1998): 155–68; John Fitzgerald, "Newfoundland Politics and Confederation Revisited," *Newfoundland Studies* 9, no. 1 (1993): 103–24 and "'The Difficult Little Island' That 'Must Be Taken In': Canadian Interests in Newfoundland During World War Two," *Newfoundland Quarterly* (Spring 2001): 21–8; Greg Malone, *Don't Tell the Newfoundlanders: The True Story of Newfoundland's Confederation with Canada* (Toronto: Knopf Canada, 2012).

43 *Secret Nation*, directed by Michael Jones, starring Cathy Jones (National Film Board, 1993); Pamela Hall, interview by author, St. John's, August 9, 2022.

eloquently of how Ron and many of his fellow Newfoundlanders felt about the process that led Newfoundland to become part of Canada: "*The prayer to which we say 'Amen' is written with a poisoned pen.*"[44]

While few historians believe that Newfoundland's entry into Confederation was accomplished through a patently corrupt process, one can readily understand why members of the broader provincial public might have had a hard time dismissing such a notion. The minutely slim margin of the 1948 referendum is one thing. Without a clearer majority, the outcome was bound to be controversial and contested either way, but the particular set of circumstances surrounding Newfoundland's loss of responsible government and eventual entry into Confederation would give any reasonably fair-minded individual some pause for thought about the potential legitimacy of the outcome. The circumstances were bitter indeed. Andy Jones spoke gravely on this point.

> We had that sense that we were a country, that we had ambassadors at one time and we had our own Parliament way before Canada did. We were a Dominion before Canada was. We lost our government in 1934. We all knew that. We all knew that there was no vote, there was no referendum. We were promised a referendum. The Parliament just dissolved itself—most illegal. It was a coup, really. We had never officially given up our nationhood.[45]

Jones is referring to the recommendations made in 1934 by the Amulree Commission, composed of a Scottish peer and two Canadian bankers, to suspend the Constitution and the responsible government of Newfoundland, turning all control over to an unelected Commission of Government. This decision stemmed from the debt crisis that had been steadily worsening since the end of World War I.[46]

Newfoundland had begun to accumulate significant debt with the building of the Reid Railroad, but it was the Dominion's obligation to the mother country during World War I and its compounding interest that eventually broke the bank. In addition to supplying men for the Royal

---

44 Ron Hynes, "The Final Breath," EMI Music (1992).

45 Jones, interview.

46 Neary, *The Political Economy of Newfoundland, 1929–1972*, 15.

Navy, dealing with wartime costs and the inevitable profiteering that comes along with them, Newfoundland was also expected to shoulder the financial burden for raising, equipping, and transporting the thousands of men who would comprise the Newfoundland Regiment. This was a challenge the relatively undiversified economy could not meet, especially considering economic conditions to come. As part of the 29th Division of the British Army, the Newfoundland Regiment served in Gallipoli before being transferred to the Western Front where they distinguished themselves at the Somme, Arras, Ypres, and Cambrai. The cruellest blow fell on July 1, 1916, the first day of the Battle of the Somme, when seven hundred and eighty Newfoundland men received orders to take the German trenches at Beaumont-Hamel. It was the deadliest day in British Army history, with over fifty-seven thousand casualties. The Newfoundland Regiment suffered a staggering casualty rate of eighty per cent, the second highest sustained by any regiment in World War I, and were later given the designation, "Royal" Newfoundland Regiment—the only outfit to receive the title. Only sixty-eight out of more than eight hundred men presented themselves for inspection the morning after Beaumont Hamel.

The Newfoundland soldier was rapidly becoming a tragic figure in the Great War, renowned for his bravery and seemingly wasted in one egregious bloodbath after another. "Lions led by donkeys" was how one commentator described them. Some twelve thousand Newfoundland men enlisted out of a population of less than a quarter of a million. By the end of World War I, roughly half of the more than six thousand men who had served in the Royal Newfoundland Regiment had been killed, wounded, or taken prisoner—cutting a hideous swathe of bereavement through the island's families and communities. Twenty per cent of the Regiment died on the battlefields of Europe, more than twice the casualty rate of the Canadian Expeditionary Forces in the same campaigns. After pouring out the lifeblood of an entire generation for the mother country, Newfoundland was left with a debt that had ballooned by thirty-five million dollars by the time World War I ended.[47]

In subsequent years, depressed fish prices and a global economic downturn worsened the financial crisis. Newfoundland's economy was heavily dependent on exports, making it precarious and highly

---

47 Noel, 122; Neary, *The Political Economy of Newfoundland, 1929–1972*, 14–15.

vulnerable to external market shifts. By the time of the Great Depression, Newfoundland's debt stood in the neighbourhood of a hundred million dollars. Bankruptcy loomed with the government unable to secure further loans and over sixty per cent of revenues given entirely to public relief. Regional merchant and finance interests, as well as those of Britain and Canada, pushed for the Commission of Government. The local press capitalized on the political and financial corruption scandals in Newfoundland's government over the previous decade to win the support of the broader public, even though these scandals had less to do with Newfoundland's financial troubles than was implied. Frederick Alderdice ran on an anti-corruption platform with the Commission of Government as the proposed solution until Newfoundland was solvent again, and was elected Prime Minister in 1932. Alderdice's victory supports the idea that the broader public gave democratic assent to the Commission of Government, but as historian Jeff Webb notes, voters might have chosen differently if they had known that this undemocratic government was going to last not for five years—as most people believed—but for fifteen years. Britain and Canada were now on the hook for Newfoundland's debt and fearful of how the burden might affect their own credit and financial systems. They could not risk a public vote, which might prevent the establishment of the Commission and potentially continue to worsen the debt crisis or lead to a default.

Instead, Alderdice was instructed by the British government to induce the Newfoundland legislature to vote in favour of adopting the recommendations of the Amulree Commission. They also specifically instructed him not to hold a public referendum as he had promised voters he would do prior to his 1932 election. Nor did he.[48] The gravity of the response expressed by Andy Jones appears, in light of these facts, to be perhaps more measured than the situation deserves. While the deed was done legally—at least insofar as those who orchestrated events were in a position to dictate what was and was not legal—it would be difficult to convincingly argue that it was done fairly.

The Great Depression proved even more debilitating to Newfoundland's economy and quality of life, regardless of the efforts of the

---

48 Noel, 189, 203, 213, 233–37; Neary, *Newfoundland in the North Atlantic World, 1929–1949*, 13–15, 25–28, 31, 35–39; Jeff A. Webb, "Collapse of Responsible Government, 1929–1934," Politics and Government Bibliography, Heritage: Newfoundland and Labrador (2001). https://www.heritage.nf.ca/articles/politics/collapse-responsible-government.php.

Commission of Government who attempted to address shortcomings in public welfare, education, health care, and worker protections in resource industries with reforms that, over time, showed some modest but measurably better outcomes. Still, the distant manner of governance by the Commission and their inability to deliver more than modest gains in the face of extreme economic conditions bred deep resentment. Alderdice himself had repented of his chosen course within a few short years. "If I had had any idea the present plan of government was to turn out as it has I am afraid I would not have been so ready to accept it," Alderdice stated in a letter to Lord Amulree in September of 1935. "And in justice to you, I feel you, yourself, would have hesitated before suggesting it. 'A word to the wise is sufficient.'" Peter Neary observed that Alderdice had always been a man of faith where the Empire was concerned, and he ultimately believed that Britain would represent the interests of the people of Newfoundland. Unfortunately, over the course of the Commission's tenure as Newfoundland's de facto government, overall economic conditions had not improved. To some observers, it seemed that Britain's care had been largely reserved for the propertied and moneyed interests who lived in dread of a default in Newfoundland's debt rather than for the general welfare of the people.[49]

To be fair, it was almost certainly beyond the ability of the Commission to solve the region's economic problems. Far richer, stronger, and less fiscally conservative economies throughout the Atlantic world and beyond were likewise struggling to survive. Like the economy of the United States, it would take a massive mobilizer of resources and finance, like World War II, to lift Newfoundland out of its economic downward spiral. When Britain declared war on Germany, Newfoundland, like the Dominions of Australia and New Zealand, was also automatically at war. Volunteers for active service were roughly similar in number to those who had volunteered during World War I, but represented a smaller percentage of the population, which had since grown by about twenty per cent. About half of the nearly ten thousand volunteers were accepted for service in the British Army, the Admiralty, the Royal Air Force, the Royal Canadian Air Force, and the Merchant Marine. The absorption of Newfoundlanders into British and Canadian military outfits was meant to ensure that any casualties would be more evenly distributed

---

49 Neary, *Newfoundland in the North Atlantic World, 1929–1949*, 42–43, 105–108; Noel, 236.

amongst the Allies. The terrible losses at Beaumont-Hamel had been instructive. An additional 3,600 men, all experienced Newfoundland loggers, served in the overseas forestry unit producing timber for the war effort and helping to rebuild in shattered communities when the conflict was over. Fewer men volunteered for service between 1939 and 1942 than they had between 1914 and 1916, it seems, because there was so much work back home. Newfoundland's economy and financial health began to rebound rapidly during World War II as the region became an important strategic location in the Battle of the Atlantic. Investment poured in from the United States, Britain, and Canada as a great deal of military, transportation, and communications infrastructure was built across Newfoundland and Labrador. Unemployment plummeted and quality of life improved markedly as Newfoundlanders began to benefit from better health care, a more varied diet, better wages, greater mobility, and greater ease of communication. By the end of World War II, Newfoundland had gained an economic surplus and its people seemed ready to face the future. The focus of public debate now centred around what that future should be.[50]

Confederation with Canada was not just controversial because of the closeness of the vote or the political polarization that such a thing implied, but also because there did not seem to be, in hindsight, a particularly fair fight between campaigns representing very different interests. The work of historians Peter Neary, David MacKenzie, and Jeff Webb has shown that the pro-Confederation camp were singularly well-organized, well-funded, and firmly supported by both British and Canadian political and economic interests.[51] Canada had long been desirous to see Newfoundland and Labrador—along with their resource wealth and now a great deal of civil and military infrastructure as well—become part of Canada and had made the first offer as early as 1868. The British government also wanted to see Newfoundland become a Canadian province,

---

50 Neary, *Newfoundland in the North Atlantic World, 1929–1949*, 116–18, 178–81, 235–36, 238, 277–79; "Number & Annual Growth Rate of Population, Newfoundland and Labrador, For Census Years 1836 to 1993," Historical Statistics of Newfoundland and Labrador. Newfoundland Statistics Agency (November 1994): 5. https://www.stats.gov.nl.ca/publications/Historical/PDF/Historical_Statistics_of_Newfoundland_and_Labrador_V2_N7_1994.pdf.

51 David MacKenzie, *Inside the Atlantic Triangle: Canada and the Entrance of Newfoundland into Confederation, 1939–1949* (Toronto: University of Toronto Press, 1986); Neary, *Newfoundland in the North Atlantic World, 1929–1949*; Webb, "Confederation, Conspiracy and Choice: A Discussion."

if only to unload the economic burden of administering a financially troubled Dominion as the broader empire was crumbling. Moreover, neither Britain nor Canada wanted to see Newfoundland gobbled up by the United States. Unlike the Confederates, the anti-Confederate camp was divided and poorly organized and lacked allies and backers as powerful as the Canadian and British governments. Anti-Confederates were in favour of a return to responsible government as a Dominion and a subgroup of them sought a measure of economic union with the United States, a prospect which, like Confederation, had also been broached and rejected in decades past. Because the anti-Confederates were so dramatically outmatched in funding or institutional support compared to the pro-Confederation campaign, many anti-Confederates looked back on the advent of Commission government and the subsequent 1948 referendum with deep outrage and a sense of the deck being quietly stacked against them.[52] A bitter outcome indeed. But, Andy Jones pointed out, Newfoundlanders weren't quite the revolutionary sort—at least not in any way that might overwhelm their democratic sense: "After the vote, there was no violence. Nobody ever shot anybody. Newfoundlanders didn't go down that road. But people did wear black armbands for a few days and in the end, joined Canada."[53]

The Aftermath

The twenty years following Confederation saw artists' first responses to a cultural landscape in flux. A notable literary voice during the earliest part of this period was that of Ted Russell. On the top floor of his house in St. John's, with the windows open to the summer breeze and surrounded by gorgeous old musical instruments and vintage posters of Newfoundland bands, Ted Russell's son, legendary fiddler Kelly Russell, told me how his dad's experience of living through Confederation influenced him.

---

52 Neary, *Newfoundland in the North Atlantic World, 1929–1939*, 351, 354–56; Jeff Webb, "Confederation, Conspiracy and Choice: A Discussion," 171–72, 175–77, 182–83.

53 Jones, interview.

> Dad loved the Newfoundland outport and the people most especially. He saw a type of small, well-knit community depending on each other . . . and a great way of life. Although you'd never get wealthy doing it, you could *get by* doing it. People who *did* get by doing that enjoyed sharing good times as well as hardships. He loved that way of life and he saw that it was going to disappear. He had inside info on that because, from 1949 to 1951, my father was Minister of Natural Resources in the first Newfoundland government under Smallwood. He ran as a member for Bonavista North. Smallwood was promising all kinds of . . . the baby bonus[54] and all that if we joined Canada. But Dad saw early on that Smallwood was not interested in Newfoundland remaining as a subsistence economy on the fishery, that Smallwood was determined to drag us, quote: "kicking and screaming into the twentieth century." And "burn your boats," and rubber factories and all these schemes that money was squandered on at the time. Dad disagreed with all that and left, he left the government. So, what was he going to do after that? He was kind of persona non grata with the existing government. He couldn't get a job as a teacher, which he was qualified for, or as a magistrate, which he'd also done. So, part of how he got by was he started telling these stories about Newfoundland outport life, and he created an imaginary community, which was called Pigeon Inlet.

"Tell me about Uncle Mose," I prompted, revealing my ignorance by giving it the wrong pronunciation—"mose" instead of "moze." "Oh, Uncle *Mose*!" Kelly gently corrected me.

> Uncle Mose wasn't from Pigeon Inlet. He came to Pigeon Inlet a little bit later in life, so he has a bit of an outsider's perspective, but he's part of the community now, and he knows everybody. So, you've got this small community in which Uncle Mose, each week, comes on the radio and tells a story about Grandpa Walcott and Grandma, and Jethro Noddy, who's a bit of a good-for-nothing. So, people got to know all these characters and in

54 Canadian federal child welfare program for low-income families.

> these stories, they saw themselves. Grandpa Walcott is in every Newfoundland community. He's the oldest guy. He's the wise fella. These stories became very popular and they preserved so much of the Newfoundland way of life and the Newfoundland humour. As early as the 1950s, my Dad was doing that. So, it was a natural thing for Breakwater to want to publish them later on. People were starting to reawaken with an interest in our past. Well, Dad had it all there in these stories. I think Dad was maybe the original renaissance man. From 1951 he started, to about '59 or '60. He wrote hundreds of stories, not all of them entertaining—some of them were more topical, like Uncle Mose would talk about the price of lobster this year.
>
> He was often asked: "Why did you stop writing about Pigeon Inlet? Why didn't you keep writing about it?" And his answer was: "I wrote about Pigeon Inlet when it was still there. It's not there anymore." And that was in 1960. He saw the change already starting to happen.[55]

During the twenty-odd years following Confederation, literature was probably the most visible and celebrated of the arts in Newfoundland and quite a few novelists, poets, journalists, and playwrights were active or became active in Newfoundland during the first few decades of union with Canada. Besides Ted Russell, others responding to the changes taking place in Newfoundland from within a literary medium include Grace Butt, Harold Horwood, Farley Mowat, and Percy Janes. Not all Newfoundland writers addressed these changes directly in their work like Mowat and Horwood did in their journalistic efforts opposing resettlement during the 1960s, or like Janes did in his exploration of conditions in industrialized company towns in the novel *House of Hate*. Rather, Ted Russell told stories about Newfoundland that served as love letters to a way of life that was fading. Russell's 1954 play *The Holdin' Ground* has been described as one which helped legitimize the outports as a dramatic and literary subject.[56]

---

55 Kelly Russell, interview by author, St. John's, August 12, 2022.

56 Ronald Rompkey, "The Idea of Newfoundland and Arts Policy Since Confederation," *Newfoundland Studies* 14, no. 2 (1998): 271; Overton, "Sparking a Cultural Revolution," 168–73, 186–87, 193–95; O'Dea, "Culture and Country," 381; Devine, 341–42.

The industrialization of the fishery and its takeover by the federal and new provincial governments hastened the demise of the outports by drastically altering rural employment arrangements. As the industry shifted from the traditional salt cure to the mass production of fresh and frozen fish, great trawlers were brought into Newfoundland waters, capable of netting more fish than any number of small, local, family-based fishing enterprises could match, making them nearly obsolete except as individual workers in the fish plants. Perhaps a more significant part of the problem stemmed from the fact that labour participation in the fishery had steadily declined by nearly seventy per cent since the nineteenth century and no other local industries were yet mature or stable enough to support an economy still struggling to diversify. In areas with few sufficiently developed industries, those who could not get work often ended up collecting unemployment cheques seasonally, if not for greater portions of each year. Efforts to diversify Newfoundland's economy were frequently no more than marginally successful or were concentrated in other resource industries such as logging and mining, or in the construction, service, or manufacturing sectors, which did not pay working-class people much better nor employ them with much, if any more security, than the fishery did. This substantially increased the number of families receiving social assistance whenever the few local employers in any one area—factories, refineries or planned development projects—either completed, went bust, or laid people off.[57] While a growing trend of welfare dependency was demoralizing enough for some, the most dramatic and controversial aspect of Smallwood's regime was resettlement.

Despite the fact that it remains one of the darker and more salient marks on Smallwood's post-Confederation agenda, resettlement was by no means Joey's brainchild. As a policy initiative to improve quality of life, it has its roots in the public welfare programs of the Commission government in the 1930s. Lean years in the fishery with the added strain of the Great Depression took their toll on many outport communities. When conditions grew too poor, outport residents applied for relocation funding assistance to give them the opportunity to rebuild their lives

57 Noel, 263–66; Neary, *The Political Economy of Newfoundland, 1929–1972*, 9, 177–78; Noel Iverson and Ralph Matthews, *Communities in Decline: An Examination of Household Resettlement in Newfoundland* (St. John's: Institute of Social and Economic Research, 1968): 2, 136–37.

in closer proximity to resources and infrastructure.[58] However, by the 1960s and 1970s, this practice had become much more controversial. Policy changes rendered it unnecessary to seek the cooperation of an entire community before executing a resettlement strategy. Increasingly, resettlement proposals began to seem like land and resource grabs to the residents of some rural communities, many of whom could not see their way to leaving the place that their families had inhabited for generations. Often, a resettlement strategy would be predicated on being able to convince the majority to move. As a result, communities were further eroded by deep and growing resentment between those who chose to go and those determined to stay. The resettlement program ended in 1975, having removed roughly three hundred outport towns from the map and having relocated approximately thirty thousand people.[59] Alongside Confederation with Canada and the disastrous cod moratorium of 1992, resettlement is among the most singular and defining events for Newfoundland political, social, and cultural consciousness in the latter half of the twentieth century. A significant proportion of the art produced in the province during the post-Confederation period is either fully or partially set in the outports, or touches on the consequences of resettlement.[60]

One of the most visible cultural responses to the resettlement policy was the Fogo Process film project, produced by a partnership between the National Film Board's (NFB) *Challenge and Change* program and MUN Extension. The nine documentary films, directed by NFB's Colin Low, sought to provide a medium for local people to address concerns within their communities and to help articulate solutions and strategies to address poverty and underdevelopment. During the late 1960s and 1970s, the people of Fogo Island faced the same challenges of economic stagnation and temptations of resettlement as many other outports had during the mid-twentieth century. Today, Fogo Island is still a thriving community, thanks largely to the residents' establishment of a locally controlled fishing cooperative following the production

58 Neary, *Newfoundland in the North Atlantic World, 1929–1949*, 64–5, 72–3, 106.

59 Noel, 264–66; Cato Wadel, "Marginal Adaptations and Modernization in Newfoundland," *Newfoundland Social and Economic Studies* (St. John's, 1969) *and* Noel Iverson and Ralph D. Matthews, "Communities in Decline" in Neary, *The Political Economy of Newfoundland, 1929–1972*, 239–40, 245–46; Raymond B. Blake, "The Resettlement of Pushthrough, Newfoundland, in 1969," *Newfoundland and Labrador Studies* 30, no. 2 (2015): 220–21.

60 Devine, 11.

of the Fogo Process films. Artists, however, also played a major role in the revitalization of Fogo Island by undertaking local projects and establishing residency programs. Admittedly, the hundred-million-dollar Fogo Island Inn, which opened in 2013, is also an economic stimulator not to be sniffed at. The Fogo Process film project of the late 1960s stands today as an international example of how art mediums like film can be used as catalysts for impressive change and development.[61]

Resettlement left its mark on visual art as well. Newfoundland's visual artists created images and pieces that spoke eloquently of the changes that the push for centralization had wrought. The works of Christopher Pratt, Gerry Squires, and David Blackwood are among the first that come to mind, but the 1960s and 1970s saw a fairly salient general theme in art emerge—that of the empty town. Images of desolate landscapes, ghost towns, abandoned houses, and crumbling churches found their way into many works of art during this period.[62]

Resettlement is also a prominent theme in Newfoundland theatre. Al Pittman's *West Moon* is an alternately humorous and heart-rending lament to the losses suffered by resettled communities. The play takes place in a cemetery in a coastal outport community in Placentia Bay. The characters, all of whom are dead and can only hear rather than see one another, awaken every All Souls' Night. They talk and behave with one another the way they did when they were alive in their community and welcome the newly deceased among them from whom they usually hear all the news about the goings-on in the world of the living. One All Souls' Night, they awaken to find that the community above has been resettled and that no one else they have known and loved from their community will ever again come to join them.[63]

The Mummers Troupe's 1973 production, *Gros Mourn*, which documents the experiences and feelings of the residents of Sally's Cove, Belldown's Point, Bakers Brook, Green Point, and Lobster Cove when they faced resettlement with the looming establishment of Gros Morne National Park, is another example of the prominence of this theme in

61 "How filmmakers and fishers saved Fogo Island," *CBC Radio* (original airdate: December 14, 2017), July 25, 2018. https://www.cbc.ca/radio/ideas/how-filmmakers-and-fishers-saved-fogo-island-1.4447208; "The NFB and Fogo Island, Newfoundland: A Continuing Story." https://www.nfb.ca/playlist/fogo-island/.

62 Gwyn, 49–51.

63 Al Pittman, *West Moon* (St. John's: Breakwater Books, 1995).

Newfoundland theatre. A deeply political group, the collectively written plays of the Mummers Troupe were far less sentimental than Pittman's *West Moon*. The conception, creation, performance, and impact of *Gros Mourn* formed a process that rendered theatre, advocacy, and social action inseparable from one another. The Troupe spent time in each of the affected communities, listening to local people voice their thoughts, concerns, and fears about the proposed resettlement. They wrote the play collectively, following a narrative of the community's crisis using the very words of community members. In a manner reminiscent of the earlier Fogo Process, the Troupe was able to provide a mirror for local residents in which to view, clarify, and articulate their unanswered grievances.[64]

Artists and a Transatlantic Rebellion

Newfoundland's political and social evolution and its cycles of economic struggle during the twentieth century helped set the stage for the rise of a mid-century cultural nationalist movement, but by the 1960s, this was something that a great many Atlantic societies had in common. Broad political and social change was on the rise in the post-World War II Atlantic basin, and many nations and regions enmeshed in various forms of decolonization and liberation were producing their own artistic and cultural movements.

South America and the Caribbean region were seeing the growth of numerous movements to throw off colonial influences and systems. The success of the Cuban Revolution stiffened the anti-communist position of the United States in the Cold War era and throughout the next two decades, the collision of decolonization or reform movements with United States foreign policy created conditions in many Latin American countries that led to the rise of military coups and autocratic governments. During the 1960s alone, Bolivia, Argentina, El Salvador, Colombia, Chile, Peru, Guatemala, and Venezuela all saw the advent of popular revolution. For most, goals were centred around democratic reform and land redistribution from feudal elites to the people. At the beginning of John F. Kennedy's presidency, nothing approaching

64 Brookes, *A Public Nuisance*, 78–96.

a pan-Latin American sensibility seemed to exist, with each country seeing itself as markedly distinct from its neighbours. Furthermore, there were stronger distinctions between Hispanic and Indigenous cultures and stronger divisions between Latin Americans of European origin and those of African origin. Throughout the geopolitical struggles of the next two decades, that sense of distinctness began to shift toward one of regional and continental multiculturalism. A broadly common experience of struggle against political and economic imperialism was accompanied by an arts movement that began to cultivate a distinctly Latin American consciousness with music, drama, visual art, and notably, literature. Like so many artistic trends that developed in the Atlantic region, Latin American literature gained a transatlantic quality. Before becoming well known on their home continent, the works of Latin American writers, like Jorge Luis Borges and Gabriel García Márquez, who were experimenting with literary forms such as magical realism, were in vogue in Paris during the 1960s and 1970s. The literature produced by South American writers of the time also contributed significantly to the formation of a broader Latin American consciousness and experience.[65]

In the Caribbean, the Cuban Revolution was probably the most visible movement towards decolonization in the region. Jamaica, however, was developing movements of its own. Jamaica gained independence in 1962, but a great deal of influence remained in the hands of elites well placed within the pre-existing colonial structure. Rastafarians in western Jamaica saw frequent repression by law enforcement at the whim of political and economic power brokers. Montego Bay in the early 1960s saw heavy investment by Jamaica's wealthiest landowners to develop former sugar plantations into resorts and hotels. They enlisted local law enforcement to harass and remove Rastafarians from this budding tourist destination. Months of these tensions culminated in violent conflict in Coral Gardens in the spring of 1963. These struggles were accompanied by the emergence of modern reggae music. Internationally popularized by artists such as the great Bob Marley, Peter Tosh, Jimmy Cliff, and Neville Livingston, also known as Bunny Wailer, this style of Jamaican

65 Mario Vargas Llosa, "Latin America from the Inside Out," *Salmagundi* 153/154 (Winter-Spring 2007): 32–6; Charles R. Hale, "Cultural Politics of Identity in Latin America," *Annual Review of Anthropology* 26 (1997): 567–69, 571; Kenneth Finlayson, "The 1960s: A Decade of Revolution," *Veritas* 4, no. 4 (2008). https://arsof-history.org/articles/v4n4_1960s_page_1.html.

music was openly political and strongly connected to the Pan-African ethos of the twentieth century.[66]

During the post-World War II period, the ongoing struggle to achieve political autonomy, social justice, and prosperity was as active on the east side of the Atlantic as it was on the west. In 1960, the vast African continent featured only nine sovereign nations. By the end of the decade, there were twenty-seven. A terrible side effect of decolonization is sometimes destabilization and, like some Latin American countries, a number of African nations fell to military juntas and autocratic power-grabs. The process of decolonization in African nations is still ongoing and has produced various cultural and artistic responses that, like the movement in Newfoundland, hearkened back to heritage and bolstered a spirit of resistance and cultural pride. In 1960s South Africa, the group that would eventually become Ladysmith Black Mambazo, formed by Joseph Shabalala, began performing in the traditional *isicathamiya* and *mbube* styles at local events in Durban and Johannesburg. The timing and particular locations of these shows—mostly Saturday nights at private venues in Black-segregated areas—was purposeful in an apartheid society as it shielded attendees from the scrutiny of employers or the oppression of law enforcement. Around the same time, singer Miriam Makeba appeared on the music scene blending traditional musical elements with the new sounds of Afro-pop and singing songs for an international audience in Xhosa and Zulu. A close contemporary of such fellow artist/activists in the struggle for Black freedom including Harry Belafonte and Nina Simone, Makeba was later lovingly dubbed "Mama Africa" and retains a legacy of devotion to the causes of decolonization and racial justice.[67] The African music produced during the 1960s and 1970s would prove highly influential to the wider culture of the Atlantic basin.

Cultural movements initiated by people of African descent throughout the twentieth century have been quite consistently rooted in the struggle for Black rights and have also invariably demonstrated an international and transatlantic quality. The artistic expression of the

66 Michele Lemonius, "'Deviously Ingenious': British Colonialism in Jamaica," *Peace Research* 49, no. 2 (2017): 79–80, 93–4; Horace G. Campbell, "Coral Gardens 1963: The Rastafari and Jamaican Independence," *Social and Economic Studies* 63, no. 1 (March 2014): 197–201.

67 Finlayson, (2008); Ruth Feldstein, *How It Feels to Be Free: Black Women Entertainers and the Civil Rights Movement* (Cambridge: Oxford University Press, 2013): 6–8, 53, 69–74; Veit Erlmann, *Nightsong: Performance, Power, and Practice in South Africa* (Chicago: University of Chicago Press, 1996): xv–xvii, 69–70, 292.

Harlem Renaissance was deeply connected to the Pan-African movement articulated by political and intellectual leaders like Marcus Garvey and W.E.B. DuBois. The art of the Harlem Renaissance found resonance in contemporary French culture. Some scholars partly attribute the rise of the *Négritude* literary movement in the 1940s and 1950s to similar developments across the Atlantic in the United States during the 1920s and 1930s. In turn, poets like Aimé Césaire and Leopold Senghor, both originally from Martinique, amplified the cultural nationalist message of Pan-Africanism for French-speaking people of African descent all around the Atlantic basin. Furthermore, one can draw a fairly clear line of influence and progression between the Harlem Renaissance and the Black Arts Movement of the 1960s and 1970s in the United States. Both arose as expressions of resistance to unequal political, economic, and social conditions for Black Americans. Each movement also embodied the rationale that art could be both a celebration of culture and identity, as well as a key stratagem in the fight for racial justice and equality.[68] The art, literature, theatre, and music created in this spirit of cultural celebration and pride found resonance elsewhere in the Atlantic basin, where it helped inspire other young artists who were in the process of discovering their own roots and passions. Sandy Morris, veteran Newfoundland musician and guitar virtuoso, was one of them.

Germinating the Newfoundland Renaissance

Sitting on his back porch surrounded by green trees and with the faint sound of traffic in the background, Sandy described his first experience seeing a rock 'n' roll band in the early 1960s and how the music coming out of the Black community in the United States had inspired him.

> I had a first cousin, Jim Hennessey, who played in a band called The Ravens, arguably the most popular band in St. John's, and Newfoundland, at the time. They were one of

68 Abiola Irele, "Négritude or Black Cultural Nationalism," *The Journal of Modern African Studies* 3, no. 3 (October 1965): 321–23, 326, 328, 342, 348; Nagueyalti Warren, "Pan-African Cultural Movements: From Baraka to Karenga," *The Journal of Negro History* 75, no. 1 (Winter-Spring, 1990): 19.

> the first bands to make an actual 45 record and they were the first band to be on television. They went to Halifax and went on *Frank's Bandstand*, so national television. So, they were a big deal locally and Jim, who we called "Jay," was extremely generous. He took me and my cousin Bryan Hennessey to see him play at a gig in a dry venue. At twelve years old, I'd never seen a live rock 'n' roll band. In fact, rock 'n' roll bands were a brand-new thing.
>
> Jay was one of the first musicians on the island to own a Fender guitar and bass, and effects pedals and stuff. He would always encourage us. I didn't know how to play the guitar, but he'd say: "Just take it out and play it!" You can imagine how space-age a Fender Stratocaster looks. It didn't look like a guitar; it looked like some kind of weapon, and in fact it is, in my opinion. Then, plugging that into an echo machine, into an amplifier, and oh the tremolo! . . . and all these weird sounds coming out of it. Even if you didn't know how to play, it was just mesmerizing, the sounds that you could get. It was kind of state-of-the-art technology at the time. It was like going to outer space.[69]

Sandy laughed, leaning back in his chair. But it wasn't just the electric guitar he had fallen in love with at his first rock 'n' roll show, he told me—it was the drums as well. The drummer for The Ravens was none other than Rocky Wiseman, who would go on to play with the Wonderful Grand Band in their early days. Undoubtedly one of the most popular acts to come out of Newfoundland during the 1970s, the Wonderful Grand Band not only fused Newfoundland folk music with rock 'n' roll, but also music with sketch comedy. Their live shows became legendary in the late 1970s and they produced an enormously successful TV show that ran on the CBC from 1980 through 1983. Sandy seemed at a loss for words to describe how electric Wiseman's performance on the drums had been to a twelve-year-old boy at his first rock 'n' roll show.

---

69 Sandy Morris, interview by author, St. John's, August 12, 2022.

> I went home from my very first experience seeing that live band and learned how to play drums with forks and knives. Jay kept that up throughout my youth; he was always taking us to shows and bringing records home. He'd be bringing home records by Black artists like Ike and Tina Turner, James Brown, and Ray Charles. He was turning us on to all this stuff that he'd been playing on the American bases. They'd be giving him these "race records" they were called at the time. He'd be bringing them home and playing them with us. I'd go out to parties as a teenager with records under my arm. Everybody else would have Bobby Vinton and Bobby Curtola, and I would have James Brown. People were like: "What? What are you bringing?" I would have jazz albums too because Jay turned us on to all of that coming out of the Black culture in the United States. The first time I ever felt high was listening to an album on my top bunk. I didn't know where I'd gone, but my mind just . . . And that got me hooked on music. So, around age fifteen, I got a guitar, an acoustic guitar, and started teaching myself to play it.[70]

In the decade to come, Sandy would be one of the musicians blending traditional Newfoundland music with broader international influences, which were themselves assertions of ethnic and regional pride.

***

Along with an international movement towards decolonization and cultural nationalism, mid-twentieth-century Atlantic societies began to feature more and more progressive voices among their bureaucrats and intelligentsia. A broadly shared perspective of optimism was emerging that placed faith in people's ability to realize a truly just society. Newfoundland and Labrador was no exception. The post-Confederation period was a time in which there were younger and notably more progressive individuals moving into development organizations and

---

70 Morris, interview.

education. There was a new focus on experimentation and autonomy, particularly at Memorial University of Newfoundland (MUN). Elevated to the status of a full university following Confederation, Smallwood had a particular vision for MUN as a resource for broad regional and community development. Ten years later, in 1959, MUN Extension was founded, seemingly in the same spirit of optimism and belief that universities could and should foster broad and positive change in their regional community.[71] Much that has been written or discussed in public forums about MUN Extension over the years tends to focus largely on its role in rural development throughout the province. Indeed, in the absence of a more comprehensive provincial bureaucracy to address such issues in those days, both the provincial and federal governments were grateful for and glad to fund the efforts of Extension's numerous field agents working in communities across Newfoundland and Labrador. The approach of Extension field agents emphasized building trust and partnership between rural communities and institutions. Therefore, Extension workers almost always went to live in the target community. In close consultation with community members, field agents aimed to help foster the conditions under which the community could begin to articulate for themselves what was needed. Extension workers then sought to empower the people with the tools and training necessary to achieve their collective goals.[72] In Extension's mission, we can clearly see the marks of a broadly progressive social agenda at MUN that could not have failed to have an impact on the first few generations to be educated there.

"When we joined Confederation, there was a sense that we were all going to be able to get an education," Andy Jones told me.

> Everyone could go to university. In fact, my generation got free university. We were all given four years for free. And then, in fact, people started getting paid to go to university, and then it died off after a while. It's too bad, it was an amazing, amazing thing.[73]

71 Webb, "The Rise and Fall of Memorial University's Extension Service," 84–5, 94, 99.
72 Webb, "The Rise and Fall of Memorial University's Extension Service," 85–6, 90–94, 100–101.
73 Jones, interview.

Memorial University during the 1960s and 1970s was crucial to the incubation of the arts and culture movement. The Memorial University Drama Society (MUDS) during the mid-1960s brought together many young artists who would help redefine the regional cultural landscape in subsequent decades. The theatre kids were soon joined by the music crowd who didn't have an on-campus office of their own, turning the newly-designated MUDS office into a forest of guitars, amps, and other musical equipment. New artistic partnerships and friendships were formed in the MUDS office as well as in MUN's Little Theatre, later known as the Reid Theatre. The Little Theatre saw some of the earliest theatrical and musical appearances by artists like Greg Malone, Janet Michael, Bob Joy, Kevin Noble, Sandy Morris, Bryan Hennessey, Noel Dinn, Laverne Squires, and Anita Best.[74] Anita described to me what it was like to meet the world through Memorial University during the mid-1960s.

> It was very exciting on all levels, not just the arts but sciences as well. I remember at the university, at that time, continental shift was being discussed by geologists. The old ideas in geology were being uprooted and the new ideas that are now the accepted norm—they were just being talked about in the science building. If you went over to the science caf, you could sit with profs who were discussing continental drift. The young geologists of the time were friends of ours. If you went into the arts cafeteria, the philosophy profs would be sitting having coffee with the students. You don't see that so much now at Memorial. I haven't really been there in a long time, but I understand from the young people I know that that kind of thing doesn't go on so much anymore. The profs tend to keep to themselves and the students get together in the student centres and stuff, but in the 60s and 70s, everybody was all together. The students went to the profs' houses for dinner. There was a mixture of generations and there was a mixture of interesting ideas, not only in the arts but in the sciences, all over. There were new things happening on every level I think.

74 Best, interview; Greg Malone and (Mary) White, interview by author, St. John's, August 16, 2022.

> Looking back now, I realize how rare it was and what a wonderful opportunity we had as young people to meet and discuss and argue and present our views and listen to people who were way more informed in their fields than we were. We had a kind of energy that they enjoyed, and they loved being with us. A lot of our good friends at school were our profs. We spent time in each other's houses and we got to know each other really well. David Alexander was a friend of mine. His wife, she was an actress. Mike Cook and his wife, Janis Spence, she was an actress. I used to babysit for their children. Edythe Goodridge remained a friend of mine to the end of her life. They were a generation older than us but they were really our friends and our close companions. I think that was how the whole thing worked. It was a real intergenerational, interdisciplinary thing.[75]

The social atmosphere and spirit of education at MUN during the mid-1960s that Best describes sounds very much like a microcosm of St. John's during the same period. Dudley Cox described the broader social environment of St. John's in much the same way. One could always find artists and academics of many and varied disciplines and age groups drinking and arguing with each other at parties and in pubs and bars in downtown St. John's, he said. "All the guys from the university, all the profs, and all the characters from the CBC—they were always involved and getting around. Patrick O'Flaherty was always at parties, swearing. He was the first one to swear really badly at parties," Dudley remarked laughing. "There was always a marvellous mixture of people. I can't speak highly enough of St. John's. What a lovely place; it was like a little Paris."[76]

Dudley's romance with Newfoundland began in the spring of 1965. While studying for his BA in Montreal, he had gotten engaged to a young woman from St. John's and accompanied her home when her term of study was finished. He went to work first as a cook and then as a waiter

75 Best, interview.

76 Dudley Cox, interview by author, Seattle/Vancouver Island, July 21, 2022.

on the Caribou CN train line nicknamed the "Newfie Bullet,"[77]—probably the best way to get to know Newfoundland and Newfoundlanders at that time—before later accepting a position teaching at the College of Fisheries. However, Dudley's original desire in coming to Canada was to attend university and he soon returned to his studies for a BA, this time at MUN. He had always longed to go to university in his native England, though he had achieved a higher national certificate and was a qualified engineer. He never, he said, viewed a BA as a qualification for employment. To Dudley, an arts education was about personal cultivation, enrichment, and mastery.[78]

> While I was in the army for two years national service, I found myself in the company of a whole bunch of university students. I never knew anybody who'd been to university and I didn't know what they were talking about half the time, especially when they talked about Socrates and Aristotle and other things like that. I mean, I could do calculus and mathematics but when it came to discussing plays and literature and stuff like that, I was a total dodo. I bought a dictionary, used to read it like a novel. I felt a need to try and make up for all the education that I'd lost.[79]

In the spring of 1966, Dudley and his wife became neighbours of Margaret Hitchens who, besides being the Newfoundland tennis champion, was also a member of the St. John's Players, which was probably the most prominent theatre organization in St. John's at the time, despite being a community theatre outfit. Unlike other Canadian provinces, Newfoundland and Labrador had no regional professional theatres until the 1970s. The St. John's Players had been founded by Newfoundland playwright Grace Butt in 1937 and since the late 1950s had more or less replaced the London Players, many of whom were community theatre transplants from England, and who had formerly

77 This line ran from Port aux Basques to St. John's until it was decommissioned in 1969. Rail travel in Newfoundland saw its demise by the mid-twentieth century in favour of a province-wide highway system, an infrastructure policy decision that is still debated for its ultimate impact on public transportation and provincial mobility.

78 Dudley Cox, "The Rise and Fall of the Newfoundland Travelling Theatre Company: A Stage Too Far" (unpublished manuscript), 2022: 1, 3–6, 8; Cox, interview.

79 Cox, interview.

been St. John's most visible theatre group. Hitchens invited Cox to audition for Tom Cahill who was soon to stage one of his *Home Brew* productions with the St. John's Players. Cahill cast Cox in a few skits and right away, he was bitten by the theatre bug.[80]

> All of a sudden, the light went on. I was taking this arts degree and I was so interested in what I had to learn, but I thought there should be some practical application for all this, this higher learning. And in fact, as I went on with the St. John's Players, I realized that all the studying that I'd done for an arts degree can be used in the theatre. The theatre needs every talent that you ever had, have, or think you might get. It's a totally absorbing, all-around kind of occupation. So, I absolutely fell in love with the theatre, not only for its own sake, but for what it draws out of you as a person. And so, I more or less became an apprentice to the theatre and I learned everything I could with the St. John's Players and made friends with most of them. There was a huge mixture of people from all over. Some were from Newfoundland, some were from Scotland, some were from Montreal. It was a wonderful group to be part of because they were very serious about what they did—they took it very seriously. I got so excited and delighted with the whole deal that I gave up my job, accepted a bursary from the university, and started studying for my master's, which was even more brilliant.[81]

For Dudley, as for so many other budding artists in the mid-to-late 1960s, an education at Memorial University was often seminal to one's development as an artist. In the next few years, Cox would go on to co-found the Newfoundland Travelling Theatre Company in partnership with David Weiser.

---

80 Cox, "Newfoundland Travelling Theatre Company," 7–8.
81 Cox, interview.

* * *

During the post-Confederation era, theatre in Newfoundland lagged behind the art forms of literature, film, and visual art in that there were fewer reflections of Newfoundland life or culture.[82] That began to change during the mid-1960s. Virtually all plays and musicals staged in St. John's or in the growing population centres of Corner Brook, Stephenville, Gander, or Grand Falls up until this time were British or American productions.[83] Occasionally, the St. John's Players would stage Tom Cahill's *Home Brew* or *Slob Ice*, reminiscent of the traditional outport concert with its skits and songs. The former London Players had followed a similar pattern: staging predominantly British plays and holding one or two *Screech*[84] nights in the course of their season. This pattern places the London Players and the St. John's Players primarily in the town-based tradition of Newfoundland theatre, which some writers and commentators have dismissed as colonial and bourgeois. Yet, it is important not to overgeneralize and mischaracterize its members as such. Systems may be seen to function in colonial ways, but the people who exist and operate within them are much more complex. The membership of the St. John's Players, and to a lesser extent, the London Players, featured quite a few proud Newfoundlanders as well as allies and lovers of Newfoundland from away.[85]

For local actors, the nationwide Dominion Drama Festival in 1966 was anticipated with great excitement. It would be the first festival in which all plays entered had to be Canadian, and it was the members of the St. John's Players who won the regional competition with Tom Cahill's adaptation of Harold Horwood's novel, *Tomorrow Will Be Sunday*. The national finalists in the 1966 Dominion Drama Festival were the first to perform in the shiny new Arts and Culture Centre

---

82 The provincial Arts and Letters competition, established in 1951, largely recognized and helped promote the work of writers and visual artists. Atlantic Films, established the same year, as well as the National Film Board and the CBC, supported the creation of regional documentaries. Theatre professionals had no equivalent infrastructure or support other than the amateur scene and Dominion Drama Festival (Rompkey, 271; Gulliver, 48).

83 Brookes, *A Public Nuisance*, 35–6; Cox, "Newfoundland Travelling Theatre Company," 22–3.

84 Newfoundland slang term and now trade name for a variety of cheap, dark Demerara rum bottled in Newfoundland. Now central to the invented tradition of "Screech-ins," whereby tourists can become honorary Newfoundlanders.

85 Devine, 91–99; Cox, "Newfoundland Travelling Theatre Company," 7–8, 22–3; Ferry, 144–45.

in St. John's when it opened in May 1967. Dudley Cox had a mere two lines in the show, but nonetheless wrote proudly of the play's success in the festival. Cahill's adaptation of *Tomorrow Will Be Sunday* made a real mark for Newfoundland literature and drama in Canadian theatre, with Alice Matheson winning Best Director, Paddy Brogan winning Best Visual, Tom Cahill winning Best Author, and John Moyes winning Best Supporting Actor in the final adjudication. However, Dudley noted, this important development did not signal a flood of Newfoundland drama about to be produced. It would be a few more years before the artistic explosion of the 1970s. In the meantime, the theatre scene remained much the same—mostly British and American fare with the occasional dash or two of the Newfoundland flavour.[86]

Yet, even if it was not yet fully visible within the arts scene, a cultural movement was already beginning to emerge. The early 1960s saw Memorial University begin to pursue a path of academic regionalism that sparked greater interest in local conditions, knowledge, and culture. An example of this academic regionalism was the development of the Folklore department during the early 1960s, which helped a great many scholars, students, and other young people rediscover the outport way of life.[87] "The culture that we were receiving after we joined Canada, I don't think it was satisfying on a really intrinsic level to many Newfoundlanders," Anita Best said pointedly. "They began to look for their own roots, their own expression. And to do that, they turned largely to the outports."[88]

Loss and Reclamation

David Ferry observed that the outports were glorified in art and academia primarily by middle-class townies and "come-from-aways" during this period, who, to quote Frankie O'Neill, "put on their grey socks, Guernseys,[89] and rubber boots and went looking for stories."[90] My own

86 Cox, "Newfoundland Travelling Theatre Company," 11–13, 23.
87 Overton, "A Newfoundland Culture?" 8.
88 Best, interview.
89 A thick, woollen, hand-knitted sweater or jumper.
90 Ferry, 144.

research might suggest that both Ferry and O'Neill have a point because only about a quarter of all respondents surveyed for this study grew up in coastal outport or inland rural communities in Newfoundland and Labrador.[91] It is also true that a great deal of art and performance activity in the province has been concentrated in St. John's.[92] However, I do have my doubts about any mid-twentieth-century Newfoundland townie's supposed lack of connection to the outports or to rural Newfoundland in general. Though they both spent the majority of their working lives as artists in St. John's, both of my parents grew up out around the bay—Dad in Ferryland and Mom in Come By Chance and later, Buchans. It is important to keep in mind that with regard to the generation under examination, the push for centralization occurred during theirs and their parents' lifetimes. With tens of thousands removed to growth centres and hundreds of towns abandoned in little more than a few decades, resident baymen were in shorter and shorter supply during the post-Confederation period and townies increasingly more common. Additionally, even if many Newfoundland families relocated to urban areas with the advent of World War II and later, Confederation, it is hard to believe that they would have thrown off all ancestral links to their original communities, provided that some incarnation of them were still in existence. Some outport fishermen who initially relocated for better employment prospects eventually began returning to seasonal fishing in their ancestral communities, leaving their families in the bigger towns for months at a time.[93] While the majority of Newfoundlanders surveyed in this study were technically "townies," many had personal experiences and opinions to share regarding life in the outports, "the soul of Newfoundland," and spoke passionately about what Newfoundland had lost during the post-Confederation era.[94] Scratch a "townie," especially one of that generation, and you might find they're only a first-generation "townie" and continue to preserve or honour familial or spatial connections in their ancestral communities. Andy Jones noted that out of the original members of CODCO, half of them had parents who were

91 See Appendices 4 and 5.

92 Boak, (1984).

93 Cadigan, 246; "Resettlement," written and edited by Jenny Higgins, Documentary Video Series (English), Heritage: Newfoundland and Labrador. https://www.youtube.com/watch?v=39SsGU1ooJI.

94 See Appendix 5.

born in outport towns.[95] Anita Best was one of the few narrators I spoke with who was born and raised in an outport community.

> I was born in a small fishing village called Merasheen in Placentia Bay. Like many, many other people who were born in small places, we had no electricity or anything like that, so entertainment was created by everybody in the room. When people got together, they didn't put on a recording. They didn't have a television set. Sometimes there were movies. The priests played films at the parish hall and people went to them. But when they visited one another in their houses, everybody was responsible for creating the entertainment for the evening, whether that would be through singing a song, telling a story, telling a recitation, doing something silly like getting up and dancing or something like that. And if there was no musician, someone would sing for a dance, that kind of thing. Without any rules being applied to it, it was kind of a collective creation that was going on in people's houses. I think that the rural people who were living in St. John's were re-creating that in the stuff that they were doing. We all had that sense of everybody contributing and there not being single individuals, as such. Everybody worked together to create something in the end.[96]

This is an interesting interpretation that differs somewhat from that of O'Neill and Ferry. In their vision, the artists are middle-class, urban tourists who discovered the outports, whereas in Best's vision, artists from the outports brought their traditions to the towns where they inspired other budding artists, not only to recapture something of the heritage of settler Newfoundlanders but also to contribute to the formation of something new.

Anita's description of outport life speaks eloquently of just what Newfoundland began to lose with the coming of World War II and later, Confederation. While these developments brought massive improvements in communications, the advent of mass media in Newfoundland

---

95 Jones, interview.

96 Best, interview.

began to threaten a domestic and community culture developed over centuries. Radio, television, and movies, primarily of American, Canadian, or British origins contributed to a shift in traditional culture. One mitigating factor was that mass media technologies were slow to take hold in Newfoundland. Even as late as the 1950s and early 1960s, there were still remote Newfoundland communities where life was nearly indistinguishable from what it had been fifty years earlier or more. People were still telling stories in the evenings, entertaining one another with music and recitations, or organizing community concerts led by the local lodge men or parish ladies.

My own mother attended elementary school in Come By Chance in the early 1960s. "It was a two-room school with a potbellied wood stove at the back," she told me smiling. "There were no paved roads." The students hauled their own water and lit the stove every morning before school. Eggs and dairy products were locally sourced and most people still made their own bread and kept kitchen gardens. Besides the Dingles, whose house was connected to the adjacent cottage hospital where Dr. Dingle worked, few if any other households in town had electricity.

"Did you ever get to see any theatre productions when you were growing up?" I asked Jane.

"No," she said, "but they did do concerts in Come By Chance. I think the first time I ever performed was when I sang "Where Have You Been Billy Boy?" with Brian Loder in grade three or four."

"So, no Shakespeare?" I asked her, laughing.

"No, definitely no Shakespeare. Newfoundland back then . . . someone would play the accordion, someone else played the fiddle, and if you could even hold a tune, you would be stuck up onstage singing."[97]

***

Considering the great changes against the marginal economic advancement that had been made by the late 1960s, the promises of Confederation must have seemed somewhat anti-climactic to many people in the province. Despite some significant gains in overall quality of

97 Dingle, interview.

life since 1949, the province still faced major challenges. Daunted by the lack of local opportunity, many families, and young people especially, began to emigrate away.[98] This outmigration trend was not new. At the end of the nineteenth century, an economic downturn heavily affected the fishery, which at that time employed at least ninety per cent of Newfoundland's working people. Newfoundlanders began to depart with their families, primarily for American and Canadian cities, a trend that continued into the post-Confederation period. By the 1960s, there were exponentially more Newfoundlanders living away than there had been immigrants to Newfoundland in several decades. Indeed, there were more Newfoundlanders in Ontario alone than there were immigrants of any origin in Newfoundland. Resettlement had cut a swathe through numerous communities and unemployment was still the highest in the Canadian federation.[99] Further, the opinions Canadians held about Newfoundlanders seemed to be little changed for the better. Anita recalls what it was like to interact with mainland Canadians in the first few years following Confederation.

> When you met a Newfoundlander, you told a Newfie joke. If you were a Newfoundlander, you were a figure of fun. I don't think that people meant it unkindly but that was just how people looked at us. We were kind of like the Dogpatch of Canada.[100]

Chris Brookes described how Newfoundland's position in Canadian society and prevalent Canadian perspectives on Newfoundlanders influenced him as a kid.

> I remember when I was twelve and I heard my voice back on a recording. I was shocked that I had a thick townie accent. I thought: "I'd better lose this accent because I'm not going to get a good job." There are no good jobs in Newfoundland,

98 Newfoundland and Labrador, Department of Finance, Population Projections—Demographic Overview, "Net Migration, Newfoundland and Labrador 1972–2043" (October 2023). https://www.gov.nl.ca/fin/economics/pop-overview/#mig.

99 Overton, "Coming Home," 86–7; Neary, *The Political Economy of Newfoundland, 1929–1949*, 8, 16, 177–79.

100 Best, interview.

> I was brought up to believe. We were told that the only good jobs are up on the mainland, so we'd all have to move up there and learn to speak like Canadians. And I shamefully tried to lose my accent when I was twelve, thirteen. Unfortunately, I succeeded to some extent.[101]

Newfoundlanders "Away"

I have had a great deal of opportunity for personal reflection throughout the course of this project. As I progressed through my reading, research, and oral history interviews, memories began to come back to me and they took on new meaning when I re-examined them in light of all I was learning. One thing that many Newfoundlanders of my parents' generation often could not help but pass on to their kids was that ever-present suspicion that they were among those at the bottom of the Canadian social hierarchy. We tend to be a sensitive bunch. I went to elementary school in Toronto during the late 1980s and early 1990s and even as late as that, the "Newfie joke" was still ubiquitous among kids. I had always been proud to be from Newfoundland, which I vaguely understood to be a unique place with a unique history and people, but as a kid who regularly heard those jokes on the playground, I knew the score. Whatever the joke, the punchline was ultimately the same: Newfoundlanders were stupid, backward, the Canadian equivalent of how middle-class and upper-class Americans refer to the poor from the southern states or the Appalachian region: "rednecks" or "poor White trash." Mom had the same advice to give as my teachers did about such jokes: "Ignore them." But there would be a minute yet perceptible shrinking in her demeanour nonetheless, a signal that a nerve had been touched. I don't recall that such teasing bothered me all that much aside from the simple fact of being teased, but I do recall one occasion sometime during the 1990–1991 school year when Dad came to school with me one morning for show-and-tell that touched what I imagine was a similar nerve for me.

Dad happened to be in town for a few weeks and had kindly offered to come and play a song for my third-grade class. I was beyond excited

101 Brookes, interview.

at the prospect; I didn't get to spend a whole lot of time with Dad and I was very proud of who he was and what he did. He had recorded his children's album, *Small Fry*, just two or three years prior and I remember him saying how much he enjoyed that project, especially working with the kids at Bishop Feild Elementary in St. John's to record the song "Okay For Us" on the album. Of course, he played "Sonny's Dream" for my class, a version of which was also recorded on *Small Fry*. As well as being a touchstone of Newfoundland art, "Sonny" really is one of those universal songs in that it can speak to anyone, regardless of age or experience. The lyrics are simple yet profound and they rarely fail to translate in a meaningful way.

I'm not sure why, but Dad's performance that day failed to translate for Ms. Simpson's third-grade class. She introduced him as "Elena's dad, who is also a singer and songwriter from Newfoundland," to which a few students snorted derisively and giggled. I heard someone snigger under their breath about his cowboy boots and hat. Ron was barely into the song's first verse when almost every student broke out into hysterical laughter, apparently in response to the phrase: "kick off your sneakers." At first I was confused, not seeing why the phrase was funny. Then, seeing the flush in Dad's face as he gamely tried to soldier on and continue singing through the laughter that went on and on, I felt a rush of sympathy for him and a deeply irrational anger at my classmates for being such disrespectful shits. I wouldn't like to believe or to suggest that someone like Dad, who always seemed so utterly secure in the craft he had spent a lifetime perfecting, could be undone in his emotions or his confidence by a gang of snotty eight-year-olds. However, I did notice that after that day, I never again heard him play "Sonny's Dream" with the word "sneakers" in the lyrics of the first verse. For whatever reason, forever after, you always kicked off your *shoes* before giving up the race.

Whatever the literary or musical preferences of Ms. Simpson's grade three class, I always admired Dad's performances. I, too, loved to perform. How could I not have with Ron Hynes for a father and Jane Dingle for a mother? Some of my earliest memories of life in Toronto involve performing. Mom constantly encouraged Rebecca and I to sing, dance, or act out a skit for the entertainment of whoever happened to be visiting at the time. She even encouraged this kind of entertainment when it was just the three of us. As a kid, I was a real ham and I loved the attention, so I performed willingly. I can now see that Mom was acting out the Newfoundland folk ethic, the collective effort and responsibility of every family and community member to entertain one another and enrich each other's lives. As I grew older, however, I recall how it began to annoy me that she kept pressuring me to perform, often to the point of what seemed like badgering: "Come on! Sing us a song," or "Do that Monty Python sketch." Unlike my parents and their parents before them, I had grown up in a world of television and movies in which family members could often manage not to interact with one another at all during their leisure time. Once screens rather than people became the focus of entertainment and communication, the culture that my mother was trying to impart made somewhat less sense to me. It now makes me sad that I sometimes grew angry with her for seemingly "treating me like a performing monkey," as I used to accuse her of doing, and I mourn the loss of opportunity to understand the shape of family and community relations that she was trying, whether consciously or unconsciously, to perpetuate.

As someone who has lived as a diaspora Newfoundlander for most of my life, I lived like many Newfoundlanders away—a tiny island of immediate family, a satellite location for other Newfoundlanders travelling through. I was raised to be proud of my birthplace, my heritage, and my culture, even though I functionally understood very little of it and as a result, felt a jarring sense of disconnection when I tried to reconcile my learned concept of home—Newfoundland—with the reality of the only home I'd ever truly known, on the mainland, in Toronto. Beginning this project gave me a feeling akin to seeing only the last thirty seconds of a movie and then being challenged to reconstruct the previous two and half hours, which I'd never gotten the chance to see. In the preface to his memoir about his experience as co-founder, director, and member of the Mummers Troupe during the thick of the cultural movement, Chris Brookes reflected upon the particularly ephemeral nature of theatre—an art form that is surely as fleeting as the past itself.

"Yesterday's performance is over," he stated and queried his reader: "Want to know what it was like? You had to be there."[102] Fair enough, let's have it straight from the lips of those who had the privilege to be there. Our story—well, a convergence of many stories anyway—begins in 1967.

102 Brookes, *A Public Nuisance,* xi.

Chapter Two
1967–1971

"There was so much excitement back then because everything was sort of new and fresh . . ."
- Don Walsh (2022)

Talkin' 'Bout My Generation

For the Newfoundland artists that came of age during the 1960s, 1967 seemed to herald the beginning of something. The new Arts and Culture Centre opened in St. John's, a magnificent thousand-seat venue in the capital city of a province that, unlike other Canadian provinces, still had no professional theatre. The St. John's Folk Arts Council had been established just the previous year. CBC television in St. John's released the first broadcast of *All Around the Circle*, bringing a program dedicated to traditional Newfoundland music to regional television for the first time.[103] The year 1967 was something of a cultural watershed in various other parts of North America as well. It was Canada's centenary year and the notions of "regional art" and "Canadian culture" were on the minds and lips of every bureaucrat looking to boost Canadian morale and stimulate tourism.[104] Montreal was getting ready to welcome the world to Expo 67. University of Toronto faculty, students, and other community members were in the process of establishing the free Rochdale College in what had previously been communal

---

103 Roger Bill, "Culture vs. Policy vs. Culture: The Evolution of Cultural Policy in Newfoundland and Labrador, 1967–2007," *Newfoundland and Labrador Studies* 24, no. 1 (2009): 93–4, 97; Rompkey, 271.

104 Bill, 93–4.

and cooperative housing for University of Toronto (UofT) in Yorkville, Toronto's hippie haven.[105] South of the Canada–U.S. border in New York City, a rich and experimental coffeehouse culture flourished. In Harlem, Amiri Baraka's Black Arts Repertory Theatre, established a mere two years before, nourished a renewed spirit of Black cultural pride and identity with new drama, literature, and music.[106] In California, the Diggers, formerly known as the San Francisco Mime Troupe, formed a coalition with roughly two dozen local residents and kicked off the Summer of Love in San Francisco's Haight-Ashbury. In Monterey, a new tradition of massive rock music festivals began with the Monterey Pop Festival, at which tens of thousands of young people heard generationally defining music for the first time, from musicians such as Jimi Hendrix, Janis Joplin, Jefferson Airplane, Simon and Garfunkel, The Who, and Ravi Shankar.[107]

It was against the backdrop of this exciting time that young Newfoundlanders who would go on to be part of the cultural movement began their apprenticeships in the arts. Memorial University and its provincial outreach arm, MUN Extension, provided a bulwark of support and cultivation for existing and budding artists while the local affiliates of the CBC began to diversify their programming creating more employment opportunities for regional artists, writers, and creators. This period also saw the beginning of provincial infrastructure to support local arts and cultural workers, a system which has since continued to develop to the present day. The primarily economically driven nature of the earliest arts and culture infrastructure in Newfoundland set a pattern for future arts funding.[108]

---

105 Roderick MacLeod, *Montreal: The History of a North American City* (Montreal/Kingston: McGill-Queen's University Press, 2017): 240–45; Barrie Zwicker, "Rochdale: The Ultimate Freedom," *Change in Higher Education* 1, no. 6 (Nov–Dec, 1969): 37–43.

106 Margalit Fox, "Amiri Baraka, Polarizing Poet and Playwright, Dies at 79," *The New York Times*, January 9, 2014. https://www.nytimes.com/2014/01/10/arts/amiri-baraka-polarizing-poet-and-playwright-dies-at-79.html; Warren, 20–21.

107 Russell Duncan, "The Summer of Love and Protest: Transatlantic Counterculture in the 1960s," in *The Transatlantic Sixties: Europe and the United States in the Counterculture Decade*, edited by Kosc et al., Transcript Verlag, 2013: 160–62; *Monterey Pop*, directed by D.A. Pennebaker (Leacock-Pennebaker, 1968).

108 Gulliver, 5, 79–80; Webb, "The Rise and Fall of Memorial University's Extension Service, 1959–91," 93, 98; Rompkey, 271.

Treading the Boards and Majoring in Coffeehouse

Young Newfoundlanders and many of their fellow Canadians were on the move in 1967. The sense of impending change and modernity was appealing, drawing people to Canada's big cities. Ron left Ferryland for St. John's and an academic career at MUN that was to last no more than a single semester. "I started majoring in coffeehouse after that," he often joked. He went up to Toronto for the first time some months later, where he discovered the diverse, vibrant, and bohemian community of Kensington Market and promptly fell in love. It remained one of his favourite haunts in Toronto. Years and years later, walking those same streets with him around Spadina Avenue between College and Dundas, we passed a kid who couldn't have been more than eighteen playing a Green Day cover with his battered guitar case hopefully placed open in front of him. Ron dug a crumpled ten-dollar bill out of his jeans pocket and dropped it into the kid's guitar case as we passed, to which the kid smiled and saluted him. "That was nice of you," I remarked. "That used to *be* me," he replied simply. "I busked these streets when I first came to Toronto at seventeen, eighteen years old. It took a while to get my foot in the door at bars and pubs. To make ends meet, I even took an afternoon shift at a strip joint once. I used to back up this daytime stripper on the electric guitar. I'd play *All Along the Watchtower* and stuff like that."

Jane's family left Newfoundland in 1967 for Montreal where the Dingles spent the next four years. Jane and her brothers and sisters attended school while their father, Dr. Dingle, pursued his medical specialization in orthopedic surgery. When she started at St. Laurent High School, Jane was painfully shy and eager to fade into the background, but by the end of her high school career, she was ready to tread the boards, Mrs. Worthington! She joined the school's drama club, read reams of Shakespeare, and took inspiration from the performances of Laurence Olivier and Sybil Thorndike. To come of age in a city like Montreal at the end of the 1960s was surely a wonderful incubation for an artist. Jane evolved into a flower child who wore love beads and worshipped Janis Joplin. In the fall of 1970, not long before the family returned to Newfoundland, Dr. Dingle took his eldest daughter to see *Hair* at the Comédie Canadienne. It's still her favourite musical, next to *Cabaret*, of course.[109]

---

109 Dingle, interview.

Like many of her fellow Newfoundlanders and Canadians, Mary Barry visited Montreal during the Expo.

> So in '67, I was twelve. That was a turning point in my life because when I went to Expo in Montreal, that's where I really got the bug—the cultural bug. By that time, I had already started to be very much into music. My uncle, who worked at Air Canada, flew me and my brother Paddy to Montreal and we spent the whole summer. It was a phenomenal time to be there. Expo 67 was really magical. Every day, we'd go to the site and we'd spend the entire day and night there. There were all these free concerts and there were amazing pavilions. The theme of the Expo was "Transportation and Communications." In fact, they even had a video phone at that point. Me and my brother lined up for three hours to get to use the first video phone. The problem was once we got the phone, all we could do was laugh. We couldn't speak. So the monitor came on and said: "Okay, that's enough of that." And we said: "We haven't even said anything!" They said: "Yes, but you've been laughing for five minutes, so goodbye."[110]

Greg Malone, having just completed his third year at MUN, also found himself in Montreal during the summer of 1967, where he interned at the National Film Board (NFB) with Bryan Hennessey before they both returned to Newfoundland as part of the NFB crew who produced the Fogo Process films. Bryan Hennessey, Sandy Morris, and Noel Dinn wrote music for the Fogo Process films and it was through Hennessey that Malone had gotten to know the music crowd who would eventually invade the MUDS office at MUN.[111] The late 1960s in Newfoundland was a notable time for coalescence and new friendships and artistic partnerships were formed among like-minded aspiring artists.

Greg recalled the first time he met Ron with barely restrained hilarity. As he told the story, it came to me that I'd actually heard Greg tell an abridged version once before—during Ron's eulogy. It really is a

110 Barry, interview.
111 Malone and White, interview; Gulliver, 98–9.

great story and it was wonderful to hear both Greg and (Mary) White tell it; voices overlapping constantly, but from long practice, without the least interruption of one another.

> **Greg:** I remember the first time I met Ron. We were all in university and we were visiting some friends in an apartment on Freshwater Road, and Ron couldn't get out of the bathroom. We only realized after he'd been in there a while. He'd either smoked too much or—I don't know, but he couldn't get out. Everyone was trying to get him out and he was getting more and more panicky . . . [starts hitching with laughter] I said: "Hang on, I think I know how to get you out. Just let go of the handle, okay?" And I talked him out of it—whatever it was—that knob—that had defeated him. He was so relieved he gave me a big embrace, and we got to know each other very well.
>
> **White:** He collapsed into your arms.
>
> **Greg:** Yes. So dramatically, right? You must have been there. Were you there?
>
> **White:** I was there.
>
> **Greg:** Yeah. I thought you were.
>
> **White:** Because I remember I gave up on trying to get him out [laughs].[112]

Nurturing the Arts: Memorial University, MUN Extension, and the CBC

It should come as no surprise that many friendships and partnerships between artists formed within environments created and nourished by Memorial University, for it was MUN and MUN Extension that constituted the most comprehensive support and professional resources for

112 Malone and White, interview.

developing artists. While it is traditionally Extension's rural development agenda that has been emphasized, the program actually provided enormously significant resources for cultivating the arts in both rural and urban communities during the years of its operation.[113] As early as 1962, Extension was recruiting local artists to teach classes in painting, drama, and music in rural communities. Celebrated Newfoundland artist Christopher Pratt taught art and painting in rural Newfoundland for the Extension service in the early 1960s and innumerable other visual artists, writers, actors, and musicians were also employed by Extension—largely on a contract basis—throughout the years of its existence.[114] It is also worth noting that the nature and shape of education at MUN at the time indicates a particular emphasis on the arts.

Academic department members readily recognized the benefits of broad interdisciplinarity and cultural richness that the elements of an arts and humanities education can provide. This was particularly true of MUN's Folklore and English departments. American folklorist Herbert Halpert and his students at MUN undertook some of the first outport oral history collections, some of the earliest of which have only recently been unrestricted to researchers in the Memorial University of Newfoundland Folklore and Language Archive (MUNFLA).[115] George Story, with the assistance of his students, assembled the first edition of the *Dictionary of Newfoundland English*, emphasizing the growing assertion of Newfoundland's uniqueness—a foundational conviction of the cultural movement.[116] Anita Best recalls how scholars like Halpert, Story, and others made important contributions to the emergence of a cultural renaissance in Newfoundland.

> They started getting people interested in collecting folkloric items and the light that they shone on those folkloric customs, songs, stories—basically the culture of rural Newfoundlanders—drew a big spotlight onto our own culture

---

113 Gulliver, 80; Webb, "The Rise and Fall of Memorial University's Extension Service," 85.

114 Webb, "The Rise and Fall of Memorial University's Extension Service," 93; Gulliver, 89, 98–100, 103–108, 129–31, 135–39, 144–47.

115 Between 2022 and 2025, I had the privilege to examine some of the earliest of these outport oral history collections, which are open to the public (MUNFLA, Memorial University of Newfoundland. https://www.mun.ca/munfla/).

116 G.M. Story, W.J. Kirwin and J.D.A. Widdowson (eds.) *Dictionary of Newfoundland English* (Toronto: University of Toronto Press, 1982).

> as opposed to the Canadian culture. Wilfred Wareham, who was from Placentia Bay, a friend of mine, was a Folklore PhD student at Memorial. He introduced people to Rufus Guinchard, for example. The people in St. John's had never heard Rufus play. Wilfred brought him into town and he arranged for him to play at the university and lots of people got interested in his music. It was traditional but yet he composed and played in his own unique style. Gerald Thomas, who was a folklorist who had come to Newfoundland from Wales, got interested in Émile Benoît and did the same thing for Émile. It also opened up an awareness of a French culture in Newfoundland, which hardly anyone on the east coast knew anything about. It was a time of discovery of various elements of Newfoundland culture that the younger people then seized and turned into their own creative endeavours.[117]

The intergenerational, interdisciplinary, and collective nature of the work being done at MUN during the 1960s helped set the tone for the artistic developments of the next decade. The local cultural reclamation that was underway helped preserve elements of Newfoundland's past, its community ethic, its music, storytelling, and theatrical traditions. Guinchard and Benoît were both legendary, self-taught musicians whose specialization was the fiddle—an instrument indispensable to the traditional Newfoundland sound. Young aspiring musicians who were exposed to the music of Guinchard, Benoît, and others helped carry forward a cultural tradition that was still in danger of disappearing. Benoît and Guinchard were in their mid-sixties and mid-seventies respectively when they began to become more widely known across Newfoundland and Labrador. The young people they inspired are today mostly in their sixties and seventies. For now, the last of old Newfoundland is still within living memory thanks to the interventions that took place during the earliest part of the cultural movement.[118]

---

117 Best, interview.

118 Best, interview; Russell, interview.

Ron Hynes, Émile Benoît, Rufus Guinchard, Kelly Russell, 1978.

Kelly Russell and Ron Hynes, 1978.

Émile Benoît, Kelly Russell, Ron Hynes at the Dingles, date unknown.[119]

119 Photographs courtesy of Kelly Russell. Used with permission.

MUN's English department during the late 1960s and early 1970s featured several "men of letters" who, like the faculty in the Folklore department, understood the value of interdisciplinarity, arts education, and support for artists. In fact, quite a few English professors at MUN during this period were artists themselves. Richard Buehler co-founded the theatre organization, The Open Group, in 1968 and continued to be a mentor to young actors throughout his career. The literature of Al Pittman was nourished by his teaching position in the MUN English department. Michael Cook began writing the first of several original plays about Newfoundland, *Colour the Flesh the Colour of Dust*, during his tenure as a drama specialist for MUN Extension. In the workaday world, MUN professors taught classes and their university paychecks supported their own artistic pursuits. In the evenings, they could be found arguing history, politics, and philosophy at parties and in bars in St. John's, perhaps performing a recitation or two. More than one MUN professor was known to moonlight as a musician in one of the local bands that could be found gigging in numerous downtown bars any night of the week. Peter Narváez, one of MUN's most celebrated folklore and music professors, was a well-known rock and blues guitarist in the St. John's music scene. He played a mean harmonica too—Narváez recorded the harmonica solo on the track *Don't Wake Me Up Too Early*, a B-side from the Wonderful Grand Band's first album.[120]

One of the best things about MUN as an institution during the cultural movement was that one did not even have to be an actual student enrolled there to receive support as an aspiring artist. "A lot of people hung around MUN who weren't necessarily registered there," White observed to me.[121] Kelly Russell concurred, and amusingly quoted Greg Thomey from *This Hour Has 22 Minutes*: "We didn't *go* to MUN—we went *up around* MUN."[122] Indeed, almost every artist I interviewed was encouraged and assisted along in their artistic development by some measure of association with Memorial University or MUN Extension, even if they dropped out of MUN, went to a completely different university, or never attended university at all.[123] More than half of all the narrators surveyed

120 Cox, "Newfoundland Travelling Theatre Company," 22; Cox, interview; Hall, interview; Ferry, 145; Devine, 96; *Wonderful Grand Band* (Clode Sound, 1978), LP.

121 Malone and White, interview.

122 Russell, interview.

123 See Appendix 4.

for this book never attended MUN at all, yet the institution still provided spaces or resources that figured largely in their artistic development.[124] The Little Theatre at MUN was given freely to the kids in MUDS who used it for experimentation, rehearsal space, and performances, but it was also given to other young aspiring artists—often through the efforts of MUN Extension—who had no affiliation with the university other than community proximity.[125] The seemingly deliberate blurring of lines between institutional space and community space made MUN's impact as a development organization all the more widespread. Sandy Morris, Greg Malone, and White all had wonderful stories to tell about the shows they used to put on at the Little Theatre during the mid-to-late 1960s. "We did a show there in 1967 called *The J. Alfred Prufrock Hour*,"[126] Sandy told me, "and the Philadelphia Cream Cheese Band would have been part of that."[127] I had to laugh out loud at the band name—that was the first I'd heard of it. "By 1967," Sandy told me, "we were almost the most popular band in town, doing like psychedelic music, you know?"

> It was really fun. We had a light show with the ink blobs, all that kind of psychedelia going on in the background, like a Grateful Dead show. We had hangers-on, fellas who would come to do the light show because they were just into experimenting with that. We would hang out and perform at what was called, at the time, the Little Theatre at MUN, which is now the Reid Theatre. It's been closed down because it was full of asbestos. It's a wonder we're even still here. But that was a great venue for us to be able to experiment with. I remember doing a show where Hennessey came up through a hole in the stage, on top of which we had placed a garbage bucket with no bottom in it. So he came up through a garbage bucket and onto the stage, you know what I mean? It was fantastic![128]

---

124 See Appendix 5.

125 Pamela Hall, "Report on the Reid Theatre History Project," (April 2016): 2.

126 This production was a musical/theatrical review written by Michael Cook, Rex Murphy, Tom Kelly, Shane O'Dea, and Elliot Leyton and featuring a large cast of MUDS theatre kids, young musicians, and dancers ("MUDS, The J. Alfred Prufrock Hour," theatrical program/handbill, Memorial University of Newfoundland Digital Archives Initiative. https://dai.mun.ca/PDFs/handbillsarts/MUDSTheJAlfredPrufrockHour.pdf).

127 Morris, interview (the Philadelphia Cream Cheese Band featured Sandy Morris, Noel Dinn, Bryan Hennessey, and Derek Pelley).

128 Morris, interview.

Greg and White recalled how the music crowd who hung around the MUDS office began to organize lunch hour concerts at the Little Theatre. The kids who would go on to form musical groups like Figgy Duff, Red Island, and the Wonderful Grand Band began experimenting with popular rock music and inviting their fellow students to see them play in between classes. Afterwards, they would pass a hat around and invite people to pay what they could.

> **Greg:** Who was it that used to do lunch hour concerts?
>
> **White:** Hennessey, Sandy, Derek [Pelley], Wayne Brace, me, Noel Dinn, Laverne Squires . . .
>
> **Greg:** They'd go around and put up signs. White would go and see Lord Thomson, the chancellor, and ask permission. He'd say: "Yes, okay." So, off we went with our signs and put them up all around. Everyone would come in with their bags of lunch and sit in the theatre and watch the show. The boys would do Jimi Hendrix or Led Zeppelin, or whatever was going on.
>
> **White:** Frank Zappa, The Who, Jefferson Airplane. Laverne did an incredible version of "White Rabbit."
>
> **Greg:** Oh my God, yes!
>
> **White:** Brought the house down.
>
> **Greg:** Just chilled you. People loved it. So, the place would be full at lunchtime. After a while, everyone was going there for lunch.[129]

Another artistic resource space at the university was CHMR, MUN's campus radio station. Don Walsh, founding member of Red Island and a major player in Newfoundland's music industry since the 1970s, spoke about how welcoming CHMR was to young musicians who were looking to record demos or have their music heard locally.

> There was so much excitement back then because everything was sort of new and fresh—the fact that you could go to CHMR radio and people would be hanging around recording things.

129 Malone and White, interview.

> I remember Sandy and Bryan Hennessey and Laverne Squires, and I think it was Derek Pelley—the four of them recorded this tape of all these traditional Newfoundland songs which nobody had done before this. You know, everything was your regular "Newfie" type songs, as much as I hate that word. But that's what people were doing back then. You know, your *Jack Was Every Inch a Sailor* and all the rest. And here's Laverne in the CHMR recording *The Bloody Gardener*, or something.[130]

While the power of the academic institution with a regional and community development mandate was indispensable to the growth of an arts movement, it is important to acknowledge the particular individuals who ran various programs at MUN and Extension. Much change and impact seems to have been driven by individuals in key positions of influence in institutions, not simply by the existence of the institutions themselves. However, perhaps it is also fair to say that institutions like MUN and Extension provided secure platforms or positions of influence from which individuals *could* encourage change should they wish to. The NFB often gets more credit for the impact of the Fogo Process films than Extension does, yet the initiative would not have taken the shape it did without the mandate of Extension and the influence of its director Don Snowden, whose first priority was to empower people to undertake change and development, yet also saw the nurturing of art or culture as key to bringing marginalized or disenfranchised others into the mainstream. The practical result was that the Fogo Process films managed to do all these things.[131]

A sizeable proportion of the narrators I consulted for this study mentioned Edythe Goodridge with deep gratitude and appreciation.[132] Curator and manager of the Memorial University Art Gallery, and later a member of the Canada Council for a number of years, Goodridge was a tireless advocate and champion of Newfoundland art and artists of various disciplines. Musicians and theatre artists who, thanks to the

---

130 Don Walsh, interview by author, St. John's, July 27, 2022.

131 Webb, "The Rise and Fall of Memorial University's Extension Service," 84, 93–5; Gulliver, 80, 95–7.

132 Best, interview; Mary Walsh, interview by author, Seattle/St. John's, September 13, 2022; Bob Joy, interview by author, Seattle/New York, September 3, 2022; Russell, interview; Hall, interview; Jones, interview; Rhonda Payne, interview by Winifred Mellor for the STAGE Project, St. John's, September 13–14, 1995.

efforts of Extension, were given free rehearsal and performance space in downtown St. John's or at MUN's Little Theatre never failed to mention particular Extension workers by name when touting the virtues of the program overall—making it clear that it was the people running the program as much as the program itself that made the difference.[133]

* * *

Memorial University may have been a dynamo in terms of artistic and cultural development during the 1960s, but the CBC was also an important institution when it came to nourishing and supporting the arts. While local CBC television programming was fairly limited until the 1970s, CBC radio had long been a significant employer for local theatrical and musical talent. In a region with no professional theatre and a mostly bar-based music scene, the CBC helped many artists pay the bills during the 1950s and 1960s in Newfoundland.[134] Local writers received commissions to write radio dramas or had their existing plays adapted for radio and many local actors were able to access opportunities for paid gigs despite the absence of a regional professional theatre. Interestingly, even after the development of a much broader theatre scene in the 1970s as well as the expansion of CBC's television programming, CBC radio in Newfoundland continued to flourish as a producer of local cultural content, continuing to air original and adapted radio plays, documentaries, and original music by local artists well into the twenty-first century, when many North Americans might argue that radio itself is past its time.[135]

Like Memorial University and many other institutions in the Atlantic region during the late 1960s and early 1970s, the CBC was open to experimentation and unique programming. If a theatrical production

133 Boak, (1984); Jones, interview; Mary Walsh, interview; Joy, interview; Best, interview, Russell, interview; Hall, interview; Joy, interview; Best, interview; Russell, interview; Hall, interview.

134 Ferry, 145; Devine, 341–42; Hall, interview.

135 Ferry, "Professional Theatre," 145; Devine, "Necessary Evils," 341-43; Michael Windover and Hilary Grant, "Chapter Nine: Tuning in to Radio Heritage in Newfoundland," in Tuuli Lähdesmäki, Suzie Thomas and Yujie Zhu (eds.) *Politics of Scale: New Directions in Critical Heritage Studies* (New York: Berghahn Books, 2019): 146–47, 152–53; Sara Beth Keough, "Canada's Cultural Media Policy and Newfoundland Music on the Radio: Local Identities and Global Implications" (unpublished PhD dissertation, University of Tennessee, 2007): 267–70.

or musical group did well locally or had a successful tour outside the province, the CBC was often receptive to creating original local programming with them. This was notably the case with CODCO and the Mummers Troupe later on in the 1970s, but even in the late 1960s, the oddest artistic partnerships could pop up between local talent and the CBC. Internationally renowned Newfoundland actor Robert Joy, known for many years to his Newfoundland artist colleagues and fans as "Bob" Joy, spoke fondly of one of his earliest theatrical experiences. Predictably, it was in high school, but rather less predictably, it was a production in partnership with the local CBC.

> I was sixteen in 1967. I was just finishing high school and coming into Memorial. There was a little sign at Brother Rice High School of something going on because Brother Bellows, the principal there, got the idea to produce Gilbert and Sullivan operettas and actually cooperate with the girls' school, Holy Heart, up the hill. But they were very separate and so, it was a bit of a radical thing. Not radical, but you know, it took us out of our comfort zone to suddenly be cooperating with the girls and the nuns from Holy Heart. The first thing we did was a concert version of *The Mikado*. He [Brother Bellows] wanted me to sing Nanki-Poo because I was one of the tenors, and I had a pretty good singing voice. The next year we did *Pirates of Penzance* and he wanted me to sing Frederic, which is the romantic lead. Looking back on it now, it seems it was the beginning of the ramp-up to the renaissance in the way that Brother Bellows felt that it was worth approaching the CBC. There's talent here. He thought: "The CBC should chip in with this and maybe if I could promise them a broadcast, they would build the sets." So, suddenly it went from being a school production to being this very professionally designed set. After we did it live for our parents and friends in the beautiful Holy Heart theatre, we were somehow—I was going to use the word "contracted" but none of us got paid—we were somehow asked or committed to doing it at CBC studios for a regional broadcast. So, there was that sense of pride: "Let's do it!" And these people at the CBC, who were eager to flex their muscles, stretch their wings—whatever you want to call

> it—they were used to making a set for a talk show or a news broadcast. Suddenly they're doing a set for *Pirates of Penzance*. Everyone had a great time. We got great feedback from that.[136]

Everywhere one looked in late 1960s and early 1970s Newfoundland, there was an emphasis on experimentation, optimism, collectivism, interdisciplinarity, and intergenerational partnership. And yet, the most visible institutional presence was mostly limited to the province's one and only university and the local radio and television broadcasting affiliates. The profusion of up-and-coming talent that was nourished and uplifted under the aegis of MUN and the CBC alone is impressive. That being said, Newfoundland artists had other local allies and venues that welcomed them during the early years of their professional development, particularly St. John's businesses in the hospitality and service industry.

The Slippery Spotlight

The existing bar and pub culture and the appearance of a limited coffeehouse culture in St. John's during the late 1960s and 1970s were important sources of cultivation and support for local musicians. The province's capital city already had a decades-long tradition of live music by the late 1960s. Most bars and pubs booked a different band every week to play live during the evenings, but of course, these establishments could not welcome musicians who were not yet of age. A few coffeehouses appeared in St. John's during the mid-to-late 1960s that helped meet this need and provided space for young musicians to experiment, network, and have their music heard. Over the course of my oral history project, I learned about two coffeehouses that showcased young musical talent from the St. John's area at this time: The Void and the Café Y.[137] Sandy Morris recalled in a 2009 interview that there had also been another coffeehouse established in the basement of a residential home in the St. John's area.[138] There may well have been other similar

136 Joy, interview.
137 Malone and White, interview; Morris, interview; Don Walsh, interview; Barry, interview; Bryan Hennessey, interview by Craig Stowe for the STAGE Project, February 2, 1998, 10.
138 Gulliver, 200.

establishments, but I was unfortunately unable to find records or mention of any others in interviews or in surviving business directories from the period.[139] Both The Void and Café Y were small venues and emerged as minor, ancillary spaces attached to larger businesses and institutions—truly, experimentation was everywhere in the 1960s. Café Y was attached to the YMCA, which back then was located at the corner of New Cove Road and King's Bridge Road.[140] The Void was located on Harvey Road in an alley between the building that once housed the C.L.B. Armoury and a Dominion supermarket before both were destroyed by the terrible Harvey Road fire in 1992.[141] Several of the narrators I interviewed for this project recalled meeting Ron and/or seeing him play live for the first time at The Void. Don Walsh saw him play at the coffeehouse for the first time as early as 1967.

> I remember the first time I ever went to a gig on my own. There was a place on Harvey Road, it was a coffee shop. There was no booze so, of course, us kids could go there and a guy named Ron Hynes was playing there that night. I sat in the audience and I heard this guy sing and play guitar and he pretty much changed my life. I was so fascinated by watching him and listening to him that night that I sort of decided it was something that I wanted to do as well. Ron was probably only a kid then too. I don't think he was that much older than me, if at all. So, if I was fourteen or fifteen, well then Ron was only fifteen or sixteen.

139 *Henderson's St. John's Newfoundland City Directory, 1968, including Mount Pearl* (Winnipeg: Henderson Directories Ltd, 1968). See also *Henderson's* 1969, 1970, 1973, 1975, 1977, 1978–79.

140 In the original theatrical program for *The J. Alfred Prufrock Hour*, "The Café Why" is listed on the advertisements page. The location given was indeed New Cove Road, and the café was billed as "St. John's oldest and finest coffee house, presenting the best in folk entertainment, Fridays 9:30 p.m." Since this ad is listed above one for Coca Cola (which almost certainly did not bankroll this production), it seems reasonable to assume this ad might be tongue-in-cheek. I am pretty sure it was called the "Café Y" and not "Café Why." What's more, most of the young musicians appearing in the show would likely have performed there regularly, and probably appreciated the opportunity to promote their other shows ("MUDS, The J. Alfred Prufrock Hour," theatrical program/handbill, Memorial University of Newfoundland Digital Archives Initiative. https://dai.mun.ca/PDFs/handbillsarts/MUDSTheJAlfredPrufrockHour.pdf).

141 *Henderson's* (1968), 120; Malone and White, interview; Barry, interview; Ryan Cooke, "25 years after Harvey Road inferno, St. John's is still nervous about fire," *CBC News*, December 22, 2017. https://www.cbc.ca/news/canada/newfoundland-labrador/harvey-road-fire-25-year-anniversary-downtown-st-johns-1.4461522.

> I think Sandy was probably doing gigs back then as well, and Bryan Hennessey and all the rest of them. But for someone like Ron to come along and all of a sudden be writing all of his own songs. I mean, nobody in Newfoundland was doing that. Who the hell in Newfoundland did gigs and filled the place and did nothing but sing their own songs? Everybody was doing covers in there somewhere, whereas Ron was doing his own stuff, which was pretty exciting at the time.[142]

Mary Barry also recalled meeting Ron and seeing him play for the first time at The Void in 1970, where she sang an impromptu duet with him.

> I was fifteen when I went to Holy Heart. I was a real lover of music, but as of yet, I still hadn't taken any training. I had this horrible experience where the nuns wouldn't let me sing because they said, quote: "Girls with deep voices can't sing." Can you imagine getting away with that today? So I was basically forced to pantomime all through school. I never sang. And in my heart, I knew they were wrong. I knew that wasn't true. I knew I could sing; I just had a deep voice.
>
> I had five or six friends and they all knew that I was really crazy about music. Anyway, we went to this place called The Void. They sold coffee and jelly donuts for ten cents. We were all just foolish; we weren't drinking or anything, we just wanted to do something different. So, we walked in and there was Ron Hynes. He would have been about nineteen, and he was singing his songs. Everyone was like: "Mary, you should get up there with him," because they all knew I was a closet singer. Anyway, they literally pushed me up. One of them, she went up and said: "We have a friend here who's really good, and really would love to sing." Ron said: "Sure, tell her to come up." I got up there, and I said: "Do you know 'The Losing End' by Neil Young?" He said: "Oh yeah, what key?" I said: "I don't know." And he goes: "Doesn't matter, let's just do it in his key." So we sang the song, we had harmonies. Anyway, it was a blast. The girls all went

142 Don Walsh, interview.

> nuts because it was really fun seeing me do it. And of course, everybody was in love with Ron Hynes because back then, Ron was already a bit of a character, you know? He wasn't famous—in that way. We didn't know anybody who was old enough to have a career, but you could tell he was already . . . this was his thing. So that completely, utterly affected my entire life because I knew that that was what I wanted to do too.[143]

Sandy Morris, with whom Ron would go on to play a-million-and-one gigs, saw him play for the first time at The Void as well. "There were a couple of coffeehouses that happened around the same time," Sandy told me. "Sixties, you know," he said laughing.

> By the time I met Ron, The Beatles had already made a huge impression on everybody and we all realized that if you were going to make any money in the music business, you had to write songs. So, we were all writing songs and none of them were any good. Then Ron came in and he was an actual songwriter, and it was a big difference between what Ron was writing and what the rest of us were writing. We were playing at being songwriters, but Ron was an actual songwriter and you could tell right away. His songs made sense, they had melody, they had shape, they had lyrical integrity, they were poetic. They had everything going that we were striving for, but this guy already had it.[144]

The small, low-key coffeehouse culture in St. John's welcomed young musicians and helped showcase their talent, but there were exponentially more bars in St. John's than coffeehouses and for most of the mid-twentieth century, they were the main employers of local musical talent in the area other than the CBC. That being said, Sandy noted, there didn't seem to be much money in it in the early days.

> All of the older guys that were pre-rock 'n' roll, who were in the horn bands and the swing bands—they all had day jobs.

143 Barry, interview.
144 Morris, interview.

> A lot of those older dudes were gigging at night so they could get out of the house. You know, get away from the wife and the kids and have a few beers. And they often picked a gig depending on what the price of beer was in the establishment. So, if they got offered a gig at The Tudor Inn[145] for fifty bucks for the whole band—like ten bucks each—and the price of beer was $1.25, but they got offered a gig for $7 each at another bar, but the price of beer was 50 cents, they'd take the cheaper beer because they'd end up owing money to the club otherwise.
>
> This year, I actually found the bookkeeping from the Philadelphia Cream Cheese Band in 1967. So, a list of every gig and how much money we made and where the money went, which was mostly to the bank to pay off the gear we had to buy. Members of the band were getting $2.50 each, so we'd go out for fish 'n' chips after a gig, and that was basically what we got paid. But see, the only guy who ever got paid any amount of money was Noel [Dinn], because he was the only one who drove. So, Noel would say: "Jeez b'y, look. I can't take the car; I've got to get a brake job." "Oh, we'll have to give you a hundred bucks tonight to get brakes taken care of or else we can't get a lift to the gig with you." Yeah, I had no idea that you could actually be a musician for a living.[146]

Packaging, Marketing and Qualifying Culture

While making a living solely as a professional artist of any type in 1960s Newfoundland and Labrador was challenging to say the least, the late 1960s did see the first development of provincial infrastructure to support artists and the arts in general, a system that has continued to grow and evolve to the present day. Ronald Rompkey has argued that

145 See Appendix 6.
146 Morris, interview.

the new focus on arts infrastructure and funding beginning at that time was primarily instituted to achieve short-term economic goals and as such, set a pattern for provincial arts policy, which working artists and their supporters still considered to be problematic as late as the 1990s.[147] It was no coincidence that some of the earliest arts and culture infrastructure in Newfoundland and Labrador was established around the same time as Canada's centenary, as well as the 1966 Come Home Year.

Come Home Year is a tourism campaign that pops up from time to time in Newfoundland, as well as in other Canadian provinces and towns, and is intended to encourage the return of expatriates who visit their families and ancestral communities while pumping some much-needed and appreciated money into the local economy. In fact, tourism campaigns were underway all across Canada as the nation's centennial year approached. In anticipation of the revenue that might be encouraged, government money was channelled into artistic and cultural efforts to showcase each province's regional uniqueness.

The St. John's Folk Arts Council was first established in 1966, a development that had been implemented in virtually every other Canadian province in recent years. Canadian government officials administering the arts were very interested in finding ways to articulate and celebrate "Canadian" culture in the wake of the nation's hundredth birthday. However, as James Overton has shown, the Canadian government was equally interested in packaging those articulations and celebrations in a medium that could be marketed to tourists.[148] This coupling of culture with capitalism is not new in Newfoundland. Significant outmigration induced by economic struggle was a phenomenon Newfoundland began to see as early as the 1880s, and it was during the late nineteenth century that the region's active promotion as a tourist destination began. Such campaigns touted Newfoundland primarily as a hunting or sightseeing destination and the emphasis on ecotourism and the commodification of the island's environmental beauty has survived to the present. Nostalgia was likewise a part of this formula from the beginning. In 1904, "Old Home Week" was launched. The newly completed railroad brought thousands of returned Newfoundland expats and their families to St. John's for a public celebration at Bannerman Park.

---

147 Rompkey, 271, 274–75.
148 Overton, "Coming Home," 95–7.

The organizers commissioned rousing and patriotic songs to be written, paid musicians to perform, and commissioned the printing and painting of pretty postcards for tourists to buy. Old Home Week survived into the 1920s but did not recur during the Depression or the years of World War II. Come Home Year of 1966 brought expats to St. John's via the newly completed Trans-Canada Highway and was meant to showcase the accrued benefits of Confederation, foster a closer sense of cultural identification between Newfoundland and Canada, and generate much-desired tourism revenue. The organizers used the old familiar strategy of hiring performers and artists for public cultural events. This repeated strategy of funding the arts primarily to achieve short-term economic goals led to a pattern of stunted development in provincial arts infrastructure.[149]

In addition to the coupling of capitalism with Newfoundland culture and history, some scholars and commentators have charged that the early part of the renaissance featured a noted preference for "high culture" among elites and bureaucracy. Exactly what is meant by this term is difficult to define precisely, but the inference behind the various criticisms seems to suggest two things: a disregard for the work of local artists and creators, and a preference for colonial repertoire of primarily British and American origins. Roger Bill, Alan Filewod, and David Ferry have commented on the development of arts infrastructure in Newfoundland and Labrador since the 1960s with a particular emphasis on the role of the late John Perlin, head of the Division of Cultural Affairs for several decades.

John was the son of noted philanthropist Vera Crosbie Perlin and Albert Perlin, one of Newfoundland's most respected and well-known journalists and a long-time political associate and friend of Joey Smallwood's. John Perlin was appointed to his position under circumstances that many have since considered to be problematic, despite the fact that nepotism and cronyism have a long and enduring presence in the history of Newfoundland's political life.[150] Walter Learning, a philosophy professor at MUN, approached Smallwood in 1966 about launching an Equity[151] theatre organization for Newfoundland in the new Arts

149 Overton, "A Newfoundland Culture?" 8; Overton, "Coming Home," 92–96; Gulliver, 49–51; Rompkey, 270–71, 279; Bill, 94–5, 98–9.

150 Bill, 91; Filewod, "The Mummers Troupe," (1998); Ferry, 146–7; Neary, The Political Economy of Newfoundland, 1929–1972, 11–13, 17, 19–20

151 In Canada, an Equity production company adheres to Canadian Actors Equity Association (CAEA) standards in terms of working conditions like health, safety, pay, and pension contributions. Having Equity status basically means that the actor is fully unionized.

and Culture Centre in St. John's. MUN Extension staff had hoped to have a hand in the new Centre's programming, a prospect Smallwood apparently rejected vehemently. Nonetheless, Joey seemed initially receptive to Learning's ideas. However, Learning was later informed in a meeting with Albert Perlin that his son John was to be appointed head of the Division of Cultural Affairs instead. Learning was offered the position of Artistic Director reporting to John Perlin, which he promptly and firmly declined. Learning's vision was eventually instrumental in the founding of Theatre New Brunswick. Following the meeting with Albert Perlin, Learning was quoted in the St. John's *Evening Telegram*: "To get a job, you either speak to Joey and his pals, or you speak to no one."[152]

John Perlin's cultural policy was much criticized during and following his long tenure as Director of Cultural Affairs. Patrick O'Flaherty observed that the entirety of the province's arts policy between the 1960s and the 1990s may largely be reduced to an "Arts and Culture Centre policy," with John Perlin seemingly calling every shot as far as funding and programming went.[153] In their respective memoirs, Chris Brookes and Dudley Cox expressed the same opinion.[154] Staff in Extension's Visual and Performing Arts section noted that the Centres failed to encourage Newfoundland culture or provide support for local professional artists, for which purposes the institution had presumably been built.[155] Greg Malone and White noted the lack of regional content on display at the Arts and Culture Centre in St. John's during the late 1960s and early 1970s, but attributed it as much to an economic bottom line as to any cultural preferences.

> **Greg:** The shows at the Arts and Culture Centre—it was all Reveen[156] and stuff from away. There was no Newfoundland culture at the Arts and Culture Centre. We couldn't get in.
>
> **White:** Well, they had the amateur theatre.
>
> **Greg:** Yeah, the St. John's Players would do a show there, or

152 Ferry, 146–7.

153 Patrick O'Flaherty, "Drawing Conclusions: A Report of the Arts Policy Committee" (1990): 1, quoted in Bill, 94.

154 Brookes, *A Public Nuisance*, 39–40, 70, 105–106, 152; Cox, "Newfoundland Travelling Theatre Company," 25.

155 Gulliver, 101–102.

156 Touring illusionist and hypnotist.

something like that. But basically it was the preserve of the Carlton Showband . . .

White: The Clancy Brothers Band . . .

Greg: It was all that Irish-y stuff. The Clancy Brothers, Anna McGoldrick, and Reveen. The big crowd pleasers. They wanted to keep money made. They weren't interested in anything that might not bring in a big crowd, untried, like Newfoundland culture. It changed after a while. It changed while we were there basically. But at the beginning . . .

White: It wasn't even considered. Who cared? No one was trying to do it.[157]

However, White went on to add, some of the young artists and musicians from MUDS did get one look-see at the Arts and Culture Centre when it first opened and apparently, it was due to the popularity of the lunch hour concerts at the Little Theatre.

White: I really don't know how this happened, and Hennessey's gone now, so he might have remembered. But we ended up with a show at the new Arts and Culture Centre that had just been opened. And for some reason, the Philadelphia Cream Cheese Band performed with costumes borrowed from . . .

Greg: . . . From MUDS. The kind of medieval stuff Hennessey was wearing—Hennessey loved dressing up.

White: And Hennessey decided to break up an amp, à la The Who or Jimi Hendrix. Now, the amp was already broken, naturally.

Greg: You could hardly afford a new amp to break.

White: They could hardly afford an amp to *play.* That wasn't even what got the attention. The fact that he turned his back on the audience to break up the amp . . .

157 Malone and White, interview.

> **Greg:** À la Marlon Brando, right? And his performance was so passionate. He was sweating and spitting and just giving everything! It was like: "Whoa! You can do this? Look at this guy go!" People were revved.[158]

The performance described here does not particularly resemble Newfoundland culture. However, it is easy to see how someone like John Perlin might be slow to book such budding artists again. Even with a rather loose understanding of just what is meant and intended by the designation of "high culture," it is probably safe to say that for John Perlin, this wasn't it. Young people may have been "revved," but it's hard to imagine anyone over thirty being so. Smashing the innards out of an amplifier dressed in a medieval doublet and hose sounds awesome to me personally, but I was born in 1982. In 1967, such a raucous, edgy, and rebellious performance was as far removed culturally from the gentle folksiness of Anna McGoldrick and The Clancy Brothers Band as it is possible to imagine. The generation gap, it seemed, had never been wider. It would be a few more years before such daring art—to say nothing of local or regional art—would find a prominent place on the stage of the Arts and Culture Centre, five more of which would be constructed and opened across the province in the ensuing years and all of which would fall under the programming aegis of John Perlin.[159]

The Arts and Culture Centre and Community Theatre

Despite the criticism of Perlin's administration of Cultural Affairs and his perceived tendency to privilege colonial art over local, and amateur acts over professional ones, it is worth noting that quite a few young actors gained mentorship and experience at Newfoundland's Arts and Culture Centres during their first few years, as well as in the amateur theatre scene. The annual Dominion Drama Festival and the

---

158 Malone and White, interview.

159 Filewod, "The Mummers Troupe," (1998).

considerable number of local theatre groups like the St. John's Players, the Freelance Players, The Open Group, the Carol Players, The Kinsmen, and The Press Club helped give aspiring artists a foundation upon which to build. In their formative years, CODCO founding members Greg Malone, Mary Walsh, and Tommy Sexton all gained experience and mentorship in the amateur theatre scene. Malone appeared as Merlin in a production of *Camelot* with either the St. John's Players or the Freelance Players (it is unclear which) as a teenager in the mid-1960s.[160] Mary Walsh made her first theatrical appearance at the Arts and Culture Centre's Basement Theatre in an original play by Dudley Cox called *Sing a Song of Sixpence* in 1971. Thirteen-year-old Tommy Sexton played the title role in *Oliver* with the St. John's Players in November of 1970. "He was outstanding," Dudley wrote many years later. "One enduring memory is of him sitting alone on a box, a candle burning beside him, singing 'Where is Love?' He was a born actor."[161]

When Bob Joy first seriously caught the theatre bug, it was the St. John's Players and the broader St. John's amateur theatre scene that helped to cultivate and nourish him artistically and inspired him to pursue the arts professionally. In 1969, while working as a summer camp counsellor near Huntsville, Ontario, Joy and two of his fellow counsellors used their four-day holiday between camping sessions to attend the Stratford Festival.

> We decided to hitchhike to Stratford, kind of as a lark. We saw Kenneth Welsh play Hamlet. We saw an amazing production of *Satyricon*. Later, Cedric Smith and a bunch of people were singing at a coffeehouse there called The Black Swan. I remember we were very much in the middle of a hippie kind of feeling. There was patchouli everywhere, incense, you know, the coffeehouse thing was big. In any case, the whole experience, especially *Satyricon*, to use the phrase from the period, "blew my mind." And when I came back to St. John's after that summer, my interest was rekindled from the Gilbert and Sullivan days of high

160 Cox, "Newfoundland Travelling Theatre," 11, 22–3, 28, 31; Greg Malone, interview by Liam O'Keefe for the STAGE Project, St. John's, March 20, 2012, 3; Gulliver, 211.

161 Cox, "Newfoundland Travelling Theatre," 28, 31.

> school. I said: "Let me get involved with community theatre." There were a whole bunch of people setting a very high bar for community theatre in St. John's. I auditioned for and got a little part in *HMS Pinafore* at the Arts and Culture Centre. Loved that. And so, when you ask what got me involved in the arts, that was the journey. By the time I was doing that, I realized that there was a family feeling—that community theatre was called that for a good reason. It's not just that you perform for the community, but the team that puts together the shows is a community. I found great confidence and solace and companionship and friendship in that community. The next summer, I successfully auditioned for *Charley's Aunt*. That would have been 1970, the next year. I got so much positive feedback from that. I guess it was after that that I started thinking: "Wow, I wonder if one can do this for a living."[162]

Jane Dingle was having a similar experience—getting involved in community theatre and exploring the possibility of becoming a professional actor. She and Bob Joy appeared onstage together at the Arts and Culture Centre in The Kinsmen's 1971 production of *The Mikado*, directed by John Holmes.[163, 164] Jane played Pitti-Sing and Joy played Koko—a production I desperately wish I could have seen, if only to have heard Bob Joy, the quirky coroner from *CSI: New York*, sing "I've Got a Little List" or "Tit-Willow." Jane performed in just one more community theatre production—*Soft Voices* with the St. John's Players—before both she and Bob Joy went on to join the cast of the Newfoundland Travelling Theatre Company's first production, *See How They Run*, in the summer of 1972.[165]

---

162 Joy, interview.

163 Former long-time member of the London Players, John Holmes had a long career in the professional and amateur theatre scene in St. John's as an actor, director, theatre critic, and mentor to young aspiring artists.

164 "Profile: Actress Jane Dingle keeps active with stage, film, television work," *The Newfoundland Herald TV Week*, November 1, 1978, 4.

165 Dingle, interview; Cox, interview; Cox, "Newfoundland Travelling Theatre," 34–5.

An Atlantic-Wide Counterculture

While undoubtedly not every participant in the cultural movement would agree, many engaged with it based on a desire to decolonize, preserve, resurrect, or innovate regional artistic and cultural forms. At the same time, it was also heavily influenced by a broad international youth counterculture movement within the Atlantic world and beyond. Within Western European nations like Britain and France and fellow Atlantic nations like Canada and the United States—the very colonizing entities that dominated the North Atlantic region politically, economically, and culturally—young people began to question the nature and legitimacy of that domination. Scholars typically note that the 1960s and 1970s counterculture originated most visibly among young, middle-class, White North Americans, probably one of the most privileged populations on planet Earth at the time. Ironically, this group of people who seemed to have everything—including everything that various post-colonial Atlantic peoples were still struggling for—had decided that much of it was either hollow, or did more harm than good. Capitalism, the middle-class lifestyle, progress, industry, modernization, the exceptionalism of Western civilization and political institutions—all of these concepts and constructs were now under indictment. The cultural and intellectual implications were far-reaching, and young people began to reject entire paradigms of living, working, believing, and being, and in turn, embraced others.[166]

The post-World War II world was one of disappointed idealism for many young people. The geopolitical configurations of the Cold War, with its competing political ideologies, exorbitant militarism, and proliferation of doomsday weapons, seemed a nearly dystopian shift from the high hopes that the end of World War II had brought. To many youth in the United States, the failure of the system seemed complete. In the world's richest nation and supposedly the most free, poverty and racism were still keeping large proportions of the population oppressed and threatened with violence. Both professional and domestic life across North America had proved patriarchal, confining, and stifling. Many members of the most privileged and gently raised generation in history had looked upon the price of that privilege, and

166 Jeremi Suri, "The Rise and Fall of an International Counterculture, 1960–1975," *The American Historical Review* 114, no. 1 (Feb. 2009): 46, 49, 53, 58, 67; Duncan, 144–45, 150.

opted to reject it rather than conform. The counterculture expressed itself in exceedingly numerous ways—too many to explore sufficiently in this, or indeed, any one study—but most embodied resistance to or rejection of the Establishment, whether that meant becoming an anti-war or anti-nuclear activist; burning your draft card or your bra; joining your local college chapter of Students for a Democratic Society; supporting the Black Power or Red Power movement, or the causes of Women's Liberation or Gay Liberation. Hippies were firmly anti-Establishment as well but, unlike their New Left political counterparts, they were less interested in reforming or improving society as it currently existed than in opting out of it entirely. Hippies envisioned a world that rejected rationalism, progress, and modernism and embraced communal, environmental, and humanistic values. Many youth, however, were neither passionately political nor deeply invested in pursuing a hippie lifestyle and expressed their opposition to their parents and the Establishment with thrifted fashion, long hair, rock music, and experimentation with sex and drugs.[167] While the various manifestations of the counterculture comprised an extremely diverse group of people and perspectives, they had something crucial in common besides resistance to the Establishment—art. The ideals of all of these intertwined movements were expressed in art and culture and in turn, their transatlantic and international nature could only galvanize more young people to embrace the counterculture.

By the late 1960s and 1970s, young people were questioning all kinds of established norms and values on both sides of the Atlantic. In the British Isles, regional independence and cultural decolonization movements in Ireland, Scotland, and Wales were the most direct expressions of the questioning that was underway, but in addition, political satire and criticism of the prevailing class system were now in vogue in mainstream entertainment. Most notable is the overt criticism or caricaturing of politicians, the monarchy, and the royal family—a glaring departure from the overweening deference on the part of the media and the broader public that the Windsors and the ruling class had always enjoyed. Television shows like *That Was the Week That Was* and *Monty Python's Flying Circus* showed that both regionalism and elements of the counterculture were alive and well, even at the epicentre of the former

167 Suri, 45–7, 51, 53–4, 56–7, 60, 67; Duncan, 144–47, 148–53, 155–60, 164–65.

Empire.[168] Britain and Ireland saw a surge in the popularity of irreverent sketch comedy, as well as a reinvigoration of traditional Celtic and regional folk music during the 1960s. Like so many other cultural trends of the day, these had a transatlantic quality as well. Newfoundlanders were strongly influenced by such art and began to experiment with it themselves, infusing it with their own culture, perspective, and humour.

During the late 1960s, Welsh, Scottish, and Irish nationalists, critical of historic and ongoing economic, political, linguistic, and cultural domination by imperial England, expressed their criticism and resistance in various ways, from cultural nationalism or political activism to outright violent resistance. The ongoing Northern Ireland conflict was the most extreme example and one that would continue for decades more. In Ireland, the political struggle and the accompanying desire for national healing from Ireland's colonial past left their marks on the art of the day, including Irish music. Along with a resurrection of regional linguistic and cultural elements, Irish musicians began to reawaken an interest in traditional music. Like Newfoundland musicians, Irish artists drew inspiration from their folk tradition but also from the jazz, blues, and rock 'n' roll influences that arose in previous decades from the Black community in the United States. The Horslips, who appeared during the late 1960s, were probably the most visible of the new Celtic Rock bands and among the first to blend traditional folk influences with the sounds of American rock, but this trend of fusing folk with jazz, blues, or rock 'n' roll influences spread still further. Soon, Britain was alive with folk-rock influences.[169] Anita Best described the transatlantic nature of traditional music and how it found its way back into vogue among young Newfoundlanders in the late 1960s and early 1970s.

> I came from a singing family, so I was always an unaccompanied folk singer, and I liked to sing the old ballads and songs that my family sang and that people around me sang. I was a big fan of rock 'n' roll and popular music, but I still held on to

---

168 Neil Hegarty, *Frost—That Was the Life That Was: The Authorised Biography* (London: Random House, 2016): 55; Caroline Langhorst, "Grannies From Hell, Daring Bicycle Repairment, Upper-Class Twits and 'Make Tea Not Love': Monty Python's Flying Circus and 1960s British (Popular) Culture," in Kate Egan and Jeffrey Andrew Weinstock (eds.) *And Now for Something Completely Different: Critical Approaches to Monty Python* (Edinburgh University Press, 2020): 125–26.

169 Britta Sweers, "Contemporary British Music Traditions," *The World of Music* 46, no. 1 (2004): 7–8; Noel McLaughlin and Martin McLoone, "Hybridity and National Musics: The Case of Irish Rock Music," *Popular Music* 19, no. 2 (Apr. 2000): 185–90.

> the traditional music. Neil Murray was a big influence in my life. He was a Rhodes scholar who had studied at Oxford. He came home in the late sixties with some albums from groups like Fairport Convention and Steeleye Span. We were listening to those songs and Noel [Dinn] and I were saying: "You know, there are Newfoundland songs that are just like these. They put them to kind of a rock 'n' roll beat, why can't we do the same?" And Figgy Duff was born out of that idea—of taking Newfoundland songs instead of English and Irish songs, and making your own music from that. I was one of the founding members of Figgy Duff. I was the first singer with them. But I was learning to be a teacher at the time and when September came, I went back to school and Pamela Morgan took over for me, later on. So Trad Rock was an idea that was germinating on both sides of the Atlantic at that time. In Ireland, it was Horslips and bands like that. In England, there were Fairport Convention and Steeleye Span. Here in Newfoundland, there was The Land of Mordor, and Figgy Duff, and the Philadelphia Cream Cheese Band.[170]

"All of a sudden, even the jigs and reels were a renewal to us," remarked Don Walsh. Don, like Anita, was born and raised in Placentia Bay.

> I grew up with that kind of music in the house all the time and hated it. The old man . . . Back in those days, there was only one or two TV stations. But on a Monday evening, *Don Messer's Jubilee* had to be on. That was it. You weren't allowed *not* to watch it, or *All Around the Circle*, when that was on. We weren't allowed to touch the TV because that's what was on. I couldn't stand that music—not realizing of course that a few years later, I'm going to completely switch and turn around, and all of a sudden, I'm going to listen to *nothing but* this kind of music. Now, traditional music is all over the place, it's everywhere. They have constant TV shows or radio shows going every Sunday with nothing but Newfoundland bands playing traditional music.[171]

---

170 Best, interview.
171 Don Walsh, interview.

The collision of folk traditions with international influences like jazz, blues, and rock 'n' roll helped shape the artistic aesthetic of the Newfoundland renaissance, but the impact of the international counterculture upon the formation of a mission and ethos for Newfoundland artists was also undeniable. In Newfoundland, the counterculture landed in force among many young people and artists in particular. By the early 1970s, it became obvious that people of this generation were determined to live their lives differently than their parents had, particularly in a social sense. Some explored feminist critiques and perspectives. Others rejected heteronormativity, choosing instead non-traditional romantic and sexual relationships, or simply accepted others who did. Some embraced environmentalism and vegetarianism or veganism, criticized or rejected capitalism, and championed the rights of working people. The marks of the counterculture and the New Left were visible on both Newfoundland art and artists alike. As these influences shaped their thinking, naturally it also helped to shape the art they created and the way they engaged with art in general. I will explore more fully some of these influences and effects on the art and practice of Newfoundland artists in the following two chapters.

Despite their determination to sit in resistance to capitalism and its worst effects, young Atlantic peoples everywhere could no more avoid being touched by it than they can today, including Newfoundland artists. Sandy Morris spoke about how he viewed the members of The Ravens, the first rock 'n' roll band he had ever seen play live and how glamorous the lifestyle of a successful musician appeared to him.

> The boys in that band, at one point they all drove Volkswagen Karmann Ghias, which were little sports cars, and they ordered clothes from Hollywood. They actually had mail-order catalogues from Hollywood and would order fancy shirts and jackets and stuff like that you couldn't get here. So, they were stars. They looked like stars; they acted like stars; they drove around town and everybody recognized them, and that was really impressive.[172]

172 Morris, interview.

The feeling of inspiration Sandy is describing here can only exist in an environment in which people are systematically moulded to view material and financial wealth as the ultimate measures of success. Yet, even from within such a system, artists like Sandy could embrace a particular work ethic and help to collectively forge a community that viewed artists as valued workers who contributed just as much as their professional counterparts, whether white-collar or blue-collar, and likewise deserved to be able to make a living.

Keeping Body and Soul Together

One interview question I posed to every narrator I spoke to for this study had to do with the economic and quality of life experiences of Newfoundland artists during the late 1960s and 1970s. The answers to this question varied widely, but taken together, they demonstrate that particular kinds of artists made more money and enjoyed greater support than others. While Newfoundland and Labrador had yet to boast a superstar among its many artists, some managed to make a decent living. However, it was writers, musicians, and visual artists that seemed to have had the most consistent paid patronage in the community. Newfoundland had had a government-sponsored annual Arts and Letters competition in place since the immediate post-Confederation period, which helped give local literary figures and visual artists a visibility boost and potentially greater professional opportunities. The CBC and other local radio affiliates aired plays by local playwrights adapted for radio as well as music by local artists.[173] By the late 1960s, according to Sandy Morris, musicians in St. John's were starting to do a bit better too. A symbiotic partnership between the St. John's bar scene and local musicians had evolved, which animated the music community and provided fairly regular work for many local bands and solo artists.[174]

"What was it like making a living as an artist in Newfoundland throughout that time?" I asked Sandy. "Was the cost of living actually affordable? Could you live well as an artist in St. John's?"

---

173 Rompkey, 271. Ferry, 145–46, 151; Gulliver, 158, 163, 165, 174, 252.
174 See Appendix 6.

> In St. John's, you could. Now, when the Philadelphia Cream Cheese Band broke up, I started playing around with a bunch of guys in a band called The Ambassadors, and that eventually evolved into a band called Garrison Hill.[175] They were the most popular band on the island for a while. We were raking in the dough, which back then probably meant about two hundred bucks each a week, but that was good money. I remember going to my father when I quit university in '68. I said: "Dad, I think I'm going to give up university. I'm making good money." He asked: "How much are you making?" I said: "As much as a plumber or an electrician." He says: "If you're okay with that boy, go for it." So I did. I never thought it would last . . . like, The Ravens, who had influenced me so much, they all had day jobs. They were musicians on the side.[176]

Encouraged by this early success and interested to see what else was out there, Sandy decided to head to England. Quite a few Newfoundland artists, both actors and musicians, were trying out the climate in London around the same time—auditioning, playing gigs locally, bunking in together, and pooling their resources—just as travelling and exiled Newfoundlanders do everywhere. Interestingly, despite its small size, limits, and challenges, Sandy found that the music scene he had left behind in St. John's was far more supportive to the artist.

> When I was still playing with Garrison Hill I was making good money, but it was all bars. By 1970 or '71, I'd had enough of bars and late nights—that whole vampire routine where you don't get to bed until dawn and then you're dead all day and you get up in the nighttime and you start drinking and you go again. So, I gave up the band and I moved to England. I knew that Figgy Duff—or members of Lukey's Boat, as they would've been known then—they had already won a contest and had gone over there on their own. Hennessey was living over there; a few friends of mine had moved there. London,

---

175 Before they were joined by Sandy Morris, Garrison Hill featured Brian McCloud, Tony Gains, Claude Caines, Jack Dooley, Eric Clarke, Ralph Parker, and Dave Parsons (Cox, "Newfoundland Travelling Theatre," 39).

176 Morris, interview.

England was where everything was happening because The Beatles were still together. They had Apple Music, which was experimenting and hiring people. It seemed like if you were going to be in the music business, that was the place to be. But it was a complete eye opener when you realized . . . I could make a living playing music here [St. John's], but nobody in England who was playing the bar circuits was making a living playing the bar circuits. They were making money at day jobs to be able to afford to buy instruments, and doing gigs hoping to get discovered. It was *discovery* that was the payoff, not the paycheck. So, we would all take turns in England doing temp jobs, like office work or loading dories or whatever, to get enough money to buy groceries for the week for the house. You'd do a few gigs, but you were basically doing them hoping to get discovered, hoping that the right guy would see you and say: "Okay, I can hook you up with this guy." That's what all the bands in England were doing, basically.

And it was *so* competitive, people would get beaten up. One band would beat up another band if they didn't want the other band to get ahead of them. If they'd figure "that guy's a better singer than I am," they'd beat the shit out of the guy, or beat up their equipment. Take their drum kit out and drive the truck over it, something like that. I saw that happen so many times, it was really demoralizing. *Nothing* like that happened here because if you were playing in a band here that was competing with another band, you knew that next year you were probably going to end up in that other band! Because the band you were in was going to break up. All the musicians played together all the time and swapped out if somebody was sick. The Ducats, they'd phone me and say: "Can you fill in tonight for Lewis Skinner?" "Yeah sure." I'd show up and play with them. The material was . . . A lot of bands played the same songs, like "Hi-Heel Sneakers." There was a whole bunch of popular tunes that bands played, and I'm sure it was probably the same tunes pretty much throughout North America. Certain songs that were easy for fellas to learn how to play when they're learning how to play guitar and that anybody could sing, that kind of thing. Swapping musicians back and forth between outfits was a pretty easy thing to do, and no one had stage outfits or costumes or anything.

When I moved to England, I then realized that this wasn't going to work out as a career move. I had previously thought: "I'm a big fish in this pond. If I go to a bigger pond, I can probably skip up the ladder." But after six or eight months, I was left in an existential crisis: "Now what am I going to do with my life? I've come over here thinking I'd make the next step up, and I can't get into a music school so I'm going to go back." I thought, "F--k, I was making good money and I was enjoying myself. Why am I fighting it? Why don't I just go back and do that until I figure out what to do next?"

Every bar had a week-long gig, almost every bar anyway, and there were enough of them that even if you weren't a great band, people still needed a band every week, so there'd be enough bars around that you could pretty much keep yourself going. Also, there were bands that toured from Vancouver to St. John's in bars and did that circuit, or from Boston, and did the eastern part of Canada. They would do Montreal, Toronto, and the Maritimes. They'd come down through here, they'd play Corner Brook, they'd play Grand Falls, they'd play Gander, then come into St. John's and play their way back again, and make their way back to Vancouver or wherever they came from. So, when I came back from England, I started doing that. I got Hennessey when he moved back home and we started another band, and that just kept going until the next big thing happened, whatever that was. Oh, the next big thing to happen after that would have been the Grand Band, of course.[177]

177 Morris, interview.

Chapter Three
1972–1976

"Do it with a bold face."
- CODCO

Curtain Up

The span of time from 1972 to 1976 saw an artistic and cultural explosion in Newfoundland and Labrador. The settler-folk tradition and the political, social, and economic developments of the earlier twentieth century had helped set the stage and provide the impetus for a cultural flowering characterized by strongly nationalist overtones, as well as elements of Atlantic-wide decolonization, counterculture, and social equality movements. Voters booted Joey out of office in 1971 in favour of Frank Moores, a clear sign that the public had lost a certain amount of faith in Smallwood's vision of a province made better and more prosperous by industrialization, modernization, and centralization. Accordingly, much of the art produced in the ensuing decade and more reflected clear critiques of the modern industrial conceptions of progress and prosperity. Despite the cultural denigration of Newfoundland and Newfoundlanders in Canadian discourse prior to and throughout the mere twenty-odd years of its membership in the Canadian federation, the province's art and artists were now beginning to gain national prominence and acclaim.

Throughout the early 1970s, many young Newfoundland artists sought to pursue dedicated careers in the arts. Differing perspectives regarding what constitutes legitimate art and what it means to be a professional artist complicated this process, as did the system of modern capitalism, which has always struggled to quantify and reward the labour and contributions of artists. Despite these challenges, together they pioneered a new artistic aesthetic and cultural ethos, the most salient characteristics of which were collectivism, interdisciplinarity, and ethnic or regional pride. While Memorial University, MUN Extension, the CBC, and other local radio affiliates continued to provide some of the most significant support and resources to developing artists, and funding bodies like the Canada Council began to take an interest in Newfoundland art, policy and infrastructure for the arts in the province remained drastically underdeveloped. There was little to no formal arts education and federal and provincial agencies as well as non-governmental organizations typically only supported artists on a piecework basis with a primary focus on short-term economic goals, with rare exceptions. It is therefore quite remarkable that the development of the Newfoundland arts scene was as active, rich, and varied as it was during the early-to-mid 1970s, for much of it was driven by the efforts of the artists themselves.

Breakwater Books, one of Newfoundland's earliest independent publishing houses, was founded in 1973 by five MUN English professors whose mandate was to promote and celebrate the works of Newfoundland writers who had little to no presence or representation in the broader Canadian national market.[178] One of the first independent feature films by and about Newfoundlanders, Gordon Pinsent's *The Rowdyman*, premiered the same year.[179] The theatre groups known as the Newfoundland Travelling Theatre Company (NTTC), the Mummers Troupe, and CODCO all formed and launched their enterprises between 1972 and 1973.[180] On the music side, the bands Figgy Duff, Red Island, and the Wonderful Grand Band all formed in fairly quick succession between 1975 and 1977.[181]

178 "Breakwater Books Ltd.: About." https://breakwaterbooks.com/pages/about.

179 *The Rowdyman*, directed by Peter Carter, starring Gordon Pinsent, Crawley Films (1972).

180 Helen Peters (ed), *The Plays of CODCO* (New York: Peter Lang Publishing, 1992): xi–xii; Brookes, *A Public Nuisance*, 43–4; Cox, "Newfoundland Travelling Theatre," 34–5.

181 Russell, interview; "Figgy Duff receives small, but enthusiastic response," *The Western Star* (Wednesday April 29, 1981): 5, Memorial University of Newfoundland Digital Archives Initiative. https://collections.mun.ca/digital/collection/westernstar/id/171683/rec/2; "Don Walsh Fonds," Memorial University of Newfoundland Digital Archives Initiative. https://dai.mun.ca/digital/donwalsh/; Malone and White, interview; Morris, interview.

Perlin vs. the Artists

Despite a significant emphasis on regional and folk traditions at MUN and in the artistic community, the existing arts bureaucracy in the province seemed to feature a preference for "high culture" of a sort that some young artists considered to be distinctly colonial. Andy Jones noted that regardless of the demonstrated public appeal of CODCO's original material in major Canadian centres like Toronto, they were still not welcome on Newfoundland's one and only "big stage."

> The Arts and Culture Centre, generally speaking, was not interested in us. We had to fight our way in, and that was a battle. We were not considered cultured enough to be at the Arts and Culture Centre. They sort of had to come around because we were obviously very popular. The way they treated us—it was as if our people turned against us.[182]

It is worth noting that under the sole leadership of John Perlin, the programming of the province's Arts and Culture Centres was not entirely devoid of Newfoundland content during the 1970s. Outside of St. John's, the Centres in Corner Brook, Stephenville, Gander, and Grand Falls each had their own local theatre groups, some of whom were producing original plays,[183] but in general, these Arts and Culture Centre spaces staged primarily British and American content often performed by visiting companies, like their counterpart in St. John's. Very few regional or Canadian plays or companies were featured at the St. John's Arts and Culture Centre before 1975. That summer, the NTTC were given the main stage for their production of *Beaumont Hamel*, written by Tom Cahill and Dudley Cox, a production for which they also received funding to stage in Québec City.[184]

---

182 Jones, interview.

183 Diane Butt, interview by Kim Frail for the STAGE Project, February 22, 1995, 6–8; Cox, "Newfoundland Travelling Theatre," 11–12, 22, 24, 33–4.

184 Dingle, interview; Cox, interview.

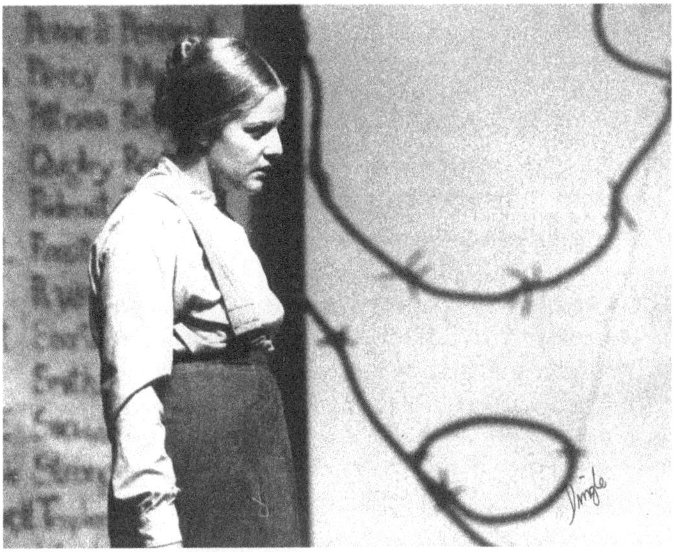

Jane Dingle in *Beaumont Hamel*, 1975.[185]

Furthermore, CODCO did eventually bring their first theatre production, *Cod on a Stick*, to the Arts and Culture Centre by 1974—but in the 90-seat Basement Theatre rather than on the main stage that, at the time, accommodated more than a thousand people.[186] In a 2010 interview, John Perlin seemed to largely take credit for the opening of the Basement Theatre, which, he said, was an idea he had gotten from Michael Cook and Al Pittman and would give local artists space to develop and perform at the Arts and Culture Centre.[187] In his memoir, Dudley Cox wrote that he and Sylvia Wigh[188] had been instrumental in carving out additional performance space and paid work opportunities for local artists with the opening of the Basement Theatre and that

185 Photo by Paul Dingle. Used with permission.

186 Malone and White, interview; Cox, "Newfoundland Travelling Theatre," 45; Devine, 112.

187 Gulliver, 58–9.

188 Drama teacher (St. John's Arts and Culture Centre), director, theatre critic for the *Evening Telegram*, former stage manager for the London Players, and long-time member of the St. John's Players.

much of the original Canadian or regional content presented at the St. John's Arts and Culture Centre during the early 1970s was staged there. Meanwhile, the programming on the main stage between 1970 and 1975 featured a steady diet of Shakespeare and British or American musicals: *Hamlet, The Merchant of Venice, Henry IV, My Fair Lady,* and *HMS Pinafore*—to name a few. The Arts and Culture Centre's main stage usually only presented Canadian or regional productions during the annual Regional Drama Festival, which featured amateur and competitive rather than professional and paid productions.[189]

One gets the sense that the Basement Theatre was where acts and actors were sent because John Perlin did not have faith in their ability to put one thousand backsides in the Arts and Culture Centre's seats. Indeed, in response to many years of criticism by local artists, Perlin contended in a 2010 interview that he had simply been doing his job as he understood it—to offer to the public an entertaining theatre program, which stood the best chance of selling out every performance.[190] This would prove to be a particular point of contention between Perlin and local artists that persisted throughout the 1970s.

According to Greg Malone and White, CODCO succeeded in securing the Basement Theatre for *Cod on a Stick* thanks, in part and indirectly, to Ron. During the winter of 1973–74, Ron had been gigging in the bars and working on his music alongside the CODCO crowd who were up in Toronto at the same time. While working on a radio program with CBC producer Jack Humphries, Ron brought him to see one of CODCO's performances. Humphries was immediately interested in producing a live performance of *Cod on a Stick* for broadcast on CBC radio, which was recorded back in St. John's at the Little Theatre a few months later, in January 1974. The success of this broadcast led to the booking at the Basement Theatre.[191]

Programming at the Arts and Culture Centres throughout the 1970s continued to lean heavily toward British and American classics and musicals. Big band shows, Gilbert and Sullivan, Shakespeare, and slick acts from "away" seemed to be the dominant order of the day.[192]

---

189 Cox, interview; Cox, "Newfoundland Travelling Theatre," 25, 28, 30, 32–3; Gail Weir and Colleen Quigley, "John Holmes Papers," Coll-127 (finding aid), Archives and Special Collections, Queen Elizabeth II Library, Memorial University of Newfoundland, 1999.

190 Gulliver, 61–2.

191 Malone and White, interview; Peters (ed.), xii; Devine, "Necessary Evils," 111–112.

192 Malone and White, interview; Brookes, *A Public Nuisance,* 36–40; Cox, "Newfoundland Travelling Theatre," 23.

That being said, the arts community was deeply interconnected and animated by a collectivist spirit, which nonetheless encouraged broader participation, collaboration, and innovation no matter what programming was on the agenda.

When Shakespeare's *The Merchant of Venice* was staged at the St. John's Arts and Culture Centre in March of 1972, Dudley Cox, whose apprenticeship in the theatre community of St. John's over the previous six years had cultivated nothing if not a spirit of experimentation, sought to extend the action and performance of the play beyond the actual auditorium. Most of the actors he enlisted for this effort would go on to work with the NTTC, which began touring that very summer, or would later go on to work with CODCO and/or the Mummers Troupe. The actors who went on to join these companies in the early 1970s became renowned for their skill at improvisation and together, they devised a short, interactive, street theatre-style show that would take place in the lobby prior to the main performance. Dudley observed that the extensive Arts and Culture Centre lobby area represented virtually wasted space and time which might be put to better, richer use. Amusingly, he called the pre-show *Foreplay* and it was meant to resemble the general atmosphere one would have expected to find outside London's Globe Theatre during Shakespeare's own time.[193] "Our group played all the whores, the beggars, the pickpockets, the Puritans . . . all the dregs of society you would have found outside the theatre at the time," Jane told me.[194]

Kevin Noble fought a mock quarter-staff battle against Bink Lash that ranged up and down the stairs. Tommy Sexton and Scott Strong were among the Bedlamites being led to their incarceration. Mary Walsh's speech as the Puritan minister was apparently particularly memorable, full of hellfire and damnation for the self-indulgent and sinful theatregoers who were bringing the wrath of God down upon themselves in the form of the plague! My mother, Jane Dingle, played a blind beggar, crouched on the floor near the theatre doors clad in filthy rags and holding up a cup hopefully in front of her. "She was unbelievable," Dudley told me, "thoroughly pitiable. She even had a string of drool coming down her chin!"[195]

193 Cox, "Newfoundland Travelling Theate," 32–3; Cox, interview.

194 Dingle, interview.

195 Cox, "Newfoundland Travelling Theatre," 32–3; Dudley Cox, email communication to author, Wednesday August 31, 2022.

Jane was cast in several productions staged at the Arts and Culture Centre throughout the early 1970s, most of which, she concurred, were indeed highly typical of programming at the time including *The Mikado* and *Macbeth*. Things would start to slowly open up by the mid-1970s, however. CODCO was finally invited to take the main stage of the St. John's Arts and Culture Centre in April of 1975 with their production of *Das Capital*, sharing the stage and billing with Figgy Duff. Prior to this, few such original, regional, and professional productions were welcomed other than the odd play by Tom Cahill or Michael Cook.[196] With the advent of the 1980s, regional content gradually began to become more common at Newfoundland's Arts and Culture Centres. Even if Newfoundland content was not yet the rule, it was now at least not the exception.[197] But until then, the Arts and Culture Centre continued to follow a seasonal pattern of repertoire that was, according to Chris Brookes, highly typical of regional theatres—not only in Newfoundland, but throughout the rest of Canada as well.

> People did American plays and British plays and sent the royalties to Britain and to America. I'm sure Arthur Miller bought himself a few cups of coffee from that. Don't forget, this was the era when it was radical, almost unheard of, to do a Canadian play in Canada. You had these things called regional theatres and they all did one American play, one Shakespeare, one British comedy, and that was their season. But trying to get a Canadian play in those seasons was just unheard of. It was imagined that Canadian plays, if they existed at all, or if we'd never heard of them, they were going to be no good. Back then, that was the climate in Canadian theatre. You had to fight and scream and push and yell to actually get a Canadian play onstage. It was smaller companies, little companies, the new companies like ours that were doing Canadian material onstage.[198]

---

196 Dingle, interview; Peters (ed.), xiv; Cox, "Newfoundland Travelling Theatre," 24–5, 30, 33.
197 Butt, interview; Boak, (1984).
198 Brookes, interview.

The Newfoundland Travelling Theatre Company, the Mummers Troupe, and CODCO

Besides the Arts and Culture Centre, there were only a few venues in St. John's that could accommodate major theatrical productions and most were school auditorium spaces, such as the Holy Heart Theatre, the Bishop Feild Auditorium, Pitt's Memorial Hall at the Holloway School, and MUN's Little Theatre.[199] With only a few viable and accessible performance spaces in their communities, young artists took their acts out on tour. The NTTC, CODCO, and the Mummers Troupe all travelled extensively throughout the province and beyond during the early-to-mid 1970s.

The NTTC itself was formed specifically because theatre groups in Newfoundland could often get no more than six or seven performances of a play in any performance space in any town, including St. John's. Dudley Cox and David Weiser reasoned that if they took their shows out on tour, they could get thirty or forty performances of a play, gain that much more experience as theatre artists, as well as bring theatrical productions to communities that did not often, if ever, get to see plays. Weiser, who had been working as a travelling clothing salesman throughout Newfoundland, used his knowledge and experience of the island to begin booking, planning, and organizing the first tour. Dudley began auditioning and casting for the two shows they'd chosen for the first tour during the early summer of 1972. During this tour, the NTTC performed Philip King's post-World War II farcical comedy *See How They Run* for adult audiences in the evenings. In the afternoons, they performed a children's matinée of *The Wizard of Oz*, adapted for the stage by Elizabeth Fuller Chapman.[200]

Less than six months after the NTTC's first tour, the original members of the Mummers Troupe launched their first production of the *Traditional Newfoundland Christmas Mummers Play* on the evening of Boxing Day, 1972, a performance that would be repeated every Christmas season by the widely varying members of the troupe for the next ten years. For those readers unfamiliar with the custom of mummering, or "janneying" or "fooling" as some communities have traditionally

199 *Henderson's*, 1968, 1969, 1970, 1973, 1975; see Appendix 6.

200 Cox, interview; Cox, "Newfoundland Travelling Theatre," 34–5.

referred to the practice in various regions of Newfoundland, it is part of a folk tradition originating in the British Isles most often observed during the twelve days of Christmas. The mummers play is the most formal expression of the tradition, which—though there are regional variations—features similar themes and character archetypes across Atlantic cultures. The version of the play adopted by the Mummers Troupe was drawn from the local research of MUN folklorists as well as from the oral histories of a small handful of elderly outport Newfoundlanders who had seen the drama performed in their communities during the early twentieth century.[201]

In brief, the mummers play begins with a surprise knock on the door of a private home. The host opens the door to a motley assortment of figures swathed in outlandish costumes designed to conceal identities, and a chorus of "Any mummers allowed in?" Once admitted, the play begins. The number of characters varies according to regional tradition, but the play generally requires a bare minimum of three people to perform and features clear echoes of Christian belief but perhaps also much older winter solstice rituals. Two of the performers, representing a polarized duality such as light and darkness, life and death, or good and evil—usually King George and the Turkish Knight in the Newfoundland tradition—begin with a mock battle in which one of the combatants is killed. Another character representing a doctor then enters and resurrects the dead man. The script is tweaked for local context and is invariably spiced with bawdy and slapstick elements.[202]

---

201 Brookes, *A Public Nuisance,* 30, 46–49; "Intangible Cultural Heritage: Mummering & Janneying," Memorial University of Newfoundland. https://www.mun.ca/ich/search-ich-collections/hearts-content/christmas-traditions/mummering-and-janneying/; Gerald L. Pocius, "The Mummers Song in Newfoundland: Intellectuals, Revivalists and Cultural Nativism," *Newfoundland Studies* 4, no. 1 (1988): 61–62.

202 Brookes, *A Public Nuisance,* 15–19; J.D.A. Widdowson, "Chasing Shadows: Retrieving the Text and Context of the Change Islands, Newfoundland, Mummers' Play," Folk Drama Studies Today, International Traditional Drama Conference (2002): 243–45. https://folkplay.info/files/papers/200207/Widdowson2002.pdf.

Cast of the Mummers Play, 1977.[203]

Less formal and more common variations of mummering still involve the outlandish costuming, concealment of identity and knocking on doors, but when admitted, the entertainment provided is more free-form and could involve instrumental music, singing, dancing, recitations, jokes—whatever the mummers' talents happen to be. As well as their bulky and bizarre costumes, which are often gender-bending and usually constituted by whatever the mummers happen to have lying around the house, they disguise their voices, their walk—anything that might help identify them. Once the hosts have correctly guessed a mummer's identity, the mummer unmasks. Regardless of the performance, there is usually an expectation that the hosts will offer the mummers some hospitality for the amusement they provide and that the mummers will offer a blessing to the hosts for their warm reception. A more common form of mummering today takes the shape of an outdoor pageant or parade in which the mummers' costumes, talents, and hobby horses are on display in

203 Photo by Kent Barrett. Left to right: Judy Parsons, Chris Brooks, Jeff Pitcher, Jane Dingle, Terry Rielly.

public streets—a far more secure arrangement for urban communities or those whose traditional isolation has decreased significantly in recent decades, when residents are far less likely to know the people knocking on their doors.[204] Founded in 2009 by coordinator Ryan Davis, St. John's hosts an annual Mummers Festival, which features just such a parade.[205]

By the time the Mummers Troupe came on the scene in the early 1970s, they could find only a few senior Newfoundlanders who could still remember having seen a performance of the traditional mummers play, or "the rhymes," as some elderly witnesses described it.[206] Less formal mummering traditions had survived in various outport communities throughout the first half of the twentieth century and some scholars believe the traditional play was probably much less common than the more free-form mummers' house visit.[207] Mummering does not seem to have been practised much, if at all, in St. John's until the 1970s. There is a concrete reason for this. Because of its history of association with sometimes riotous working-class protest in Newfoundland, particularly during the first half of the nineteenth century, mummering in all its forms was made officially illegal in 1861.[208]

In addition to its cultural significance to settler Newfoundlanders as a folk tradition of theatre, the illegality of mummering must have made the practice that much more attractive to Mummers Troupe co-founder Chris Brookes as both a central feature and guiding philosophy for the fledgling theatre company. The mummers play is a near-perfect incarnation of guerilla theatre. One does not "attend" such a production but rather is confronted with it unexpectedly. Its subversive working-class character has the power to discomfit those with a more middle-class mentality of what theatre is or perhaps should be. It probably also pleased the founders of the Troupe to help resurrect a tradition

---

204 "Intangible Cultural Heritage: Mummering & Janneying," Memorial University of Newfoundland. https://www.mun.ca/ich/search-ich-collections/hearts-content/christmas-traditions/mummering-and-janneying/; Craig T. Palmer, "Mummers and Real Strangers: The Effect of Diminished Isolation of Newfoundland Christmas House Visiting," *Newfoundland Studies* 8, no. 2 (1992): 125–26, 131–32; Brookes, *A Public Nuisance,* 53; Devine, 82.

205 "Bras needed for mystery reason, says Mummers organizer," *CBC News,* Nov 28, 2013. https://www.cbc.ca/news/canada/newfoundland-labrador/bras-needed-for-mystery-reason-says-mummers-organizer-1.2444034.

206 Brookes, *A Public Nuisance,* 15, 18, 46–7.

207 Pocius, 62–3.

208 Kelly Best, "Making Cool Things Hot Again: Blackface and Newfoundland Mummering," *Ethnologies* 30, no. 2 (2008): 215, 231–32.

that had been used in the past as a means for poor fishermen to air grievances and demand redress from rich and privileged merchants in an anonymous way. Drama professor Michael Devine, anthropologist Melvin Firestone, and Brookes himself, however, have all posited that the mummers play served other community needs that went deeper than politics or economics.[209]

Aristotle's concept of the social utility of theatre was one in which demonstrated violators of social conventions are punished and a sense of righteous civic and moral order is reinforced. Instead, the practice and theatrical tradition of mummering allows small and historically homogeneous communities to confront the concept of the "Stranger" safely and comfortably. The figure of the Stranger is a powerful symbol in Newfoundland settler culture and drama. In most cases in small and rural communities, mummers would have been the hosts' neighbours and friends who temporarily became strangers by virtue of their costumed anonymity. In addition to reducing social tensions and reaffirming community ties and trust, mummering provided a symbolic process by which strangers are demystified. This theatrical approach is reflective rather than instructive or pedantic making it the perfect symbol and vehicle to suit Brookes's vision, one in which theatre would not be created for the sake of art itself, or for the elevation or edification of an audience seeking cultural refinement, but as a very purposeful tool to *move* people, to shift consciousness, and stimulate change in communities. Co-founded by Lynn Lunde, John Doyle, and Brookes himself, who together established the Resource Foundation for the Arts, the Mummers Troupe would go on to write and perform some of the most overtly political theatre ever staged in the province and I dare say in Canada.[210]

Not to be outdone, CODCO's vision and original material was likewise deeply political. Helen Peters observed that CODCO's status as a comedy troupe often served to obscure just how rabidly political the group was. Their first production, *Cod on a Stick*, employed a brand of humour and dramatic strategy that aptly expresses the ethnic and nationalist tone of contemporary regional theatre at the time. *Cod on a Stick* was first performed for a Toronto audience in December of 1973.

---

209 Best, "Making Cool Things Hot," 233; Diane Tye, "At Home and Away: Newfoundland Mummers and the Transformation of Difference," *Material Culture Review* 68 (Fall 2008): 50; Devine, 79–82.

210 Brookes, *A Public Nuisance,* 7–8, 13, 17, 42; Devine, 79–82; Palmer, 126; Tye, 50.

Cast of *Cod on a Stick*, 1973.[211]

The show initially seems to send up Newfoundlanders in much the same ways that mainlanders typically used to do via the "Newfie joke," but as the performance progresses, it becomes clear that it's the audience of mainlanders who are the figures of fun and that the actors onstage are the ones laughing, holding up a mirror to their fellow Canadians and exposing their misconceptions.[212] "We were making fun of Newfoundland all the time," Andy Jones remarked.

> We were always making fun of ourselves, but also making fun of the audience who were watching us. We were determined to present Newfoundland, to be hard on Newfoundland, but also to be hard on everybody else for being hard on

211 Photo by Kent Barrett. Left to right—Top: Diane Olsen, Mary Walsh, Greg Malone. Bottom: Cathy Jones, Paul Sametz, Tommy Sexton.

212 Peters (ed.), xii, xx, xxii–xxiii; Jones, interview.

> Newfoundland. We could do it ourselves, but they weren't allowed to. We were aware that we had a job to do, in small "p" politics, and it was to tell the Canadians that they got a good deal when we joined them, to tell Newfoundlanders that we didn't necessarily get that great a deal, and to be cautious not to give everything away.[213]

Peters reflected that CODCO's tendency towards an almost "drawing-room style" comedic action paired with their raw, dark brand of humour served to blunt the edge of their political views, but only a cursory reading of CODCO's work is required to reveal a collective as strongly committed to political and social criticism as the Mummers Troupe. While they may have mocked the earnestness and outrage of other political theatre groups, CODCO's critical commentary on long-standing social problems in Newfoundland and Canadian society remained consistently audacious.[214] Between 1973 and 1976, the CODCO[215] collective wrote, performed, and toured five theatre productions that explored a variety of issues and problems, from class inequality and exploitation of the working poor to the corruption and institutional abuses of both government and the Church. The international counterculture and concurrent social and political movements strongly influenced CODCO's members. Throughout the years the group was active, their plays and their CBC television show (which ran from 1986 through 1991) addressed feminism, queerness, environmentalism, and Indigenous/settler relationships.[216]

The interconnectedness of the 1960s and 1970s countercultural generation in the Atlantic world was manifest in a small community of young Newfoundlanders at the time, of whom roughly half of CODCO's original members formed a part. "You know about the Rastafarian thing?" Andy Jones asked me during our interview. I did, in fact. My mother, Jane, had told me stories for years about the summer of 1976 during which she, Beni Malone, and Kent Barrett had worked out in Eastport where they had collectively written, rehearsed, and performed *The Madman's Cabaret*.

---

213 Jones, interview.

214 Peters (ed.), xx.

215 CODCO's membership over a nearly twenty-year period (1973–1991) comprised the talents of Greg Malone, Tommy Sexton, Diane Olsen, Mary Walsh, Cathy Jones, Paul Sametz, Scott Strong, Bob Joy, Andy Jones, and manager/administrators White and Maisie Rillie (Peters [ed.], xi–xiv, xix).

216 Peters (ed.), xxiii–xxix.

Jane Dingle, 1976.[217]

217 Photo by Ron Fitzgerald.

Jane Dingle, Kent Barrett, and Beni Malone, 1976.[218]

Beni and his partner, Marian White, rather than come into the boardinghouse where Kent and Jane were staying, had elected to spend their summer in Eastport in a tent outside. "They were much more comfortable out there, they said," Jane recalled. "They had Bob Marley on the record player out there and they ate a mostly vegan diet, which was actually really hard to do in Newfoundland back then."[219]

"Anyway," Andy Jones continued, "there was a big thing happening, the most bizarre thing." A sizeable group of young Newfoundlanders had embraced elements of Rastafarianism. "Some of them had spent time in Jamaica and had made all of these friends down there," Jones recalled. The extraordinary popularity of the roots reggae movement throughout the Atlantic world had likewise landed in Newfoundland. In a clear example of just how culturally interconnected the Atlantic world was becoming, health and lifestyle beliefs from as far away as Jamaica appear to have influenced some young

218 Photo by Ron Fitzgerald.

219 Jane Dingle, interview by author, Seattle/St. John's, September 5, 2022 (private collection).

Newfoundland artists a great deal. When CODCO was invited to shoot a half-hour TV spot for CBC's *Peep Show* in 1975, which showcased the work of theatre groups across Canada, it reportedly led to a tussle of wills between some CODCO members and CBC staff. "They refused to wear makeup and they refused to eat the food unless it was vegan. So, CBC staff were forced to make chicken out of tofu and make it look like Kentucky Fried Chicken because that was what the piece we wrote was all about!" Andy laughed heartily. "They were furious with us. Furious. Who did we think we were?"[220]

In the context of the Mummers Troupe and CODCO, the NTTC is sometimes rather unfairly maligned for supposedly perpetuating what some budding artists and cultural nationalists at that time viewed as colonial culture at the expense of regional culture. This response is an understandable one in the context of the time, and one I will return to and examine in more detail later in this chapter. However, I contend that both the NTTC and Dudley Cox himself had far more significance to the development of regional theatre and to the broader Newfoundland renaissance than some have given them credit for. Chris Brookes once referred to the NTTC as a theatre company formed to stage "light British comedies."[221] Brookes's status as a true believer in the cause of cultural decolonization explains his particular perspective in this case, but his characterization lacks some important nuance.

The NTTC was a crucial training ground for many actors and notably, for the corps of artists who, fresh from their experience on the first two NTTC tours, soon went on to form CODCO. Mary Walsh, Tommy Sexton, Bob Joy, Andy Jones, and Diane Olsen were among the actors cast in the theatre group's first production, *See How They Run*, and Cathy Jones and Greg Malone joined the cast during the NTTC's second tour of *Pool's Paradise* the following summer. "We talked a lot at that time about getting a company together and writing our own material. That was a general theme of our discussions at the time," Andy remembered. The professional experience and opportunities for self-cultivation provided by the NTTC helped give these young artists the foundation and the confidence to strike out on their own.

---

220 Jones, interview.
221 Brookes, *A Public Nuisance*, 103.

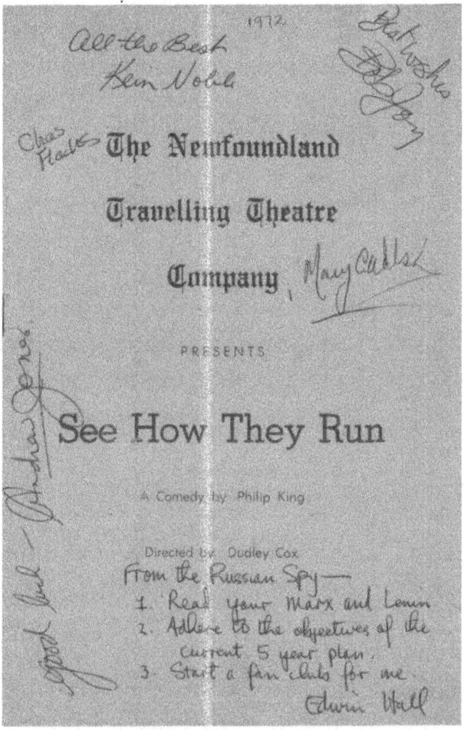
1972

All the Best
Ken Noble

The Newfoundland
Travelling Theatre
Company

PRESENTS

See How They Run

A Comedy by Philip King

Directed by Dudley Cox

From the Russian Spy—
1. Read your Marx and Lenin
2. Adhere to the objectives of the current 5 year plan.
3. Start a fan club for me.
Edwin Hall

See How They Run theatrical program with cast autographs.[222]

"That experience took us up another level," Bob Joy recalled.

> This was the first time I was ever paid to be an actor and I remember Dudley Cox saying very early on what it means to be a professional. He laid it out very simply: "It doesn't matter what mood you're in, or if you're having a bad day or a good day. You show up and you do your work." It sort of struck me and I said: "Yeah, this is the threshold that I'm crossing," for whatever it was, thirty-five dollars a week. And it felt *great*. What an experience that was. We had the security of a script

222 Private collection.

> which, later on, of course, with CODCO, we didn't have—or rather, we didn't have it in the same way—but there was a lot of other variables that we had to juggle. The size of the theatre, the kind of audience we were facing varied wildly from community to community as we went through. It was an occasion for solidarity in the group.[223]

Another important experience that such provincial touring provided was the opportunity to travel widely throughout Newfoundland and Labrador and see the remnants of outport life and culture in various far-flung and still-remote places. Undoubtedly, this experience could only have proved educational and most likely influenced and/or reinforced the political and social perspectives of that generation of young actors which, in turn, shaped the art they went on to create.

Collective Theatre and the Tradition of the Crew

The unique local conditions under which artists developed and pursued their careers strongly influenced the artistic practices they employed and the content they produced. With only a few art academies and no theatre schools, music schools, or film schools yet in existence in Newfoundland and Labrador, young artists of the time simply pursued what amateur or professional experience they could, either by travelling outside the province or by carving out spaces within their own communities. Across various artistic mediums, the Newfoundland art being created, shown, and performed began to feature distinctive characteristics.

When it came to regional theatre, collectives largely seem to have been the order of the day. This trend in theatre during the 1970s extended well beyond the Newfoundland arts community and was observable among independent and alternative theatre groups across Canada.[224] Theatre Passe Muraille is the example most commonly cited

---

223 Joy, interview.

224 Alan Filewod, *Collective Encounters: Documentary Theatre in English Canada* (Toronto: University of Toronto Press, 1987): 182-83.

by the Newfoundland artists who began their careers in the early 1970s. In interviews with founding members of both the Mummers Troupe and CODCO, the collective work of Theatre Passe Muraille is frequently referenced as an inspiring influence.[225] In fact, the theatre group's director, Paul Thompson, actually gave the founding members of CODCO their first bit of funding, with which they wrote and staged *Cod on a Stick*—three hundred dollars left over from Theatre Passe Muraille's most recent Canada Council grant.[226] What the fledgling group then went on to do with Thompson's kind contribution was impressive. I asked Greg Malone if he sensed the importance of what CODCO was doing at the time. "I know it probably seems foundational now, but did it feel similarly significant to you at the time?" I asked him.

> When I saw the response to *Cod on a Stick*, yeah. It was different. It was not just theatre. It was something else. People were liberated almost, by the show. It was a cultural happening. Everyone jumped on it. Newfoundland rules! Newfoundlanders are funny, they're saucy, they can handle themselves onstage with anyone. So, it was a real coming out, a waking up to the huge creative potential that's here. And people thought: "Oh, you can do that? I can do that!"[227]

The Mummers Troupe and CODCO were among the first Canadian theatre groups to thoroughly adopt the collective model and run with it, and it remained a defining characteristic of Newfoundland theatre throughout the following decade. Companies established later like Rising Tide Theatre, Sheila's Brush, and Resource Centre for the Arts, all of which had members who had previously worked with the earlier two troupes, continued the collective theatre tradition until well into the 1980s.[228] There were practical reasons for the fairly common use of the collective process in Newfoundland and one of them, according to Chris Brookes, was the relative dearth of regional playwrights.

---

225 Joy, interview; Jones, interview; Butt, interview; Malone and White, interview; Payne, STAGE Project, 68.

226 Peters (ed.), xi.

227 Malone and White, interview.

228 Gulliver, 30–31, 206; Devine, 115.

> Back then, it was a much smaller pool of ability and we were all in our twenties. We just sort of made do with what we had. In the Mummers Troupe, we didn't work with a playwright. There was nothing like that then—there was nobody that was really prolific—so we just sort of improvised stuff together. I loved improvisation at the time—still do. That was the method that I chose. It was imagined that somehow, it couldn't be done here, but we did it and it was different from elsewhere. We didn't have to do Arthur Miller plays. We could make our own.[229]

In July of 1975, Ron Hynes acted in and wrote the music for *East End Story*, the first of five productions he would work on with the Mummers Troupe. The St. John's chapter of the Community Planning Association of Canada (CPAC) commissioned the troupe to write a play to bring attention to the corporate gentrification and decline in the condition and availability of affordable housing in the downtown east section of St. John's, and to make local residents aware of government programs to which they could apply for funding to improve their homes, install parks, green spaces, or other infrastructure to encourage the health of the residential community.[230] To my knowledge, Ron had no prior acting experience, collective or otherwise, but perhaps his close relationships with the members of CODCO and his exposure to their creative and writing process was instructive. Greg Malone recalled that Ron came to see *Cod on a Stick* in Toronto virtually every night it played and the two of them usually discussed and analyzed the performance afterwards.[231] Brookes observed that Ron took to the Mummers Troupe's collective model right away, and easily translated it into his songwriting process.

> He was great to work with. He was just really open. I didn't know how to work with a musician, you know? We were all just improvising, we didn't know. So, when Rhonda Payne first dragged Ron into rehearsals, I thought: "Oh great, here's a musician. What do we do now?" But then Ron had us, at one

229 Brookes, interview.

230 Brookes, *A Public Nuisance*, 128–29, 236–38.

231 Malone and White, interview.

> point, sitting on the floor in a circle around him. He closed his eyes and said: "Everybody close your eyes," and he just started strumming. Then he said, "Now, throw out stuff about downtown. Just words, phrases, ideas, anything." And so we'd say: "Cop on the corner, streetlights . . ." This went on for a good twenty minutes, maybe half an hour, and Ron would just be strumming and fingering and occasionally joining in. What would come out of it was the bare bones of lyrics for a song. This was a young guy, how old was he? Twenty-four or something? He wasn't experienced in this at all. He'd never worked with a theatre company before. I thought it was remarkable that he did that, and it worked for that show.[232]

While the collective impulse among young Newfoundland artists of the 1970s may have stemmed partially from a dearth of writers, the potential influence of a collectivist and communitarian spirit inherent in the Newfoundland folk tradition should not be overlooked either. Don Walsh commented on the extraordinary camaraderie between aspiring and working artists in St. John's at the time and both their willingness and desire to help one another get ahead. Often, Don observed, "People really want to put other people down."

> I don't know if it was just the fact that it was the sixties and the seventies, but it was different. We were all trying something new, we were all struggling, and we all wanted to help each other. If somebody needed you to lend them some gear because they were going to be doing a gig, or if you were at the gig and, all of a sudden, a mic stopped working and you had a mic, you'd tear off home. You'd get it and you'd bring it back to them just so their show was going to be good. We were all sort of part of the same family, you know?[233]

This description is a far cry from the contemporary professional artistic environment in London, England that Sandy Morris described. A literal and figurative Atlantic lies between Don's anecdote of

232 Brookes, interview.
233 Don Walsh, interview.

community support and Sandy's tale of battered band members, smashed instruments, and destroyed equipment. What was different about Newfoundland? About St. John's? Could it simply have been the fact of a smaller population with fewer degrees of separation? Or was there also something else at work here? During my interview with visual artist Pam Hall, I asked her from whence she thought the strongly salient trend of collective creation in that era of Newfoundland art emerged. Hall ascribed not only the collective impulse, but also the tendency toward interdisciplinarity or multidisciplinarity, to Newfoundland and Labrador's history as a collection of predominantly rural and isolated communities.

> I know where it comes from! I've thought about this so much. First, there's the rural tradition of no specialists, all right? If you are living in Carbonear and you need to build a house, you need to ask somebody for help. Our interdisciplinarity here comes from this collective impulse or tradition, if you like, of what I call the tradition of the crew. When you think about it from within a disciplinary context—music, theatre, and film—those are all crew things. Visual art and writing kind of sit *over here* because they're creative arts where you're making something from nothing and you're usually doing it entirely by yourself. All those other art forms are collective and collaborative by nature. You do not make a piece of theatre by yourself. You do not make a film by yourself. You don't choreograph a dance by yourself. You don't actually make visual art or literature by yourself either, but try telling that to a visual artist or a writer. You've got to realize that what's always there is the history of the form you're working with and the materiality of the space you're working in. You are not alone. It doesn't matter if I spend hours by myself in a field flying 150 fish-shaped windsocks. Some guy in a mechanic's office cut that sixteen-foot fence pole for me, you know? Somebody made the flour bags that I cut up and turned into fish. Now, that's not a common perspective. I'm one of the few visual artists who will tell you that art is not made alone.[234]

234 Hall, interview.

Whether or not these elements emerged from Newfoundland's folk tradition, they are clearly visible in the artistic perspectives, processes, practices, and in the art created throughout the 1970s. Accounts of narrators I interviewed personally and those whose interviews I read from the STAGE Project invariably illustrated a clear tendency toward collectivity and interdisciplinarity.[235] We have already observed how MUN professors of the period were rarely just teachers and academics—they were poets, novelists, playwrights, musicians, and actors as well as historians, archivists, sociologists, philosophers, and antiquarians. There is a notable ring of plausibility to the notion that the multidisciplinarity of the 1970s arts community stems from the rural tradition that Pam Hall describes. In a region with few specialists and a small pool of people, both the collective impulse and the ability to wear more than one hat, so to speak, must be essential to the achievement of any goal worth pursuing.

Interdisciplinarity and Artistic Breadth

Newfoundland artists of the 1970s demonstrated an impressive breadth of interdisciplinary practice. Virtually no narrator interviewed for any of the three oral history projects used in this study was *just* a writer, or *just* an actor, a painter, a musician, or a dancer.[236] Part of the reason for this was the difficulty many artists experienced making a living solely from their art. Many, as Sandy Morris observed, still needed to work a full-time or part-time job to support themselves and their artistic pursuits.[237] Many would have worked in the hospitality and service sectors as so many artists continue to do today. Some were teachers as well as artists. Others became involved in art education in their area of expertise or even moved into local and provincial councils and policy-making bodies to influence the development of arts infrastructure. Aside from the challenge of making a sufficient living solely in the arts, the interdisciplinarity of Newfoundland artists was remarkable for the ease with which so many of them engaged with multiple artistic

---

235 See Appendices 4 and 5.

236 See Appendices 4 and 5.

237 Morris, interview.

occupations across the industry. The Newfoundland arts scene was one of those rare places where not just a few, but *most* artists might start out working in one artistic milieu, like a theatre company, and end up playing in a band; acting in films; writing plays, poetry, or literary fiction; or joining a dance troupe or even a circus! Additionally, Newfoundland artists frequently seized opportunities to blend artistic mediums in unique ways.[238]

There was a charmingly bizarre mix of art mediums and entertainment forms in vogue in the 1970s Atlantic world, and elements of what was happening throughout the region were well represented in Newfoundland art and artistic process. Collective theatre, political and guerilla theatre, sketch comedy, satire, puppetry, mime, clowning, folk art, and traditional music—all of these artistic expressions found a place in Newfoundland's burgeoning cultural landscape, further aiding the already widespread tendency toward multidisciplinarity. Jane and Ron alternately wore the mantles of actor, musician, playwright, songwriter, singer, and teacher but their fellows had just as much or more artistic breadth. "You weren't a 'triple threat,' you just *were* a triple threat," Mary Barry remarked dryly.[239]

The literary, dramatic, musical, and theatrical talents of Greg and Beni Malone extend far beyond comedy and clowning. Chris Brookes and Lynn Lunde were actors, writers, administrators, activists, and, prior to the establishment of the Mummers Troupe, even puppeteers.[240] Songwriter, musician, and singer Mary Barry also trained and worked as a puppeteer in Toronto in 1974. Her roommate at the time, Tommy Sexton, proved to be an interdisciplinary virtuoso—an actor, singer, dancer, writer, and comedian. While his castmates of CODCO were putting together their own commissioned production for CPAC's urban development campaign in St. John's, titled *What Do You Want to See the Harbour for Anyway?*, seventeen-year-old Tommy was pursuing studies at Toronto Dance Theatre.[241] Back in St. John's, he'd even fronted a folk-rock cover band with Kelly Russell called Rakish Paddy. "Tommy wasn't a great fan of Fairport Convention, not like me," Kelly told me, and if Jane's stories of herself and a teenaged Tommy belting out the

---

238 Gulliver, 242–43.
239 Barry, interview.
240 Brookes, *A Public Nuisance*, 7–10; Brookes, interview.
241 Barry, interview; Peters (ed.), xiv.

soundtrack of *West Side Story* in her parents' basement are to be believed, then I'm sure Kelly is right. "But Tommy would go for anything," he continued. "He was just open to whatever, he had no bias about anything. He wouldn't say: 'No, I'm not going to do that, I don't like that song.' Tommy just loved everything. If it got him onstage, he was all about it."[242] Kelly Russell himself has likewise always demonstrated impressive interdisciplinarity. Musician, writer, storyteller, collector, and antiquarian, Russell's contributions to the cultural life of the province over the last fifty years have been enormously significant.[243]

The enthusiasm for personal breadth and artistic and cultural exploration translated easily to those who came to Newfoundland from away and promptly fell in love with it. Dudley Cox's years of experience and entrenchment in Newfoundland theatre by the early 1970s landed him on various successive committees, including that of the 1972 Provincial Drama Festival. After his mini-production of *Foreplay* during the run of *The Merchant of Venice* the previous month, he intended to continue making use of the Arts and Culture Centre's extensive lobby, recruiting visual artists of various disciplines to showcase their craft and process throughout the six days of the festival. This bundling of artistic mediums is a clear example of the communitarian and multidisciplinary spirit of the Newfoundland arts scene and gave these visual and craft artists the chance to be seen and to potentially stimulate more interest in their work. Cox called the program Peripheral Activities and it featured weavers working on looms, sculptors working with clay, potters at their wheels, and painters plying their craft in real time. Gerry Squires was given an entire section of the lobby in which to work continually on a twenty by thirty foot canvas throughout the festival. Dudley remarked that the Peripheral Activities program was merely an extension of the culture he had observed throughout his years in St. John's and in Newfoundland generally. "That's how we used to hang about in the bars and in the pubs. Everybody wanted to talk and everybody was interested in what everybody else was doing. That was the way wherever I went. People were interested and they had time to listen."[244]

---

242 Russell, interview.

243 Russell, interview.

244 Cox, "Newfoundland Travelling Theatre," 33; Cox, interview.

Actor and Toronto native Shifra Zisman was equally inspired by the uniqueness and richness of Newfoundland and its burgeoning cultural landscape. Technically, students enrolled in York University's Bachelor of Fine Arts program were not permitted to do professional theatre, but Shifra, who went by the name Sheila at the time, apparently decided that was more a suggestion than an edict. By the time she started sending out her CV in the spring of 1974, most summer shows had already been cast. Defiantly, she hitchhiked to Nova Scotia to work front-of-house at a local theatre and continued sending out résumés. She soon got a call from Dudley Cox, offering her a part in the NTTC's summer touring production of the *Newfoundland Pageant* written by Grace Butt. Shifra spoke glowingly of her years working in St. John's and of the impressive breadth and interdisciplinarity of Newfoundland's art scene.

> I didn't feel it at the time—that this was unique. I had the chance to work with actors, with musicians, with dancers. Where would that happen? You know what I mean? In Toronto, you're an actor. Okay. That's it. You're an actor and the others don't really mesh, but in Newfoundland that didn't exist.
>
> It was really amazing for me, being a mainlander. You know, when I got there, I couldn't understand anybody. Oh my God, it's like a different language. A world opened up that I had no idea about and I was building these intense friendships. Because we were touring around on the bus together, and later, living together, Jane and I were like sisters in this crazy world. And Ron was at the bars, being very hip and cool, playing his music, and every single woman had a crush on him! I wish I could find the scripted words to try to tell you what that era was like. I was there from '74 to '78 and it changed my life. It *changed my life*.[245]

245 Zisman, interview.

Regional Pride

In addition to collectivity and interdisciplinarity, pride in Newfoundland was also a defining characteristic of art produced during the 1970s. Nearly seventy-five per cent of the interviews I personally collected or reviewed from the STAGE Project referenced a conscious intention to pursue not only cultural reclamation but also to assert their regional pride among their Canadian counterparts on the mainland.[246] "Everybody was determined to shake off that mantle of the stupid-Newfie stereotype that we were painted with at that time, to reclaim our place and to present it with pride rather than shame," commented musician and songwriter Pamela Morgan, former long-time lead singer of Figgy Duff.

Figgy Duff, 1982.[247]

246 See Appendix 5.

247 Photo by Kent Barrett. Left to right: Derek Pelley, Dave Panting, Geoff Butler, Noel Dinn, Pamela Morgan. Band members at various times also included Anita Best, Kelly Russell, Art Stoyles, Philip Dinn, Bruce Crummell, Frank Maher, George Morgan, and Rob Laidlaw.

> I think that, in retrospect, I was on that path before I even ran into Noel [Dinn]. I was already looking into the Peacock books[248] for the undiscovered folk song gems in Newfoundland and when I met Noel, he was doing the same thing. It seemed a natural fit. Figgy Duff was determined to do something very specific and what it was doing was very close to my heart.
>
> I was so proud of everybody, of us, of CODCO, of the writers, and the painters, and everybody who was doing it. I think that's partially the reason why so many Newfoundland artists in this day and age have been able to make it on a national and international scale, because those doors got opened and the perception of Newfoundland and Newfoundlanders changed. Instead of being laughed *at*, we were in control of the laughter and what was funny, do you know what I mean? In those days, people laughed *at* us, but we produced some of the best comedians ever and they dictate what is funny. And that's really great, that's really fantastic.[249]

There is an evident desire for reclamation in the efforts and perspective that Morgan describes, which ties the Newfoundland effort clearly to the broader Atlantic push for decolonization and continued resistance to political, economic, and cultural colonialism. The presence of regional pride as an essential ingredient in Newfoundland art also signals, in my view, a desire for articulation—for *actualization*. Andy Jones seemed to touch on this directly when he explained the motives behind the conception and production of the film *The Adventure of Faustus Bidgood*,[250] created by Andy and Michael Jones.

---

248 See Kenneth Peacock, "The Native Songs of Newfoundland," *National Museum of Canada Bulletin* 190, Ottawa, 1960 *and* "Songs of the Newfoundland Outports," Vol. 1–3, *National Museum of Man Bulletin* 197, Ottawa, 1965 (The Canadian Encyclopedia. https://www.thecanadianencyclopedia.ca/en/article/kenneth-peacock-emc.)

249 Morgan, interview.

250 While this film was not released until 1986—several years after the period under examination—conception and production began as early as 1976 or 1977 (Jones, interview). *Faustus Bidgood* had an enormous cast of characters; the film seemed to feature almost every working actor in Newfoundland at the time, an aspect that contributes to the strongly salient theme of regional collectivity and community support.

> We were so political that we didn't even want to explain who we were in that movie. We said: "Let's make a movie as if we're in New York, or we're in London, just make our own movie for ourselves," which was a strong post-colonial thing, I guess. Usually, we would always have to say: "Oh, by the way, this is where we're from. We sort of lie right off the coast . . ." But we said: "No, no, no, we're just going to do it. And then, if you can't follow it, you're not one of us." We made it for ourselves. Everything that we did had a political edge, like Ron's singing.[251]

The attempt at actualization is apparent here and the filmmakers clearly would not have cared had any consumer of their art disliked their strongly nationalist perspective, especially its potential for exclusion—"*you're not one of us*." This attitude seems to crop up in just about every movement pursuing decolonization, liberation, or cultural reclamation and it's one that outsiders, even outsider allies, tend to find intimidating. For a time, everyone's identity credentials come under scrutiny. Those whose sense of belonging is cast into doubt may find themselves feeling hurt and isolated. Yet, these growing pains are utterly necessary. Until a people who perceive themselves as colonized has undergone cultural reclamation, articulation, and actualization, that intense and sometimes adversarial sense of pride and nationalism is essential to the process. Identifying and solidifying a common history and culture is crucial to a people's "psycho-affective equilibrium," or their ability to self-regulate as a cohesive social unit.[252]

As for Andy's characterization of Ron's music as political, I'm not sure that's true in and of itself. The subjects and voices he employed in his songwriting were as diverse and various as one can imagine. Although Ron does have quite a few patently political songs in his catalogue, some were written for regional theatre and film productions that were political on the face of them, like *Secret Nation*, Mary Walsh and Rick Boland's *High Steel*, or the Mummers Troupe's *East End Story* and *I.W.A.* But perhaps Andy meant something different when he described Ron's music as political, something more in keeping with the pursuit

---

251 Jones, interview.
252 Warren, 19.

of cultural actualization. Pam Hall expressed it quite elegantly, as one would expect an artist to do.

> One of the things that I loved about your dad's music—inasmuch as it wasn't like Phil Ochs or Bob Dylan protest folk—is that because of its cleaving to location, there was a kind of resistance in your dad's music that carved *place* out of *space*. Big difference between those two things. It was just his ornery determination to tell stories in his own voice, in his own way, his own stories, whether they were popular or not. That's a total act of resistance.[253]

According to Sandy Morris, Ron's dedication to that goal appears to have intensified significantly during the period under examination. Sandy showed me a few archival treasures during our interview, but two of them were very telling in terms of Ron's progress as a musician committed to performing and recording *only* his own original music. Somewhere among his papers and old notebooks, Sandy had found two handwritten set lists—one from a 1974 gig he and Ron had played together at The Hideaway, a bar that was once housed in the St. John's airport,[254] and another from a 1976 show they played together at the LSPU Hall. The 1974 set list is predominantly cover tunes, although roughly half of the songs from Ron's 1972 debut album, *Discovery*, appear on it. However, the 1976 set list, created only two years later, is all Ron's original music, including "Sonny's Dream."[255]

---

253 Hall, interview.

254 See Appendix 6.

255 While it would be very difficult to confirm this for certain, I believe that the 1976 LSPU Hall show to which Sandy is referring might have been among the first, if not *the* first time Ron ever played "Sonny's Dream" live in public. Dad stated on multiple occasions that he wrote "Sonny" in 1976 on a bus while travelling somewhere in western Canada. This was most likely during the Mummers Troupe's tour of the production *What's That Got to Do With the Price of Fish?* Dad both acted in and wrote music for the show and according to Chris Brookes's memoir, the troupe did indeed take the tour to western Canada in 1976 (Brookes, *A Public Nuisance*, 175).

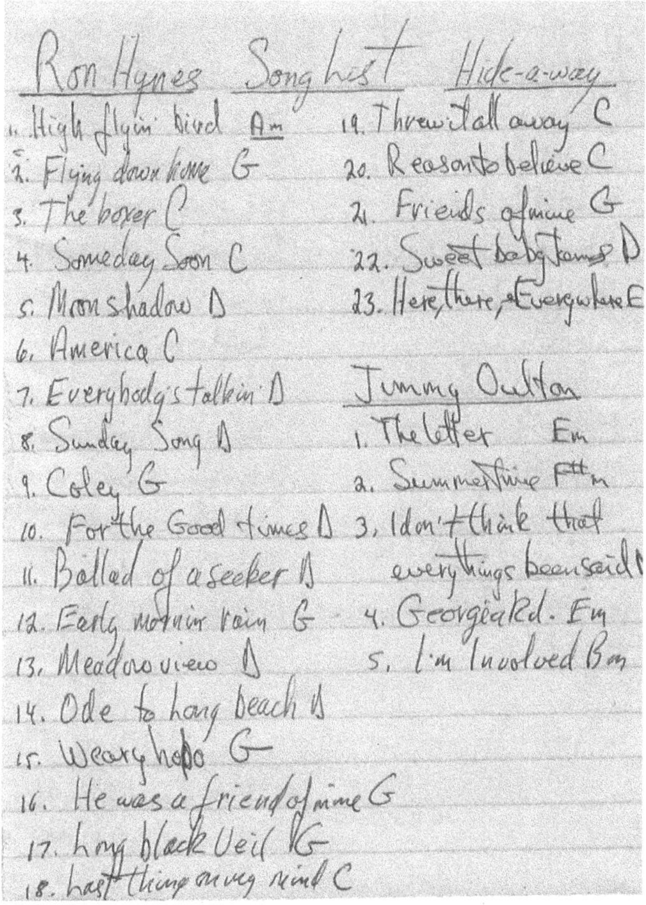

Ron Hynes Songlist Hide-a-way

1. High flyin' bird Am
2. Flying down home G
3. The boxer C
4. Someday Soon C
5. Moonshadow D
6. America C
7. Everybody's talkin' D
8. Sunday Song D
9. Coley G
10. For the Good times D
11. Ballad of a seeker D
12. Early mornin rain G
13. Meadow view D
14. Ode to Long beach D
15. Weary hobo G
16. He was a friend of mine G
17. Long black Veil G
18. Last thing on my mind C
19. Threw it all away C
20. Reasons to believe C
21. Friends of mine G
22. Sweet baby James D
23. Here, there, & Everywhere E

Jimmy Oulton

1. The letter Em
2. Summertime F#m
3. I don't think that everythings been said D
4. Georgia Rd. Em
5. I'm Involved Bm

Hideaway Set List, 1974.

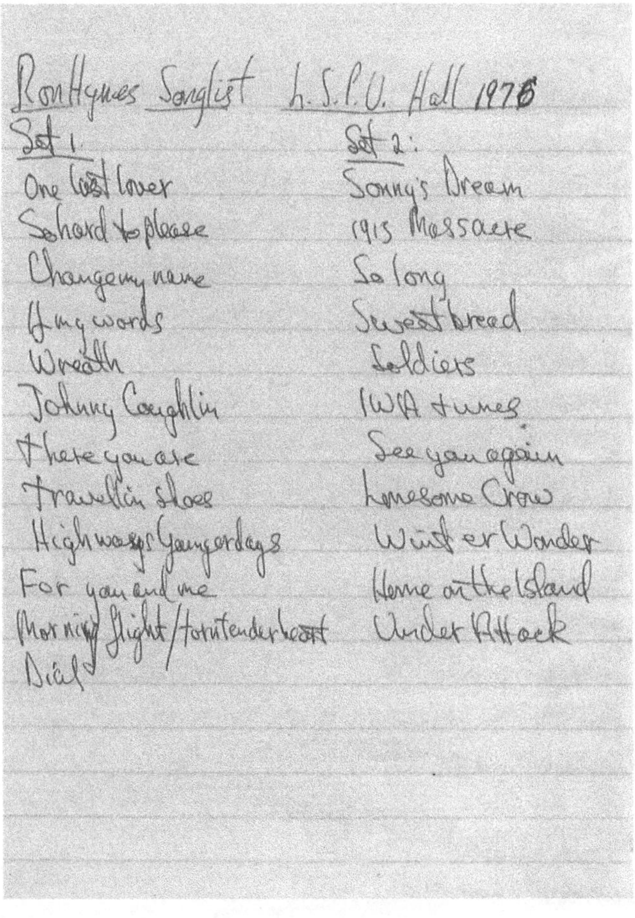

LSPU Hall Set List, 1976.[256]

256 Images courtesy of Sandy Morris. Used with permission.

When Sandy showed me the set lists following our interview, he exclaimed: "Must have been a busy two years!" The following years would be even busier—that 1976 show at the LSPU Hall featured a few more of the musicians, besides Ron and Sandy, who would soon form the Wonderful Grand Band, including Bryan Hennessey and Bawnie Oulton.[257] "I tried to talk him into doing covers in shows at the Hall in later years," Sandy later wrote, "but he didn't want to do covers!"[258]

The kind of focused development that Ron required as a songwriter, dedicated to performing only his own original music, almost certainly went beyond personal motivation or will, and I'm sure that his friendships and professional relationships with those in the broader arts movement underway in Newfoundland helped to sharpen his intentions and shape his perspective. In just the previous two years, he had had a front row seat to CODCO's creative and performing process up in Toronto. He had acted in and written songs for four out of the five Mummers Troupe shows that he worked on during the 1970s.[259] All about him, fellow artists were engaged in intentional cultural reclamation and actualization. To Pam Hall, this intentionality was readily apparent across the arts community.

> I think I was aware that there was a conscious intention or impulse to grow, to reclaim the Newfoundland voice. Clyde Rose was quite articulate in some cases about that. Dick Buehler, Michael Cook . . . People were self-aware of their mission, which was: "It's local, let do it. Let's write a play called: *Head, Guts, and Soundbone Dance*." I mean, come on. They knew what they were doing, or they knew that their impulse was about this reclamation—in many ways, very much what Indigenous folks are doing now. There was pressure against which Newfoundlanders were building. Nobody would publish them on the mainland, so they said: "F--k you, we're going to publish ourselves."
>
> Don't forget, some of these were university employees. They had the wherewithal to have a university salary. Al Pittman taught in the English department, Michael Cook taught in the English department, Dick Buehler taught in the English

257 Morris, interview.

258 Sandy Morris, personal email communication to author, Thursday June 23, 2022.

259 Malone and White, interview; Brookes, *A Public Nuisance*, 236–38.

> department, Clyde Rose, Pat Byrne . . . These guys were a bunch of academics saying: "We have a mission; we're going to pull this back together." Meanwhile, down in the gutter were the ordinary folks who had songs they wanted to write, had plays they wanted to write. Andy and Mary and Bob . . . I mean, that crowd were just dying to get stuff done and were poking around and trying to find a way to do it. The Reid Theatre [Little Theatre] at the university, again, was receptive. They said: "Okay, let's give these kids a key, so they can come in." Certainly, Edythe Goodridge on the visual arts side, at MUN Extension and the university art gallery, was very vociferous about the cultural renaissance.[260]

Carrying this intentionality before them like a shield, Newfoundland artists used their communitarian impulse both to support one another and, as Bob Joy put it, to feed off one another's success. "If there was any motto in CODCO, it was to 'do it with a bold face,'" Bob Joy told me during our interview. "Do it with a bold face" seems to have been something of a mantra for some of the CODCO folks I spoke with.[261] This short slogan seems to perfectly encapsulate the temper of an arts community with little formal training or funding infrastructure to support them, whose only professional experience had largely occurred in spaces they had, to a significant extent, carved out for themselves and who had long felt the weight of a chip upon their shoulders caused by Canada's history of cultural denigration for them. "There was an inferiority complex, it seemed to me, as I was growing up," Joy admitted.

> People would say: "If you're any good, you go to the mainland," or "If you want to buy anything really good, go to the mainland." Certainly, cultural products from the mainland had a lot of prestige and part of what I was beginning to realize was that St. John's culture and Newfoundland culture deserved as much praise as anything else, anywhere in the world.
>
> We had to have that boldness because otherwise you can't do it. When you think about the kind of boldness that CODCO

260 Hall, interview.

261 Joy, interview; Malone and White, interview; Jones, interview.

went forward with, there was a related kind of boldness that Noel Dinn and Figgy Duff had to go forward with. They said: "Okay, last month we were playing Jefferson Airplane covers, and maybe we're not going to do that. Maybe we're going to use our chops to present traditional Newfoundland music, and see what happens there." And then we fed off each other's confidence. Then there's the confidence of the Mummers. Chris Brookes had this idea, partly I think, based on the Passe Muraille model, that you could go into a Newfoundland community, into a Newfoundland narrative of some kind, and write your own show. There was the tradition of the Newfoundland concert, where there'd be sketches and recitations that had been handed down orally. That was the Arts and Culture crowd. St. John's Players would put on a bunch of sketches, Tom Cahill would write some monologues, and there'd be songs and hilarity, goofing around. With all of that combined, we felt not just our own boldness, but we felt that somehow, after all the economic difficulties and the Commission of Government and the feeling that Newfoundland was one of the poor provinces that was getting handouts from Canada . . . There was a feeling that our pride wasn't there as strongly as we thought it could be. There was a whole history, a cultural history, that met this new wave and the new wave, I think, brought it higher.

When you do things with a bold face you can end up inventing, perhaps from a source of panic, fear, excitement or danger, but that kind of confidence that we had as a community, where we fed off each other and we believed in our work . . . When you think about how important that is for each person on Earth as an individual, and certainly each culture on Earth, to believe in your own worth . . . So, we believed in the worth of what we were doing and we surged ahead. We forged ahead and that makes things happen that wouldn't otherwise happen. So, whether we were full of ourselves or what, it doesn't really matter. What it means is, it *made* happen what happened.[262]

---

262 Joy, interview.

Institutions: The Artist's Lifeline

While I have great admiration for the passion, drive, and motivation of these artists despite the challenges they faced, do not mistake me: I am not attempting to laud or promote any kind of bootstrap philosophy or policy perspective by any means. The value that institutional and government support can have to a regional arts community and therefore the wider society is both important and immense, in my view. Memorial University and MUN Extension, the Canada Council, the CBC, and other governmental and non-governmental organizations engaged in funding and supporting the arts during the 1970s were utterly essential. The vast majority of narrators I interviewed were unequivocal about the fact that without that institutional baseline of support, the cultural movement might not have gotten off the ground.[263]

One of my interview questions concerned the importance of interactions with funding bodies for Newfoundland artists in the 1970s. "Huge," Kelly Russell replied. While the Newfoundland and Labrador Arts Council wasn't formed until the early 1980s, there had been some national support in the meantime.

> Back in 1975, 1976, I know that Figgy Duff accessed Canada Council money several times. There was a tour that we did which we always referred to as "forty days in the wilderness." We got a grant to go around to small Newfoundland communities to perform and collect music. The mission was to meet musicians, singers, accordion players, fiddle players, and learn and record their music, but also to perform in these communities to show: "This is what we're doing with the music"—interpreting it in a more modern sense. I got several Canada Council grants myself in the late seventies. I went around Newfoundland collecting fiddle tunes, recording them, transcribing them, and eventually publishing them in music notation, and a couple of small Canada Council grants were essential for me to be able to do that. I couldn't have travelled. There's gas, there's food, there's accommodations, and I didn't have any money. I was a fiddle player looking for work. So, Canada Council was great for that. Lots of people were accessing Canada Council money in

263 See Appendix 4.

> the seventies. I'm sure Canada Council was in the background of every artist that was on the go back then. In those early days, the funding that was available was key.[264]

The role of the Canada Council in supporting developing artists was evidently crucial and worked in tandem with the frequently unpaid efforts artists were making on their own behalf, giving them a leg up in projects they wanted to develop. Like the Canada Council, Memorial University and MUN Extension also provided infrastructure and assistance, which was consistent with their communitarian and community development mandate at the time. Mary Walsh spoke just as enthusiastically as Kelly Russell about the support of Canada Council, as well as that provided by MUN Extension.

Mary Walsh on the set of *Faustus Bidgood*, 1978.[265]

264 Russell, interview.
265 Photo by Kent Barrett.

> Oh my God, the MUN Extension Service saved our lives! We would not be here at all without them because when we came back to Newfoundland as CODCO, we didn't come back as a company. There was no structure. There was nowhere to go except MUN Extension and they gave us a place to rehearse. They let us do the shows at the Little Theatre. It was free. It was free help that we got from Extension's services. I think we did pay some rent to do a public show, but boy, without the university and Extension particularly, I don't know how we would've gotten by.
>
> As for Canada Council, I remember they gave CODCO a grant even though we shouldn't have gotten one because you could only get a Canada Council grant if you received provincial government money—but there was no way to get provincial government money. The Canada Council set up a cross-Canada tour for us because we didn't know what we were doing. Things are different at the Canada Council now, I think, for sure, and MUN Extension is gone. I don't know who people can turn to now.[266]

Andy Jones had a very similar outlook on the contributions of MUN Extension and Canada Council to CODCO's early success.

> MUN Extension was absolutely golden and fabulous to us from the very beginning. We settled right in there and they were aware of community. They gave us free rehearsal space at 77 Bond Street[267] for about fifteen years. They were our champions, our supporters. They encouraged us, they helped us with our grants, they took telephone messages for us.
>
> The Canada Council, when we finally applied, were very supportive, and they really saw us. One hundred per cent of our material was Canadian, whereas there was a movement across Canada to try to get theatres to do four per cent or six per cent Canadian material. We were saying: "F--k, we don't

266 Mary Walsh, interview.

267 See Appendix 6.

> have that problem." Everyone in Newfoundland was putting out their own material, so we fit into their mandate very well—better than anybody in some ways. And here's another story that's the God's truth: *They* called *us* . . . to see if we'd be interested in applying. Imagine. People wouldn't believe that today, but that's the truth. Not only did they support us, but they *promoted* the cross-Canada tour we did in 1976. They called people up and got the gigs for us. The touring office did that. Generally speaking, it seemed like they were positive towards Newfoundland.[268]

I remarked to Bob Joy during our interview that it was great to see that government and educational institutions of the time seemed to be in agreement with artists and others about the value of the cultural products being created, the value of the talent being promoted, and the importance of the actualization that was taking place. He agreed, noting that Memorial University staff and administration were often as willing to help as those at Extension.

> When I was working as the locations manager on *Faustus Bidgood*, I remember approaching Memorial to use one of their collective offices, where a whole bunch of desks are in the same office. That was a very important location for us for *Faustus Bidgood*. I went to the administration and they let us go in there! To shoot scenes at night in their office spaces. And we didn't pay them anything. Consider that today a location fee is standard, but they just gave it to us. It was extraordinary.[269]

In examining these accounts, not to mention the excellent academic work that has also previously been completed on the subject,[270] it is clear that the assistance of institutions provided necessary impetus to the development of artists and of an arts industry. Yet even though the motivation and drive of artists could not have been vindicated without

268 Jones, interview.

269 Joy, interview.

270 See Mekaela Gulliver, "Preserving the Best," and Jeff Webb, "The Rise and Fall of Memorial University's Extension Service, 1959–91."

the support of institutions, it seems quite a stretch to characterize the existing resources and infrastructure during the 1970s as anything approaching sufficiency. In considering and weighing the narratives and experiences of artists throughout this period, it is apparent that much of what was produced throughout the most active part of the cultural renaissance was heavily driven by the often painstaking efforts of the artists themselves with institutional support providing more of a lifeline rather than the means to make a secure living.

Grit, Endurance, and the Artist-Run Centre

When David Weiser and Dudley Cox launched the NTTC in 1972, there was no provincial arts funding to tap and as has already been noted, artists were usually required to have already received provincial funding to qualify for Canada Council funding. Though they were able to secure a little assistance from MUN Extension and a few local businesses,[271] Cox and Weiser more or less personally bankrolled the launch of the NTTC by taking out a loan from the Bank of Montreal for forty-six hundred dollars.[272] As if the interest on a personal loan wasn't enough to make any group of young artists sweat, the efforts involved in ensuring that the shows generated enough revenue to pay salaries were just as daunting. In that sense, Dudley told me, "the first show we did was highly significant."[273]

> We opened in Arnold's Cove and it was a huge success. Everybody loved it. That was great but I was in a shattered state in a sense, somewhat disillusioned with the harsh realities of trying to put on a play around the bay without any real preparation going into it. I think we went out of Arnold's Cove with about thirty-five or forty dollars total. I think it was the Lion's Club in Arnold's Cove—they took sixty per cent of the house. You know, I guess we hadn't really clarified . . . We

271 "The Newfoundland Travelling Theatre Company Presents, *See How They Run*, A Comedy by Philip King, Directed by Dudley Cox," theatrical program (1972), private collection.

272 Cox, interview; Cox, "Newfoundland Travelling Theatre," 35.

273 Cox, interview.

> were just trying to get a foothold and I thought to myself: "Oh my God, we're going to go around Newfoundland and we're going to make thirty or forty bucks every time we go into a place and we're not even going to cover the wages." We *were* paying the wages, every actor got fifty bucks a week. I think they got thirty-five during the rehearsal and now they were getting fifty. So anyway, we went all around Newfoundland and that was pretty much the lesson that we learned. Every place we went, it was very difficult to take any money out of that community and go on with it, because they wanted it. They wanted a big take, and so wherever we went we were at the mercy of this club or that club or this group or that group. We completed the tour. We went all the way up to St. Anthony. We didn't miss any shows. When we got back I think we'd lost a bit of money, but more or less, we still owed the bank what we'd borrowed, forty-six hundred dollars, which was a lot more money than it is today.[274]

While reminiscing about that first tour with the NTTC, Jane was effusive in her appreciation for Dudley and David's leadership and how hard they worked at the myriad tasks involved in carting around a travelling theatre production—tasks that could only have been more challenging in rural Newfoundland half a century ago.

> We'd get to a place and the actors would be allowed to roam free and maybe run lines in a pasture outside somewhere. And there's Dudley and poor Derek [Butt] unloading the frigging truck with all the sets. They would work right through until we opened. Those guys worked their tails off. As for us actors, Dudley said: "Sit down, go over your lines, or relax," and they'd do all the work. There were no roads to get to Jackson's Arm, for example. To go to Jackson's Arm, you had to go over by boat. So, some fella from Jackson's Arm would come get you in a boat and you'd have a bunch of actors sitting in the boat, going across, and then trekking up a path to get up to the community. And there was Dudley and Derek

274 Cox, interview.

> loading all this stuff onto a boat and trekking it up. They even set up all the lighting and everything. I can't believe they used to do that.[275]

Pamela Morgan communicated a similar perspective about the grit and endurance required to live as a dedicated professional artist in 1970s Newfoundland. I asked her how often as a young artist she had interacted with institutions, arts infrastructure, or funding bodies for the arts. "Hardly ever," she replied. "Figgy Duff once had a Canada Council-sponsored tour," she told me, but aside from that, the band members were pretty much on their own.

> What a lot of people don't understand is nowadays there's an infrastructure for the music industry. There's management companies . . . there's no labels anymore, but there was a period later when there was an infrastructure with management and labels and all that kind of stuff. But when we started, there was nothing and to get off the island of Newfoundland with a six-piece band and your gear was no small feat. We were on the road in a Chevy van and sleeping on floors and pool tables, stuff like that. That was the reality of our existence. We would be picking up gigs as we went. We'd stop in a town and the first thing Noel would do is go find a phone booth, call ahead to whatever city we were going to hit next and try to find a place to play. Literally, that was the kind of life it was, with the exception of the occasional thought-out tour. We never had anything like agents or managers or labels and certainly no financial input from anywhere. So, it was kind of hand to mouth, but the shows were great, the band was great, the reaction was fantastic and it was never any problem to find someone to take you home after and give you a bed. People were very kind.
>
> Noel and Philip [Dinn], they were scrappers, but out of necessity. They fought for everything they wanted, and they had

275 Dingle, interview.

> to. Before Figgy Duff, Noel Dinn brought Lukey's Boat[276] to Montreal. They won this national contest, this battle of the bands thing, and their prize was to go to England and play. But achieving that when you came from Newfoundland in that time was absolutely remarkable because there was no infrastructure and it was so hard to get off the island. If you lived in Ontario and you had to go to Montreal, you'd manage it. If you were in central Canada where there's a bigger population base, it was much easier to tour. But if you were in Newfoundland, first of all, you had to get off The Rock.[277] Then you had to drive a couple of days in order to get to Montreal and that's where the population density starts. But even to get there, you're talking three days on the road and six people to feed and put up. So it was really, really difficult.[278]

Coping with the kinds of working conditions that Cox, Dingle, and Morgan describe not only highlights the need for provincial arts funding and infrastructure at the time, but also the need for a measure of autonomy for artists within their professional communities. In other words, they needed supportive and accessible programs and spaces to develop, showcase or perform their work that were artist-run. An artist-run centre will invariably do more and on a longer-term basis for their community of fellows than simply continuing to compete with one another for extraordinarily limited grant money. A cooperative or artist-run centre will also have established mentorship, scholarship, or artist-in-residence programs that engage and support artists at all levels of experience and mastery.

Pam Hall spoke very decidedly on this point. From her perspective, the artist-run centre or co-op in Newfoundland was the next most logical step in the progression of how the cultural movement unfolded. This progression begins, of course, with Memorial University and Extension. "It started earlier," Hall observed. "It was interdisciplinary and almost

---

276 Lukey's Boat featured Noel Dinn, Laverne Squires, Neil Bishop, Al Smith, Ron Tilley, and Nelson Boland. The band was formed roughly five years prior to the formation of Figgy Duff (Tara Bradbury, "CDs of '60s songs," *The Telegram*, March 22, 2017).

277 If one could not afford airfare, the only way to leave Newfoundland for the mainland in the 1970s was to drive to either Port Aux Basques or Argentia and take a ferry to Nova Scotia (a trip that, even today, can take between eight and sixteen hours).

278 Morgan, interview.

everybody came out of it. The second one was the literary community."[279] I am inclined to agree with Hall here. The connections between the MUN English department and the literary arm of the cultural movement in the 1960s and early 1970s resulted in the establishment of Breakwater Books, a for-profit publisher that was probably the closest thing to an artist-run centre outside of Extension that Newfoundland could boast in 1973. Breakwater was founded by Clyde Rose, Tom Dawe, Richard Buehler, Al Pittman, and Pat Byrne. Closely connected to and intermingled with these literary circles was the performance community with their live music and recitations. Committed to the same goals of reclamation and representation, together they publicly amplified the message of the cultural movement that Breakwater was attempting to communicate with the publication of writers like Ted Russell, Ray Guy, Art Scammell, and Des Walsh. Pat and Joe Byrne were part of the performance community as well, as the Breakwater Boys, and might be found on a weeknight in a downtown bar playing traditional Newfoundland music. In Hall's view, Breakwater was the first of a number of important artist-run and artist-focused institutions that, once matured, went a long way towards helping realize comprehensive arts resources for the province. Important cooperatives and artist-run centres created in the years to follow included St. Michael's Printshop, established in 1974; the Newfoundland Independent Filmmakers Cooperative (NIFCO), established in 1975; and the Eastern Edge Gallery, established in 1984.[280] For artists of various disciplines, but most especially the theatre community, the first and probably the most significant artist-run centre was the LSPU Hall.

When Chris Brookes first wandered into the Longshoremen's Protective Union Hall, he was merely on the lookout for a venue to stage his theatre troupe's next production, *East End Story*. Just as the troupe's previous productions of *Gros Mourn* and *Buchans: A Mining Town* had been researched, written, and staged in the locales in which the troupe sought to amplify the voices of local people and encourage change, they believed it was important to do the same for a show about the east end of St. John's. When Brookes first inquired at the Hall, he had no notion of finding a permanent home for the Mummers Troupe,

279 Hall, interview.
280 Gulliver, 188–89; Hall, interview; see Appendix 6.

and much less of establishing an accessible piece of arts infrastructure that would serve and support innumerable working artists for the next half-century and more.

> We kind of fell into it. It was purely by accident. All of our work was being done outside of St. John's, which I thought was important because that's where Newfoundland's soul lives—outside of St. John's. I don't think quite so doctrinaire about it now, but I did then, even though I was a townie. So, I went sniffing around downtown in the east end to look for some school or hall and I never actually noticed the LSPU Hall on Victoria Street before. I went in and met Peter Breen, who was the father of Danny Breen, the current mayor of St. John's. Just a lovely man. They were the only place in St. John's at the time who ran up the Pink, White and Green.[281] The Pink, White and Green is everywhere now! Back then, you had to *make* one. You had to *sew* the damned things! You couldn't buy them. Anyway, the LSPU had one and Peter Breen would go out on his deck and he would run it up every morning and run it down every evening. He was a fount of wisdom and history. I think they had heard of us because we had done shows with unions several years before. So anyway, they said sure, they'd rent the hall to us for rehearsals and ultimately, for performance.[282]

The Mummers Troupe staged their next three productions at the LSPU Hall throughout the spring, summer, and fall of 1975. The run of *East End Story* was followed in July by *Dying Hard*, a play about the poor working conditions and terrible health outcomes of workers in the mining industry, and in August by *I.W.A*. This last production saw only a couple of performances at the Hall before city inspectors arrived to close it down. In his memoir, Chris Brookes expressed a strong suspicion that the city's closure order was politically motivated. The opening night of *I.W.A* had been attended by both long-time labour leaders and

281 This tricolour flag is the unofficial flag of the "Republic of Newfoundland." While Newfoundland is not and never has been a republic, this flag has been flown by opponents of Confederation and by independence-minded Newfoundland nationalists for more than a century.

282 Brookes, interview.

politicians. The play's highly critical take on the handling of the historic Newfoundland strike by the Smallwood government stimulated a front-page theatre review in *The Daily News* with the headline: "I.W.A: Reopening the Wounds."[283] Moreover, the earlier production of *East End Story* had criticized Mayor Dorothy Wyatt's city planning policies directly. Two days after opening night, Brookes claimed to have received a discreet tip that city authorities planned to close the Hall. The city inspectors arrived with the closure order a few hours before showtime the following evening. For nearly seventy years, Brookes noted, the LSPU had hosted numerous meetings and varied events with similar numbers of attendees and the Mummers Troupe had been rehearsing and performing at the Hall for seven or eight months already. According to this reasoning, Brookes's suspicion that the closure order might have been political is easy to understand.[284]

> The International Woodworkers of America [IWA] strike in Newfoundland in 1959 was still a very touchy subject for a lot of people. It had broken families and careers. It seemed very fitting to do it in a union hall. Within a few days we were sold out. A few days later the city hall inspectors came and decided that the Hall was not suitable for public performance because it didn't have a sprinkler system.
>
> In the meantime, the LSPU were really supportive. They were outraged and pissed off. Gerald Abbot was the president and he basically said: "F--k this. If they won't let you have the show here, then I'll call a membership meeting. We'll block the f--king place and let's see them try to throw us out." Anyway, of course, he couldn't do that and we had to move the show up to the university.
>
> But there was the Hall. Suddenly it had to have a sprinkler system and the LSPU wanted to sell it. It was not officially on the market, but they wanted to sell it. The Bank of Montreal wanted to buy it and turn it into a parking lot for the bank and the LSPU didn't really want that. It was the second-oldest

---

283 William R. Callahan, "IWA: Reopening the Wounds," *The Daily News*, November 5, 1975.
284 Brookes, *A Public Nuisance*, 143-45.

> union in Newfoundland; it was a historic building. So, between the jigs and the reels, we realized we could buy it from them. We had a terrific administrator, Lynn Lunde. There were no theatre administrators in Newfoundland at the time. She was the only one, I think. She'd had some training at the Manitoba Theatre Centre. Anyway, she sniffed out a fund from the Secretary of State Department that provided homeless theatre companies with a home, basically. So, we tapped into that and bought the Hall for forty thousand dollars.[285] We scrounged up five thousand dollars for a down payment and the rest came from the Secretary of State money, and that's how the Hall came to be. But it was by accident, it wasn't planned. It was only because City Hall came in and closed down the Hall. I don't think anyone had any idea it would survive. How long is it now? Decades and decades. Andy Jones once called it the Newfoundland National Theatre, and it kind of has been.[286]

The LSPU Hall filled a real and urgent need for an accessible and welcoming performance space, and virtually every artist ever to come out of Newfoundland since 1975 has had some association with it whether they were playwrights, actors, musicians, dancers, or visual artists exhibiting their work. It continues to be a crucial piece of arts infrastructure and an important community resource today. As Brookes himself pointed out: "Everyone went through there."[287] The administrators of both the NTTC and the Mummers Troupe personally went into debt in order to carve out space for themselves and their fellow artists to work and continue their development.[288] These examples help make a compelling case that existing funding sources at the time represented a minimum rather than a sufficiency and that much of the development that occurred in the arts was artist-driven. That being said, the provincial government did contribute forty-five hundred dollars toward the LSPU Hall's purchase. It may be that John Perlin viewed the establishment of a new

285 The Secretary of State Department provided $57,500 for the Hall's purchase and renovation (Gulliver, 228).

286 Brookes, interview.

287 Brookes, interview.

288 Cox, interview; Brookes, interview; Brookes, *A Public Nuisance,* 106–107.

400-seat theatre downtown as an ideal initiative not only to increase resources for the theatre community that could not access the Arts and Culture Centre, but perhaps also to lessen some of the ill feeling that had persisted between himself and local artists.[289]

The Darker Side of Funding

Throughout the 1970s, federal and occasionally provincial funding bodies, non-governmental organizations, and private businesses provided financial support at critical moments. However, the piecework nature of grants and the reality that artists lived virtually unpaid in between projects—even if they were working full-time on their art—made daily life and professional development difficult and stressful. Dudley Cox noted that things began to get easier for the NTTC by 1974, when the Canada Council began to fund them.

> The actors' wages could go up to a hundred a week and I could pay for them to sleep in hotels and motels, but at no time was I allowed to divert any of the Canada Council grant money towards the debt. The general welfare of the group improved and I was glad to see it happen, of course, and me along with them. Now I was earning fifty bucks a week, which was a lot better than before, but the debt just hung there like the Sword of Damocles and it simply wouldn't move. That went on for a few years.[290]

Part of the attraction that the NTTC likely held for the Canada Council was their commitment to touring their performances throughout rural Newfoundland and hosting workshops in schools. Governments invariably prefer to fund projects with economic and social utility demonstrable beyond the aims of art. "We were sort of surviving doing that," Cox said. In 1976, the Canada Council commissioned him to undertake a cross-Canada study tour on the use of theatre performance and

289 Gulliver, 228.
290 Cox, interview.

workshops in schools. He had gotten as far as Toronto in his study tour when he received the rather abrupt news that the NTTC's funding had been cancelled. "There was no way we could have carried on without any help from Canada Council," he explained.[291] By 1978, the NTTC was officially defunct and Dudley had to accept a job out in British Columbia so he could eventually settle the NTTC's debt.[292] The lack of sufficient arts infrastructure created a funding dependency that could kill artistic ventures quite suddenly when the support ran out or starve others before they had a chance to get off the ground. "I was always suspicious of funding," Dudley said.

> I was at an arts conference once and Peter Bell[293] was there. I loved Peter, such a bloke he was. Everybody was going on about: "Oh, we're not getting enough funds for this," and "Why don't they fund that?" Funding, funding, funding. They were all getting up one after the other. And at the end Peter Bell got up and said: "Has anyone ever thought that funding is not really such a good thing?" There was an enormous silence . . . and then everybody carried on chanting for funding. But I remembered Peter, and I think he's absolutely right because it's a double-edged sword, you know. People are building a life. You're building for your lifetime, but funders, they're only funding for a couple of years. To pin your life to that kind of support . . . it's like an iron lung. If it stops working or the electricity dies, you're dead![294]

The funding patterns characteristic of both governmental and non-governmental entities who supported the arts during the 1970s is consistent with a mandate of achieving short-term economic or development goals using art, much in the same vein as artists have always been recruited to produce or perform content for Come Home Year or Old Home Week. The year 1974 marked the twenty-fifth anniversary of Newfoundland's

291 Cox, interview.

292 Ferry, 147.

293 Artist, curator of the Memorial University Art Gallery from 1966–1972 and art columnist for the *Evening Telegram* from 1973–1980 ("AGNL: Peter Bell," Bibliothèque et Archives Canada. https://epe.lac-bac.gc.ca/100/205/301/ic/cdc/agnl/bell.html).

294 Cox, interview.

Confederation with Canada and John Perlin had placed Robert Nutbeam, Premier Frank Moore's brother-in-law, in charge of organizing the acts and performances for the official summer celebrations. This might have been the perfect opportunity to showcase some of the original content that was being produced all over the province. Both the NTTC and CODCO received funding from the organizers to perform their work, but not in any of the official celebrations in St. John's. Greg Malone and White had heard that acts and performances were being planned and that funding was available for local talent. Fresh and fairly confident from the success of *Cod on a Stick*, Malone and Diane Olsen paid Nutbeam a visit.

> **Greg:** We went to Bobby Nutbeam and he said: "We think you are the heart and soul of Newfoundland, but unfortunately we spent all our money on mainland acts." There was no Newfoundland entertainment in the whole program that the government of Newfoundland had planned. Nothing. That's what it was like in those days. Everything was brought in. There was no feeling that *we* could do these things.
>
> **White:** So, they hauled eight thousand dollars out of the hat.
>
> **Greg:** We got eight thousand dollars and we did an eight-week tour of Newfoundland in the frozen spring, from the north tip of the Northern Peninsula, St. Anthony, all the way down to Bay d'Espoir in the south.
>
> **White:** That's what we did with the eight thousand dollars—we bought a van.
>
> **Greg:** We bought a van and lived off the box office on the road.[295]

The NTTC likewise received funding from the Confederation jubilee organizers to conduct a provincial tour of Grace Butt's *Newfoundland Pageant* rather than participate in the official celebrations. At John Perlin's behest, Nutbeam, Dudley said, had given him "a script as thick as a Bible that was a history of Newfoundland from day one right through

295 Malone and White, interview.

to Joey Smallwood."[296] While these commission and funding efforts provided key support to both theatre groups at important times, the particular approach to funding meant that local artists frequently faced a condition of feast or famine. Additionally, one could argue that the almost exclusive booking of mainland acts for the official celebrations of Newfoundland's Confederation jubilee demonstrates the continued preference either for "high culture," or "colonial culture" depending on one's perspective. But then again, perhaps the primary concern was for an economic bottom line. Perhaps Perlin and Nutbeam did not have faith that the available local talent was capable of bringing in the kinds of crowds and revenue the organizers hoped to realize.

Andy Jones echoed the frustration of his fellow artists with the nature of the funding structure that prevailed in Newfoundland and Labrador into the 1980s.

> The government was slow to take off. They couldn't understand the Hall: "What are you guys doing down there anyway at the dirty old Hall?" That was a big challenge to get over that. "Well sure, if we give you money for the Hall, why do we have to give you money for shows?" And you'd say: "Gosh, you know, you've got to pay the actors to be in the shows." So, it took years trying to educate them.[297]

In the meantime, Jones noted, Canada Council and MUN Extension continued to be "pillars" for the artistic community. CODCO received their first direct Council funding for their second theatre production, *Sickness, Death and Beyond the Grave*. The group showed success early on with their ability to generate enough revenue from the box office on their tours to cover salaries, but a troupe of that size (seven members at the time) still sometimes needed assistance with the costs of transportation, accommodation, and meals—expenses that could promptly wipe out box office revenue on an extended tour. With the exception of two Canada Council-sponsored tours between 1973 and 1976, Malone commented: "Everything we did was on our own dime."

---

296 Cox, interview.
297 Jones, interview.

> **Greg:** We were the only theatre company in Canada that toured the country from coast to coast. We went from Victoria to St. John's.
>
> **White:** Nobody else did it.
>
> **Greg:** Nobody!
>
> **White:** Well, Winnipeg Ballet would make tours some places but they were heavily subsidized.
>
> **Greg:** They wouldn't go coast to coast either.
>
> **White:** No, there was no theatre company . . .
>
> **Greg:** They didn't cover the territory we did or as regularly.
>
> **White:** They certainly didn't come here.
>
> **Greg:** No, they certainly never came here. So we were the only Canadian theatre company doing that and that was noticed by Canada Council. We were very popular in Vancouver, Edmonton, and Toronto. We had a good following.[298]

Institutional Faces

CODCO did get great reviews across Canada in the early years, stimulating a good deal of mainland support.[299] As a Newfoundlander, whether one loved or hated that "Newfcult" was in vogue in music, theatre, and quaint folksy magazine spreads across the country, it certainly was helpful in attracting the attention of national arts funders to the pool of readily available and hungry talent in Newfoundland. Institutions contributed a great deal to the eventual success of this vanguard of artists, but the mandates and goals of such institutions are frequently shaped by the individual people who guide, manage, and administer them. It is noteworthy in my view that two-thirds of the narrators I interviewed personally mentioned institutional figures *by name* and often with a

298 Malone and White, interview.

299 Peters (ed.), xv, xx.

good deal of emotion when expounding upon the role and impact of institutions in either supporting or starving the arts during this early period.[300] This suggests that it was often the individual bureaucrats or staff members who went the extra mile for artists as much as the existence of the institutions themselves that made the difference.

Greg and White did not forget the kind assistance of Anna Stratton in helping to secure their first Canada Council grant.[301] Andy Jones referred to the Canada Council's John Cripton with warm gratitude for organizing and promoting one of CODCO's cross-country tours.[302] Both Jones and Mary Walsh spoke with deep appreciation for Extension workers Ray Cox and Mina Hickey, who along with many others tirelessly supported the motley crew of artists who used the free space and services provided at 77 Bond Street in St. John's throughout the 1970s.[303] Artists of multiple disciplines, not just those on the visual arts scene, recognize the mentorship contributions of artist and Extension worker Don Wright, who went on to co-found St. Michael's Print Shop with fellow artist Heidi Oberheide.[304] When I asked Kelly Russell to describe the quality of interactions with institutions and funding bodies during the 1970s, he replied: "I'm going to start with one person's name—Edythe Goodridge. She was the arts community's strongest supporter."[305]

Goodridge's name was the one most frequently invoked among institutional champions for Newfoundland arts and culture. She was either mentioned or discussed at length with notable appreciation by more than a third of narrators I interviewed personally and by nearly a fifth of those I surveyed from the STAGE Project.[306] Those who worked directly with her or were the beneficiaries of her generosity spoke of her commitment to Newfoundland artists of all disciplines. "She was extremely influential," noted Anita Best, "not only in the visual arts but in getting writers, musicians, and actors together."

> She was a real catalyst for the arts in Newfoundland. She was just a spectacular person. She had a flair, she had a presence, and

300 See Appendix 4.
301 Malone and White, interview.
302 Jones, interview.
303 Jones, interview; Mary Walsh, interview; Gulliver, 80, 103, 145–46.
304 Brookes, *A Public Nuisance,* 6; Hall, interview; Gulliver, 130–31.
305 Russell, interview.
306 See Appendices 4 and 5.

> she was so generous. She was the head of the Canada Council, the visual arts section, for a long time. She used that position to really encourage Newfoundland artists and to introduce them on the mainland, arranging concerts for them and things of that nature. People slept on her floor when they went to Ottawa.[307]

In the same vein, MUN English professor and orator Shane O'Dea commented on Goodridge's commitment to advocacy for artists in a speech before Goodridge received her honorary doctorate from Memorial University during their 1998 Commencement.

> In St. John's, she so frequently entertained the Flying Feds (as the bureaucrats were known) that her house became a byword in Ottawa. It even came to the ear of Jim Coutts, Trudeau's chief of staff, who asked, "What is this *Edythe's* like? Is it the only restaurant in St. John's?'"[308]

In 1984, Goodridge gave an interview to Cathryn Boak for the MUN Pathways program about her experiences and achievements as a cultural impresario. When asked why she approached her role as curator of the Memorial University Art Gallery the way she had, Goodridge replied that in the context of a place like St. John's during the 1970s, the concept of a multidisciplinary artistic and cultural forum was the best approach, not the typically more "narrow, defined, effete, and elite" role of more typical art galleries.[309] Further, she believed that it had to reflect the collective and communitarian mandates of Extension and the broader body of the university.

> What we tried to do was establish the notion of a forum, not a traditional gallery with strict curatorial and custodial functions. In those days, there was no alternate theatre space. There was no alternate *anything*. All these emerging activities and expressions were starting to evolve . . . Young people were

---

307 Best, interview.

308 Shane O'Dea, "Oration honouring Edythe Ryan Goodridge," Memorial University of Newfoundland, *Gazette* 31, no. 6 (October 29, 1998): 5. https://dai.mun.ca/PDFs/mun_gazette/MUNGaz_V31No6.pdf.

309 Boak, (1984).

> very committed to exploring the traditional art forms with great dignity and devotion and they wanted a place to express their findings and to bring some of that traditional expression to a larger audience. I think it was *that*—that broadening of the role of the gallery into alternate spaces, ideas, expressions that were not strictly formal or *colonial* for that matter—which were some of the arts being perpetuated in an official capacity. That caused all the furor and the debate and the noise level. It was a very exciting time.[310]

At the beginning of his oration during the 1998 Commencement address, O'Dea described Goodridge as the "mother" of the "New Newfoundland," the father being Joey Smallwood.[311] If Goodridge may be said to be the patron saint of the 1970s Newfoundland arts community, then John Perlin resided at an opposite pole as far as many artists were concerned. Indeed, Perlin once described his decision to place Goodridge in charge of the Memorial University Art Gallery, including the programming of the related Arts and Culture Centre exhibition spaces, as "the biggest mistake [he] ever made."[312]

Throughout a significant number of the sources I employed for this study, even if Perlin was not mentioned by name, then the Arts and Culture Centre or the Division of Cultural Affairs over which he presided for several decades was referenced as colonial in character and uninterested in promoting original regional cultural content for either political, aesthetic, cultural, or economic reasons. Multiple oral history interviews, the memoirs of Chris Brookes and Dudley Cox, as well as Alan Filewod's examination of the Mummers Troupe's interactions with arts and funding institutions during the 1970s all highlight the sharp political differences between the province's top bureaucrat for the arts and provincial artists, and the Mummers Troupe most especially.[313]

The overtly political theatre of the Mummers, with its process and values sunk deep in the New Left counterculture, was bound to clash with John Perlin's vision of what regional theatre in Newfoundland

310 Boak, (1984).

311 O'Dea, "Oration honouring Edythe Ryan Goodridge," 5.

312 Bill, 95.

313 Brookes, *A Public Nuisance,* 39-40, 70, 97-106; Cox, "Newfoundland Travelling Theatre," 26; Filewod, "The Mummer's Troupe," (1998); see Appendices 4 and 5.

should look like. With his lifetime appointments of Canadian Secretary to Her Majesty Queen Elizabeth II, protocol officer for Royal Visits, and Chairman of the annual Royal St. John's Regatta, John Perlin and his family appear as close to provincial aristocracy as it seems possible to get, and these facts almost certainly influenced his critics among emerging artists, many of whom identified as working class. Perlin had grown up in the amateur theatre scene of post-World War II, mid-twentieth-century St. John's, and seemed to have been thoroughly inculcated with the "town" tradition of theatre. The community theatre scene as it existed up until the mid-1960s with the London Players and the St. John's Players was predominantly aimed at a sedate middle-class audience with no expectation of being confronted with activism, protest, or even much controversy, much less by seemingly semi-Marxist, pro-labour critics of government, industry, and progress.[314] "At the time," Brookes told me, "our provincial Director of Cultural Affairs seemed to think that I was a Communist and that I should be run of out of town."

> I thought that was extremely funny and I was quite proud of the fact that he considered me to be that dangerous. I still wonder, did he really think I was a card-carrying Communist? Because I was accused of that. All of that's changed. All of us in the movement, right across the arts . . . I guess we were challenging the status quo, so it was a big push, but it was also kind of a gas to think, "Oh, we're pissing people off. The Old Guard is not liking this, oh! So we must be doing something right." You can always judge yourself by your enemies, I guess.[315]

In his unpublished memoir, Dudley Cox remembered Perlin's sincere attachment to the community theatre scene in St. John's ever since his youth. Perlin had taken personal ownership—and now sole charge as well—of an artistic arena that had, in his experience, typically adhered to the town tradition of theatre.[316] The theatre of the Mummers Troupe was virtually opposed to John Perlin's concept of theatre and therefore it is unsurprising that Perlin became, as Alan Filewod put it, "an

---

314 Brookes, *A Public Nuisance*, 39–40, 97–8; Cox, "Newfoundland Travelling Theatre," 25–6, 49; Gulliver, 59, 61–2, 102, 123.
315 Brookes, interview.
316 Cox, "Newfoundland Travelling Theatre," 25; Devine, 76–7.

ideological antagonist as well as a competitor for audience support."[317] Compared to other contemporary and later theatre groups, Perlin did little to support the Mummers besides his assistance in the purchase of the LSPU Hall. The Mummers were welcomed at the Arts and Culture Centres only twice during their decade of existence, the first time for their 1978 production of *They Club Seals, Don't They?*[318] Indeed, as we have already observed, both the NTTC and CODCO received touring grants from provincial funds by 1974, support that was not given to the Mummers, whose then-current production of *Buchans: A Mining Town* was, Brookes claimed, "too hot to touch." Instead, Brookes wrote, the Mummers secured their 1974 touring funds with the kind assistance of steelworkers unions in Baie Verte and Labrador City.[319] Furthermore, both CODCO and the NTTC had been welcomed on a limited basis by this time at the Arts and Culture Centre, even if only in the Basement Theatre. While the NTTC could not be fairly accused of being a bastion of the town tradition of theatre (a charge I shall discuss in more detail in due course) and neither, certainly, could CODCO, the Mummers seem to have been the most offensive to bureaucratic sensibilities.

Dudley Cox recalled reminiscing with Chris Brookes about Chris's one and only attempt to submit an entry at the Dominion Drama Festival. During the 1969 adjudication session, Brookes had jumped out of his seat unannounced and begun handing out pamphlets detailing his "gorilla" theatre entry to the Dominion Drama Festival. Unfortunately, Brookes remembered, the adjudicator had refused to read or acknowledge his entry and John Perlin himself had appeared "apoplectic in the wings" at Brookes's perceived temerity.[320] Cox, whose vision and perspective on theatre was almost certainly more comprehensible to Perlin than Brookes's own, nonetheless found the Director of Cultural Affairs challenging to work with, remarking during his STAGE Project interview that continued appeals for support to the Division of Cultural Affairs always felt like "begging."[321] Perlin himself did not approve of the manner in which some artists seemed to approach him with an expectation of being fully funded, and wanted them to "help themselves

---

317 Filewod, "The Mummers Troupe," (1998).
318 Brookes, *A Public Nuisance,* 200; Gulliver, 62.
319 Brookes, *A Public Nuisance,* 125.
320 Cox, "Newfoundland Travelling Theatre," 26.
321 Dudley Cox, interview by Gail Weir for the STAGE Project, April 13, 1995, 20.

first" before coming to him for help "with the rest."[322] It was Cox's opinion that Perlin's administration of the arts effectively stymied the development of professional regional theatre and comprehensive arts infrastructure for more than a decade.[323] "We put in a whole bunch of hard work in those early days," Dudley told me during our interview.

> I think we proved ourselves to John Perlin, who was a big cheese in many ways at the time, and he stood between the government and us riffraff there struggling away. Everywhere I went, people did not speak highly of John Perlin. He was a very difficult figure to deal with, but, you know, I understood . . . I was a bit older than most of these people, and I sort of knew that he had a job to do and he had bosses and so on and so forth.[324]

Perlin's desire to see artists "helping themselves first" before approaching him is an attitude consistent with a mandate of making sure that the Arts and Culture Centres—merely the first of which had cost a staggering eight million dollars to build—turned a profit and paid for themselves. Perlin himself pointed out that he did not actually have the power to enlarge the budget he was given and neither did he have the power to use the Centre's profits to fund further programming beyond that which he thought would pay the Centre's bills. All profits were returned to the provincial coffers. More programming meant more labour, which further depleted the Arts and Culture Centre's allotted annual budget. In this context, Perlin's perspective is easy to understand. Yet, his attitude fails to empathize with the frustration of regional artists and creators who could not afford the rental rates to stage their shows at the Centres. Meanwhile, the often imported programming on the main stage was chosen by Perlin and funded with taxpayer money in a venue that many felt was supposed to encourage and celebrate Newfoundland culture and artists.[325] "I understood," Dudley recalled of Perlin. "There was a limit to what he could do. I used to rail against him like everybody else, but you know, Canada Council was not so perfect either."[326]

---

322 Gulliver, 62.
323 Cox, "Newfoundland Travelling Theatre," 25-6.
324 Cox, interview.
325 Gulliver, 57, 62.
326 Cox, interview.

Canada Council and Resistance to the Regional Theatre Model

Cox experienced the precariousness of Canada Council's funding structure firsthand and developed his own reservations about it based on the unpredictable financial existence it could produce for the artist. But beyond this, Cox was also concerned that the nature of the funding structure had shifted the relationship dynamics between the members of the Newfoundland theatre community, a concern that Chris Brookes shared. Both Cox and Brookes wrote at length of how the onset of Canada Council funding for Newfoundland theatre was simultaneously helpful but also problematic. It helped keep their nascent artistic endeavours afloat and something was certainly better than nothing, on the one hand. On the other hand, it had engendered competition and resentment in an environment that both Cox and Brookes observed was previously much more cordial.[327] Indeed, it stands to reason that in such an environment with limited resources and many hungry artists, the camaraderie and collectivity that significantly animated the movement at the outset might have been threatened.

In their respective memoirs, Cox and Brookes each described Canada Council's efforts to organize the growing number of newly formed theatre companies into a Newfoundland regional theatre organization. Sometime during the summer of 1973, the two met with Michael Cook of the Open Group to discuss the prospect. An administrative merger of the Open Group, the Mummers Troupe, and the NTTC would require that each individual company shelve certain personal ambitions or mandates in order to access sustained and stable funding for all three.[328] According to Brookes, Cook and Cox asked him to form a school-touring arm for the proposed organization and to move away from the more politically inflammatory artistic processes and productions like *Gros Mourn*, which had stimulated a significant media response regionally but had alarmed and aggravated provincial and federal bureaucrats, including members of the Canada Council. One member had observed to Brookes and Lunde upon reading the script, which had criticized and caricatured Canadian politicians: "As soon as you use real names, your theatre becomes political rather than creative."[329]

---

327 Cox, "Newfoundland Travelling Theatre," 48–50; Brookes, *A Public Nuisance*, 103–107.

328 Cox, "Newfoundland Travelling Theatre," 49; Brookes, *A Public Nuisance*, 103–104.

329 Brookes, *A Public Nuisance*, 99.

"*Well yeah, no shit,*" I can hear Chris and Lynn thinking in response to this critique, "*of course it's political.*" As far as they were concerned, art for the sake of art was pointless. It was, they believed, the duty of the artist to be faithful to their subject and neither art nor culture existed simply to vindicate bourgeois political values.[330] Brookes, of course, refused to consider toning down any aspect of the Mummers' mission or approach, which did not surprise Cox in the least. Dudley later wrote that the description of the meeting between himself, Brookes, and Cook in Chris's memoir was "not entirely accurate," but he refrained from going into specific detail. It does seem, however, that the Mummers' political warfare style of theatre was at issue and was viewed as a potential impediment.[331]

To Brookes, it seemed that the Canada Council had found a mechanism to force the Mummers to tamp down their radical politics in exchange for the "dangled carrot" of stable funding.[332] Brookes's commitment to his cause resembled zealotry to Cook and Cox, both of whom dreamed of founding a Newfoundland regional theatre. Cox and Cook had come to Newfoundland to work and attend school, respectively, and neither had initially planned to stay as long as they did. Both had fallen in love with the place and joined the ranks of Newfoundland's most ardent allies and supporters. Cook's commitment to making room in Canada for Newfoundland's unique culture and artistic voice is manifest in his many years of contribution to the provincial theatre and literary scene as a drama professor, playwright, actor, and director. Cox himself dreamed of helping to found the Newfoundland equivalent of Ireland's Abbey Theatre, to illuminate the "deeper emotions of Newfoundland," a goal he believed transcended partisan politics.[333] All three of these individuals were equally passionate and united in their love for Newfoundland's people and culture. They were equally devoted to what they each believed would lead to the province's development and betterment and in their belief that the arts had a key role to play in that effort—they simply had different incarnations of that vision in mind. Minus the competitive and adversarial environment engendered by limited and intermittent funding structures, these differences might have simply added the mere spice of variety and diverse dialogue to the community rather than antagonism.

330 Brookes, *A Public Nuisance*, 100.
331 Cox, "Newfoundland Travelling Theatre," 49.
332 Brookes, *A Public Nuisance*, 103–104.
333 Ferry, 102, 253; Cox, "Newfoundland Travelling Theatre," 48-9.

In early 1974, numerous artists of varied disciplines met in St. John's for two arts conferences at which the goal of securing stable funding was at the top of the agenda. What was needed, the arts conference attendees agreed, was a provincial arts council to which members of the community could be elected to influence policy and support their fellow artists, not, both Brookes and Cox wrote, unfettered governance by a single appointed bureaucrat.[334] What artists ultimately sought was the beginning of a comprehensive arts infrastructure, one that gave artists representation, autonomy, voice, and support in their professions. The conference attendees together submitted a petition to the provincial government for the creation and funding of a provincial arts council.[335]

Alan Filewod observed that the nature and shape of funding policies can profoundly impact both the artistic process and its final product. As they existed in the early 1970s, federal funding policies proved particularly challenging to navigate for the administrators of the Mummers Troupe, which could then in turn make the creative process more difficult to navigate also. "We feel that Council funding concepts should be tailored to fit theatre structures as they exist in Canada, not vice-versa," the Troupe's administrators wrote in their 1974 grant application.[336] Newfoundland and Labrador theatre was not the regional theatre of other provinces. It was going far beyond the Canadian regional model of predominantly British and American content with the occasional Canadian play, and was increasingly producing original content with each company doing something quite different from the others. The models that federal funders employed to organize support for the arts imposed binary definitions of regional theatre and alternative theatre, neither of which described the Newfoundland theatre scene at all.[337]

An important related consideration was that most of this original content was being created collectively, which presented difficulties for Council members who wanted precise timeframes and reports. Such demands are easier to make on a single writer, but the collective process is long, fraught, and messy with multiple writers all working to reach creative consensus. "Our projects, for the most part, don't have

---

334 Brookes, *A Public Nuisance,* 105; Cox, "Newfoundland Travelling Theatre," 49.

335 Filewod, "The Mummers Troupe," (1998); Brookes, *A Public Nuisance,* 105; Cox, "Newfoundland Travelling Theatre," 49.

336 Filewod, "The Mummers Troupe," (1998).

337 Filewod, "The Mummers Troupe," (1998).

a clear beginning and end. . . . This means, in part, that we prefer not to predict, eight or nine months in advance, where we will be in this process and exactly what we will need to do," Brookes explained in a communication to Canada Council.[338] Due to the agency's mandate for regular reports and detailed timelines far in advance of a project, the Canada Council were never really equipped to adapt themselves to the reality of the collective theatre process as it existed in Newfoundland. The Mummers managed the best they could, often shifting grant funds from one project to another when necessary—a level of informality that, Filewod noted, would have shocked the Council had they known.[339]

An additional problem with the structural nature of arts funding is the potential impoverishment of the creative impulse. Sandy Morris remarked critically on the impact of a corporate-style streamlining of the artistic process. "You can't say: 'Well, between nine a.m. and ten tomorrow, we'll write a play.' That doesn't happen, not if it's going to be a good play."[340] From Sandy's perspective, musicians require just as much space and time as do theatre collectives in order to allow the creative process to play out. "It would have been a bunch of fellas getting together and jamming until they came up with something that clicked, that everybody agreed clicked," Sandy said. "In the Grand Band, you could toss out a thousand ideas and all of them would get rejected until something happened that made everybody say: 'Oh yeah, we can do that!'" Knowing that the Wonderful Grand Band never played with fewer than six members and that at their most numerous, with the addition of the CODCO contingent, the band toured with no less than ten performers, I observed to Sandy that it must have been crazily difficult to secure creative consensus in an act of that size. He laughed and agreed:

> And look who you had to get to agree with you! Ron, for one. And everybody had their own biases or preferences, like different kinds of music, different styles of bass playing, or whatever. But that's part of the reason why it was so good, because we all had to convince each other that something was worth doing. So, your first audience was the other fellas in the band.[341]

---

338 Filewod, "The Mummers Troupe," (1998).
339 Filewod, "The Mummers Troupe," (1998).
340 Morris, interview.
341 Morris, interview.

Food and a Roof

Keeping their professional artistic efforts funded and afloat was challenging enough, but there was also the added stress of meeting the cost of living as a professional artist. I asked the oral history narrators I interviewed to describe what it was like to make a living as an artist in 1970s Newfoundland. Answers varied, as did experiences, but taken together, these narratives indicate that by the mid-1970s, it was challenging but quite possible for a young artist to survive and make a basically decent living as a single person. Still, conditions were often less than ideal.[342] As the administrators of the NTTC, Dudley Cox and David Weiser had learned some hard financial lessons during their first tour, and they were determined they would do better during their second. They made a little more money with the 1973 *Pool's Paradise* tour than they had made touring *See How They Run* the previous summer. "But again," Dudley admitted, "it was really rough with the money situation. We never slept in a hotel or a motel or anything. We slept on the floor of the stage where we did the show and ate what we could where we could find it. David used to make up Spic sandwiches every day."

"*What* kind of sandwiches, sorry?" I asked Dudley.

"Spic!" he exclaimed laughing. "Andy Jones had a monologue about Spic sandwiches. You must ask him, but Spic . . . it's a meat, like a processed meat."

"Like Spam?" I clarified, unable to suppress a smile.

"Spam! Yeah, it's like Spam," he said, and I smothered my laughter at a mental image of the Monty Python boys singing with a superlative men's choir costumed as Vikings.[343]

Greg Malone described CODCO's 1974 Newfoundland tour of *Cod on a Stick* as similarly gruelling.

> We did an eight-week tour in the frozen spring, from the north tip of the Northern Peninsula, St. Anthony, all the way down to Bay d'Espoir in the south and it nearly killed us. In the van, uninsulated, sleeping on floors of schools and gymnasiums. We never had any kind of motel or hotel and we just did it because we thought everyone should see this.

---

342 See Appendix 4.
343 Cox, interview.

> We needed to get this place going. That was our long march. It didn't destroy us, maybe it made us stronger, I don't know. I lost my health on that tour. I lost all my weight. I had digestive problems and stress problems after that. That's when I went veggie because I had nothing to lose. It was either that or go the medical route, all the injections and all that kind of stuff. We were quite bold and brazen in doing that. It kills you, of course, if you take on too much.[344]

Pamela Morgan provided a similarly extreme description of the kind of arduous sacrifice sometimes required to pursue a career as a professional artist.

> We didn't make any money and we spent our lives on the road, so rent wasn't an issue. My parents kind of disowned me when I joined the band. They wouldn't allow me to come back to Grand Falls unless I stopped hanging out with those "Catholic hippies." So, I used to go and stay with one of the guys I learned music from in Bonavista Bay, in Lethbridge, Uncle Mose. I didn't have an apartment. Everything I owned fit in a trunk. It was literally a nomadic kind of existence. I would get a room somewhere occasionally, but there were no possessions, no home, no nothing. But that didn't matter! Life was on the road. We were always travelling. There were not a lot of creature comforts involved with that either. There were six of us in a Chevy van, perched on top of the gear, driving across Canada and back. My favourite place was with my back against the engine between the two seats in the front, sitting on the floor.[345]

Clearly, more than a few artists had to struggle, but some were doing a bit better than others. Thanks to the steady increase in the appearance of pubs and bars in downtown St. John's between 1968 and 1979,[346] and the seeming conviction of proprietors that live music was what brought

344 Malone and White, interview.

345 Morgan, interview.

346 See Appendix 6.

in the crowd, some musicians in St. John's appeared to have somewhat more reliably steady work and income than other artists. "Back in those days," Don Walsh remembered, "you were playing seven nights a week in the bars."

> We used to get a gig at The Strand that was three weeks [long] because there were three Strand lounges here. So, you did the Avalon Mall for seven nights, but you also did the start of the afternoon matinée. Then you'd pack up all the gear and bring it to The Strand Lounge in Atlantic Place downtown and you'd do seven nights there. And then, you'd pack up all your gear from there and you'd go to The Strand Lounge in the Village Mall and do another seven nights there. Whereas now, if you get one night, you're lucky, but back then, everything was a week-long gig. So, everybody was busy and getting lots of work because all bars had live music, whereas it's not too much like that now.[347]

Andy Jones admitted that by late 1974, the CODCO members were also making pretty decent money—when they were performing. "Two hundred dollars a week in 1974 was a lot of money," he affirmed. "We were doing quite well, but we all had unemployment insurance to get ourselves through." What used to be called UI rather than EI in Canada was one of the primary means by which many artists supported themselves between paid projects. Working a full-time job, or even a part-time job, can be very taxing for an artist who nonetheless continues to invest a regular and often equal amount of labour into their art, for which they are not paid. Those Newfoundland artists who wished to dedicate themselves full-time to their art often made decent money when they were actually performing, but in between projects, quite a few had to resort to the UI loophole. "All you had to do," Andy said, "was work for twenty weeks, and then the next year you only had to work for ten weeks."[348] Both Jones and Don Walsh shared anecdotes that demonstrated how significant the Canadian UI program was to keeping working artists supported. "My brother Vince, who had a head for figures, decided to manage Red Island one year," Don told me.

---

347 Don Walsh, interview; see Appendix 6.

348 Jones, interview.

> We did a three-month tour of the Maritimes. We were on the university circuit out there, going to all those different universities and playing in the odd bar. What Vince did was start the business. He wanted to give us a year of not having to worry and just work on the music and so, he started the company and he hired the band to do this tour. Then he paid us from the tour and we got UI stamps. Of course, after the tour was over there was no more work, so Vince laid us off and we collected UI for a year. So, we didn't have to worry about where the next money was coming from or where the next gig was coming from.[349]

"We kept working," Andy Jones concurred. "We never stopped working. We weren't sitting around; we were working all the time." Jones explained that as far as many full-time dedicated artists were concerned, UI functioned in their lives very similarly to a project grant.[350]

Those artists who worked jobs unrelated to their art met the cost of living with varying degrees of efficacy. Anita Best was one of those artists who managed to work a full-time job and still found ways to continue developing her craft as a musician.

> Nobody made a living exclusively as an artist because you didn't get paid that much for things that you did. You ended up taking other jobs. A lot of artists were waiters or bartenders. Me, I was a teacher in training, so I taught school in the fall and winter. The way you were paid as a teacher in Newfoundland was that your salary was split over twelve months. You worked for ten months but your salary was split over twelve months . . . I could afford to pay the rent.[351]

I asked some of the narrators I interviewed what it cost to rent an apartment in the 1970s, particularly in St. John's. Most could not recall specific figures, but Jane and Mary Barry recalled that they had paid between one hundred and one hundred and fifty dollars per month for your average studio, one-bedroom apartment, or room in a shared house depending on

349 Don Walsh, interview.
350 Jones, interview.
351 Best, interview.

amenities and location.[352, 353] In Anita's opinion, wages at the time were more or less commensurate with the cost of living, but goods and services probably represented more value for one's money during the 1970s. Plus, she allowed, "There was a kind of self-sufficiency ethic on the go."[354]

Owing to advancing inflation and decline in the value of real wages over the last fifty years, one's money went a good bit further in 1970s North America than it does today—despite the economic downturn impacting North America at that time. It is also true that many Newfoundlanders of the baby-boomer generation received a tuition-free education from Memorial University as part of the institution's provincial development mandate. And yet, quite a few of the interviews I conducted referred to the artist's frequent need to couch surf or otherwise temporarily co-habit with a more stable fellow while trying to find their own financial feet. White remembered that wherever she and Greg lived, they had always sheltered temporarily unhoused or travelling artists. "If a Newfoundlander went somewhere and set up, everyone else would descend on them."[355] The apartment that she and Greg shared on Pembroke Street in St. John's had hosted virtually every fellow artist of their acquaintance whenever one was between apartments, or just back from a tour with nowhere to crash. It was the same, they said, when they were living in England in 1971. Fellow Newfoundland artists who were also sampling the climate of opportunity in London invariably spent a number of weeks or months with Greg and White. When the corps of artists who went on to form CODCO landed in Toronto in the fall of 1973, several of them descended on Mary Walsh's apartment. "Mary was studying at Ryerson," Greg recalled. "She had an apartment all set up and they all bunked in together. Mary was the only one who had a bed.

---

352 Dingle, interview; Barry, interview; see Appendix 4.

353 According to provincial government statistics based on a sample of 316 families in St. John's, the average full-time income earner or family unit paid about fifteen per cent of their income to housing during the mid-1970s. Food absorbed another seventeen per cent, while utilities cost slightly more than housing if one were a renter. The average income earner or family unit paid a little less than two hundred dollars per month, but likely for accommodations with more space and privacy than a studio or rented room. If one was making at least a hundred dollars a week as a single person, then they were likely able to meet the cost of living ("Historical Statistics of Newfoundland and Labrador," Vol II [1], July 1977, 121–22. https://www.stats.gov.nl.ca/publications/Historical/PDF/Historical_Statistics_of_Newfoundland_and_Labrador_V2_N1_1977.pdf.)

354 Best, interview.

355 Malone and White, interview.

The others were sleeping on couches and floors."[356] Anita Best related a similar experience. As a teacher with a regular and reliable salary, she could afford, she said, to have people living with her if they needed to. "Nobody lived alone," she observed. "You always had four or five people living with you if you had an apartment."[357]

I am inclined to view this trend of constant "crashing" not only as a sign of the economic precariousness of artists' lives in general, but also as another manifestation of Newfoundland's communitarian impulse. Most of what Greg, White, and Anita revealed was distinctly familiar to me, having grown up on the mainland with a regular flow of travelling visitors from home. White's description of visiting Newfoundlanders descending on whatever exile had an apartment made me laugh knowingly, thinking of our first days in Toronto when Mom, Rebecca, and I had crashed with Barry Greene in his apartment for two months before his landlord finally evicted him. The four of us ended up sharing a two-bedroom house together for the next two years. Mom's bed was in the hallway, I remember, so that Rebecca and I, and Barry, could have our own rooms. Barry's room as I recollect, God bless him, was little bigger than a closet. Our experience as a family is a perfect example of why the development of infrastructure and comprehensive support for artists can be so crucial. An artist may be able to eke by or even live in decent comfort as a single person, but once they have families, kids, aging parents, or others to support, the situation changes dramatically. "That's what drove the band apart later," Pamela Morgan said, referring to the break-up of Figgy Duff.

> People started to have kids and responsibilities and wanted to have a life and all that. So, we couldn't continue following the dream forever with no financial compensation. We didn't really think much about it until everybody got older and went: "Hang on, we can't keep this up forever.[358]

The political, social, and economic context in which the Newfoundland cultural movement germinated shaped the way that regional artists saw themselves. Against the backdrop of continually high unemployment,

356 Malone and White, interview.
357 Best, interview.
358 Morgan, interview.

welfare dependency, increased labour union activity, and ongoing resettlement programs, many artists could only see themselves as little different from their fellow Newfoundlanders and workers in other provincial industries—industries dominated by a seemingly elite and dictatorial few bureaucrats and corporate entities. Ironically, both Alan Filewod and David Ferry observed, these pro-labour Newfoundland theatre artists were resistant to allowing the Canadian Actors Equity Association (CAEA, commonly referred to simply as Equity) to regulate and normalize their employment policies, which on its face seems the most direct route to unionized protection for local theatre professionals. Unfortunately, just as Canada Council's bureaucratic structure was little equipped to adapt and respond to the reality of the regional theatre situation in Newfoundland in the 1970s, so too was Equity.[359] In true countercultural fashion, many young artists of the time distrusted Equity, seeing it as part of what David Ferry referred to as "the big bad mainland theatre establishment."[360] Moreover, local artists were keen to preserve their eligibility to apply for UI between projects, which they would have lost under an Equity contract. Finally, artists were resistant to the idea of paying dues from budgets and salaries that were already fairly modest to begin with, and for which they could not foresee receiving any discernible benefit. Full-time theatre artists in Newfoundland typically only got around sixteen weeks of work per year and were loath to part with the rough equivalent of two weeks salary to maintain an Equity contract.[361]

Invented Concepts? Nationalism, Culture, Capitalism, and the Starving Artist

Along with political and class tensions, the 1970s cultural movement was infused with an often intense nationalism. Harry H. Hiller posited that these nationalist and occasionally separatist views emerged in response to the province's "regional economic subordination to a wealthier, ethnically-different core . . . . When cultural particularity and economic

359 Filewod, "The Mummers Troupe," (1998); Ferry, 149–50.
360 Ferry, 148.
361 Filewod, "The Mummers Troupe," (1998); Ferry, 148–50.

disadvantage coincide in a locality," he wrote, "nationalist movements result."[362] Hiller makes a reasonably good case for his thesis with regard to Newfoundland, arguing that the region's "history and socio-cultural identity have combined to produce a nascent ethnicity." He cited two opinion studies, one from 1979 and another from 1982, which each suggested exceptionally elevated levels of provincial loyalty over national loyalty. In the 1979 study, fifty-five per cent of Newfoundlanders surveyed saw themselves as Newfoundlanders first and Canadians second with fifty-eight per cent indicating that they saw themselves as either "somewhat different" or "very different" from other Canadians. The 1982 study found that fifty per cent claimed their first loyalty was to Newfoundland while only eight per cent claimed the same loyalty to Canada first.

"In a Canada-wide sample," Hiller noted, "Newfoundlanders were more likely to identify with their own province than even Quebecers, and Newfoundlanders had the lowest level of satisfaction with federal treatment of their province."[363] Hiller further argued that the discovery of regional oil resources and the future prospect of their development galvanized the nationalism of Newfoundlanders, giving them "new confidence in confronting the outside world" and making them "more aware of their own group identity," a phenomenon, he wrote, that Brian Peckford seized upon and carried forward.[364] James Overton likewise observed that by the end of the 1970s, newly-minted Premier Peckford had neatly incorporated this intense sense of nationalism into his political platform and rhetoric. "He can wax lyrical about the mystical experience of rabbit catching in Green Bay or his roots in the area and link such things to this stance on oil resources and the need to preserve Newfoundland's unique identity," Overton amusingly wrote.[365] I would argue that it was rather the 1970s arts community in Newfoundland that performed the function that Hiller attributes to the possibility of economic betterment, as well as to Peckford's amplification of widespread nationalist feeling. The work of artists is almost always in some sense a reflection of the place and the people it comes from, which is quite obviously connected to the broader formation of group identity as well as to greater confidence as a regional cultural entity.

362 Hiller, 257.
363 Hiller, 265–66.
364 Hiller, 267.
365 Overton, "A Newfoundland Culture?," 7.

By helping to solidify a sense of who they were and of the historical conditions that had led them to that point, the regional academics, visual artists, writers, actors, and musicians of the late 1960s and 1970s not only gave their fellow Newfoundlanders new confidence and a strengthened sense of group identity, but also the means to articulate a new dialogue, which might help them choose the best path forward in times of change. Peckford may have used the powerful platform and machinery of the state to amplify the nationalist message, but it should be acknowledged that he jumped on a train that began moving more than a decade before. The day after the Mummers Troupe staged *Gros Mourn*, nine years before Peckford's election, the company joined residents of Sally's Cove to protest the official opening of the national park. Listening to the residents soon to be displaced from their homes, Brookes wrote that he was struck by how often he heard the protestors use language and perspectives that had been featured in the play. The Mummers' theatrical production had been written based upon the experiences and struggles of the residents, and the process of creating and performing the show had helped the people of Sally's Cove articulate their grievances to visiting politicians and media with greater directness, clarity, energy, and confidence.[366]

The question of whether Hiller is correct that such a thing as Newfoundland "ethnicity" exists is beyond the scope of this book, but a distinct Newfoundland settler culture is certainly real enough, albeit somewhat problematic in an historical and economic sense. Overton wrote that the regional culture that has developed over the past half-century or so is, to a certain extent, an invented concept.

> The aim is not to expose culture as an empty abstraction and to suggest that Newfoundland culture is an illusion. Rather it is to suggest that culture is a particular lens through which the world is "seen" and to raise some questions about how this lens was ground and the nature of the vision it allows.[367]

The Newfoundland culture as it exists and is understood today is not the same Newfoundland culture that existed in the mid-twentieth century, or

366 Brookes, *A Public Nuisance*, 88–9.
367 Overton, "A Newfoundland Culture?," 15–16.

indeed the early twentieth or the mid-nineteenth century for that matter. While I did not pose the question specifically in my interviews, I strongly doubt that any narrator or any other Newfoundlander of their generation would say that the cultural flowering that occurred during the 1970s was a true renaissance or rebirth of traditional Newfoundland culture. Shane O'Dea's 1998 commencement address at Memorial University honouring Edythe Goodridge also seemed to acknowledge what Overton noted about Newfoundland culture as both a real phenomenon and an invented concept.

> She came to the gallery at a time when the Canadian government had gone mad over multiculturalism; so mad that if you were part of a distinctive ethnic group you could get enough funding to run the Newfoundland Railway. Edythe Goodridge had been long enough in the parlours of power to see an opportunity in this. For her, Newfoundland was not just a province. Newfoundlanders were a distinctive people with a five-hundred-year-old history, a unique language and were one of Canada's newest immigrant groups. They were a people with a culture as deep as their soil. Now the fact that the then-visible culture was only six inches deep did not worry our Edythe. She was never one who would allow a dull fact to get in the way of a great fiction. She would help build up that cultural soil. She convinced Ottawa that Newfoundlanders should be treated as a distinct ethnic group and made sure that Canadians saw what was distinctive about us.[368]

The historically problematic concept of Newfoundland culture is apparent in O'Dea's speech. By the time people like Edythe Goodridge came on the scene, Newfoundland life and culture was already dramatically changed with a mere "six inches" of what it once was still visible. O'Dea's speech also highlights the problematic system of modern capitalism, which encompasses virtually all life and activity. Artists and cultural champions for Newfoundland, like Goodridge, were compelled, like all the rest of us, to operate and pursue their goals within a system that really only cares about the extent to which a producer is economically

---

368 O'Dea, "Oration Honouring Edythe Ryan Goodridge," 5.

viable. As Goodridge and others clearly understood, the machinery of the modern state can do much to ameliorate some of capitalism's worst side effects, but we are still left with the implicit rationale of the broader system: if it's not economically viable or if its returns cannot be fully quantified and justified financially, it's not a real job and whether or not it makes a useful contribution is up for debate. We are thus brought to the threshold of some uncomfortable questions: Where do the artist's labour and products rank on the capitalist scale of usefulness? Further, can the artist's indisputable gifts to society of articulation, actualization, and a nourished sense of group identity and fellowship even be quantified in an economic sense? The fact that the concept of the starving artist is ubiquitous in our lexicon throughout the English-speaking world should be fairly self-explanatory.

Insiders and Outsiders

Just as there are complex historical and economic elements that influence conceptions of Newfoundland culture, there are, of course, potentially problematic sides to nationalism as well. Newfoundland nationalism, as I've discussed, was both a salient feature and essential ingredient in the cultural movement. As many oral history narrators have related, their regional pride was, they believed, a significant and necessary aspect of the process of cultural actualization and decolonization.[369] However, a frequent side effect of nationalist movements is the identification of what theatre professor Michael Devine described as "insiders" and "outsiders," and the potential exclusion or marginalization of the latter. In his doctoral dissertation, Devine explored these archetypes in Newfoundland drama, linking them to the region's history as an exceptionally "short-lived nation," which was largely ruled by "strangers" from without for the majority of its settler history. The additional and widespread fact of individual community isolation and relative homogeneity reinforced the strong psychic distance between the two archetypes. Like the outport setting, Devine notes, the archetypes of insider and outsider proliferate in a majority of literary and dramatic

369 See Appendices 4 and 5.

works produced in Newfoundland during the latter half of the twentieth century and beyond. If we accept the notion that art frequently reflects the reality of the society in which an artist lives, then the proliferation of this theme suggests that to a certain extent, Newfoundland's "strong sense of local identity [is] based, to some degree, on perceptions of otherness." Through a process of social and community negotiation, however, strangers can negotiate a level of acceptance.[370]

Of the seventeen people I interviewed for this project, three were born elsewhere and came to Newfoundland as adults. A few others, including Jane Dingle and Chris Brookes, were also not born in Newfoundland but emigrated to the island with their families as very small children[371] and so enjoy the status of unqualified insiders.[372] My mother's parents came to Newfoundland during the summer of 1959. My grandfather had just completed medical school with a full ride scholarship to University College London and it was the established custom for such graduates to give two years of service to the Empire in an overseas region with few specialists in a graduate's area of expertise. By 1959, the Empire was already in a very real state of dissolution and I doubt that anyone would have chased Papa down if he had decided to duck his term of service. However, young Dr. Dingle had grown up in council housing in Jersey in the English Channel islands. His upbringing and childhood experience encompassed the Great Depression and the Nazi occupation of Jersey. Grateful that he had accessed merit-based opportunities in spite of childhood poverty, he felt compelled to give back. The Dingles initially came to Newfoundland intending to stay only a few years, but the largest contingent of the family has never left. Three out of their five children, a majority of their grandchildren and now, their great-grandchildren as well were born and raised in Newfoundland and Dr. and Mrs. Dingle themselves were laid to rest there. As a general practitioner, Papa treated every diverse medical complaint that came his way during his years as one of the very few doctors serving rural communities like Come By Chance and Buchans and delivered literally hundreds of babies. As a surgeon, Papa performed numerous therapeutic and life-saving procedures for people all over Newfoundland and mentored several generations of young healthcare professionals

370 Devine, 1–8.

371 See Appendix 4.

372 Devine, 27.

throughout his career. His bedside manner was legendary, full of kindness, compassion, and often wicked good humour. Whereas their children would have been regarded as virtually unqualified Newfoundlanders, some might have viewed Dr. and Mrs. Dingle as what Devine called "necessary outsiders," those who provide important service or resources to the community.[373]

Outsiders, both necessary and otherwise, can be accepted and embraced by demonstrating a personal investment or commitment to the community, which Papa and Nanny certainly did throughout their years in Newfoundland, but they could never enjoy the status of unqualified insiders. Insiders need outsiders implicitly, for their own self-identification, as well as explicitly for the social and economic contributions that outsiders make. Newfoundland settler society had always been predominantly working class as well as relatively homogeneous ethnically, and the identification of otherness served to reinforce the position of insiders and thus social and community stability. However, in a society that has seemingly always been ruled from without, the outsider can sometimes have a steep hill to climb to find acceptance.

For those who didn't really know them well, my grandparents' British accents, customs, and Papa's income as a doctor marked them as different, and made them resemble the middle and upper-class Protestant elite. Those who saw them attending the symphony at the Arts and Culture Centre and chatting pleasantly with John Perlin might be forgiven for thinking of the Dingles in a certain way, but many wouldn't have known that Nanny and Papa had dear friends in numerous communities up and down the Avalon Peninsula and beyond. Jane recalled her first few professional encounters with Chris Brookes, which left her with the distinct impression that he thought she was bourgeois beyond endurance, an opinion that appeared to moderate significantly upon longer acquaintance.[374] Her good friend and fellow actor Shifra Zisman remembered that Jane had been sensitive to such resentment and was hesitant to invite just anyone home.

> There was sort of this embarrassment because her father was a doctor and they had this beautiful house. It was like, compared to everyone else . . . I was invited to go there because

373 Devine, 9.
374 Dingle, interview.

> she didn't think there would be this judgment. And you know, she went to theatre school in England, but she was so not *that*. And your grandparents weren't either.[375]

Shifra recalled her own personal experience as a perceived outsider in Newfoundland in the 1970s.

> I'm Jewish. Newfoundlanders didn't know a lot of Jews. They were often the merchants in the town, so they had money.... It's like worldly views, you know? We don't all have big noses. It also took time for me to be accepted because initially it was: "Oh, a mainlander's come to take a job." Well, I didn't know anything about that when I landed here, right? I had no way of knowing that. I think it was Beni Malone who explained it to me, this thing about "mainlanders." I think because I had made a commitment to Newfoundland, a commitment to the people, then it became less: "She's a mainlander." And people *were* coming and taking jobs. That's a reality.[376]

David Ferry noted that sometimes the nationalist desire to decolonize Newfoundland and the suspicion and lack of trust for mainlanders or other outsiders could extend to instances of seemingly xenophobic behaviour. In an interview with Ferry, David Ross recalled being pulled aside a few days into rehearsal for *Buchans: A Mining Town* and being called a "scab, comin' here and taking jobs away from Newfoundlanders."[377] Another account detailed a Mummers' Troupe meeting in which some members demanded "that only actors born in Newfoundland should be allowed to work for Newfoundland theatre companies." According to this account, "tempers flared and a whole pot of boeuf bourguignon got dumped on someone's head."[378] Clearly, there was some conflict within the Newfoundland psyche between the very real need for outsider allies and the desire to resist economic and cultural colonialism. However, young artists of the day were already beginning to think more deeply and critically about such issues.

---

375 Zisman, interview.
376 Zisman, interview.
377 Ferry, 148.
378 Ferry, 148–49.

Andy Jones spoke at length about how CODCO's creative process was influenced by a broad, frequent, and ongoing discussion of ethics, which suggests that the group's mindset had already extended far beyond the simple dialectic of insider and outsider.

> We had a lot of talk. We weren't just writing sketches. We hung around together and we analyzed what we did. There was a strong ethical discussion always on the go. "Should we do this? Is that making fun of the wrong people?" And sometimes we went too far, I think, and made fun of people who were more innocent. We tried to stick it to politicians, to the Church, and to people in power and it was to kick up, not kick down. So we were quite aware of that. We weren't just doing fart jokes.[379]

Jones's description highlights a more thoughtful perspective than the heat of nationalism often allows. When a nationalist climate evolves to an insular us or them mentality, there's less room for discernment or ethics. Bob Joy's sense of nationalism seems to have been similarly tempered and in such a way that he could appreciate the merits of seemingly colonial art without any thought of denigrating or obscuring that of Newfoundland.

> There was always a feeling in St. John's that we were in a unique position, an enviable position, because we could admire and be influenced by literature and culture from all around the world without being swept away by it. Like Peter Cook and Dudley Moore, *Beyond the Fringe*, and then when Monty Python came along. But then, we were also very much taken by *The Mary Tyler Moore Show* and *I Love Lucy* and *The Honeymooners*. And then all of us reading Russian novels in translation, and British and American novels, and Canadian novels. We could take in whatever the world had to offer us and not be colonized by it. So, I think that colonization issue is very interesting. We could sort of then push back and say: "Well, what we have to offer is just as good as that."[380]

379 Jones, interview.
380 Joy, interview.

Joy's perspective highlights an important point about the value and importance of the cultural products of outsiders. While the justice inherent in the cause of cultural decolonization is undeniable, quite a few outsider cultural influences were instrumental in shaping the movement in Newfoundland. It would have been harder to envision the creation of an act like CODCO without *Beyond the Fringe* or *Monty Python's Flying Circus.* It would be nearly impossible to imagine the existence of Trad Rock without the influence of American rock 'n' roll or the Atlantic-wide folk roots movement. Not all outsider influences are strictly colonial in nature. While such cultural products may seem to have diverted attention from local or regional ones, they were often expressions of other regional movements sunk deep within the 1960s and 1970s counterculture, like *Beyond the Fringe* or Monty Python. Or, they may have been deeply connected to rights, equality, and cultural decolonization movements as blues, jazz, rock 'n' roll, and reggae music created by Atlantic peoples of African descent has frequently been. These art forms carried the language and implicit message of resistance and hope for change that galvanized a generation on an international scale.

Outsiders themselves likewise played important roles in Newfoundland's cultural movement. From MUN's Folklore and English departments to Extension, a great many staff members at the university came to Newfoundland from elsewhere and provided essential assistance to developing both necessary infrastructure and a sense of pride in place. Herbert Halpert, Richard Buehler, Don Snowden, Michael Cook—the contributions of these individuals to the broader arts and cultural movement were far-reaching. This does not mean that their presence would not have sparked a certain amount of understandable resentment among native Newfoundlanders. I am reminded of Greg Malone when he described his dismayed reaction to the news that none of the artists and entertainers hired for the twenty-fifth anniversary of Confederation were actually from Newfoundland: "There was no sense that *we* could do these things."[381] Michael Cook himself, as well as his work, were appreciated to varying degrees by different members of the Newfoundland community and its contingent of artists. Not everybody was ready to appreciate the fact that a British man could

381 Malone and White, interview.

come to Newfoundland and so quickly become a prominent regional playwright, while many local artists were still struggling to find the means to have their own regional work shown. Cook, however, was one of those emigrants who came and stayed. His loyalty to and love for Newfoundland was manifest in his life's work. Many years on, it has become more possible to appreciate that fact now that the nationalist need to carve out space for insiders is less urgent. "I remember being very bitter about Michael Cook," Mary Walsh admitted, "because his plays were being produced all over Canada."

> He was an Englishman who wrote *Colour the Flesh the Colour of Dust*, and *Head, Guts, and Soundbone Dance* and a number of other plays. I remember feeling very angry because his was the only voice that was heard out of here. I didn't actually forgive him for that—even though there was nothing to forgive him for—till he was in the coffin in the middle aisle of the Basilica, and I thought: "Oh, he just wanted to be a Newfoundlander. I could've been more accepting." But you know, there were a lot of "goofy Newfie" jokes. We were considered to be backward and stupid. We were writing in CODCO against that notion and still we would get reviews that said: "A dory-load of fishy fun," and "Newfies turn Newfie joke on its ear." You know what I mean?[382]

Time, deep thought, and hindsight have shifted and nuanced the sense of nationalism shared by young artists in the 1970s. In a similar manner of deliberation, we can today more clearly see the impact of the contributions of outsider allies of whom Michael Cook was just one.

Pam Hall first came to Newfoundland in 1973 at the age of twenty-two. Having completed her bachelor of fine arts degree in Montreal, she accepted a job teaching art in two St. John's-area middle schools. There being no formal art education in Newfoundland at the time, art teachers were invariably hired from elsewhere. Hall did not intend to stay more than a year before going on to begin her master's degree at The Slade art academy at University College London.

---

382 Mary Walsh, interview.

> Halfway through that first year, I was pretty sure that I wasn't going to grad school anytime soon. I got involved in the politics of teaching. Art education was really disorganized. I grew up in the sixties, you know? Every bone in my body is political, small p, and I thought: "Well, you know, I can always be an artist, but I can't always make change." That was what a lot of my generation came out of art school feeling. So, I swung over into education for what turned out to be more than ten years before I finally found my way back to my own studio.[383]

Hall is a true interdisciplinarian and, as such, in 1970s Newfoundland, she fit right in. As an artist, educator, administrator, and policy-making committee member, she seems to have had her hand in every corner of the cultural movement. She has always been committed to the development of art education and infrastructure in the province throughout her career and seems to have worked with everyone on the arts scene at some point. She took promotional photographs for CODCO and photographed album covers for Terry Rielly and Rufus Guinchard. She created illustrations for Breakwater Books, and had her own works published as well. She travelled the province on behalf of the Department of Education interviewing the province's most celebrated visual artists for the creation of a media resource, which would help teach young students about Newfoundland art and artists like Reginald and Helen Shepherd, Christopher and Mary Pratt, Heidi Oberheide, and Frank Lapointe. She sat on numerous committees and boards with fellow administrators and artists and championed measures for greater development, support, and access for the arts.[384] When I asked Hall to tell me about the first time she met Ron, she related a singularly lovely and quirky story that told me much about her growing attachment to Newfoundland and her decision to remain here permanently.

> I'll never forget it. I tell this story all the time. I was sharing my apartment with Rhonda Payne and one day, I came into my apartment and there was a young man sitting on the couch in the living room. He had a guitar case by his feet.

---

383 Hall, interview.
384 Hall, interview.

He was kind of good-looking in his way. You know, your dad was a funny kind of guy. He wasn't handsome in the conventional sense of the word handsome, but he was quite magnetic. He was probably sexier looking than handsome.

I said: "Who are you?"

He said: "I'm a friend of Rhonda's." I never asked did she give him a key. I never asked how the f--k he got in the apartment. I never asked him did he want a cup of tea. I mean, I was like twenty-three years old. I wasn't that polite then. I just said: "Who are you?'"

He said: "Ron."

I said: "Is that your guitar?"

He said: "Yeah, I'm a musician."

I said: "So, if you're a musician, play me something." And God bless his heart, he leaned down and he opened up that case, he took the guitar out and played "Back Home on the Island." It pierced me. I hadn't even been here that long. I wasn't sure if I was going to stay, but I had already started building those threads of unshakeable connection, which is what that song is about. That unshakeable, unchosen connection. He finished singing, and I went: "Shit. What's your last name?" He said: "Hynes. Ron Hynes." I think I bought every album that your dad ever made. I think I connected with him more through his music than through any personal encounters, although we had plenty of those.[385]

385 Hall, interview.

Ron Hynes, 1978.[386]

386 Photo by Kent Barrett.

Pam Hall is one of many outsider allies who found a home, a true community of like-minded fellows and a place to belong in Newfoundland. The contributions she has made to the arts in the province have had far-reaching effects and I would rank her alongside any of the artists and administrators referenced in this book.

Among these pioneering artists, Dudley Cox's efforts during the 1970s were crucial, despite the fact that his contributions to the development of Newfoundland theatre were somewhat undervalued at the time and for quite a few years more. While he was dismissed by some of his contemporaries for his seeming conformity to a rather more colonial tradition of theatre, a closer examination of the part Cox played reveals a far more complex picture.[387] The majority of the plays staged by the NTTC were not regional or Canadian. Neither were many of them "overtly political or focused on social and historical inequities," like the productions of CODCO or the Mummers Troupe. Yet, as David Ferry has noted, Cox hired far more local actors than the Mummers Troupe did during the early 1970s. While none of the NTTC's productions were collectives, Cox was always open to staging or co-writing original regional content. Even the more "colonial" repertory choices like Molière's *The Doctor in Spite of Himself* were tweaked for local audiences. Cox significantly modified the language in the script to be more colloquial to the Newfoundland ear.[388]

Outside of his work with the NTTC, Cox's efforts to help develop the Basement Theatre of the St. John's Arts and Culture Centre as an additional performance space for local artists expanded opportunities for the development of regional theatre. Jane and Shifra Zisman both commented on how valuable Dudley's repertory programming in the Basement Theatre was to their development as actors. In the late winter and early spring of 1975, Cox's repertory theatre provided steady work for professional actors who, from week to week, would perform one play each evening and rehearse another during the day. The rehearsed production would then premier the following week while the actors began daily rehearsals for next week's production. While it sounds gruelling, the opportunities for professional cultivation, not to mention steady income,

387 Cox, "Newfoundland Travelling Theatre," 41; Brookes, *A Public Nuisance,* 103; Filewod, "The Mummers Troupe," (1998); Ferry, 147–48.

388 Ferry, 147–48; Dingle, interview.

are obvious. Moreover, Dudley's administrative involvement in multiple regional, provincial, and high school drama festivals throughout the 1970s demonstrates his commitment to fostering new theatre and new actors.[389] There is, in the final summation, something to be said for being among the first to attempt such bold ventures for a vision of greater good.

Feminism in Art and Artistic Process

While the bulk of the NTTC's repertoire was not nearly as political or hard hitting as that of CODCO or the Mummers, the marks of Atlantic-wide countercultural change were clearly visible in the group's interactions and artistic process. Interviews with narrators who worked with the NTTC in the early days related incidents that spoke eloquently of changing attitudes regarding feminism and women's liberation during the early 1970s.

When Dudley Cox started handing out the scripts to the actors he'd cast for Grace Butt's *Newfoundland Pageant*, he was immediately cornered by Rhonda Payne and Shifra Zisman. Their main problem with the script, Dudley said, was that "all the parts were male figures."

> It was like Newfoundland history was only dealt with by the men. The women were there for the ride but it was the men who were dealing with the history, which is ridiculous. They came to me and they said: "Dudley, this is no good at all. You're giving all the parts to the men, and what's there for us? Why are we here? What's the deal? This is ridiculous." And they were absolutely right. So, I got to work on that script, night and day, sorted it out. I got the costume mistress to make a costume for us that was the same for male and female actors, I made no differentiation. The parts, whatever they were, were just divided up evenly amongst the actors. If a woman played a man's part, too bad. It was totally egalitarian and you know, that was a great thing. That was a lovely thing that happened there.[390]

389 Zisman, interview; Dingle, interview; Cox, "Newfoundland Travelling Theatre," 30–33, 46–8.
390 Cox, interview.

The NTTC followed a similar pattern when they staged *Beaumont Hamel* in the fall of 1975, the subject matter of which would seem to naturally point to an almost exclusively male cast. Accordingly, Dudley used a gender-blind strategy for casting and costuming.[391] The effect reinforced the opportunities for creative exploration for female actors as well as mirrored the broader social change underway both within Newfoundland and far beyond.

Feminist influences were not only visible in the artistic process, but also in some of the repertory choices of the NTTC. During the summer of 1975, Cox and Weiser toured Myrna Lamb's one-act play *But What Have You Done For Me Lately?*[392] First performed at Berkeley in 1968, Lamb's play explores the experiences of a man who, following a medical procedure, is awakened by a female doctor and informed that he has been implanted with a uterus, is now pregnant and prohibited from accessing an abortion.[393] In the outports, Cox admitted to David Ferry, Lamb's play created a "Balkanisation of the audience." While the male contingent "hooted out derisive commentaries," the female patrons "angrily advised the male element to shut their cake holes."[394] Dudley and Shifra both spoke at length about the complexity and importance of the post-performance discussions during the tour. Female cast members would often be invited to visit the homes of local women who had seen the play the night before to talk further about the issues raised. Ferry described Cox's decision to stage such a production as "risky"[395] and indeed, Shifra seemed to agree. "We were travelling to Catholic communities and not quite knowing what the response would be," she said. Surprisingly, Shifra noted, some women seemed to feel liberated enough by the show to admit that they themselves had quietly chosen to end pregnancies. "Some of them had twelve children," Shifra remembered, and simply could not support any more. "Basically it was: 'Don't tell anyone, but I went to Boston for an abortion.' It was just . . . enlightening."[396] It was only during the late 1960s that women in

---

391 Dingle, interview.

392 Ferry, 148.

393 Neil Genzlinger, "Myrna Lamb, Feminist Playwright in an Unwelcoming Era, Dies at 87," *The New York Times*, September 22, 2017. https://www.nytimes.com/2017/09/22/theater/myrna-lamb-feminist-playwright-dead-at-87.html.

394 Ferry, 152–53.

395 Ferry, 148, 152–53; Zisman, interview.

396 Zisman, interview.

Canada first gained legal access to the birth control pill and a life-saving abortion, and that women in Newfoundland and Labrador gained the means to divorce.[397]

A Magical Time and Place

1972 to 1976 was a watershed period in the Newfoundland cultural movement in which numerous artists, administrators, bureaucrats, and educators of varied disciplines came together with a common purpose. Despite internal divisions inherited from the region's complex history and the minimal sufficiency of supportive infrastructure for the arts, those in the vanguard of the cultural movement forged ahead, bold faces firmly in place and to a very real extent, made something out of nothing. Chris Brookes spoke movingly to this point while reminiscing about an interview he'd once conducted with Kevin Blackmore, lead singer of the musical trio Buddy Wasisname and the Other Fellers. "It was an interview in which he started to cry partway through it," Brookes remembered.

> He was talking about a wooden boat in a song . . . He was explaining how it used to be the case where Newfoundlanders could go up into the woods, they could cut down a tree, they could shape it out, they could build a boat, they could go out on the boat, on the water, they could catch a fish, that was their livelihood. And it was all: "We can do it," from basic materials, from what we have. We use what we have and we can do remarkable things, and I think that's how it was in the arts.[398]

While the spaces artists carved out for themselves were hard-won, almost every narrator I interviewed spoke with warm and wistful nostalgia of this unique moment in their youth when they were each part of a broader wave of creativity, pride, and agency that extended across the

---

397 Kimberley E. Liu and William A. Fisher, "Canadian physicians' role in contraception from the 19th century to now," *Journal of Obstetrics and Gynaecology Canada* 24, no. 3 (March 2002): 239; Kristen Douglas, "Divorce Law in Canada," Law and Government Division, Revised March 27, 2001. https://publications.gc.ca/Collection-R/LoPBdP/CIR/963-e.htm.

398 Brookes, interview.

arts community of Newfoundland as well as far beyond.[399] One of the greatest privileges of working on this book was the opportunity to hear, and now to share with you, dear reader, some of these terrific stories, all of which highlight the extraordinary friendships and partnerships that were formed between and among artists of the period. Perhaps it's because almost everyone in the vanguard of the movement was young and full of a sense of possibility or perhaps it has something to do with that indefinable spirit of the 1960s and 1970s, but narrators really made their time and place seem magical.

Donna Butt reminisced warmly about her first appearances in the *Traditional Christmas Mummers Play* in December of 1973, knocking on doors unannounced and being invited into the homes of strangers, almost all of whom gave the Mummers a great reception. "We mummered ships in the harbour!" she exclaimed with a laugh. "In those days, you could actually get near ships in the harbour, so there were all the men from Portugal and Spain, and all these different places. We were adventuresome, to say the least."[400]

Shifra Zisman recalled the singularly Newfoundland experience of giving a recitation before a bar crowd in downtown St. John's one night. Dudley Cox had admired Shifra's delivery of a poem called "The Face on the Barroom Floor"[401] and had asked her to perform it. The fact that Ron was playing at the bar that night made no difference. Shifra remarked upon how normal and appreciated such a romantic and impromptu thing seemed to a St. John's bar crowd and how radically differently such a performance would have been perceived in a contemporary Toronto bar, where everyone was just a little bit too cool.[402]

Mom and Dad

Listening to and recording such stories is a privilege for any collector or historian, but it was especially meaningful to me that these stories helped me locate my parents in the history I was researching. I'm very

399 See Appendix 4.
400 Butt, interview.
401 Written by Henry Titus (1872), later revised by Hugh Antoine D'arcy.
402 Zisman, interview.

grateful that I have been able to collect stories from my mother while she's still with me, but the opportunity to do the same with my father is irrevocably gone. It therefore strikes me as a very great privilege indeed to hear one's own history, a part of my parents' story, from those who loved, respected, and worked closely with them in their formative years.

"What was Ron like as a young man?" I asked Kelly Russell.

"Foolish," Kelly replied with a faraway smile.

> Happy. Always carrying on, joking. Really lighthearted. I noticed such a change in him over the years. But back in those days, he was really kind of happy-go-lucky, always making little quips and puns and jokes. Anytime he could make a rhyme or a poem about something, he was all about that. Always playing with the language. And I'm a bit like that myself, so we used to banter stuff back and forth.[403]

"I remember a very gentle person," Donna Butt said of Ron.

> We were always so strong about the politics and stuff. Ron was too, but he was rooted in whatever his personal thoughts of the world were, I think. He'd always be trying to console us if he thought we were getting too upset or too angry. Ron always managed to walk both sides of that whole Mummers conflict that was going on. That's the person I remember. A gentle person.[404]

"Dad, diplomatic? Really?" I asked Donna with a note of playful mockery.

"Well, you know what? A bit," she replied.

> It was a weird kind of thing. Ron wasn't, by nature, certainly in those days, a fighter. That wasn't his approach to things. He always said: "You guys get all wound up like this, you're going to be at each other's throats all the time." The Ron that I remember and experienced is not necessarily everybody's Ron as the years went by, but that's the Ron that I knew.[405]

---

403 Russell, interview.
404 Butt, interview.
405 Butt, interview.

Dudley Cox cast Jane as Ida, the Cockney maid in the NTTC's first show, *See How They Run* when she was just seventeen. "I didn't know she was that young actually," Dudley recalled.

> She was totally professional. Totally on time, totally with her lines, totally into character, always interested if there was any discussion about acting going on. She was there listening, listening, listening, soaking it up. Some actors are very difficult for directors and sometimes you don't get along with them very well because they're so ornery but she's quite the opposite. I don't think we ever had a cross word. It was always lovely to have her in a play, so I cast her as often as I could."[406]

In fact, this supposed picture of professionalism and confidence had to be dragged to the audition kicking and screaming by a thirteen-year-old Tommy Sexton, who almost certainly never assimilated the concept of shyness. "If it wasn't for Tommy, I probably wouldn't have found out about Dudley Cox and the Newfoundland Travelling Theatre Company," Jane told me.

> We both wanted to go sing on Broadway and do musical theatre. We used to listen to records and sing—*West Side Story* and stuff like that. Tommy came over after school one day and said: "This guy named Dudley Cox is doing this thing called the Newfoundland Travelling Theatre Company. He's paying! I'm going to audition. You should come too. There's actually a part in there for you. You can do any British accent. They want a Cockney maid. You should go!" He had to talk me into it. Believe it or not, I was very shy, but I still desperately wanted to act. Tommy was anything but shy, so he dragged me to the audition. And I got it! I thank him to this day. God bless you Tommy because if it wasn't for you, I would never have had the opportunity. I wouldn't have gone out by myself to audition.[407]

---

406 Cox, interview.
407 Dingle, interview.

"Jane was the best person I ever improvised with in my life," Andy Jones recalled. "We didn't go in for comedy that much. Now, it seems like all improv is always about comedy, but we did it straight, serious. And Jane was right there, no hesitation. I could just dive in, and she would just go."[408] Jane likewise remembered discovering what an incredible improvisation artist Andy was as well during the tour of *See How They Run*. In one scene, the maid, Ida, has just stashed the drunken Miss Skillon in a closet to keep her away from the disapproving eyes of the Bishop of Lax, played by Andy. Unfortunately, after Jane closed the closet door and Andy made his entrance onstage, Jane found she could not get the door open again. Hilariously, both had to improvise and ad-lib with one another through the closet door for what felt like forever until, through their combined efforts, they finally managed to get the door open again and continued the scene.[409]

Andy became very good friends with Ron as well. In fact, he told me, he had heard a great deal of secondhand information about him a few years before he met him. As a teenager, Ron was already becoming known locally as a musician and a songwriter with a touch of the rebel about him.

> I taught school in Ferryland in 1971 and '72. I had already heard of Ron Hynes because I was going out with Monica Ryan, who was best friends with Ron's sister, Evelyn. She told me about this boy, how he was kind of a troubled guy and had been into drugs and stuff like that. He was already a major figure in the community and a mythical figure, but definitely a bad boy. But obviously, a very attractive bad boy.[410]

Aren't they all, Andy? Aren't they all?

"We were all just out for a good time," Andy continued in reference to his early years in theatre with the NTTC. "We were drinking and there was lots of sexual tension as you can imagine. We were all falling in love with each other and out of love. So, it was great fun."[411]

---

408 Jones, interview.
409 Dingle, interview.
410 Jones, interview.
411 Jones, interview.

Jane confided to me during our interview that she had had an enormous crush on Bob Joy during the tour of *See How They Run*. In her eagerness to impress him she nearly gave him a black eye, which sounded just about right for Jane.

> This one time, I think we were in Colinet touring and Mom, Dad, and the kids, everybody came out. They drove everybody out to see the show. Dad brought a couple bottles of champagne and Mom packed this amazing picnic hamper for us to have after the show. There was pâté and there was Dad's bread and all kinds of goodies. For starving actors on the road eating cans of stew, it was really lovely. I was thinking of how to impress Bob, and so I said: "Oh, I'm going to open the bottle of champagne now." I popped the cork and it hit him right in the eye! I thought I frigging blinded him. "Oh God, oh God!" I was thinking in my head: "I blinded Bob Joy!" "I'm so sorry! I'm so sorry!" I said. He said: "I'm okay, I'm okay." Yeah, I was trying to be ever so sophisticated. Hit the person that you really like, and have a crush on, in the *eye—that's* really good.[412]

412 Dingle, interview.

Chapter Four
1977–1982

"You've got to run with the idea
before you know where the idea's going."
- Bob Joy (2022)

A Vanguard of Artists

The late 1970s saw a great many artists who had begun their careers five to ten years previously reach their first peak in development with regard to their craft. In theatre and music particularly, there was a heightened focus on creating original content. Artist-run organizations continued to appear and existing ones continued to mature throughout this period, giving increasingly greater professional support to the arts community. Meanwhile, regional institutions like Memorial University, MUN Extension, the CBC, and other local radio affiliates continued to nurture the development of regional art and helped provide the means to develop and showcase it. Provincial infrastructure and funding shortfalls still presented challenges, spurring many artists, particularly in the theatre, to take their professional conditions and labour issues in hand personally. Broader international political and social trends continued to influence regional art including the feminist movement, as well as the Red Power movement for Indigenous rights, sovereignty, and decolonization. The late 1970s saw the first examples of "feminist" theatre in Newfoundland, as well as drama that brought greater attention to the contemporary conditions of Indigenous communities across Newfoundland and Labrador and reflected changing perspectives on Indigenous history and settler colonialism. By the end of the decade, the establishment of Premier Brian Peckford's government saw many of the critiques of cultural, economic, and political colonialism, which had issued from the cultural movement throughout the past decade and more, become part of mainstream political discourse.

Trad Rock and the Wonderful Grand Band

On the music scene, Trad Rock began to move to the front and centre. The first independent and artist-run music studios established themselves, including Echo Music in St. John's and Clode Sound in Stephenville, attracting local bands and solo artists seeking to have their music produced and recorded for release without having to go to the mainland. During the late 1970s and early 1980s, Clode Sound, operated by legendary blues and rock musicians Neil Bishop and Claude Caines, produced the music and other recorded works of dozens of Newfoundland artists, including Red Island and the Wonderful Grand Band.[413]

Both Red Island and the Wonderful Grand Band appeared on the scene more or less fully formed by 1977 and each recorded their first albums with Clode Sound in 1978. Added to the popularity of Figgy Duff, who had been touring and playing traditional music with some rock 'n' roll influences since 1974, Trad Rock began to become much more defined and familiar to the Newfoundland ear. The music created by Newfoundland Trad Rock artists during this period was a major contribution to the cultural movement, representing both exciting innovation in art and the nationalist desire for the preservation of traditional music. Like their counterparts in the theatre, Newfoundland musicians absorbed and reflected in their art many of the anti-modernist and anti-colonial perspectives that united a vast swathe of the cultural movement. The title track on Red Island's 1978 album, *In Pursuit of the Wild Bologna*, shows that the tendency and

413 "Two Legendary NL Recording Studios Receive MusicNL Honorary Awards For Industry Builder of the Year," (MusicNL press release), February 4, 2021. https://musicnl.ca/two-legendary-nl-recording-studios-receive-musicnl-honorary-awards-for-industry-builder-of-he-year/.

talent Newfoundlanders have for couching social commentary or criticism in a comedic context was certainly not limited to CODCO. The song calls to mind the old Maple Leaf Bologna radio and television commercials made for the Atlantic provinces in the post-Confederation years, which parodied nature documentaries and positioned the "wild" bologna as game hunted by native Newfoundlanders—a gag still employed by comedic YouTubers in the province. Like CODCO, Red Island clearly had no trouble making fun of themselves as Newfoundlanders in such a cultural context.

Searchin' for the wild bologna
In the jungles of Newfoundland
If I get 'im
I ain't gon' let 'im
Jump out of my frying pan![414]

Despite the implied colonial critique of the easy accessibility of a highly processed meat product for people who often couldn't afford much else,[415] Newfoundlanders as a group really do love bologna. Nearly thirty-two per cent of the Maple Leaf Bologna currently produced in Canada is sold in the Atlantic provinces, about one-third of which is sold in Newfoundland.[416] *In Pursuit of the Wild Bologna* was among the first "rock 'n' reel" albums by a Newfoundland band ever to be released.

Sandy Morris remembered Red Island making a huge impression on him. "I had heard Red Island that summer [of 1977] at the Atlantic Folk Festival, which was a big deal. It was like Woodstock," Sandy said of the festival, which ran from 1975 to 1981, "only for Atlantic Canada and not nearly as huge, but it was an enormous event and all the popular bands were there. We were camping and it was raining. It was lovely. It was muddy, if I remember correctly."[417] Sandy had admired Red Island's integration of traditional reels and fiddle tunes with the power and energy of a full rock band.

414 "In Pursuit of the Wild Bologna," written by Jamie Snider, track 1 on *In Pursuit of the Wild Bologna*, Quay Records, 1978 (LP).

415 The second verse, which begins: "Wild bologna came to Newfoundland in 1949 . . ." directly references the Confederation watershed.

416 Maple Leaf Foods, email communication with author, November 16, 2023.

417 Morris, interview.

By 1977, Morris had amassed more than a decade of experience in the music industry, not only playing with various bands in bars, clubs, and out on tour, but also composing and performing music for films and local television shows. Due to his considerable entrenchment in the Newfoundland music and media scene, he was approached by Kevin O'Connell of the CBC to consult on potential future programming. Sandy recalled the producer telling him: "We've been trying to recreate the success of *All Around the Circle*, and we haven't come close." *All Around the Circle* showcased traditional Newfoundland music in a half-hour variety show format. Running on the CBC from 1967 through 1979 in Newfoundland and Labrador, this program did a great deal to keep regional culture alive during a critical time when American, British, and Canadian content dominated mass media in the province.[418] Since that time, O'Connell told Sandy, "None of our shows have taken off. You're out there in the community. You work with all the different people. Come up with an idea for a TV show."

"So," Sandy said, "I went to Greg and White because they were my best friends." Greg recalled that Sandy had been hesitant to take the conceptual lead that O'Connell had offered him, which made White "hit the ceiling" that they might pass up the opportunity to fill a prime CBC timeslot. "What are you talking about? Of course you have a show!" Greg remembered her insisting.[419] "Well, I'd like to put a band behind Ron," Sandy began.

> I had always wanted to hear Ron's songs with bass and drums and harmony and guitar solos . . . as opposed to say, a folk singer, or what we would call today a singer/songwriter—somebody playing by himself with an acoustic guitar. I always thought: "No, that stuff would sound great with a band behind it." I was a band guy. I said: "I'd like to do that, and I'd like to do Newfoundland fiddle tunes."[420]

The strong collectivity of the Wonderful Grand Band in practice makes it difficult to identify a "leader," "lead singer," or "creative lead" in the

418 Bill, 96–7.

419 Malone and White interview; Mary White, interview by Danine Farquharson for the STAGE Project, St. John's, September 23, 1996, 66–7.

420 Morris, interview.

typical sense because everyone in the band wrote or helped write songs, sang and/or played an instrument. Ron frequently fronted the band as lead singer, but so did Glenn Simmons, Jamie Snider, Greg Malone, and Tommy Sexton. It might be hard for a casual observer to pin down that it was actually Sandy Morris who was band leader, despite his sideman's clothing. It was Sandy who originated the band's name and basic musical concept. He was one of the most experienced as a professional musician, but this was not the only reason why the position of band leader eventually fell to him. He laughed heartily while telling me the story about the person who was originally supposed to be band leader.

> He had just moved in from Grand Falls. He was a hotshot piano player and knew a lot more about music than I did. He got hired as band leader and the very first gig, he didn't show up. I found out what happened after. He had a convertible at the time, a beautiful convertible. He was parked at a red light and a really good-looking girl rolled up on a bicycle. He invited her for a drive, and he never showed up to the gig![421]

Such a thing was fairly common among musicians, Sandy recalled with amusement. He usually had his share of doors and windows to go knock on when it was time for the band to rehearse.[422]

Greg and White had remembered that, besides his interest in putting a band behind Ron, Sandy had also been keen to bring Glenn Simmons into the band. Glenn was a terrific fellow guitarist with an exquisite tenor voice. Sandy also wanted Kelly Russell, who had only recently left Figgy Duff, to play the fiddle. Pianist and bassist Bryan Hennessey and singer Bawnie Oulton, both of whom had been playing together live with Ron and Sandy since 1976, also joined the band and Rocky Wiseman, former drummer for The Ravens, was hired to complete the initial ensemble. As impressive as the Wonderful Grand Band ultimately proved to be, however, there had to be more to the proposed television show than just the band's music. A central concept was needed.

421 Morris, interview.
422 Morris, interview.

Wonderful Grand Band, 1978.[423]

Bawnie Oulton and Ron Hynes.[424]

423 Photo by Kent Barrett. Left to right: Sandy Morris, Kelly Russell, Bryan Hennessey, Rocky Wiseman, Bawnie Oulton, Ron Hynes.

424 Photo by Kent Barrett.

Sandy originated the band's musical concept and coined their whimsical name—apparently based on an offhand remark from Kelly Russell's mother: "Well, it must be a wonderful, grand band because you're never home fighting about it."[425] White and Greg took the creative lead in developing the sketch-comedy component of the show. They delved into CODCO's repertoire for one of their most memorable recurring characters, the opportunistic, unprincipled, crass, bigoted, and hilarious Mr. Budgell, played by Malone. Together, they sketched out a basis for the program in which the Wonderful Grand Band plays in a bar owned by Mr. and Mrs. Budgell who would interact with both the band and the guests. Mary Walsh joined them as a co-writer and to play Mrs. Budgell in the series. "So, I went back and I pitched that to Kevin O'Connell and he loved it," Sandy said. "We called it *The Root Seller*."[426]

The concept and premise of *The Root Seller* was only a few creative tweaks away from becoming the *WGB* television show, which later enjoyed a three-year run as well as unprecedented ratings and popularity. Why then, was *The Root Seller* cancelled after only six episodes? Sandy recalled the serious cultural and professional clashes between the cast and the CBC staff who produced the show. "They were used to telling people how to dress and how to look because that's part of being on TV," Morris remembered.

> When it came to dealing with the Wonderful Grand Band, we were already, individually, all out successfully playing live. "You can't tell me to wear that shirt. I'm not putting that on. I wouldn't be caught dead in public with that." So, there was always this tension and similarly, Greg and Mary had *very* specific ideas about how they wanted to do the show. They were brilliant actors and directors and everything else . . . writers! They knew exactly what they wanted and they had no trouble at all speaking up and saying: "No, no! Don't shoot it from over there. Move the camera over here." Of course, this didn't go over well at all and people were saying: "Who's producing this f--king show?" So, the CBC dropped that show.[427]

---

425 Malone and White, interview.

426 Malone and White, interview; White, interview for the STAGE Project (1995), 66–7; Morris, interview.

427 Morris, interview.

Of the six episodes of *The Root Seller* that were made, only two are left in existence. Sadly, this short-lived television show fell victim to the same fate as many shows aired on publicly funded broadcast networks all over the Atlantic world prior to the digital age. With only a limited amount of physical space in broadcasters' archives for previously aired programs, many were erased to accommodate new recordings, or simply destroyed to create more storage space. The exceptionally long-running *Dr. Who* series similarly has lost episodes—108 of them—some of which may never be seen again due to the insufficient funding or storage space available for the BBC at the time.[428] The two episodes of *The Root Seller* that survive are only extant thanks to Kelly Russell, who requested copies of them from the CBC early on because they featured performances by Émile Benoît and Newfoundland singer Minnie White that he wished to preserve.[429] I was particularly disappointed to hear about these lost episodes because my mother guest-starred in one of them—a performance I will likely never get to see.

Jane and Ron

"Tell me about when you first started seeing Dad." I asked my mother this question rather late in life. When one's family has long existed in a state of estrangement, such memories and their narration are usually coloured by the enduring pain of parting. It's the kind of thing you think about carefully before asking. Jane was more than happy to tell me the whole story however, and we laughed quite a bit. Jane's good friend and fellow actress Shifra Zisman was dating Kelly Russell at the time, who was just beginning work with Ron and the rest of the nascent Wonderful Grand Band on *The Root Seller*. One day after rehearsal, Ron asked Kelly and Shifra where they were off to and they told him they were going to hang out at Jane Dingle's apartment.

Ron remembered Jane from his regular shows at Bridgett's. During a recent tour with Dudley Cox and the NTTC, Jane had discovered an

428 "Doctor Who—The Lost Episodes," *Archive on 4*, hosted by Shaun Ley, produced by Chris Ledgard, BBC Radio 4, December 26, 2009. https://www.bbc.co.uk/sounds/play/boopjoy2.

429 Russell, interview.

outport clothing store with absurd amounts of overstock fashion dating from the World War II period and was often turned out in a 1940s dress and hat. Bridgett's was Jane's favourite St. John's bar and she and the rest of the crowd residing at 100 Patrick Street came out one or two evenings a week for a drink and some live music. She had been struck by Ron's performance and stage presence and the two would chat occasionally when he was making the rounds after his set. "That's really the first time I got to know him," Jane told me. Ron promptly invited himself along with Shifra and Kelly to visit her. "So, he started coming over to my apartment," Jane recalled.

> I was actually dating somebody else at the time, but we used to hang out. We used to play cards and talk a lot. Everybody would be talking about what they were doing and how *The Root Seller* was going. Shifra and I used to talk about what we were up to. And they kept bringing him back, and bringing him back. He just showed up. Then he started bringing presents. First it was a J.D. Souther album, *Black Rose*. Then it was something else. That went on for a while. I said to him: "But, I'm dating someone Ron. Why are you giving me presents?" He said: "Because I like you. I want to give you presents."

After about a month of coming and going with Shifra and Kelly, Ron asked Jane out on a date. He was met with the same protestations, which seemed only to add fuel to his resolve. "He bugged me for about three weeks," Jane remembered, "and I finally said: 'Oh God, okay!' The movie he took me to was neat; I loved Liza Minelli. *New York, New York*, how appropriate," she added with a smile that was both wry and warm all at once. "Anyway, we went to the movie and afterwards we talked and talked and talked." By this time, Jane started to notice that she had been hearing from her boyfriend less and less. "He stopped calling," she said, "and I thought: 'I wonder what's going on with that?'"[430]

While Mom rarely talked to me about her relationship with Dad when I was younger, Dad himself had few such reservations. What's more, Dad's easy relationship with a good buzz meant that he often told me more than I wanted to hear. "Your mother was *gorgeous*," I remember

430 Dingle, interview.

Dad telling me once after a glass or two of Jameson. "She looked just like Angela Lansbury in *The Picture of Dorian Grey*. I had to have her. I told the fella she was dating to f--k off and leave her alone because she was mine. I said I'd kick his ass if he didn't." I couldn't have been more than seventeen when Dad told me this story and having been the generational beneficiary of an established feminist movement, I had serious reservations about whether I should laugh and encourage him. But honestly, the thought of a skinny little dude like Dad who stood no taller than five feet, seven inches in his socks threatening to kick anyone's ass quite tickled me. It was I who finally answered Mom's questions, years later, about why her boyfriend at the time stopped calling.

The Wonderful Grand Band

After *The Root Seller* series wrapped, the Wonderful Grand Band went out on the road as a purely musical act throughout the province for several months. They were generally well received by audiences in St. John's, but out on tour "it just didn't go over very well," Sandy remarked. "We were doing fiddle tunes and people weren't used to that."[431] While Figgy Duff had made significant headway re-popularizing traditional music, Trad Rock was still fairly nascent. Like their counterparts in the theatre, many young musicians were committed to a similar cultural reclamation. However, that did not necessarily mean that all Newfoundlanders were ready to come along with them. Don Walsh, lead guitarist for Red Island, recalled that sometimes regional innovations in art and music such as "wild guitar solos in the middle of jigs and reels" just didn't land with some Newfoundlanders, no matter how proud and patriotic they might have been.

> I remember one night Red Island were playing . . . I can't remember where we were to—I think it was out in Boyd's Cove or something like that—but we just *emptied* the place. By the time we finished the first set, there was nobody left. Finally I'd gone up to the bar and the man says to me: "Boys, what are you *playing*? What kind of music are you guys playing?"

431 Morris, interview.

> Me, being sarcastic and snotty, I said: "Well, we're playing a variation of traditional Newfoundland Celtic music in a jazz/rock idiom."
>
> And buddy looked at me and said: "Boy, that's not what your f--king manager told me you were going to play."
>
> I said: "Well, what did my manager tell you?"
>
> And he said: "He told me you were going to play old rock 'n' roll with country and western."
>
> I'm thinking to myself: "Jesus, here we goes again with this." So, I went down and I said to the boys what buddy was up there saying. We asked: "Should we go back to the room and watch TV?" But then, Jamie took his guitar, and I had a guitar, and Derek and Shawn or Des, whoever was at the gig that time, I can't remember . . .[432] We just turned around and said, "Okay, who knows 'Mansion on the Hill?'" So, the rest of the night was country music and rock 'n' roll, but they were not too keen on Red Island. In the city, in St. John's, we would block the place. In Halifax, there used to be lineups to get in to see us, but you go out around the bay somewhere . . . I used to say to the boys, "Boys look, this crowd been working their asses off all week. They just want a Friday night out. They don't really want to sit in the audience and *decide* whether or not they like this music. They don't want to have to think about it. They just want to have fun." So, sometimes we would try to throw in a few country and rock 'n' roll songs when we were playing out around the bay like that.[433]

Walsh's anecdote is very interesting and adds weight to the concerns that many Newfoundlanders had at the time that elements of traditional culture were still at risk of being lost. Walsh himself recalled how as a kid he had rolled his eyes at the traditional music on *Don Messer's Jubilee* and the early episodes of *All Around the Circle* before going on

---

432 The members of Red Island were Don Walsh, Jamie Snider, Derek Pelley, Shawn Power, and Bruce Crummell. Poet, playwright, and musician Des Walsh also played with the band at various times.

433 Don Walsh, interview.

to embrace it as a young musician.[434] Mass media reached the outports quite late in the twentieth century and apparently, even by the mid-to-late 1970s, traditional music was still considered passé and tired by more than a few Newfoundlanders. By the end of the decade however, Trad Rock would secure a prominent and ultimately long-lasting presence in Newfoundland's musical repertoire.

Despite the CBC promptly cancelling *The Root Seller* after a mere six episodes, which aired in the spring of 1978, the Wonderful Grand Band still managed to make an impression on the public significant enough to receive the offer of a gig from Toronto Caravan that summer. "Do you remember Toronto Caravan?" Sandy asked me during his interview.

> It was kind of a precursor to Caribana.[435] The idea was that each of the various diverse cultures in Toronto would have their own pavilion and feature their own food, their own musicians, their own storytelling, or whatever culture they wanted to share. The Caribbean community were a big part of that and a lot of other ethnic communities too. Newfoundland was the only province that had its own pavilion and the people that had organized it invited the Grand Band because they had seen us on television.[436]

Building on the success of the concept from *The Root Seller*, Greg Malone once again joined the Wonderful Grand Band as a Mr. Budgell-esque character and emcee for the run of their Toronto Caravan show. "It was the old Masonic Temple[437] where Hendrix had played, and The Who . . . So, it was a fantastic room to be gigging in, and it's a big room. I think that when it was full we had six or seven hundred people in there. We did three half-hour shows a day."[438]

What the Wonderful Grand Band created is fully emblematic of the shape and spirit of the broader cultural movement, featuring the clear marks of regional pride, interdisciplinarity, and collectivity. The format and style in which the band presented itself strongly resembles

---

434 Don Walsh, interview.
435 Annual summer festival of Caribbean culture in Toronto.
436 Morris, interview.
437 Historic Toronto concert hall at 888 Yonge Street.
438 Morris, interview.

a re-creation of the traditional outport concert, with its music, songs, and sketches, its comedic and interactive hosts, as well as the highly direct audience engagement, which narrows the distance between performers and spectators. The band's music could occasionally be contemplative, but was more often toe-tapping, designed to get audiences on their feet while the sketches and comedic monologues by the CODCO contingent of Greg Malone and Tommy Sexton, and later, Mary Walsh and Cathy Jones, also kept the audience and band members enmeshed in a theatrical experience, which invariably resembled the outport tradition rather than the town tradition.

"I realized," Greg recalled of that first Wonderful Grand Band show at the Masonic, "that Ron was my guy onstage. He was the most vocal, he'd talk back. So, I used to pick on him. Ron loved it and the crowd got to know him. They played *Joe Smallwood's Reel* and that was the first time I danced. That was the first time the Wonderful Grand Band all came together."[439]

"It was amazing the difference you could see in the way people reacted to Ron after he became a character," Sandy concurred, "and not just a singer in the band. People sympathized with him because he was being picked on by Mr. Budgell, you know what I mean? That show went over like a house on fire and Toronto went mad for it, just loved it. So, when we moved back, we thought: 'We're going to have to do a show with Greg.'"[440]

---

439 Malone and White, interview.
440 Morris, interview.

Wonderful Grand Band theatrical program, Toronto Caravan, 1978.

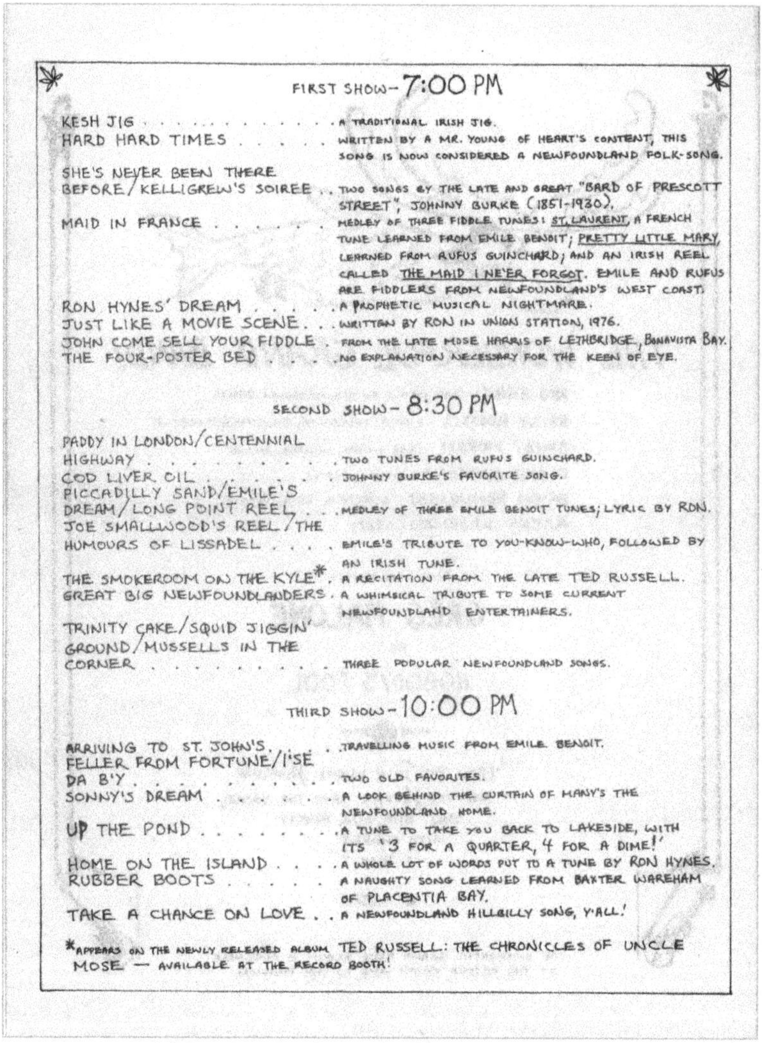

FIRST SHOW – 7:00 PM

KESH JIG . . . . A TRADITIONAL IRISH JIG.
HARD HARD TIMES . . . . . WRITTEN BY A MR. YOUNG OF HEART'S CONTENT, THIS SONG IS NOW CONSIDERED A NEWFOUNDLAND FOLK-SONG.
SHE'S NEVER BEEN THERE BEFORE / KELLIGREW'S SOIREE . . TWO SONGS BY THE LATE AND GREAT "BARD OF PRESCOTT STREET", JOHNNY BURKE (1851-1930).
MAID IN FRANCE . . . . . . MEDLEY OF THREE FIDDLE TUNES: ST. LAURENT, A FRENCH TUNE LEARNED FROM EMILE BENOIT; PRETTY LITTLE MARY, LEARNED FROM RUFUS GUINCHARD; AND AN IRISH REEL CALLED THE MAID I NE'ER FORGOT. EMILE AND RUFUS ARE FIDDLERS FROM NEWFOUNDLAND'S WEST COAST.
RON HYNES' DREAM . . . . . A PROPHETIC MUSICAL NIGHTMARE.
JUST LIKE A MOVIE SCENE . . . WRITTEN BY RON IN UNION STATION, 1976.
JOHN COME SELL YOUR FIDDLE . FROM THE LATE MOSE HARRIS OF LETHBRIDGE, BONAVISTA BAY.
THE FOUR-POSTER BED . . . . NO EXPLANATION NECESSARY FOR THE KEEN OF EYE.

SECOND SHOW – 8:30 PM

PADDY IN LONDON / CENTENNIAL HIGHWAY . . . . TWO TUNES FROM RUFUS GUINCHARD.
COD LIVER OIL . . . . JOHNNY BURKE'S FAVORITE SONG.
PICCADILLY SAND / EMILE'S DREAM / LONG POINT REEL . . . MEDLEY OF THREE EMILE BENOIT TUNES; LYRIC BY RON.
JOE SMALLWOOD'S REEL / THE HUMOURS OF LISSADEL . . . . EMILE'S TRIBUTE TO YOU-KNOW-WHO, FOLLOWED BY AN IRISH TUNE.
THE SMOKEROOM ON THE KYLE*. A RECITATION FROM THE LATE TED RUSSELL.
GREAT BIG NEWFOUNDLANDERS . A WHIMSICAL TRIBUTE TO SOME CURRENT NEWFOUNDLAND ENTERTAINERS.
TRINITY CAKE / SQUID JIGGIN' GROUND / MUSSELLS IN THE CORNER . . . . THREE POPULAR NEWFOUNDLAND SONGS.

THIRD SHOW – 10:00 PM

ARRIVING TO ST. JOHN'S . . . . TRAVELLING MUSIC FROM EMILE BENOIT.
FELLER FROM FORTUNE / I'SE DA B'Y . . . . TWO OLD FAVORITES.
SONNY'S DREAM . . . . A LOOK BEHIND THE CURTAIN OF MANY'S THE NEWFOUNDLAND HOME.
UP THE POND . . . . A TUNE TO TAKE YOU BACK TO LAKESIDE, WITH ITS '3 FOR A QUARTER, 4 FOR A DIME!'
HOME ON THE ISLAND . . . . A WHOLE LOT OF WORDS PUT TO A TUNE BY RON HYNES.
RUBBER BOOTS . . . . . . A NAUGHTY SONG LEARNED FROM BAXTER WAREHAM OF PLACENTIA BAY.
TAKE A CHANCE ON LOVE . . A NEWFOUNDLAND HILLBILLY SONG, Y'ALL!

*APPEARS ON THE NEWLY RELEASED ALBUM TED RUSSELL: THE CHRONICLES OF UNCLE MOSE — AVAILABLE AT THE RECORD BOOTH!

Wonderful Grand Band theatrical program, Toronto Caravan, 1978.[441]

441 Private collection.

"The band felt good together," White remembered. "The impact was great. Everyone's game was up when they got together. Glenn and Ron singing together—it was dynamic—and Ron had a few really amazing songs to bring into it."

"Which excited everyone in the band," Greg interjected. "Original stuff, and it's good! It's not just traditional stuff." After the Toronto Caravan show, the Wonderful Grand Band went on to do several months of live shows back in Newfoundland featuring the band's music with Greg doing sketch comedy, which went over extremely well.

"There were lineups around the block," Malone recalled. It was at one of those shows during the winter of 1978/79 that Tommy Sexton first came to see the band play in St. John's.

"I was doing Mavis, with the long blonde hair," Greg remarked laughing, "and Tommy just about came out of his *skin*, that I was daring to do that onstage! He just *had* to do it. He said: 'I can be your friend, Carmel-Anne.'"[442] Sandy recalled a similar exchange between Tommy and Greg after Tommy had seen the show for the first time:

> "Oh no. You're not getting a band, Malone. You can't do that without me." That's literally what he said. And so, the two of them created what they created and that became what the Grand Band was—which all of us were totally gobsmacked at. Even though we were all sure we were on to something, we didn't expect it to take off. The band became so popular, the CBC came back and said: "We're just going to take your live show and put it on TV."[443]

442 Malone and White, interview.
443 Morris, interview.

Left to right: Greg Malone (Mavis), Tommy Sexton (Carmel-Anne), Ron Hynes, Sandy Morris. (n.d.)[444]

444 Photograph courtesy of Kelly Russell.

The Wonderful Grand Band's adoption of traditional music and the resemblance of their act to the outport concert signals the cultural reclamation side of the renaissance movement, as well as the artistic interdisciplinarity of the broader movement. We see evidence of collectivity not only in the band's creative process as previously described by Sandy Morris, but also in their membership over time, which was quite extensive. No less than seventeen performers have played as regulars at one time or another with the Wonderful Grand Band whether in live performances, on their studio albums, or on *The Root Seller* or *WGB* TV shows.[445] According to Malone, the collectivity and interdisciplinarity of the Wonderful Grand Band were representative of the experience of the larger arts community in the province, a place where both the communitarian impulse and the arts in general have always been equally valued.

> We're a small group, five hundred thousand of us, but we punch way above our weight culturally compared to any other province. I guess, to stay in the arts, you often had to do more than just what your primary passion was. Maybe it was music, but maybe you got a chance to be in a musical show, so you started to act. Or maybe if you were an actor, but you could play guitar or you could sing, you'd be drafted into a band. Whoever was interested in the arts knew about each other in such a small group. There was that support and that interdisciplinary movement where actors and musicians went back and forth between stage shows and bands in clubs. Wonderful Grand Band was a big example of that.[446]

445 These include Sandy Morris, Ron Hynes, Kelly Russell, Glenn Simmons, Bawnie Oulton, Bryan Hennessey, Rocky Wiseman, Howie Warden, Ian Perry, Steve Annan, Jamie Snider, Paul "Boomer" Stamp, Kevin McNeil, Greg Malone, Mary Walsh, Tommy Sexton, and Cathy Jones. This list does not include those who did not regularly play with the Wonderful Grand Band, but who nonetheless played musical accompaniment, songwriting, or production roles on either of the band's albums, such as Émile Benoît, Peter Narváez, or Declan O'Doherty. It is also worth noting that numerous other Newfoundland artists guest-starred on episodes of *The Root Seller* or *WGB* in singing or acting roles.

446 Malone and White, interview.

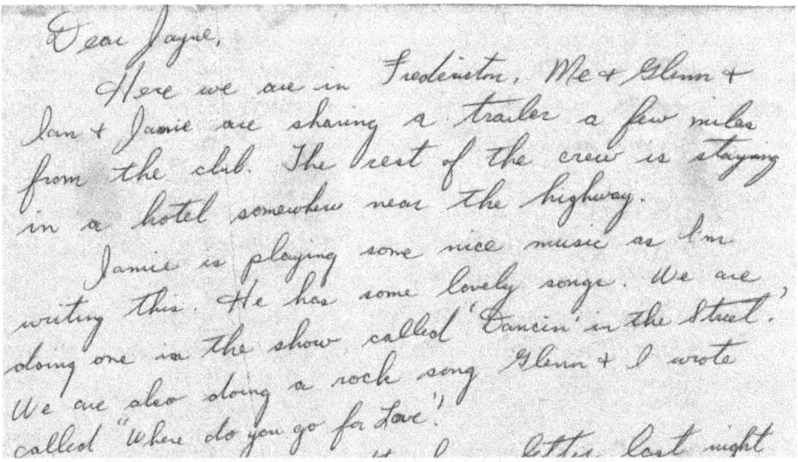

Dear Jayne,
Here we are in Fredericton. Me + Glenn + Ian + Jamie are sharing a trailer a few miles from the club. The rest of the crew is staying in a hotel somewhere near the highway.
Jamie is playing some nice music as I'm writing this. He has some lovely songs. We are doing one in the show called 'Dancin' in the Street.' We are also doing a rock song Glenn + I wrote called "Where do you go for Love".
... letter last night

Dear Jayne, undated letter from Ron Hynes to Jane Dingle, 1979–80.

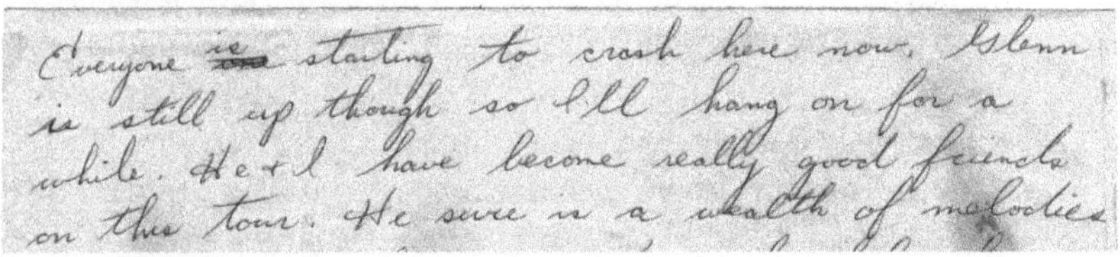

Everyone is starting to crash here now. Glenn is still up though so I'll hang on for a while. He + I have become really good friends on this tour. He sure is a wealth of melodies

Dear Jayne, undated letter from Ron Hynes to Jane Dingle, 1979–80.

The Wonderful Grand Band was just one piece of a much broader artistic and cultural movement, but both the response to the band and the broad reach of the television show seemed to signal its own distinct cultural phenomenon. Many young Newfoundlanders who would one day join the ranks of the arts community as actors, musicians, writers, and comedians watched *WGB* on television and felt seen for the first time. Newfoundland playwright and theatre director Jillian Keiley once wrote of the feeling of pride in reading the single chapter devoted to the province in her high school Canadian history textbook.[447] One can therefore imagine how powerful the experience must have been when a young generation of future artists like Rick Mercer, Alan Doyle, or Mark Critch saw *WGB* on television for the first time.[448] "Schools began doing shows with Mr. Budgell and Nanny Hynes in them. They had changed the lines, but they had adopted the characters," Greg recalled. "We'd become part of the culture."

"And certainly songs like 'Sonny's Dream' and 'Back Home on the Island' . . ." White began.

"They drove it home," Greg finished. "He [Ron] was singing our songs. He was singing about us, our life, people we knew." The *WGB* TV show brought a sense of cultural representation to numerous Newfoundlanders.[449] "We were all very excited that we had somehow gotten into that stream and we knew we could do this," Greg continued.

> We could be ourselves onstage, sing our songs and get the crowd going. Ron was from Ferryland. He had self-esteem troubles as Newfoundlanders generally did, vis à vis Canada and the States and the mainland. We were only a small, poor little outpost. So, this was a revelation to all of us that we were as good, or better, than anyone else and maybe even unique in some ways, with something new to offer. Ron's songs were exciting and CODCO was too, and they were both coming at the same time. They met in the Wonderful Grand Band, and that was like: "boom!" It was like an explosion. The *Wonderful Grand Band* TV show was the most watched show the CBC ever made. Eighty per cent viewership. Nothing like it ever had eighty per cent viewership. It beat out *Dukes of Hazzard*, which was on at the same time, and that was *the* number one show.

---

447 Jillian Keiley, "Review of Helen Peters (ed.) *Stars in the Sky Morning: Collective Plays of Newfoundland and Labrador*," *Newfoundland Studies* 15, no. 3 (1999): 132.

448 "Bigger than Elvis: Rick Mercer praises Wonderful Grand Band in Q interview," *CBC News*, January 15, 2017. https://www.cbc.ca/news/canada/newfoundland-labrador/rick-mercer-tom-power-radio-q-1.3934950; Alex Kennedy, "Alan Doyle shares the struggles of pandemic life and his connection to a Ron Hynes classic," *CBC News*, May 11, 2021. https://www.cbc.ca/news/canada/newfoundland-labrador/alan-doyle-back-to-the-harbour-first-listen-1.6017777; "Return to the Babylon Mall! Mark Critch featured in remake of Wonderful Grand classic," *CBC News*, December 7, 2017. https://www.cbc.ca/news/canada/newfoundland-labrador/babylon-mall-covered-for-avalon-s-50th-s-1.4437039.

449 Bill, 97–98.

> We even beat the News. So, the band was very happy about that. On Monday mornings in Newfoundland, everyone would stop and talk about the show.[450]

***

Listening to White, Greg, and Sandy describe their experiences and achievements with the Wonderful Grand Band, I felt again a strong sense of how special a time and place Newfoundland in the 1970s was for artists. I listened to a great many stories throughout the course of this project, most of which painted a picture of hopefulness and excitement among a passionate and strong community of fellows, but the story that Sandy Morris told me about the night after the Wonderful Grand Band recorded their first album at Clode Sound in 1978 is probably my favourite. I'm certain its impact is infinitely greater delivered by Sandy himself in a warmly lit bar over a glass or two than by my poor pen, but I'm glad to have the privilege to preserve it here.

> When we finished the recording, we decided we'd drive down to see Émile [Benoît] who lived on the Port au Port peninsula. It was only an hour's drive from Stephenville where we were recording. I had this big old international travel truck, almost like an armoury vehicle. Émile had one of those cattle things over his front gate, of a sort that cattle can't walk between, and when my vehicle went over it, boof! It stopped, it shut off and I couldn't get it going again. Kelly said: "Don't worry, Émile knows all kinds of stuff about cars." So, Kelly went down to Émile's house and knocked on the door.
>
> He said: "Émile, the truck's broke down, could you have a look at it for us?"
>
> We opened the bonnet and Émile looked in and said: "I can't do nothing with that till tomorrow morning, eh? So, you're going to have to spend the night." So, we all went in with him.

450 Malone and White, interview.

> Then he got on the phone and called everybody; everybody he knew. "Hey! Ron Hynes is here! Sandy Morris! Kelly Russell! The Grand Band!" Next thing, the biggest party I've ever seen in my life. The house was . . . you couldn't move. You literally couldn't. Beer and rum and fiddle tunes, unbelievable. Fantastic, biggest party ever on the Port au Port peninsula.
>
> Next morning . . . I slept in the kitchen on one of those little settles by the stove because there was nowhere else to sleep. I don't know where everybody else crashed, I have no idea. At seven o'clock in the morning, Émile shows up, comes down and puts the kettle on the stove. I wake up and say: "Hey Émile." He has a cup of tea and he starts playing the fiddle. I said: "You think you could have a look at the truck now? We're going to have to get back today and we're driving across the island." He said: "Sure, come on up." We opened the bonnet . . . and then he put the battery clip back on. So, he kidnapped us for the night! And we had the party of our lives! I wish we had a video of that.[451]

The band Ryan's Fancy filmed a similar experience of a party with live music at Émile Benoît's home on the Port au Port peninsula for television, but, Sandy allowed, that particular program was fairly "cleaned up" compared to the time the Wonderful Grand Band had after recording their first album.[452] I'd give a great deal to have been a mere fly on the wall for that particular party.

A Fresh Aesthetic in Theatre

The Newfoundland and Labrador theatre scene at the time was equally exciting. "That's when collectives really boomed," Jane recalled of the drama produced between 1977 and 1982. The Mummers Troupe, Rising Tide Theatre, and what eventually became known as the Resource

451 Morris, interview.

452 *Ryan's Fancy*, CBC St. John's, produced by Jack Kellum, original airdate: June 5, 1979.

Centre for the Arts staged some of the best original Canadian theatre of the period. As we have previously observed, collective creation was a widespread trend in North American theatre during the late 1960s and 1970s, but in Newfoundland it was particularly pronounced.[453] The collective tradition seemed to be part of every professional theatre company's process until well into the 1980s. CODCO, however, which ceased touring as a theatre troupe by 1976, was virtually the only example of a strict collective in every sense: creatively, administratively, and regarding ownership.[454]

Clearly, these young artists didn't mind a challenge because collective theatre is a colossally tricky beast. It not only involves group conception of ideas, shared research, exhaustive improvisation, and collective writing, but the artists also face the difficulties of ensuring the egalitarian conditions that the label collective implies. This latter goal was indeed ambitious and one which several artists of the time admitted to struggling with. "I sing the praises of collectivism, but it's difficult and it takes it out of you to be in a collective," observed Mary Walsh. "But so does an autocracy. These days, many of us say: 'I'd just as soon have the one big asshole make all the decisions.' Every system has its own flaws, but as a creative tool I think the collective, especially for comedy, is just the best."[455]

As far as a smooth road toward collective creation, CODCO seems to have been best placed to make the process work. The group had a fairly closed membership during their nearly five years together as a theatre troupe, which meant greater professional familiarity and potentially greater working cohesion over time. It also helped that the members of CODCO were friends to begin with and, in the case of Andy and Cathy Jones, family. Still, Sandy Morris recalled, CODCO's writing sessions had been fraught with both personal and professional issues, which had to be settled among the group before they could all sit down and create together.[456] One could argue that the Mummers Troupe, whose membership was constantly shifting with each new play, faced a much stiffer challenge in collective creation. Like musicians with the Wonderful Grand Band, virtually every Newfoundland actor in the 1970s seems to

453 Dingle, interview; Gulliver, 206, 209–210.
454 Peters (ed.), xix–xx.
455 Mary Walsh, interview.
456 Morris, interview.

have worked on one Mummers Troupe show or other. By Chris Brookes's own reckoning, no less than 106 theatre artists had performed, written, directed, or provided technical services in a Mummers Troupe production during the ten years of the company's existence.[457]

The Mummers Troupe—alongside the Resource Centre for the Arts (RCA Theatre) who succeeded them—operated out of the LSPU Hall until 1982, where an impressive series of original productions inspired by regional history, life, and culture were staged for the first time. During the fall of 1977, the Mummers Troupe produced *The Bard of Prescott Street,* a musical show about the life and times of late nineteenth-century folk musician and balladeer Johnny Burke. Ron Hynes played Burke alongside a cast that included Mary Walsh, Bob Joy, David Ross, Janet Michael, Bryan Hennessey, and Jane Dingle, with Chris Brookes directing. *The Bard of Prescott Street* was collectively written and, like many contemporary theatrical productions, it featured original music played by resident musicians who also acted in the show. Sometimes, however, music in these productions was collectively written as well.[458] For *The Bard of Prescott Street,* each member of the cast penned their own broadside ballads to familiar airs. They were sold on the streets for five cents to advertise the show, just as Burke had sold his songs on the streets of St. John's for pennies.[459] Following our interview, Chris Brookes kindly sent me an image of a framed, mimeographed copy of the broadside ballad that Dad had written to advertise the show. In true Burke fashion, Ron had taken a popular air and made it relatable to the community with a song about a recent local news item. "The year before," Brookes recalled, "about six or eight bars downtown mysteriously burned down. The police said: 'It's pure coincidence.' 'Course it must have been an insurance job, you know," Chris noted with a small knowing smile.

---

457 Brookes, *A Public Nuisance,* xii–xiii.

458 Brookes, *A Public Nuisance,* 191, 238; Dingle, interview.

459 Brookes, *A Public Nuisance,* 191–92.

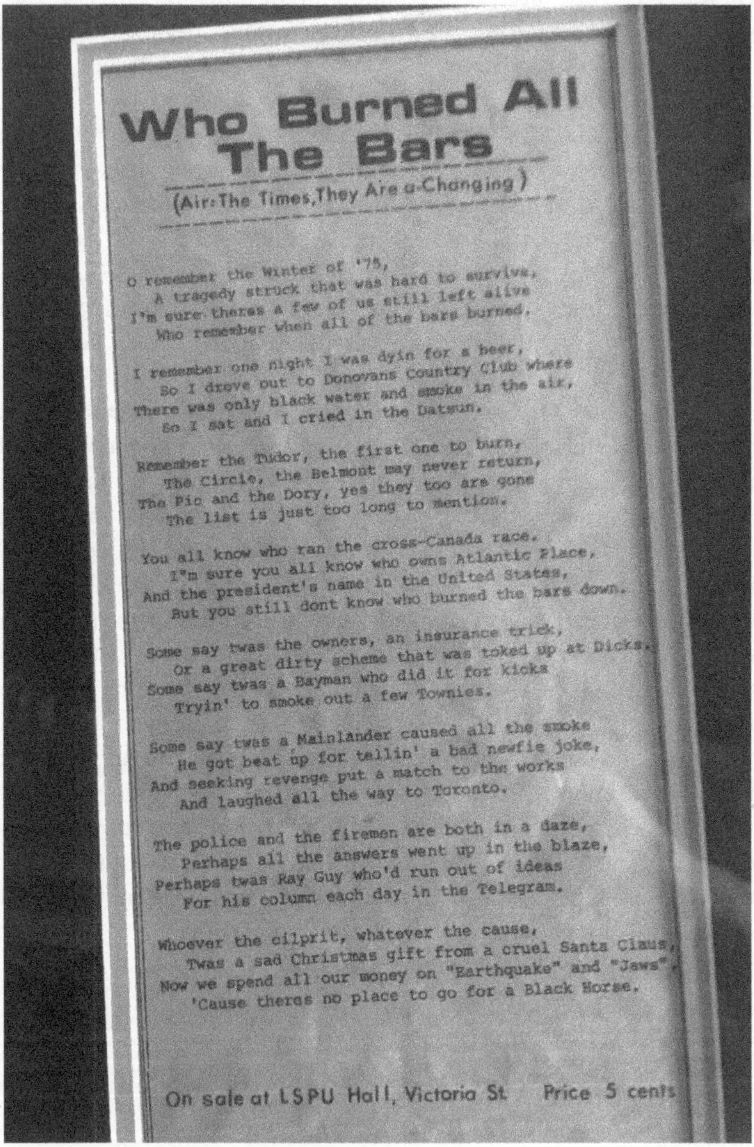

Who Burned All The Bars

(Air: The Times, They Are a-Changing)

O remember the Winter of '75,
A tragedy struck that was hard to survive,
I'm sure theres a few of us still left alive
Who remember when all of the bars burned.

I remember one night I was dyin for a beer,
So I drove out to Donovans Country Club where
There was only black water and smoke in the air,
So I sat and I cried in the Datsun.

Remember the Tudor, the first one to burn,
The Circle, the Belmont may never return,
The Pic and the Dory, yes they too are gone
The list is just too long to mention.

You all know who ran the cross-Canada race,
I'm sure you all know who owns Atlantic Place,
And the president's name in the United States,
But you still dont know who burned the bars down.

Some say twas the owners, an insurance trick,
Or a great dirty scheme that was toked up at Dicks,
Some say twas a Bayman who did it for kicks
Tryin' to smoke out a few Townies.

Some say twas a Mainlander caused all the smoke
He got beat up for tellin' a bad newfie joke,
And seeking revenge put a match to the works
And laughed all the way to Toronto.

The police and the firemen are both in a daze,
Perhaps all the answers went up in the blaze,
Perhaps twas Ray Guy who'd run out of ideas
For his column each day in the Telegram.

Whoever the cilprit, whatever the cause,
Twas a sad Christmas gift from a cruel Santa Claus,
Now we spend all our money on "Earthquake" and "Jaws",
'Cause theres no place to go for a Black Horse.

On sale at LSPU Hall, Victoria St Price 5 cents

Who Burned All the Bars? [460]

460 Image courtesy of Chris Brookes. Used with permission.

Several narrators I spoke to remembered *The Bard of Prescott Street* fondly.[461] The production featured beautiful music both traditional and original, which blended seamlessly with one another as well as with the drama of the production. It had a far more developed and lavish set than the necessarily more sparse and mobile productions the troupe were used to staging. *The Bard* incorporated more than a few interesting visuals, including Ron swinging vigorously in a swing hung high above the stage to simulate aerial flight, an insurance nightmare that could only have flown in the 1970s, so to speak. Jane also recalled a lovely tableau that she and Ron had staged of the shy shopgirl and her smitten young man while he performed *Old Brown's Daughter*.[462] There was a good deal of new love among the cast; Jane and Ron had only been dating a few months when *The Bard* was staged and fellow cast members David Ross and Janet Michael began their relationship during the course of the production as well.[463]

Cast of *The Bard of Prescott Street*, 1977.[464]

461 Dingle, interview; Joy, interview; Mary Walsh, interview.

462 Brookes, *A Public Nuisance*, 191; Dingle, interview; *The Bard of Prescott Street* (1977), directed by Chris Brookes (original theatre script), 37–8, Memorial University Libraries, Archives and Special Collections, Coll-126 4.02.

463 Dingle, interview; Mary Walsh, interview.

464 Photo by Kent Barrett. Left to right: Bob Joy, Ron Hynes, Jane Dingle, Janet Michael.

The show was well received in St. John's with every single performance quickly selling out. Encouraged by the initial public interest and conscious that the production needed an ample stage, Chris Brookes offered to bring *The Bard* to the Arts and Culture Centre. The Division of Cultural Affairs refused Brookes's offer on the grounds that the subject matter was "too local," Brookes claimed. Instead, the St. John's Arts and Culture Centre was preparing to stage a full run of the 1962 American musical *A Funny Thing Happened on the Way to the Forum.*[465] The following year, however, the Mummers would finally be welcomed at the St. John's Arts and Culture Centre with, interestingly, one of the most controversial plays in their repertoire.

In the spring of 1978, the Mummers Troupe staged *They Club Seals, Don't They?*, a defence of the Newfoundland and Labrador sealing industry which, Brookes wrote, pitted him rather uncomfortably against most of the Mummers' regular supporters and political fellows. International animal rights and environmentalist groups were aligned against them. Middle-class urbanites across Canada and several other countries in the Atlantic basin recoiled in horror from the very notion of the seal hunt, while rural residents and producers wondered what all the fuss was about. The majority of the private sector funders that had previously supported the Troupe's shows flatly refused to touch this production. To Brookes's complete lack of surprise, the Division of Cultural Affairs initially refused support as well, but once the provincial Department of Rural Development agreed to provide what amounted to twenty per cent of the show's budget, the Arts and Culture Centre finally booked its very first Mummers Troupe production—if only to avoid the appearance of political tension, Brookes thought.[466] Like *The Bard, They Club Seals Don't They?* was a collectively written musical with a resident musician, this time Terry Rielly alongside a cast including Donna Butt, David Ross, Rhonda Payne, Glenn Tilley, Jeff Pitcher, and Pierre Beaupre. The interdisciplinarity of art forms employed in this production was even more pronounced than *The Bard* had been, incorporating film and audio collages as well as drama and music. As part of a broader commentary on the annual protests against the seal hunt with its international camera crews and American and European celebrities mobbing the Labrador

465 Brookes, *A Public Nuisance,* 192–93.
466 Brookes, *A Public Nuisance,* 195–200.

shores every spring, the Mummers employed a circus theme in multiple scenes, for which Jan Henderson and Ian Wallace were brought in to give the actors workshops on clowning. Finally, this unique show always ended with the cast facilitating detailed discussion and debate with the audience about the issues and misconceptions around the Newfoundland and Labrador sealing industry.[467]

The last Mummers Troupe show staged before the group finally folded a few months later was the spring 1982 provincial tour of their World War II-era musical, *Makin' Time with the Yanks*. Produced for the first time the previous spring, *Yanks* was collectively written, directed by Mary Walsh, and starred Kay Anonsen, Brian Downey, Janis Spence, Rick Boland, Jane Dingle, and Paul Steffler, who was also the production's resident musician and composer.[468] Like *The Bard of Prescott Street*, *Makin' Time with the Yanks* was quite clearly not the political theatre that the Mummers had traditionally produced.

A larger proportion of the shows the Mummers (and other emerging companies) staged during the late 1970s and early 1980s had marked local and regional historical significance, but lacked the political immediacy of the Mummers' usual community documentaries. Not everyone viewed this as a necessarily negative point. Many artists who worked on collectives with the Mummers were interested in exploring beyond political theatre. Brookes viewed the theatre not only as a vehicle for culture but more importantly, as a practical tool, a means to a political end. Yet, art that is not political on its face can still awaken or galvanize us both as individuals and as a group. One could argue that all drama and literature, all stories, are in some way political or reflective of social issues nonetheless. One simply has to be looking through the right lens.

World War II had been over for less than forty years and it is likely that for many, those memories were still relatively fresh when *Makin' Time with the Yanks* premiered at the LSPU Hall in March of 1981. The show's producer, Rhonda Payne, and Brookes himself observed that roughly ten per cent of St. John's residents bought a ticket to see *Yanks* during the run of the show.[469] "It was something that local people could relate to," Jane remarked. "It's not like going to the theatre

467 Brookes, *A Public Nuisance*, 195–96, 201–203.

468 Brookes, *A Public Nuisance*, 224, 234, 240.

469 Brookes, *A Public Nuisance*, 222–24; Payne, STAGE Project, 120–21.

and seeing British farce."[470] Indeed, considering the significant number of Newfoundland women who formed relationships with and married American servicemen stationed on the island during World War II, a great many local people would have related personally to the premise of the show. *Yanks* was the last of only two Mummers Troupe productions to play the main stage at the St. John's Arts and Culture Centre. Brookes had taken off for Nicaragua by this time, having left Rhonda Payne as artistic director to shepherd the company through its last two years. Payne appealed to John Perlin to give *Yanks* a three-night run at the Arts and Culture Centre to help recoup an unexpected budget shortfall. Perlin agreed and all three performances promptly sold out.[471]

In *Yanks*, the demands on cast members encompassed dance as well as music and drama. Not one cast member had a background in professional dance, so director Mary Walsh brought in dancer, teacher, and choreographer Cathy Ferri to teach the actors the jive and the lindy hop. Jane remembered that the cast acquitted themselves admirably during the choreographed swing dances, especially considering their relative lack of experience. Jane recalled a moment of doubt during the choreography stage when she confronted her dance partner Rick Boland, who was almost exactly her own height, unlike Downey and Anonsen who had been paired together. "Brian Downey was six foot and Kay Anonsen was a slip of a thing," Jane recalled, and so it had been relatively easy for Downey to lift, turn, and flip his partner as swing dances typically demand. When it came time to choreograph Jane and Rick however, Jane was quick to point out: "Jeez, he can't lift me up. I'd be dropped on my arse!" To which Cathy Ferri observed musingly: "Jane, *you're* pretty strong." "Yes, she is, isn't she?" Mary Walsh concurred. Ferri choreographed an impressive dance sequence that included Jane flipping Rick over her hip and appearing to swing him around to her other side. "Rick was really subtle and quite athletic," Jane remembered. "I would hold him in a certain way, like you would a woman, and flip him over my hip while he helped me with the momentum. That was a show-stopper every night! Rick Boland and I used to get a standing ovation every night for that one. Sure, Mary loved that."[472]

---

470 Dingle, interview.
471 Payne, STAGE Project, 119–120.
472 Dingle, interview.

Industry Gatekeepers, Tight Incomes, and Tough Choices

The profusion of original art in Newfoundland during the late 1970s shows that artists were definitely working—and productively. Many were doing better financially than in previous years, but shortfalls in provincial arts funding and infrastructure continued to pose challenges to both arts-oriented organizations and the artists they employed. The Division of Cultural Affairs did not start issuing funding grants to regional theatre organizations until 1978 and they were invariably offered in the same piecework structure as most federal or private sector funding, leaving artists in a familiar and ongoing rhythm of struggle between gigs or funding cycles. On the positive side, theatre organizations could now operate more securely with sources of funding (if not levels of funding) comparable to other Canadian theatres. The Mummers Troupe, however, never received any "sustaining" funding from the Division of Cultural Affairs. This was complicated by the fact that unlike other Canadian theatres, like Toronto's Factory Theatre or Tarragon Theatre, whose Canada Council funding had increased significantly throughout the 1970s, the Canada Council funding provided for the Mummers had remained the same since 1975, during which time Brookes estimated that the annual operating grant's value had shrunk by thirty per cent due to inflation while the cost of salaries had increased forty per cent during the same period. The stress of operating within a constant budget shortfall was part of the reason the Mummers Troupe closed by 1982.[473]

Chris Brookes and Alan Filewod have attributed the fall of the Mummers Troupe not only to financial and administrative difficulties, but also to clashes of ideology, personality, and culture. Both have asserted that part of the reason the Mummers had such difficulty securing sufficient federal funding was because the Canada Council was unable to reconcile their binary model of "legitimate" regional theatre and "political" theatre (assumed to represent an "oppositional minority") with the reality of what the Mummers Troupe actually was—both a political theatre troupe *and* a legitimate expression of regional culture. The arrival of organizations like Rising Tide Theatre and RCA Theatre, which aligned more closely with the Council's definition of

473 Filewod, "The Mummers Troupe," (1998).

regional theatre, made it easier for the Council to employ their binary model, which continued to leave the Mummers underfunded as the decade came to a close.[474]

Rising Tide Theatre was able to cultivate and maintain a much more cordial and collaborative working and funding relationship with the Division of Cultural Affairs and with John Perlin in particular, who sat on the theatre's board for several years. While Rising Tide Theatre continued the collective theatre tradition and regional focus that had come to typify Newfoundland theatre, they also performed and encouraged the production of single-authored works and were much more open to exploring and performing non-regional content.[475] Jane was cast in several Rising Tide Theatre shows during the early 1980s, including the collectives *I Was a Teenage Love Doll* and *A Big Fat Lie*, Arthur Miller's *The Price*, a stage adaptation of Bram Stoker's *Dracula*, and Tom Cahill's *So Oft it Chances*. Ron was part of the collective that produced and staged Rising Tide Theatre's *Newfoundlanders Away*, a musical depicting the experiences of exiled and dispersed Newfoundlanders trying to make a go of it up in Canada.[476]

474 Filewod, "The Mummers Troupe," (1998).

475 Gulliver, 273–74.

476 Dingle, interview; Butt, interview; "Rising Tide Theatre Presents: Arthur Miller's *The Price*" (original theatrical program); "Music, Romance, Wanderlust, and 'a time' for all in Rising Tide Theatre's *Newfoundlanders Away*" (theatrical advertisement); "Cultural Affairs Division, Department of Culture, Recreation and Youth present Rising Tide Theatre's Production of *So Oft it Chances (The Bond Years: 1898–1919)* by Tom Cahill," May 10–12, 1984, Memorial University of Newfoundland Digital Archives Initiative. https://collections.mun.ca/digital/collection/a_posters/id/421/rec/2.

Cast of *I Was a Teenage Love Doll*, 1981.[477]

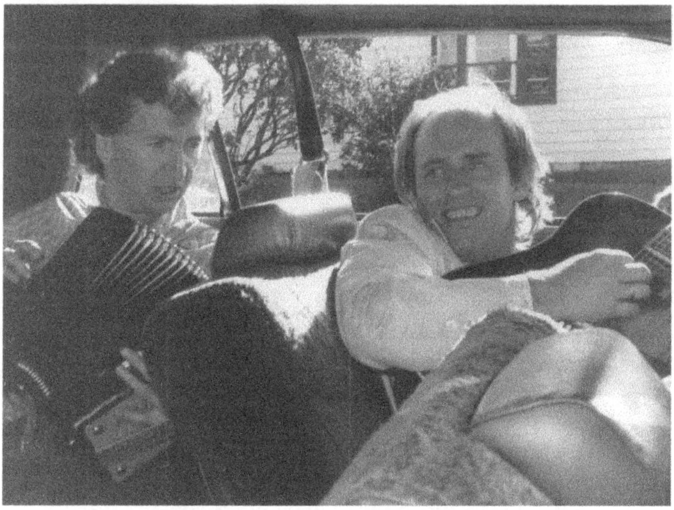

Jim Payne and Ron Hynes, *Newfoundlanders Away*.[478]

477 Left to right: Denis Parker, Mac Furlong, Jane Dingle, Brian Downey, David Ross. Image courtesy of Donna Butt. Used with permission.

478 Image courtesy of Donna Butt. Used with permission.

Brookes and Filewod have both maintained that in contrast to Rising Tide Theatre, the Mummers were held back by cultural and ideological clashes between themselves and gatekeepers to the theatre industry. John Perlin was not the only bureaucrat or Canada Council officer to clash with Brookes politically, culturally, or artistically. Filewod's essay on the rise and fall of the Mummers Troupe highlighted internal communications between Canada Council officers and third-party assessors of the work of grant recipients. In theory, Canada Council officers function neutrally as part of the grants process, but the Council itself decides who their third-party assessors will be, and will ostensibly use their report to judge the quality of the company's work and their ability to meet the obligations of their grant. In the fall of 1977, the Canada Council tasked Walter Learning, who incidentally would succeed to Theatre Officer at the Canada Council the following year, with assessing *The Bard of Prescott Street* on the Council's behalf.

> The Mummers finished work always seems, to me, to have a "work-in-progress" quality about it. My usual reaction is—"now there's the basis for a really fine and exciting production." They always seem to lack really tight script editing and direction. This, of course, is in part the result of their work method and perhaps this would be adversely affected if another element were introduced into the process. Maybe they need a chance to work with some really experienced directors from the collective creation area.[479]

Learning's assessment, Filewod observed, failed to acknowledge that Brookes was among the most experienced directors of his generation with the collective process and that Learning's criticisms "rested on aesthetic assumptions" that didn't really apply to the "political theatre for action" model.[480] The cultural and artistic clash is apparent here and ongoing interactions of this sort probably contributed much to the financial struggles of the Mummers throughout their years of operation, as well as those of other theatre companies or entities that did not align with federal or provincial gatekeepers' conceptions of art or culture.

479 Quoted in Filewod, "The Mummers Troupe," (1998).
480 Filewod, "The Mummers Troupe," (1998).

According to one account, the Canada Council made their funding for the Mummers' 1981 season conditional upon Chris Brookes not returning to the organization.[481]

Yet even artists whose art inspired no controversy or criticism from Canada Council officers found it difficult to rely on their support. This should not suggest that the funding provided by Canada Council was not key to furthering the work of Newfoundland artists. With the near-absence of provincial infrastructure for the arts it was downright essential, but its inflexible structure continued to pose problems.

Sandy Morris recalled that the Wonderful Grand Band occasionally applied for Canada Council funding for extended tours, "But we never really availed ourselves very much of that because we were so successful commercially."

> We were making enough money, but if we decided to go on a tour to Vancouver, we'd tap the Canada Council because you could never afford it without support. In fact, that's eventually what broke the band up—touring Canada, and there not being enough support. If anything happened on a tour like that, if it was really well-planned with precision and backed up, you're not going to lose money. But then, something gets cancelled in the middle of the tour, and you've got ten, twelve people . . . We had fourteen people on the last tour, on the road. Four crew and ten people onstage. Then we pulled into New Brunswick and the guy whose place we were supposed to play, his father had died. He said: "I can't open. My father just died today. I'm sorry, I can't do anything for you." So, that's fourteen people got to be put up and fed and are expecting to get paid, and there's nothing coming in. A number of things like that happened and it just got too expensive and everybody got too tired. We were slogging across the country for not really a lot of money and it just got too much.[482]

With funding structures and institutions that better understood the realities of artists' lives and working conditions, it might have been possible

481 Payne, STAGE Project, 121.
482 Morris, interview.

to avert such barriers, which continue to drive so many artists out of their industries and discourage them from pursuing their passions today.

Individually, artists continued to cope with the gap between their incomes and rising costs. "Could you make a living?" I asked Jane regarding the state of actors in the late 1970s. "Could you make rent and buy groceries?"

"Yeah, but it was tight," she replied. "You had to do all kinds of stuff. If I hadn't been working on different things—not just in the theatre—it would have been more difficult. I was doing a bit of television, a bit of radio, but it was tough because sometimes there was nothing for you."[483] Twenty-two-year-old Jane, who had already been working as a professional actress for the last five years, rented a room at 100 Patrick Street in St. John's in 1976. By mid-1977, she was doing well enough to afford her own little basement apartment downtown. After she and Ron moved in together, they rented a shared house with Kelly Russell and Shifra Zisman for most of 1978.[484]

The effort of trying to be a full-time artist remained difficult and often involved making tough economic choices. In 1976, Don Walsh held a job at the post office.

> It was a situation more than a job because I used to work from five o'clock in the evening until nine o'clock at night. It was perfect because back in those days, the gigs started at nine-thirty. So, I'd go right from the post office to the gig and start playing. Then we could be up drinking, going mad all night long and then I didn't have to be at work until five o'clock the next evening. So, it was a perfect situation.[485]

When the Mummers Troupe approached Don about replacing Ron Hynes for the Newfoundland tour of *What's That Got to Do With the Price of Fish?*, Don was immediately interested and tried to get the time off.

> They [the Mummers Troupe] came to me and they said: "Can you learn all of Ron's songs and do Ron's part in the show?"

483 Dingle, interview.
484 Dingle, interview.
485 Don Walsh, interview.

> I said: "Sure!" I went to the boys at the post office and said: "Boys, I'd like two weeks off. I'd like to do this show," and they wouldn't give me the two weeks off, so I quit. Well, the old man, Jesus . . . You can imagine. You know, I had a government job at the post office, and I *quit* to do a show for two weeks with the Mummers Troupe. But I learned all these great Ron Hynes songs and I sang them all for that show for two weeks. It was a great bit of fun, although I didn't have a job at the post office to go back to, but it was probably the best thing that ever happened to me because otherwise I could've been stuck at the post office for the rest of my life. Not that there's anything wrong with that, but I had some wonderful, fabulous experiences because I *wasn't* working at the post office.[486]

"Would you say that you were able to make a living wage as a regularly working musician during the seventies in St. John's?" I asked him.

"You could pay your rent," Don allowed. "We weren't jet setting it off to Florida for the holidays, but you could get your rent paid if you were living in, you know, a downtown hovel," he remarked wryly.

> I remember myself and Jamie [Snider] had a place out on Portugal Cove Road. I remember the guy that we were renting from—I won't say his name—he owed back taxes or something. So, the sheriff came and put a sticker up on the side of the house and said that we had to pay the rent to the sheriff's office and not to the landlord. So, I followed up with the landlord about it. He said: "Don boy, f--k 'em. Don't give them nothing. Just stay, look after the place for me." So, we had the whole winter in that place with no rent. Plus, the electric company got something screwed up and the electric bill was in the name of Jamie Sidew, or something weird like that, so we didn't pay any electricity and they can't cut you off in the winter.
>
> So yeah, you could make a living, and we did. We survived because there was so much work on the go back then. Seven nights a week, the gigs were always for a week. Even the little

486 Don Walsh, interview.

> pubs would hire you for a week so you got the full seven nights. So, we just worked all over the city basically. All the bars had music going constantly. There were little places like Freddie Michaels and the Cochrane Hotel and Bridgett's, small pubs. There were dozens and dozens of bars all over the city that had live music every night. We were all getting loads of gigs. A lot of these pubs now are not even open on a Monday or Tuesday night and even if they are, there's probably no live music until Thursday, so you might get three or four nights of live music and that's it. I don't know how the hell they make a living now. Whereas back in those days, it was steady.[487]

A Labour Movement Among Artists

During the course of my examination of the St. John's business directories spanning the years 1968 through 1979, I made an interesting observation that speaks volumes about the growth of the labour movement in the province throughout this period. Though St. John's boasted a huge number of bars and pubs relative to its modest population, there were often roughly as many unions and labour organizations with headquarters in St. John's listed in the business directories as there were bars. In 1968, the *Henderson's* directory listed a total of eighteen "cocktail lounges" or "taverns" and an equal number of "professional" or "labour" organizations.[488] The cultural movement of the 1970s happened against a mid-twentieth-century regional political backdrop of strong labour activity in multiple industries including fishing, logging, mining, and skilled trades, as well as among public service employees such as teachers and health care workers.[489] This helped set the stage for a labour movement among artists, many of whom viewed themselves as little different from their fellow workers. Beginning in the mid-1970s, individuals and groups of artists began endeavouring to take their own labour issues and professional conditions in hand personally. In the

---

487 Don Walsh, interview.
488 *Henderson's* (1968), 119–20, 131.
489 Cadigan, 235, 242–44, 250–51, 255–58.

absence of infrastructure or regulatory bodies for their professions that could adapt themselves to the realities of working in the arts in Newfoundland, some artists attempted in various ways to create fairer and more stable working conditions and working relationships.

The Resource Foundation for the Arts, the non-profit entity that functioned as the legal and administrative face of the Mummers Troupe, purchased the LSPU Hall in 1976. Its purpose was creating an exhibition space that would support artists no matter the whims of the Division of Cultural Affairs, which controlled programming at every major regional performance space not belonging to MUN, a local school, or a church.[490] Policies set early on by Brookes and Lunde provided that all workers in theatre productions at the LSPU Hall would be paid a living wage regardless of the nature of their work, whether they were actors, directors, technical artists, ticket-takers, or caretakers. Lunde insisted that they not solicit volunteers—that everyone who worked for the company in any capacity was entitled to a salary.[491] Both CODCO and Newfoundland Travelling Theatre Company had similarly egalitarian internal wage policies as well.[492]

Mindful that few artists could likely afford to pay market rental rates to stage their original work at the Hall, the Mummers allocated ten thousand dollars in annual subsidies from their revenues (which rarely exceeded one hundred forty thousand dollars annually, including box office take, Canada Council funding and private sector funding). Consistent with their vision of moulding and nourishing a downtown cultural centre to support and enrich both the artistic and broader community, the Resource Foundation for the Arts undertook separate fundraising efforts to provide small grants to emerging or experimental local theatre artists with no prospects of receiving funding elsewhere, called the FISH Fund (Fund to Initiate Stage Happenings). Chris Brookes, Andy Jones, and Dudley Cox formed a "mini arts council" to assess applications and allocate funding to independent artists undertaking experimental performance projects.[493] Incidentally, Jane, Kent Barrett, and Beni Malone were the recipients of one of these grants, with which they

490 Brookes, *A Public Nuisance,* 151–53; see Appendix 6.

491 Brookes, *A Public Nuisance,* 44, 153.

492 Cox, interview; Mary Walsh, interview.

493 Brookes, *A Public Nuisance,* 153–4.

wrote and staged *The Madman's Cabaret* at the 1976 Eastport Festival.[494] The LSPU Hall long outlasted the Mummers Troupe, but remains an important legacy of their vision for artists and community.

While Chris Brookes and Alan Filewod ultimately attributed the fall of the company to ongoing funding shortfalls and a fundamental lack of understanding between the company and bureaucratic gatekeepers to the theatre industry, the internal struggles between individual members of the Mummers Troupe also contributed to its fragmentation and decline.[495] "Eventually we had a huge falling out, a group of us, with the Mummers," Donna Butt told me. "It was pretty bitter at the time. There were a lot of internal differences and most of it was around the idea that we thought we were a collective, that we were in it together, and it didn't turn out to be quite the case."[496]

In his memoir, Chris Brookes wondered to what extent the subject matter of the Mummers' plays shaped the interactions between members of the company.[497] Their work was heavily pro-labour and consistently anti-Establishment, yet due to operational and funding exigencies as well as significant clashes of ideology and personality, the company seemed to struggle to avoid replicating the sorts of hierarchical relationships that they, as a group, tended to oppose in general. The Resource Foundation for the Arts was incorporated using vague and seemingly arbitrary conditions for membership on the board of directors, which since its inception had remained a three-member committee of Brookes, Lunde, and Doyle, who never had an official "board of directors meeting" until 1975. As early as 1974, actors who worked with the Mummers Troupe for varying degrees of longevity presented their first "Mummers Manifesto" to Brookes, identifying their professional grievances with management. Brookes's suspicions that in this instance life was imitating art were not far-fetched; the actors who wrote and presented the manifesto had only just completed the Troupe's production of *Buchans: A Mining Town*, during which they had lived in miners bunkhouses and worked directly with miners involved in the local labour dispute to produce the show.[498]

---

494 "Sun Theatre Presents A Madman's Cabaret" (theatrical program) Eastport, July 1–August 15, 1976 (private collection).

495 Brookes, *A Public Nuisance*, 157–62, 170–74; Filewod, "The Mummers Troupe," (1998).

496 Butt, interview.

497 Brookes, *A Public Nuisance*, 159.

498 Brookes, *A Public Nuisance*, 152–53, 157, 159–60; Filewod, "The Mummers Troupe," (1998).

The cast acknowledged that working many long hours for meagre pay throughout the production had been necessary owing to timing and funding constraints. However, they noted, going forward, they wanted to set a standard minimum wage for company members and identified a number of other changes they believed would help the company function as a true collective, administratively as well as creatively. These included separation of the positions of administrator and artistic director (both held at the time by Chris Brookes while Lynn Lunde was completing her graduate studies on the mainland), membership on an executive committee that met regularly, and finally, transparency regarding company finances.[499]

Although their creative sphere had always been a collective one, Brookes was apprehensive about extending that to the Troupe's administrative and governing sphere. Convinced that they had only a few years left to stem the tide of cultural colonialism, he wrote of his fears that the original mission and vision of the company might be compromised if taken over by a board of directors. He also expressed concern that the quality or impact of their plays might suffer should company members always be assured of a part in the latest show and fall into complacency and stagnation.[500] Eventually, Brookes was persuaded to shift the company's administrative model to an executive committee format in which members who had regularly and consistently worked with the Mummers Troupe might have both steady employment with the company and a voice in the committee. Donna Butt and Rhonda Payne joined Brookes and Lunde on the board in 1975.[501]

The Mummers were quite ingenious at fundraising and once they acquired a regular operating budget from Canada Council the same year, everyone's wages at the company increased and enjoyed greater stability. The executive committee model seemed to work moderately well for a while, but the personal and professional disagreements between members, exacerbated as they were by creative differences, financial headaches, and arduous tours, eventually led to a permanent schism.[502] Several of the Troupe's members including Donna Butt, Rick Boland, Maddy Williams,

---

499 Brookes, *A Public Nuisance*, 160; Filewod, "The Mummers Troupe," (1998).

500 Brookes, *A Public Nuisance*, 37–41, 171, 173; Gwyn, 54.

501 Brookes, *A Public Nuisance*, 160–61; Filewod, "The Mummers Troupe," (1998).

502 Brookes, *A Public Nuisance*, 139, 153, 170–82; Filewod, "The Mummers Troupe," (1998); Payne, STAGE Project, 102.

and Wayne McNiven presented another manifesto to Brookes in 1976, detailing their discontent with the company's failure to operate as a collective administratively and their belief that the situation was potentially exploitative. The group broke with the Mummers to form a short-lived company called Community Stage. Butt returned to the Mummers Troupe in 1978 at Brookes's request to join the cast of *They Club Seals Don't They?*, after which she left the organization for good to form Rising Tide Theatre in 1979.[503] Their first production, *Daddy, What's a Train?*, chronicling the demise of the Newfoundland railroad, continued the development of theatre with strong political undertones, marked regional significance, and a distinctly Newfoundland voice. Rising Tide Theatre has maintained that theatrical tradition with their annual theatre season in Trinity, where the company have made their home for more than thirty years.[504]

In 1980, a group of local theatre artists, Andy Jones and Mary Walsh among them, managed to secure ownership and control of the LSPU Hall under an elected, artist-led board in what Walsh called something of a "revolution."[505] By the fall of 1978, it was clear to the chronically underfunded Mummers that they could no longer afford to support the cost of running the Hall and they began to look around for a community group to take it over. Several of the artists who eventually did so had previously worked with the Mummers and shared some of the concerns of former Troupe members, including Brookes's seeming determination to remain artistic director without having to be accountable to a traditional board.[506] There was also concern that despite subsidies, rental rates were still too high for many independent artists interested in staging their work.[507] Finally, there was the Hall itself—the only really viable artistic exhibition venue in St. John's not administered by the Division of Cultural Affairs or the university. Most contentious was the negotiated separation of the Mummers Troupe itself from the legal entity, Resource Foundation for the Arts, which actually owned the LSPU Hall. After a very public and political fight, the Mummers Troupe

---

503 Brookes, *A Public Nuisance*, 180–82, 198, 223; Butt, interview.

504 Butt, interview; Cynthia Martin, "Donna Butt: 'That sense of wanting to belong to something is universal,' *The Globe and Mail*, October 23, 2017. https://www.theglobeandmail.com/report-on-business/careers/management/donna-butt-that-sense-of-wanting-to-belong-to-something-is-universal/article36676794/.

505 Mary Walsh, interview.

506 Brookes, *A Public Nuisance*, 154–55; Filewod, "The Mummers Troupe," (1998).

507 Gulliver, 232.

finally became a separate organization and the artist-led group took over control and ownership of the Hall. The new non-profit became known as the Resource Centre for the Arts.[508] RCA Theatre, like Rising Tide Theatre, continued the development of a distinctly regional theatre tradition focused on Newfoundland life, history, and culture with original productions like *Terras de Bacalhau* and *High Steel*. Like several later Mummers Troupe productions and those of Rising Tide Theatre, RCA Theatre productions continued to nourish a developing nationalism and cultural identity without the immediacy or marked divisiveness of political theatre.[509]

All of these examples highlight the efforts of both individuals and small groups of artists to advocate for themselves and carve out space for better and fairer working conditions in the relative absence of regulatory or supportive infrastructure for the arts. As contentious as the schism among the Mummers Troupe and the battle over the Hall proved to be, there remained a notable solidarity within the arts community nonetheless, which presents itself very clearly across a range of oral history interviews. There may have been bitter disagreements and differences, but in terms of the overarching motivation for the cultural movement as a whole, artists stood shoulder to shoulder.[510]

A United Perspective

Despite being opposed on many other issues, Donna Butt's overall perspective on the cultural movement differs little, if at all, from that of Chris Brookes. Both described similar views on how it developed and similar personal motivations for engaging with it, particularly a desire to oppose economic and cultural colonialism from Britain and Canada. Both spoke of a vast unifying mission across the arts and academia.[511] "There was a desire to create your own voice in your own place," Butt observed. "We all did it in different ways, but I think that was definitely

508 Brookes, *A Public Nuisance*, 154–55; Andy Jones, "LSPU Hall—There's nobody can touch us!" *Showtime* 1, no. 1 (Spring 1981): 2.

509 Mary Walsh, interview; Devine, 117.

510 See Appendices 4 and 5.

511 Brookes, interview; Butt, interview.

at the heart of the so-called Newfoundland renaissance."[512] Brookes and Butt were also in total agreement about the profoundly underdeveloped state of the arts in Newfoundland during the 1970s. Both spoke of a cultural elitism, a prolonged intransigence towards original regional art within the Division of Cultural Affairs, and a conviction that for most of the decade, artists had managed to pioneer a rich regional arts scene in spite of these barriers.[513] The fact that these views were echoed in multiple other interviews shows solidarity across a broad milieu of artists that transcended personal, ideological, or creative differences.[514]

"I'll never tell you everything that went on in the renaissance period, believe me," Donna remarked with a laugh.

> Much of it is better left to history. I don't know how much you know about that time but there were a lot of divisions within the artistic community. Many of us are still here, but we've lost so many people that were so dear to us. I guess as you get older and you go through loss, you begin to really reflect back on what mattered and who we all were. Some of us who were really at loggerheads at the time have come to understand that everybody was making a passionate contribution in a passionate way to what we believed. So, there's been a real respect that has grown amongst us all over time, but it was pretty . . . iffy for a while, for sure. We were young. We had a lot of energy and spirit and passion, and it was in the days when everything was said and done. Political correctness had not been heard of, even thought of, at that point and so everybody wore their heart on their sleeve, and every other emotion. That's the way we were.[515]

Despite the many thorny creative, administrative, financial, or personal issues complicating their relationships, artists continued to pursue their work collectively and as collaboratively as they could. If they could agree on nothing else, they could at least all embrace an overall mission and message of reclamation and change in their art.

---

512 Butt, interview.
513 Brookes, interview; Butt, interview.
514 See Appendices 4 and 5.
515 Butt, interview.

The Red Power Movement

Just as the rising tide of regional labour activity influenced the political and ideological positions of young artists as well as their art during the 1970s, so too did broader international movements including what some revolutionaries and historians have called the Red Power movement. For the purposes of this discussion, we will examine the United States and Canada as representing part of a unified geographic space many Indigenous nations view as the borderless Turtle Island. While governments and academics have traditionally compartmentalized Indigenous issues and policy between the two nations, many groups make no such distinction since the various facets of settler colonialism have affected their communities on both sides of the border in very similar ways.

During the 1960s and 1970s, the continent saw a renewed wave of activism for Indigenous sovereignty, rights, and decolonization. Regional political and development organizations began to advocate for themselves to bring greater attention to concerns shared by a broad majority of communities including the enforcement of historic treaty and land rights, environmental and resource stewardship, and resistance to brutal policies of assimilation.[516] Much of this political resistance took place at the local level, but there were several high-profile organized protest actions throughout the 1960s and 1970s that signalled the beginning of a much more unified pan-Indigenous movement in North America, including the 1969 occupation of Alcatraz Island; the 1972 Trail of Broken Treaties protest, which ended in a two-week occupation of the Bureau of Indian Affairs in Washington, D.C.; the Fish-In Movement in Washington state; and the 1973 armed occupation of Wounded Knee on the Pine Ridge Reservation in South Dakota. The relocation of hundreds of thousands of young Indigenous people from reservations to urban areas as part of the disastrous Termination Policy in the United States and the pervasive impact of the Sixties Scoop, or forcible removal of Indigenous children from their families in Canada to residential schools and White foster families, had unintentionally created conditions both on reservations and in major cities alike for the flourishing of Indigenous nationalism, militancy, and sincere desire and effort to resurrect traditional culture.

---

516 David B. MacDonald and Graham Hudson, "The Genocide Question and Indian Residential Schools in Canada," *Canadian Journal of Political Science* 45, no. 2 (June 2012): 427–49.

Indigenous activists from all over the continent travelled to sites of protest to join the fight.[517] The impact of the movement was amplified in an age of mass media and many young people responded with solidarity, as many did to the movement for Black freedom and civil rights during the same period.

Artists play active roles in articulating shared ideological and cultural positions as well as providing important representation for their communities. During the late 1960s and 1970s, seeing brilliant musicians and songwriters like Robbie Robertson on *The Ed Sullivan Show*,[518] or Buffy Sainte-Marie on Sesame Street,[519] or the hugely popular blues/funk band Redbone on *The Midnight Special* or *American Bandstand* bolstered the visibility of Indigenous peoples and helped amplify the messages of the movement. This kind of exposure can lead not only to cultural revival and reinforced group identity within communities, but may also encourage increased "resistance to external oppression."[520]

Of course, expression of the Red Power movement and Indigenous perspectives in art was happening all over the continent and on a much smaller, more local scale than that implied by the reach of international television programming. Art has always been central to Native cultures. Music is often ceremonial and visual art and storytelling are particularly important means by which Indigenous peoples "have portrayed the land and propagated their history."[521] As early as the mid-1960s, small regional art galleries and museums began to pursue greater collection of contemporary Indigenous art, to hire Indigenous curators, and invite local Indigenous artists to exhibit their work for the community. From the Canadian north to the American southwest, the movement for change

---

517 Donna Hightower Langston, "American Indian Women's Activism in the 1960s and 1970s," *Hypatia* 18, no. 2 (Spring, 2003): 114–119, 122, 125; MacDonald and Hudson, 445–46.

518 Stephen Thomas Erlewine, "15 Essential Robbie Robertson Songs," *LA Times*, August 9, 2023. https://www.latimes.com/entertainment-arts/music/story/2023-08-09/15-essential-robbie-robertson-band-songs.

519 While the recent revelations alleging ethnic fraud by Sainte-Marie have proved deeply troubling and painful, particularly to Indigenous Canadians, Sainte-Marie nonetheless had an enormous impact on awareness of Indigenous issues during the latter half of the twentieth century. (Geoff Leo, Roxanna Woloshyn, and Linda Guerriero, "Who is the real Buffy Sainte-Marie?" *CBC News*, October 27, 2023. https://www.cbc.ca/newsinteractives/features/buffy-sainte-marie).

520 Laura Graham and H. Glenn Penny (eds.), *Performing Indigeneity: Global Histories and Contemporary Experiences* (Lincoln: University of Nebraska Press, 2014): 11–12.

521 Ian C. Hartman, "Violence, Culture and Resistance: New Directions in the Study of Settler Colonialism and Indigeneity," *American Studies* 55, no. 1 (2016): 142.

was amplified as common experiences and goals among numerous nations found expression in the work of painters, sculptors, and other visual artists. While the most prominent national museums and art galleries in North America often still struggle to either integrate Indigenous art without tokenism, or to incorporate Indigenous vision or interpretations into their exhibitions, smaller regional institutions like university galleries, independent galleries, and local museums have played an important role over the last fifty years supporting artists and working with communities towards a decolonization of what have traditionally been highly Westernized institutions, moulded from within a colonial mindset.[522]

That the Red Power movement found expression in Newfoundland art seems inevitable in the context of the revolutionary and countercultural Atlantic world of the 1970s. Newfoundland and Labrador is the traditional homeland of Mi'kmaq, Inuit, and Innu nations, and of the Beothuk, for whose cultural extinction many settler Newfoundlanders have for nearly two centuries carried deeply rooted and highly complex feelings. Conceptions of Indigenous history were shifting in real time during Newfoundland's cultural movement and settler communities were gaining greater awareness of their First Nations and Inuit neighbours. A robust and multi-armed cultural movement was germinating in Labrador just as it was in Newfoundland. Like their counterparts on the island, Labradorians were working with limited to nonexistent funding resources and, largely through their own efforts, were pioneering their own cultural landscape. In 1975, the Labrador Heritage Society and the Old Timers' League established the magazine *Them Days*, to explore and celebrate Labrador's history, culture, and art. Though its editor Doris Saunders had to borrow typewriters from offices that had already closed for the day during the magazine's early days, this publication is still alive and well, and last year released their fiftieth-anniversary issue. Craft studios and artistic associations were formed and organized in Labrador during these hopeful and productive years, oral histories were collected, and local and ancestral knowledge were preserved for future generations.[523]

522 Kathleen Ash-Milby and Ruth B. Phillips, "Inclusivity or Sovereignty? Native American Arts in the Gallery and the Museum since 1992," *Art Journal* 76, no. 2 (Summer 2017): 10–38.

523 Amy Chaulk, "How Them Days Magazine Has Kept Labrador History Alive," *Inuit Art Quarterly* (June 19, 2024), https://www.inuitartfoundation.org/inuit-art-quarterly/iaq-online/how-them-days-magazine-has-kept-labrador-history-alive; Heather Igloliorte, "Back to the Future: What Nunatsiavut Art History Reveals About Inuit Art in the 21st Century," in *Future Possible: An Art History of Newfoundland and Labrador* (Goose Lane Editions, 2021): 56.

As Indigenous-led political and development organizations began to emerge in the province as part of a larger continental groundswell of action, the expression that the Red Power movement found in Newfoundland art helped shift and mould the overall perspective of settler society on Indigenous history, and helped bring attention to contemporary conditions in Indigenous communities. Dudley Cox noted that by the early 1970s, the regional theatre community, both professional and amateur, began to explore repertoire centred on Indigenous life, history, and experience. Cox directed Labrador-born Minnie Aodla in a one-woman show based on her memoirs called *Survival in the South.* He also recalled a growing interest among young aspiring actors at the Provincial High School Drama Festival to explore regional Indigenous stories.[524] Interest in Indigenous experiences continually developed and persisted in Newfoundland art into the following decades. CODCO's television sketches poked fun at bigoted Newfoundlanders who insisted that the Mi'kmaq rather than White settlers were responsible for the demise of the Beothuk.[525] The 1988 film *Finding Mary March* directed by Ken Pittman called upon White settlers to grapple with both their historical and contemporary relationships with Indigenous communities in the province.[526] The 1977 Mummers Troupe production *Silakepat Kissiane* or *Weather Permitting* was rather more immediate as political theatre tends to be, highlighting the challenges then facing Inuit and First Nations groups in three communities in northern Labrador.[527]

Sometime during the last few weeks of 1976, Chris Brookes wrote Jane a letter offering her a part in the upcoming show, which would be researched, written, and staged over a two-to-three-month period in the northern communities of Nain, Makkovik, and Hopedale. It had been Don Snowden, formerly of MUN Extension and the Fogo Process film project who, after researching and writing the most recent Report of the Royal Commission on Labrador for the provincial government, had suggested that the Mummers undertake a political theatre project there. "His viewpoint on it all," Brookes wrote, "is that the most important problem on the coast which the show should bring out is that many of

524 Cox, "Newfoundland Travelling Theatre," 33–4, 46–7.

525 *CODCO*, Series 1, Episode 3: "The Beothucks," CBC Television, 1988.

526 *Finding Mary March*, directed by Ken Pittman, starring Andrée Pelletier, Red Ochre Productions in association with CBC, 1988.

527 Brookes, *A Public Nuisance*, 186–90.

the fifteen-years-ago-resettled Hebron Inuit want to go back up north to their former fishing/hunting grounds and former lifestyle."

> Snowden feels this to be imperative within the next five years. They don't want oil jobs, or saloons, or all that. They want their land to hunt on, not to dig for uranium on. Within the next five years there may be huge resource developments on the coast that will totally change ways of life, and people aren't prepared for that. Also, the outside world isn't prepared to accept that Labradorians are intensely proud of the place, see island Newfoundland as an imperialist power (like we see the mainland) and that they are getting a rotten deal as citizens of the province. The idea of concentrating on the three communities is that the northern coast as an area must focus on their common concerns and face the future as a unit, rather than three separate entities, since the massive changes that are descending on them are common. The cultural changes are not to be underestimated—they are rapidly becoming a people stranded between two lifestyles, two cultures, belonging in neither and all the expected social problems will attend.
>
> It won't be easy, but if we can bring it off it could be an incredible show, which is why I'm really concerned that the people involved with the project be somewhat special—and why I really hope that you'll do it. Jane—I encourage you to do this show. Aside from the fact that I'd really like the opportunity of working together with you, it will certainly be the first time in Canadian theatre for a group to produce a play on and directly about northern life in this way. It's important.[528]

As a people who had witnessed and experienced painful and problematic resettlement policies and resource exploitation from the federal government, settler Newfoundlanders were well positioned intellectually and emotionally at this juncture to see marked similarities between themselves and Labradorians—a frame of mind well suited to a shift in perspective. "I can see where that was the beginning of a lot of those

528 Letter to Jane Dingle from Chris Brookes, December 1976 (private collection).

feelings for us," Andy Jones said in reference to the cultural movement. "We felt we were colonized by Canada and Britain. Of course, now we realize in retrospect that we ourselves were the colonizers of Indigenous people."[529] With a commission from the Labrador Inuit Association and the Labrador Resources Advisory Council, and with their full support and logistical assistance, the cast of *Weather Permitting*, which included Chris Brookes, Jane Dingle, Jeff Pitcher, Judy Parsons, and Terry Rielly boarded a tiny plane for northern Labrador at the end of January 1977. "It was a life-changing experience for all of us," Chris Brookes recalled.

> We went to Army Surplus and got big snow boots and stuff. We got off this little single-engine Otter in Makkovik, and people looked at us like we'd come from the moon. I remember Jane in her puffy snow boots and people were shaking their heads and saying: "No, no, no . . . let me give you a pair of proper sealskin boots. Those things, they're not going to keep you warm." They took us all in . . . idiot White townies, from the south.
>
> None of us had any inkling of what that would be like, you know. I mean, I went to school in Newfoundland, but it's not like now. We didn't learn *anything* about Native people. I knew nothing about Labrador and it was wonderful to see this whole other view of the cosmos, a totally different way of being, of seeing, of understanding. I thought my life would never be the same again after.[530]

Jane likewise spoke of her time in Labrador as both life-changing and eye-opening. The cast stayed in the homes of local families during their time in each of the three communities and travelled either by means of bush plane, snowmobile, or dog-drawn *komatik*.[531]

> We went out to Web's Bay, Jeff Pitcher and I, on *komatik*. I was in the women's *komatik* and Jeff was up front with the man driving. There was one house in Web's Bay. There were

---

529 Jones, interview.
530 Brookes, interview.
531 Brookes, *A Public Nuisance*, 188; Dingle, interview.

> hunters and trappers, but there was nothing else there. No trees, not a single landmark in sight. I said to Jeff: "We're going to get lost. We're never going to be seen again. Holy cow, how do they know where they are?"
>
> We went to the land claims court hearing in Goose Bay and we heard Bill Edmunds, the Inuit representative, speak. We saw the Innu representatives, who were also there for their land claims in northern Labrador and they were militant, led by a guy named Bart Jack. It was really interesting to see the different ways the Native people were expressing themselves and trying to navigate . . . fighting for their land claims. We did research into big oil companies that were doing things up there, and the government that was ripping the people off and putting them on welfare and taking away their hunting and fishing rights. They could only hunt or fish at certain times of year, so it was very political. Inuit people were chucked off at Hebron and told to live in Nain because they wouldn't help them bring medical supplies or anything back to those old sites. The government just said, "Sorry, we're not doing it." They moved them like a ghetto. They put them on welfare and they moved them down to the other side of the community, so you had the Whites and then you had the Native people.
>
> My research was with the Native people and I lived down on the other side of town with a woman named Mary and her husband and kids. They rented a room out to me. I learned a lot from Mary. I was really interested in the whole Moravian mission that was there and the fact that they were taught in Moravian-run schools. Mary had an Inuktitut/English dictionary, and she showed me some words. She said: "We had no word in Inuktitut for this word" and she was upset because the term she was referring to was venereal disease. So, I got to learn about that side of it.[532]

Weather Permitting was a deeply affecting show that, Chris Brookes later reflected, landed differently on different ears. The drama of

532 Dingle, interview.

the production encompassed not only the Indigenous perspective on sovereignty and land rights, but other problems that attended colonization and resettlement as well, including welfare dependency, alcoholism, violence, and the over-policing of Native communities by the RCMP. Those representing the southern White establishment in Labrador, such as law enforcement and education officials, hated the production for what they viewed as its divisiveness, Brookes wrote, while the majority of permanent residents in the three communities, both Indigenous people and White settlers alike, seemed to love it. "They thought we were telling it like it was," Brookes recalled.[533] *Weather Permitting* also did very well in St. John's. As a production that was meant to bridge cultures, the drama was conducted in both English and Inuktitut. Whether the performance was in Labrador or Newfoundland, the cast invariably confronted audience members who only spoke one of the two languages. Since some scenes were delivered entirely in one language or another, the cast had to find creative ways to provide translation. This was largely accomplished with visual symbolism, including the use of puppetry, mime, and string games to illustrate Labradorian cultural and historical perspectives. Moreover, this collectively written piece aptly captured a near-perfect reversal of the exploitative Newfoundland–Labrador relationship in a scene in which the Labrador government, heedless of the protestations of Newfoundlanders, was determined to demolish the entire commercial centre of downtown St. John's to make room for caribou grazing. This particular scene, Brookes observed, translated extremely well to audience members in St. John's when *Weather Permitting* was staged at the LSPU Hall in April of 1977.[534]

Second-Wave Feminism

Another international movement that began to find clearer and more pointed expression in Newfoundland art beginning in the late 1970s was second-wave feminism. As we have observed, the movement for

533 Brookes, *A Public Nuisance*, 186.
534 Brookes, *A Public Nuisance*, 188–90.

women's rights and equality was visible at the grassroots level of the Newfoundland cultural movement, with often just as many women as men entering the arts in various roles, from creating and performing to administration and management. This was not necessarily a remarkable trend since women's roles in Newfoundland settler society—particularly those of working-class women—have traditionally been as important as men's to individual household economy as well as to the fishing industry. As early as the mid-eighteenth century, women had played production roles in the fishery that were every bit as key as those played by their male counterparts.[535] The entrenched cultural notion of a married couple as equal contributors and partners in the broader tradition of a rural industry supported by the labour of both sexes makes the notable participation and leadership of women in the mid-twentieth-century arts movement less remarkable than it might have been elsewhere. This should not suggest, however, that the ideas and reforms of the feminist movement were not being debated, contested, or even ignored in Newfoundland and Labrador, or that the province did not still have a great deal of work to do towards women's liberation and equality.

It was only in 1968 that women in the province first gained the right to file for a no-fault divorce. The following year, Canadian women as a group first gained legal access to reproductive health care including therapeutic abortion and birth control when both were federally decriminalized in 1969.[536] In 1970, the Royal Commission on the Status of Women in Canada released their report, prompting widespread public discussions of discrimination in the areas of women's employment and pay equity, political representation, and personal freedoms. All across Canada, local councils and women's groups formed with a view to overseeing government response to recommendations outlined in the Royal Commission's report, as well as to advocate and lobby for further change. Newfoundland and Labrador was no exception.[537]

After the release of the report in 1970, newly formed women's groups across the province began to organize workshops, events, and

535 Willeen Keough, "'Good Looks Don't Boil the Pot': Irish-Newfoundland Women as Fish (-Producing) Wives," *Signs* 37, no. 3 (Spring 2012): 536–37.

536 Douglas, (2001); Liu and Fisher, 239.

537 Linda Kealey (ed.), *Pursuing Equality: Historical Perspectives on Women in Newfoundland and Labrador* (St. John's: Institute of Social and Economic Research, 1993), 10–11.

campaigns. In consciousness-raising workshops, women explored how their common experiences represented facets of broad and far-reaching patriarchy. Some groups published magazines and other literature exploring contemporary issues through a feminist lens. Annual conferences that brought together many and diverse women's groups from across the province nourished and reinforced a sense of unity over time among women who, despite significant differences in politics, class, culture, and ethnicity, actually had a great deal in common nonetheless. The challenges and concerns of their daily lives and the discrimination they faced were often similar, which helped to bring together women from the conservative, liberal, and radical-left persuasions, rural and urban women, Anglophone and Francophone women, as well as Indigenous and settler women. Despite their differences, they found support and consensus in their common concerns, such as women's and children's education and health, reproductive freedom, domestic and sexual violence, barriers to employment, and childcare for working mothers. Isolation, poverty, and addictions were exceedingly common experiences for rural women that transcended racial, ethnic, and linguistic differences.[538]

In 1970, women in Newfoundland and Labrador could not serve on juries, women were paid roughly two-thirds the wages of their male counterparts for the same jobs, and Memorial University refused to extend permanent employment to women after they married.[539] By 1980, things had changed significantly with the promulgation of a Provincial Advisory Council on the Status of Women and a Women's Policy Office to monitor, conduct research, and advise government on women's issues, reforms, and legislation. More and more women were campaigning for and being elected to public office. Dorothy Wyatt, a former registered nurse and one of only three women from the province to have submitted individual briefs to the Royal Commission on the Status of Women in 1968, was the first woman to become mayor of St. John's, winning election in 1973. With more women in government came reforms and legislation, which began to bring the province closer to a feminist vision of equality.[540]

---

538 Sharon Gray Pope and Jane Burnham, "Change Within and Without: The Modern Women's Movement in Newfoundland and Labrador," in Kealey (ed.), 164, 167–180, 184–85.

539 Pope and Burnham, 167–68.

540 Pope and Burnham, 168, 177.

In 1978, St. John's was a hopeful time and place for the local feminist movement. The struggling St. John's Women's Centre, which had changed location several times since its establishment in 1972, finally found a permanent home at 83 Military Road, where it remained for the next thirty years. The down payment for the property was crowdfunded by twenty of the organization's members, each of whom contributed a small loan of one hundred dollars. The mortgage and renovation costs were covered by, interestingly, two government funding sources that were also key to supporting the local arts movement: the Secretary of State Department and the Local Initiatives Program.[541] The new women's centre hired nine salaried staff and established a 24-hour rape crisis hotline. Despite the frequent public derision they faced as "women's libbers" and the demeaning questions from hostile members of the community asking: "What do you *want* anyway?" women breaking ground during the early feminist movement in Newfoundland and Labrador reported a sense of deep faith and purpose, a conviction that their goals and their rhetoric rang so true and were imbued with such common sense that many believed discrimination could be a thing of the past within a decade.[542] Provincial culture was now well situated for the advent of feminist theatre. In the fall of 1978, *Stars in the Sky Morning* kicked off its Newfoundland tour with a run of performances at the LSPU Hall.[543]

Pam Hall described *Stars in the Sky Morning* as Newfoundland's "first piece of feminist theatre" and she may well be right.[544] In terms of a women's literary tradition prior to the late 1970s, a few women come to mind, such as Cassie Brown or Grace Butt, but neither produced much in the way of literature that might be called feminist. Grace Butt's short play *Mom*, which was staged in the Basement Theatre in 1980 as part of Barbara Barrett's *Faces of Women*, certainly qualifies. Throughout the piece, the title character never speaks, but simply continues to acquiesce to the whiny, petulant, and ridiculous demands of her unruly and ungrateful family members while haltingly trying to eat her breakfast.[545]

541 Pope and Burnham, 172, 175, 181–82, 190; Brookes, A Public Nuisance, 149; Brookes, interview; Filewod, "The Mummers Troupe," (1998).

542 Pope and Burnham, 174–77, 181–82.

543 "Stars in the Sky Morning," Presented by Molly Grub Productions, 1978 (theatrical program).

544 Hall, interview.

545 Annette Clark, "Newfoundland: Downtown Views," *Canadian Theatre Review* (1984): 117.

The works of Margaret Duley produced during the pre-Confederation period are among the few examples of early-to-mid twentieth-century feminist literature.[546] My research has not uncovered a regional play written prior to *Stars in the Sky Morning* that was exclusively written, performed, and directed by women, or that transported the audience into a world inhabited entirely by women with the story filtered through a woman's perspective. The piece was collectively created, starred Rhonda Payne and Jane Dingle, and was directed by Jan Henderson. Payne had written the outline based upon extensive interviews conducted with elderly family members from King's Cove, and she and Dingle developed the final script through character development and improvisation.[547] Whether or not it was the province's first, *Stars in the Sky Morning* is undeniably feminist theatre, featuring deep explorations of the joys and sorrows of the lives of girls and women in early twentieth-century rural Newfoundland. Descriptions of childhood games quickly give way to the pressures of marriage that, in a rural seasonal migrant-worker economy like the cod or seal fishery, meant that women coped alone for significant portions of every year with extreme isolation and long, gruelling daily domestic work under pre-industrial conditions. The almost total lack of birth control information and methods available meant that married women often conceived a child every year while their husbands were home, making each successive year of marriage more difficult as women aged and their burdens grew heavier during the seasonal absence of their husbands. Jillian Keiley noted that *Stars in the Sky Morning* is an expository rather than a plot-driven piece and, as such, "May lend itself more to a wonderful read than performance."[548] Indeed, with only two women playing eight characters there are predicably more than a few monologues throughout. However, as a result, the play also offers a clear and rich glimpse of the lives of female settlers a century ago. "It is as important as a piece of Newfoundland's mostly unwritten women's history," Keiley observed, "as it is an important theatrical work."[549] In subsequent years, numerous other Newfoundland women joined the provincial arts community as single-author playwrights to tell their own stories.

546 Marian Frances White, *The Finest Kind: Voices of Newfoundland and Labrador Women* (St John's: Creative Publishers, 1992), 50–51.

547 "Stars in the Sky Morning," (theatrical program), 1978, private collection; Dingle, interview.

548 Keiley, 133.

549 Keiley, 133.

The feminist movement of the 1970s and 1980s saw women in Newfoundland and Labrador make impressive strides toward equality in a relatively brief span of time, but everyday gender politics and attitudes towards women would take quite some time to catch up. Canadian women went from gaining the legal right to a life-saving abortion in 1969, to gaining the right to end a pregnancy entirely by their own choice by 1988, less than twenty years later.[550] Such relatively rapid change is noteworthy when compared to the nearly century-long suffrage movement in North America between the early nineteenth and early twentieth centuries. Yet, just one year prior to the R. v. Morgentaler case, which secured near-total reproductive freedom for Canadian women, the minister of social services for Newfoundland and Labrador demonstrated that a great many people continued to nurture sexist and patriarchal attitudes quite blithely despite the changes taking place around them. The minister responded publicly to a question about the government's pledge to increase the provision of daycare services, saying that "the province needed more conscientious mothers to sacrifice their careers and stay home to take care of their children," not expanded daycare programs. If more women did so, he added, perhaps there would be "fewer (juveniles) in correction institutions."[551] It would indeed take far longer than a decade to even begin to unravel a patriarchal political and social structure that feminists increasingly began to recognize as systemic. Even the most progressive institutions and entities of the time could not avoid replicating patriarchal structures and attitudes within the scope of their operations or the communities they served.

Linda Cullum, Margaret Davis, and Laura Jackson spoke about their experiences as some of the very few women to serve as MUN Extension field agents during the 1960s and 1970s. Cullum observed that while the predominantly male administrators of Extension were highly progressive regarding class issues and analysis, they were very "conservative and sometimes hostile" when it came to confronting gender inequality or women's issues.[552] In fact, the hiring of individual women Extension agents was so uncommon that both Davis and

---

550 Liu and Fisher, 239; R. v. Morgentaler, 1988 (SCC), 1 SCR 30. https://www.canlii.org/en/ca/scc/doc/1988/1988canlii90/1988canlii90.html.

551 Pope and Burnham, 216.

552 Webb, "The Rise and Fall of Memorial University's Extension Service," 95–6.

Jackson were hired alongside their respective husbands as teams. In 1974, when Jackson sought to persuade Extension administrators to allow her to work specifically with the women in her upcoming posting in the Labrador Straits, Davis warned her to "be prepared for a rough ride 'cause they [the men who run Extension] don't like to hire women, they don't see the need. They see the traditional community, the traditional power structure, and they are not thinking outside that box." Anticipating a battle, Jackson researched the area extensively prior to her pitch, and in true Extension fashion, identified needs and issues about which women in that community were concerned including farming efficiency, nutrition, childcare, and handicraft production. Her pitch was approved and while her husband focused on the "bread and butter" concerns of the local fishery, Jackson was able to respond directly to the needs of the community's women by running educational workshops and helping to set up childcare centres.[553] With so few women Extension agents however, many women's problems and concerns may have gone significantly overlooked as part of the province's rural development agenda.

Mary Barry reflected during her interview that, while women in the province have come a long way since the 1970s, the process of unravelling traditional gender politics on the smaller scale of families and communities is, in her view, still underway.

> My mom was a librarian. She worked at the Arts and Culture Centre, and every single person that worked at the library was British. They would make sixty thousand a year. Mom made forty dollars a week and that's because she was local. We're talking maybe sixty years ago. She was at the mercy of colonialism—and sexism because she was a woman and a widow. Do you know how they treated women who were widows back then? You were ostracized because you might steal someone's husband. And do you know that that's still true in some places out around the bay? If a bachelor on his own moves into a community, every Sunday he'd have not one but two Sunday dinners delivered to his door. Everybody would take care of him because he's a bachelor, right? If a single

553 Webb, "The Rise and Fall of Memorial University's Extension Service," 96–7.

> woman shows up . . . not necessarily like a single mother, but someone who doesn't have a husband or a partner, I'd say they usually last about eight months. They're a threat to the community because they may steal someone's husband. That's the truth.
>
> I'm talking about gender politics and only a woman who's a feminist would notice things like this. I've been to five or six turkey dinners and honestly, the women spend eight hours preparing this dinner—and it's perfect. You know those people that make food, and it's perfect? Well, I'm not one of them, at all, but every woman around the bay, they all have the most perfect food and the perfect lemon meringue pie or whatever, but it's because they've spent forty years developing it. They spend eight hours as a team getting it all ready. Well, guess what happens after it's all eaten? They all clean up! And the boys, they all go out into the living room and drink. Excuse me? F--k off![554]

Pam Hall recalled what it was like to operate in an arts community that was exceptionally attuned to some progressive ideas but often deaf to others. "They were not a widely feminist crowd . . . is the way I could say it politely, with some lovingness and also some bite to it," she remarked. "Nobody was wildly feminist in the seventies. And we weren't even really using the word that much in those days. We were just struggling, just trying to get a gig, you know?"[555]

Hall makes an important point here. Subsequent generations of women, myself included, have been able to readily and publicly identify as feminists without much fear of any cultural baggage hanging from the label, but I imagine that the women who were part of feminism's second wave might have encountered more scrutiny or hostility for such self-identification. In a 1984 interview for the *Canadian Theatre Review*, Mary Walsh was the only one out of four pioneering women theatre artists that readily self-identified as a feminist. Grace Butt said she was interested in the advancement of women, but was not an "activist"

554 Barry, interview.
555 Hall, interview.

because it interfered with artistic "objectivity." Donna Butt described herself as deeply political, an independent woman and an "individualist," but not a feminist. Jane replied to the question with what seemed in print to be admirable evasiveness: "What *is* a feminist?"[556] "I was just being snarky," she told me when I asked her about it later. "I meant: 'Of course I'm a feminist!'"

That women as a group have come a long way towards equality since the 1970s is undeniable and perhaps one of the reasons for it concerns timing. The feminist movement germinated within an historical context that included the civil rights, Indigenous rights, and gay liberation movements, in the context of which earlier struggles helped pave the way for subsequent ones. The rhetoric of liberation, of decolonization, of equality and fair treatment crosses all boundaries of identity. Indeed, I think it would be difficult to imagine the feminist or gay liberation movements unfolding how and when they did without the earlier context of the movement for Black freedom and civil rights or the movement for Indigenous rights and sovereignty. Hall expressed the notion very well when describing how the predominantly White, male literary community in 1970s Newfoundland seemed to unintentionally create an environment in which other groups could begin to have their voices heard also.

> There is a through line . . . that sits upon the principle of autonomous voice in place: "We'll tell our stories." That is a strange thing for a White settler to say about a bunch of other White settlers, most of whom were men, most of whom just wanted to publish each other. It was about making space for *them*. This was the group that claimed Newfoundland for themselves: "*My* seven generations of ancestors." Never occurred to them that a Mi'kmaq person out in Grand Falls might think differently. These guys were kind of progressive in some ways and not so progressive in others.
>
> I think one of the things that they *did* inadvertently create is this commitment to an impulse to favour authentic voice and authentic, "in-placed," connected voice, which of course,

556 Clark, "Downtown Views," 118.

> makes a fabulous foundation to support Indigenous writers, filmmakers, and dancers, people of colour, and queer and trans people . . . All these others are building on a foundation which was made by a bunch of privileged white guys who felt they were not being well enough served by the large colonial cultural infrastructure of the country. They were doing it for themselves and their own generation, just as the women, the feminists, are doing it for other feminists, and just as Indigenous folks are not really worried about you publishing or me publishing. They're working towards carving out a space for them to publish. So, it may have been inadvertent, but I think that's healthy and inevitable and entirely appropriate.[557]

I observed to Pam that her description brought to mind a series of nested dolls, with each layer of decolonization and liberation peeling back to reveal another, which it had previously obscured.

The Atlantic world saw momentous social and political change between the mid-1960s and the mid-1980s and it had an enormous impact on art and culture. Strongly influenced by the changes taking place around them, artists of all disciplines explored and reflected these in their art. Whether in the form of literature, film, visual art, music, or theatre, artists of the period helped define and articulate a new public dialogue and shifted their own community's sense of itself. Artists in Newfoundland and Labrador played an important role in facilitating public discussion and shifting perspectives concerning feminism, Indigenous history, rights and sovereignty, and the movement for organized labour throughout the study period.

Jane and Ron

The fall and winter of 1978/79 was full of promise. For Ron and Jane, career life seemed to be on an upswing. Ron was elated that the *WGB* television show was about to be launched. Jane had been working on a

557 Hall, interview.

steady stream of projects including *Stars in the Sky Morning* and a guest spot alongside Ron on the CBC's *Come All Ye*. Andy Jones cast her in the film *The Adventures of Faustus Bidgood* and she shot scenes throughout the fall and winter. She also had another television guest spot lined up in the new year for the CBC's *Up At Ours*.[558] Suffice it to say, work seemed plentiful and both Jane and Ron were doing better financially than they ever had. They had a beautiful apartment on the top floor of a converted and renovated house on Old Topsail Road. They began to talk about marriage and children.

> I remember your Dad saying: "We have everything we want. We really love each other. We're doing well in our careers. Why don't we get married and have a baby?" And we *were* in a great place. He was writing songs like crazy, I was doing show after show, we lived in a gorgeous apartment and I kept thinking to myself: "I can't believe everything is so wonderful. Maybe it *is* time to have kids." It seemed to make sense all of a sudden.[559]

Ron and Jane were married at St. John's City Hall on April 12, 1979. Jane's sister Midge and her husband Paul Blackwood accompanied them as their witnesses and Paul took all of their wedding photos. Jane wore a tea-length pink silk dress and Ron wore a suit with a ruffled collar the likes of which could never have been worn unironically after 1983. Mayor Dorothy Wyatt performed the ceremony and afterwards gifted the couple with a flowering plant and a pen emblazoned "St. John's City Hall."

"Ron loved that!" Jane recalled, "That Dot Wyatt was marrying us. She was a real character."[560]

---

558 Dingle, interview; "Profile: Actress Jane Dingle keeps active with stage, film, television work," *The Newfoundland Herald TV Week*, November 1, 1978, 5.

559 Dingle, interview (private collection).

560 Dingle, interview (private collection).

Ron and Jane, April 12, 1979.[561]

561 Photo by Paul Blackwood.

> We went back to Mom and Dad's afterward for a reception with just the family. Mom took a cake out of the freezer that she had put down for Christmas—they always made extra ones in Britain. She decorated it with pink flowers and stuff, and that was our wedding cake. Mom had a huge spread up at the house for everybody, a buffet. She had everything decorated and Dad had tons of champagne. And that was our wedding. It was a funny ceremony, but we were really happy.[562]

Peckford, Nationalism, and the "Renaissance" Bandwagon

Just a few weeks before Ron and Jane married, Brian Peckford became Newfoundland and Labrador's third premier. Peckford carried forward various perspectives and convictions that had featured prominently among the rhetoric of the cultural movement and amplified them by connecting them to his own political platform. "The government of Newfoundland were not very sympathetic at all until Peckford," Andy Jones recalled. "Peckford saw the Quebec model and knew: 'Hey, our culture is going to get us a sense of ourselves and then we can fight—when we need to fight Ottawa to get what we want.'"[563]

Chris Brookes also appreciated Peckford's interest in building up the arts and culture industry in Newfoundland. Following the national success and acclaim of *They Club Seals, Don't They?*, Brookes wrote and distributed a pamphlet to all of the province's Members of the House of Assembly, urging them to reform administration of the arts and address the poverty of artists. He pointed out that theatre companies in other provinces received roughly a third of their funding from provincial sources while their own province provided nothing to its artists, leaving them constantly struggling. Newfoundland actors, Brookes explained, had worked extremely hard writing, rehearsing, and touring a play that defended the sealing industry, one of great value to the provincial government, and they had significantly shifted public opinion across the

562 Dingle, interview.
563 Jones, interview.

country. Brookes pointed out the irony that the actors in the show (and in the province generally) actually made significantly less income than the sealers they were defending. Seal hunters at the time supported themselves and their families on an average annual wage of seventy-five hundred dollars, well below the national poverty level. Seal hunters don't ply their trade "for fun," Brookes wrote, and neither do actors. They have to support their families and pay the bills just like any other workers. He warned that if this situation remained unchanged, talent would continue to trickle steadily out of the province to the mainland, where artists stood a better chance of making a living. The only MHA who seemed at all interested in Brookes's pamphlet, he recalled, was Brian Peckford.[564]

Scholars and other commentators have expressed varying perspectives in their analysis and judgment of Peckford's historical legacy of cultural nationalism—and no small amount of ambivalence. MUN English professor Ronald Rompkey credited Peckford with being the first Premier "to openly embrace the arts as an expression of the provincial culture,"[565] and Roger Bill observed that Peckford used his political power to reorganize government departments and specifically prioritize provincial funding of the arts.[566] Peckford's government instituted the Department of Tourism, Recreation and Culture, commissioned artist Christopher Pratt to design the province's first official flag, established the Heritage Foundation of Newfoundland and Labrador and the long-awaited Newfoundland and Labrador Arts Council (NLAC).[567] However, both Rompkey and Bill identified problems with Peckford's approach and wrote critically about the manner in which arts initiatives were prioritized.

The Peckford government seemed to see no problem with funding celebrations of historical milestones that bolstered the association of art and culture with tourism—and thus with capital. Yet, in 1983, they "deflected a proposal for a cultural and educational broadcasting authority on the model of Radio-Québec and TV Ontario," a resource that could have provided provincial communities—many of which remained geographically isolated—with an immense public educational resource accessible to anyone with a television. According to Rompkey,

564 Brookes, *A Public Nuisance*, 207–209.

565 Rompkey, 272.

566 Bill, 98.

567 Rompkey, 274; Bill, 98.

Peckford began a policy tradition that "entrenched Newfoundland arts and culture in an industrial model," a tradition that would continue into the 1990s and 2000s regardless of changes in the province's political regime.[568] Bill's assessment of the NLAC identified several shortcomings despite his assertion of its overall importance, including the fact that while artists would have some influence, it would not be an artist-run board. Further, the board was seemingly given some independence from government, yet continued to face what Ken Pittman, the council's first full-time Executive Director, called "paternalistic" conditions that impeded artists' attempts to help shape cultural policy. The province's long-time top cultural bureaucrat, John Perlin, had been appointed to the newly created NLAC board and had been given "signing authority on the Council's bank account." Perlin later insisted that despite his position and function on the board, he "certainly was not controlling the Council," but Pittman recalled that "when the NLAC made recommendations to government they landed on John Perlin's desk."[569]

The advent of the NLAC meant that regional artists and artistic companies finally had a funding structure comparable to those elsewhere in Canada, with support from not only the Canada Council and whatever private sector funding they could raise, but also from their home province. However, some artists took issue with levels of funding offered and choices around how funding was allocated. Additionally, artists charged that government budgets continued to allocate the lion's share of provincial arts funding to the Arts and Culture Centres, institutions that still had a reputation for favouring "culture with a capital C" over original regional art.[570]

Musicians, as well as theatre artists, now began to organize as well. In the spring of 1981, Wayne Hynes, Don Wherry, Glen Tilley, Johnny Barela, Peter Gardner, and Terry Rielly formed the executive board for the Newfoundland and Labrador Musicians Association to provide a "united voice" for musicians to negotiate wages, group insurance, and contracts.[571]

In 1987, a broad coalition of artists met in Gander to discuss the formation of a body to represent their interests to government.

568 Rompkey, 274.
569 Bill, 98–9.
570 Bill, 99–100.
571 Terry Rielly, "Musical Notes," *Showtime* 1, no. 1, Spring 1981.

Anita Best made a strong oration on behalf of her fellows, criticizing the government's funding and handling of the NLAC and insisting that the Council's board be controlled by artists. In any other profession, Best asserted, common sense dictates that representative positions on a council board would be filled by members of that profession. The group would go on to found the Artists Coalition of Newfoundland, yet another example of the grassroots action of individuals and small groups to address their own issues and challenges in the absence of sufficient institutional or government support.[572] "I've always been a committee person," Anita remarked. "I always took a leaf from Edythe's book that somebody has to turn up at the meetings, otherwise nobody knows what going on."[573]

Sociologist and MUN professor James Overton, writing during the last year of Peckford's term, was far more critical of the premier than Rompkey or Bill later proved to be and his wariness of some of Peckford's initiatives and rhetoric was clearly expressed. According to Overton, the intellectual linchpin of the so-called Newfoundland renaissance was criticism of "mass civilization and urban industrial society" from the vantage point of "culture and tradition." While Newfoundland culture itself had often traditionally been viewed as the very culprit in the region's continued underdevelopment—something to be conquered by means of training or education—Peckford's perspective offered a more positive spin. The "rugged individualism," "independence," "self-reliance," and neighbourly communitarian qualities of outports were now touted as economically and socially ideal. Newfoundlanders armed with these attributes, Peckford argued, would make excellent oil entrepreneurs. The recommendations in the 1986 report of the Royal Commission on Employment and Unemployment encouraged rural Newfoundlanders to pursue "do-it-yourself" job creation strategies and "production for use" in such traditional rural occupations as fishing, hunting, or carpentry. Overton observed that such recommendations seemed typical coming from a Conservative political platform in which social spending and government responsibility for job creation are often first on the chopping block.[574]

572 Bill, 99–100.
573 Best, interview.
574 Overton, "A Newfoundland Culture?" 13–14, 18–19.

Economic and social elites, Overton further charged, often capture the spirit of grassroots cultural or nationalist movements, channelling them into reforms that ultimately suit broader political or economic goals, and sometimes discarding elements that do not, such as the encouragement of labour unionization, environmental stewardship, or reforms that expand democracy. In "capturing the cultural question for the Conservatives," Peckford managed to unite a broad swathe of the province despite the exceptional political diversity among Newfoundlanders and Labradorians at the time. Overton is one of few scholars to point out how deeply the resurgence of Conservative politics in Newfoundland and Labrador during the 1970s was intertwined with the cultural movement. A decades-long dynasty of Liberal politics in Newfoundland and Labrador had died particularly hard when Joey Smallwood was voted out in 1971, and the ensuing cultural nationalist movement had encompassed "many deeply conservative assumptions" even among those who were largely progressively minded or openly left wing. In Overton's view, Peckford adopted a dialogue that posited the existence of a "natural" cultural community in the province, a political community of folk who would be a stopgap against encroaching change. When a leader comes to be seen as "unproblematically representing" the will of a political and cultural community, Overton warned, that "more critical perspectives may get lost."[575]

Historian Jerry Bannister concurred with Overton regarding the tendency of elites to co-opt nationalist movements, pointing out that the middle and upper classes representing local business and finance interests had been instrumental in bringing the movement for responsible government to fruition during the first half of the nineteenth century.[576] Moreover, the intellectual premise of this movement was not so different from that of the 1970s cultural movement, both of which stressed an ongoing history of exterior or foreign control. Labelled the "conflict thesis" by historian Keith Matthews, who wrote the first real challenge to prevailing Newfoundland historiography during the mid-1970s,[577] this historical perspective has its origins in the late eighteenth-century writings of John Reeves, Newfoundland's first

575 Overton, "A Newfoundland Culture?" 16–18.

576 Jerry Bannister, "Making History: Cultural Memory in Twentieth-Century Newfoundland," *Newfoundland and Labrador Studies* 18, no. 2 (2002): 148.

577 Keith Matthews, "Historical Fence Building," *The Newfoundland Quarterly* 9, no. 3 (1978): 21–30.

Chief Justice. It was Reeves's contention that since the seventeenth century, fishing merchants and imperial elites had purposely and continuously sought to inhibit both permanent settlement and local control of the fishery. This rhetoric served middle-class reformers well during the early nineteenth-century campaign for a self-governing colonial legislature, but in reality their election did very little to reduce the pervasiveness and tyranny of a credit/truck system that was the primary means by which most settler Newfoundlanders experienced economic and social domination, a system that persisted into the early twentieth century.[578] By the end of the nineteenth century, the conflict thesis was still alive, well and prominently featured in D.W. Prowse's *History of Newfoundland*, undoubtedly still one of the most popular and widely read works on the subject. Prowse's book looked back to a familiar history of colonial domination but also looked hopefully forward with a Whiggish conviction that, with the continued development of civilization and industry, life in Newfoundland would only improve. Prowse's perspective strongly influenced that of Joey Smallwood who, like Prowse, saw Newfoundland's climb toward prosperity as inextricably tied to nation building in the modern, industrial model. By the mid-1960s, the wisdom of this modernist approach was being openly questioned, but the core of the conflict thesis remained. Distilled down to its most simplistic form, the intellectual premise of the conflict thesis states that it is foreign colonial influence—British, Canadian, or American—that has always kept Newfoundlanders and Labradorians from enjoying full control of their own political and economic fate. Without such domination, their innately hardworking nature and rich resource wealth would certainly have ensured their prosperity as an independent nation—a historical notion, Bannister notes, which is still open to question.[579]

Whether or not the conflict thesis has real historical merit ultimately matters little for the broadest part of the community in the province. The premise of the conflict thesis contributed to a unifying effect that helped galvanize much of the activity during the cultural movement and continued to do so throughout the remainder of the twentieth century. It has provided a key piece of scaffolding in the construction of a modern cultural identity—one largely articulated by

578 Cadigan, 108–109, 119, 142, 152.

579 Bannister, "Making History," 176–180, 182.

artists. The conflict thesis is also a key element in a larger process of decolonization that may grow or continue to decline in prevalence or intensity in the future depending on both regional and national economic or social conditions. Still, Bannister warns, the motives of elites ought to be "critically evaluated" for the ways in which they serve political and economic expediency, especially when they champion nationalism as Peckford and other leaders have done since jumping on the bandwagon of the cultural movement. "Historians," Bannister observed, "tend to be wary of the notions of truth and certainty."[580] And yet, the basis for Newfoundland nationalism "is a view of the past rooted in historical certainty." Any nationalist will be utterly convinced that their version of history is correct. Moreover, despite the unifying effects of nationalism, sustaining a cohesive political coalition "has necessarily entailed the masking of social cleavages," such as race, ethnicity, gender, and social class.[581]

Bannister's line of argument does not suggest that the culture of grievance that has long existed in Newfoundland and Labrador has no foundation. On the contrary, where such a culture exists, it usually signals legitimate grievances long unaddressed. But beyond this, there is something of a dissonance between the values and convictions expressed in the art produced during the cultural movement, and the manner in which that rhetoric was carried forward and employed by Peckford and subsequent political leaders both Liberal and Conservative. Many of the young artists in the vanguard of the cultural movement leaned toward anti-modernism and quite baldly questioned industrialism and corporate capitalism. Peckford's conception of Newfoundland nationalism embraced the conflict thesis and championed greater regional autonomy, just as the broader cultural movement did, but neither he nor any premier since has seemed to perceive any moral issue with the commodification of Newfoundland's culture or natural environment to benefit the resources, tourism, or entertainment sectors. The particular brand of rhetoric critical of such things, once so visible during the cultural movement, seemed to fall by the wayside once Establishment politics began to pick up the message and run with it. Consider this refrain from CODCO's 1974 production, *Cod on a Stick*.

---

580 Bannister, "Making History," 185.
581 Bannister, "Making History," 186.

Wild cod lie dead in the ocean,
The wild cod lie dead in the sea,
They all died of water pollution,
Caused by the oil companies.[582]

Peckford neatly incorporated into his platform the broad discontent with Canada's exploitation of Newfoundland and Labrador's resource wealth as well as the underlying conviction that the region's long history of economic hardship could finally be overcome if Newfoundlanders and Labradorians themselves had control of their own resources and economic affairs. With the discovery of the Hibernia oil reserves by the end of the 1970s, the oil industry seemed poised to become a major marker of coming prosperity and the anti-industrial message of environmental stewardship seemed to recede into the background—but not before the Mummers Troupe had one last word on the matter with their 1979 production, *Some Slick*.

A unique piece of theatre, *Some Slick* more closely resembled a cabaret or rock opera than a musical, with the drama presented almost entirely through music with very brief dramatic interludes. It was collectively written and starred Paul Steffler, Mac Furlong, Brian Downey, and Denis Parker, who together formed an excellent blues/rock combo. Director Chris Brookes envisioned the show as a production that could play exclusively in bars. He hoped to reach a target audience of working-class people in the province, those who thought conventional theatre was stuffy but would be more likely to appreciate a rock 'n' roll show with a few beers. This was the audience whose livelihoods and communities would likely be most affected by the building of new oil infrastructure, the quality of new industry jobs, and potentially, by any environmental disaster that might result from the pursuit of oil.

Ultimately, *Some Slick* sought to urge people in the province not to—as Andy Jones put it—"give everything away." It was the people of Newfoundland and Labrador, Brookes wrote, who should have the final say on whether or not these resources should be developed and who should also control the manner and pace of development, not oil companies or international investors. Ironically, both the Newfoundland

582 Peters (ed.), 55.

tour and Canadian tour of *Some Slick* were heavily financed by Petro Canada. The offer—the largest private sector grant any Newfoundland arts organization had ever received up until that point—gave Brookes significant pause, but the fact that Canada Council had cut off the Mummers' funding as a result of this latest production forced his hand toward acceptance and his mind toward rationalization. Brookes comforted himself, he wrote, with the thought that at least Petro Canada's interest in the show was based on a nationalist notion of resource control by Canadian companies and authorities. Anyway, he further rationalized, government regulations compelled oil companies to contribute a certain amount of annual funding toward education or development initiatives.

Some Slick played to sold out crowds when it opened at the LSPU Hall in April 1979, for which the Hall was turned into a beerhall during the run of the show. Both the Newfoundland and Canadian tours were very successful and, in 1980, the local CTV affiliate shot and aired a ninety-minute special of the show adapted for television. *Some Slick* stimulated significant public dialogue on the burgeoning oil industry throughout the province. Still, the part that seemed to resonate most with the Peckford government was the question of control and ownership for Newfoundlanders—for exactly *which* Newfoundlanders was less clear to Brookes.[583]

Like the environmental message, the deeply pro-labour stance of those in the vanguard of the cultural movement did not quite translate into the Peckford government's initiatives on behalf of the arts community. In terms of economic stability, artists fared marginally better throughout most of the 1980s, but the initiatives of the Peckford government were hardly a panacea for all of the challenges facing them. It is very telling that by the end of Peckford's term, the official report on the condition of the provincial arts community still found it necessary to state quite baldly: "The arts are not a frill." Tax money to fund the arts was "no more a 'subsidy'" than that contributed to the provincial "fishery, agriculture, mining, forestry, post-secondary education, and offshore oil." Why, questioned the artists who contributed to the report, should they be considered less worthy of security and a decent living? It is equally revealing that the report went on to advocate heightened

583 Brookes, *A Public Nuisance*, 214–18.

investment in the arts on the grounds of its economic value. Patrick O'Flaherty, Donna Butt, and many, many others who contributed to this report clearly understood that emphasizing economic value was the only way to convince bureaucracies to regularly fund the arts and to cease forcing artists into poverty, thereby inducing them either to abandon their careers or betray their own artistic vision in order to obtain support.[584] Artists have arrived at a complex and seemingly irresolvable impasse with the entity and force that is capitalism. We are all enmeshed in social and economic systems in which we can still appreciate the human, cultural, and community significance of art, yet we simultaneously and blithely admit that it is a product to be sold, and often without much thought for the well-being or protection of the artist as a worker or producer like any other.

Despite this uncomfortable dissonance, this nagging sense of a revolution incomplete, it is undeniable that arts infrastructure and education in Newfoundland and Labrador saw slow but steady improvement ever since Peckford's advent as Premier and the creation, soon thereafter, of the long-sought-after Newfoundland and Labrador Arts Council. Today, schools of art, music, theatre, and film are now much more familiar institutions in a province that only fifty years ago did not even have the educational resources to train visual art teachers for middle schools and high schools.[585] Today, nine voting members of the province's arts community sit on the board of what is now known as ArtsNL, which also features a single, non-voting government appointee. At the time of this writing, an annual budget allocation of five million dollars supports numerous artists and companies across Newfoundland and Labrador.[586]

---

584 Drawing Conclusions: The Report of the Provincial Arts Policy Committee, St. John's: Department of Municipal and Provincial Affairs, 1990, quoted in Rompkey, 275.

585 Hall, interview; see Appendix 6.

586 Independent Appointments Commission of Newfoundland and Labrador, Newfoundland and Labrador Arts Council, Department of Tourism, Culture, Arts and Recreation. https://www.exec-abc.gov.nl.ca/public/agency/detail/?id=566&; "Release: ArtsNL announces temporary changes to Professional Project Grants Program funding for fall 2023," ArtsNL: Newfoundland and Labrador Arts Council, September 13, 2023. https://artsnl.ca/release-artsnl-announces-temporary-changes-to-professional-project-grants-program-funding-for-fall-2023/.

Jane and Ron

1982 brought something of a professional hiatus for Jane and Ron, as well as for the larger community of artists surrounding them. The *WGB* television show had been cancelled, though episodes continued to air on the CBC into 1983. Ron returned to touring and gigging for a few hundred bucks a night at best, which did not go very far when travel and accommodations were factored in.

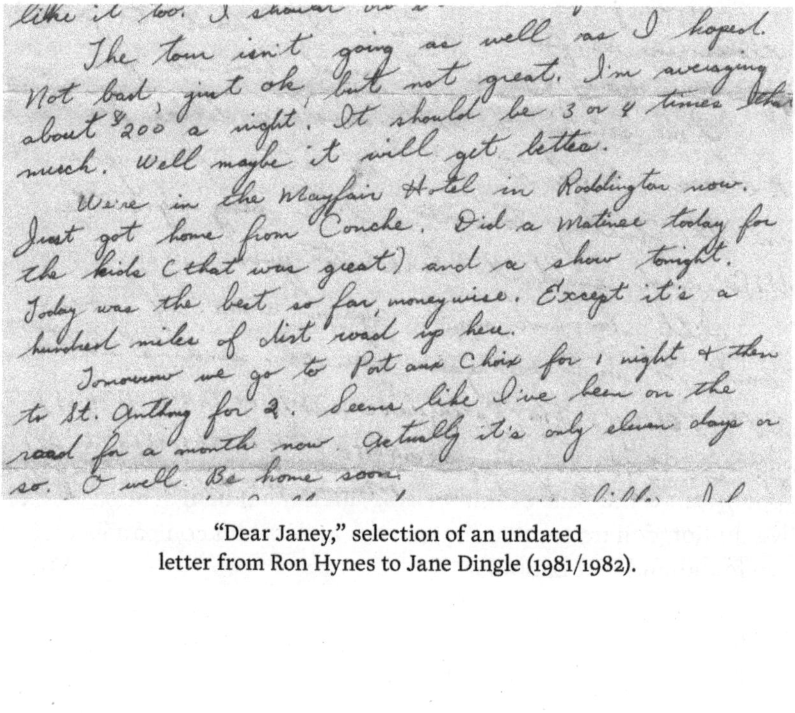

like it too. I

The tour isn't going as well as I hoped.
Not bad, just ok, but not great. I'm averaging
about $200 a night. It should be 3 or 4 times that
much. Well maybe it will get better.

We're in the Mayfair Hotel in Roddington now.
Just got home from Conche. Did a matinee today for
the kids (that was great) and a show tonight.
Today was the best so far, moneywise. Except it's a
hundred miles of dirt road up here.

Tomorrow we go to Port aux Choix for 1 night & then
to St. Anthony for 2. Seems like I've been on the
road for a month now. Actually it's only eleven days or
so. O well. Be home soon.

"Dear Janey," selection of an undated
letter from Ron Hynes to Jane Dingle (1981/1982).

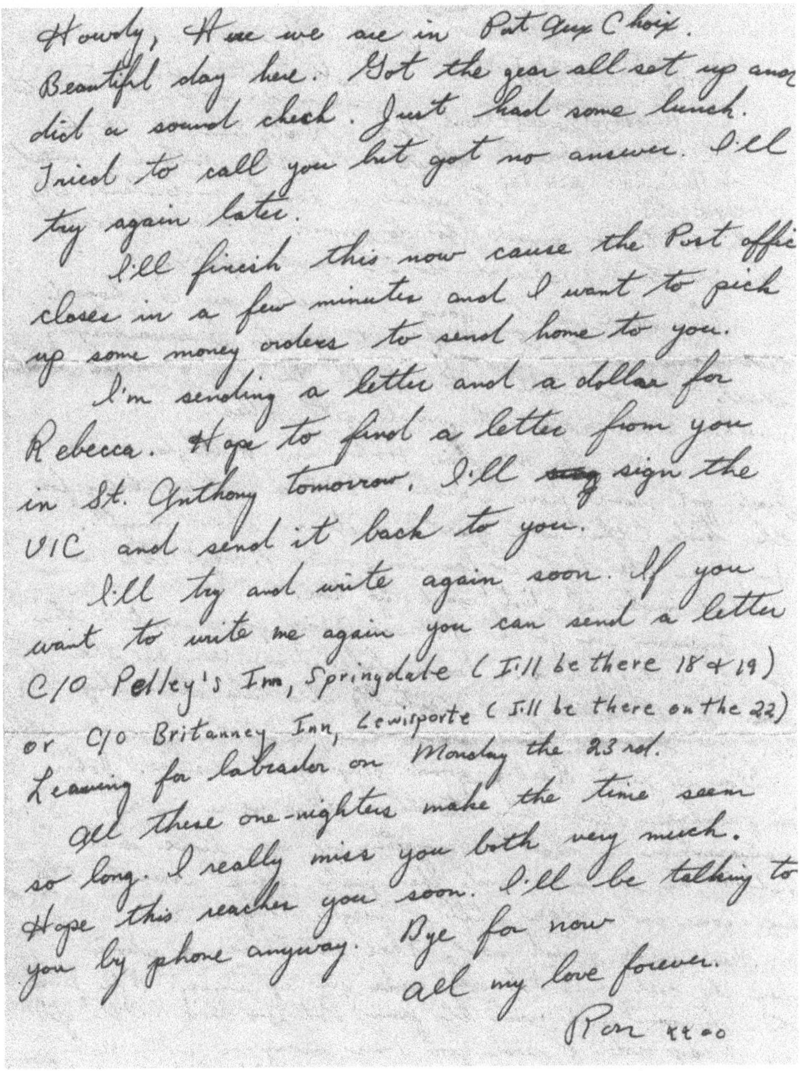

Howdy, Here we are in Port Aux Choix.
Beautiful day here. Got the gear all set up and
did a sound check. Just had some lunch.
Tried to call you but got no answer. I'll
try again later.
I'll finish this now cause the Post offic
closes in a few minutes and I want to pick
up some money orders to send home to you.
I'm sending a letter and a dollar for
Rebecca. Hope to find a letter from you
in St. Anthony tomorrow. I'll ~~say~~ sign the
UIC and send it back to you.
I'll try and write again soon. If you
want to write me again you can send a letter
C/O Pelley's Inn, Springdale (I'll be there 18 & 19)
or C/O Britanney Inn, Lewisporte (I'll be there on the 22)
Leaving for labrador on Monday the 23rd.
All these one-nighters make the time seem
so long. I really miss you both very much.
Hope this reaches you soon. I'll be talking to
you by phone anyway. Bye for now
All my love forever.
Ron xxoo

"Dear Janey," selections of an undated letter from Ron Hynes to Jane Dingle (1981/1982).[587]

587 Private collection.

Jane had given birth to two children during the previous three-year period, returning to work within weeks of each delivery. In fact, she rehearsed for and appeared in *Stars in the Sky Morning* while she was pregnant with my sister Rebecca.[588] Unfortunately, the theatre scene in St. John's seemed somewhat stalled in 1982 and Jane was cast in fewer shows over the next three years. These financial problems exacerbated other marital struggles, and Jane and Ron finally separated in the early spring of 1983.

> I don't want to paint a picture that he didn't care. He did. He loved you so much. He loved Becca so much. But in retrospect, I think he had a lot of demons. I also think he couldn't deal with the fact that we were broke, that the band had split up, that he had to go on the road by himself after having had so much success, and play bars all up and down Newfoundland and Labrador. He hated it. He hated being away from us, but that's the only way he could make enough money. You could only play so many bars in St. John's, right? You could make a decent living if you were a single person living in a room, playing in the bars in St. John's. But he wasn't getting enough gigs. He couldn't pay the mortgage. There were lot of things in retrospect—now that I can think about it sensibly. There was a *wearing down* with him being on the road, being away from us, and having the demons that he had.[589]

And then they came to part. Ron exited stage left before I was out of diapers. Did their marriage dissolve because of their financial situation or because of the declining economic climate for artists? Not at all. Ron had his demons and Jane had her limits, but again, this is not a memoir. Suffice to say however, their precarious finances and the general economic climate for artists did not help the situation, nor did it make the aftermath of their separation easy.

588 Dingle, interview (private collection).
589 Dingle, interview (private collection).

Feeling the Pinch

Jane was not alone in feeling that the theatre scene seemed somewhat stalled. In September of 1982, the Mummers Troupe disbanded permanently. Rising Tide Theatre and RCA Theatre still remained, but most actors were finding work harder to come by during the early 1980s. Political regime changes across Canada were impacting arts funding everywhere, including the Canada Council. As regional and national politics shifted in favour of the Progressive Conservatives, the arts community across Canada launched public campaigns in favour of ending the Council's funding freeze, which had lasted for most of the late 1970s. However, since it was from the federal government itself that Canada Council received ninety per cent of its funding, there was little the Council could actually do once Canada's political establishment decided that the "discourse of economy" now outranked any "discourse of culture."[590] By 1981, Brookes wrote, most Canadian theatres had an average funding deficit of seventy thousand dollars. The pinch was particularly felt in underfunded Newfoundland and Labrador, where the arts community received less than fifty per cent per capita of what some provinces received, and as little as five per cent of what the most generously funded provinces received. Artists and companies were advised to canvass the private sector to make up the shortfall. Because of the concurrent economic slowdown, private sector funders were less keen than ever to invest in the arts and thus this strategy produced limited results.[591]

Mom and Dad

Mom was part of the collective that wrote and staged the very last Mummers Troupe show to be performed while the group were still in existence, *Makin' Time with the Yanks.* When the troupe began their Newfoundland tour in March of 1982, she was nearly two months pregnant with me, which makes her athletic swing-dancing and constant travel throughout the tour all the more admirable in my eyes. After the

---

590 Brookes, *A Public Nuisance,* 211–214; Bill, 98.
591 Brookes, *A Public Nuisance,* 221.

Mummers Troupe folded, literally the same month I was born, Jane began to find regular theatre work increasingly difficult to get. When her marriage dissolved several months later, conditions became still more difficult but would certainly have been much worse without the close and supportive family network she was lucky enough to have nearby. By 1984, Jane was beginning to consider pursuing her career further on the mainland and with my sister and I in tow, she left St. John's for Toronto in October of 1985.

I was born into a family and a community that was in some respects crumbling or otherwise in flux—in the process of becoming something else. Leaving Newfoundland was a wrench for Jane and for Rebecca who, at six years old, was old enough to be deeply affected and apprehensive about leaving Newfoundland, the Dingles, and Dad. I, of course, knew nothing of any of this, being barely able to locate much more than my mother's nursing breast when Dad moved out, and barely old enough for nursery school by the time we left St. John's. I've largely experienced my family's separation simply as a learned fact, one imbued with the trauma-memories of both my mother and sister: we fell away from each other. We came apart. Circumstances were accompanied by rationalization, justification, hope that it was all for the best, but there was still the pain of separation, of leaving.

***

By the 1980s, Jane's decade and more of experience in Newfoundland theatre had equipped her with a perspective, a set of skills and habits of mind that shaped every decision she ever made subsequently as an actor, a teacher, a drama coach, and a member of her community. She went on to have a rich and varied acting career primarily in theatre, but also in various television and film roles. Being a single actor's daughter was exciting and often unpredictable. It was amazingly fun sometimes. When Mom was cast in two episodes of the CBS documentary/re-enactment television show, *Top Cops*, in 1991, I got to spend the weekend on set. I spent a particularly fun Saturday in the makeup trailer getting a makeover and several false tattoos. Sometimes, having to bring her kids to work was a more arduous experience for all of us. I remember little of her performance in a theatre production of *Jane Eyre* for Young People's Theatre.[592] Rebecca and I had fallen asleep backstage during several rehearsals leading up to the performance—most of which I also slept through. Despite some of the grander productions in which I have seen her perform, my absolute favourite performance I have ever seen from Jane was a tiny workshop production of a play called *The Hanging Sheet*, based on the memoirs of Theresa Anne Glaremen, which explored the traumatic and cruel conditions for Indigenous women in Canadian prisons. This play was performed before less than twenty people on a virtually bare stage at Eastview Community Centre, but it's still one of the most affecting theatrical performances I have ever seen. With most actors, I find it difficult to buy in to their performance if they can't make me forget who they are. *The Hanging Sheet* truly made me forget that Jane was the mother I'd known all my life. She does that a lot.

Life came with the kinds of highs and lows one would expect for an artist with two kids in an expensive city like Toronto. Mom secured her Equity status quickly after moving to the mainland and she never stopped pursuing a professional acting career, but like any artist, she had good years and bad years. Sometimes she worked steadily on well-paying projects for months and we'd get to enjoy a vacation or two. But the vagaries of artists' lives invariably lead to leaner times. When acting work was thin on the ground, Jane was quick to land either a service or clerical job. Even when she was getting semi-steady acting work, like most artists, Jane almost always worked a regular job in addition, sometimes two or three. Single parents rarely have much choice in the matter.

I am very proud of the career and body of work that Jane built as an actor. Yet, perhaps just as much, I admire the way she carried forward the communitarian, neighbourly qualities of Newfoundland and the determination of her generation to pursue the development and betterment of all communities of which she was a part. As a family, we lived at the mercy of the rental market in Toronto until 1987, when we moved into public housing. The all-hands attitude of Newfoundlanders served her well in this new and far more diverse world and Jane quickly became involved in varied work for the community. Most committed initially to safety and governance, she spent evenings patrolling the streets

---

592 Jane Dingle, interview by Alicia Hartley for the STAGE Project, St. John's, November 16, 2012, 18.

with fellow moms, or served on the Tenants Association to advocate for better conditions or funding.

Eventually, Jane applied for a government grant to offer free drama and other arts programs for the neighbourhood kids at the local community centre. This program ran for nearly eight years, giving low-income, at-risk kids access to activities and skill-building opportunities other than the inevitable after-school sports programs—which seemed to be the only activities regularly funded at Boys and Girls Clubs at the time. The Blake Boultbee Drama Group staged scripted plays at Eastview Community Centre for the first few years, including *The Wizard of Oz*—incidentally, the same script that the Newfoundland Travelling Theatre Company performed during their first tour in 1972. As the kids in the drama group grew older, Jane began to teach them the same lessons she had learned at theatre school and as a young actor in Newfoundland: character development, improvisation, collective writing. Between 1991 and 1995, the group wrote and staged original productions for school tours and for the annual festival at Toronto's St. Lawrence Centre for the Arts. These original plays focused on issues of concern to the young actors themselves, including domestic abuse, addictions, and community violence. I had no idea what the Mummers' Troupe was at the time, but upon completion of this book, it is crystal clear to me how deeply Jane was influenced by the Mummers' model of theatre for community action and development. It is easy to understand why the phrase "the personal is political" immediately struck home to me the first time I heard it from a veteran feminist professor during my first year of college. I'm certain that at some point, I absorbed it through osmosis.

Jane's career shared the fate of many of her fellow artists. She has an unbelievably crammed resumé, which encompasses more than three decades of performing. She's a great talent, a foundational contributor to the establishment of Newfoundland's arts community and she's well known across the industry for her abilities and professionalism, but such bona fides don't always translate into financial success. Many of the artists who pioneered during the cultural movement who are still around today are still working. A few of them did really well, but almost no one went on to make tons of money. The most successful few have managed to make a respectable living and pay the bills and the luckier still have secured a decent retirement. Yet, some of the issues they face as artists and as workers are burdens they still share with younger artists in the province—and indeed, across Canada. I doubt there is an artist working in Canada today who would disagree with Edythe Goodridge's insistence that "the arts must have some status." Speaking to Cathryn Boak for the MUN Pathways Program in 1984, Goodridge's words ring every bit as clear and true today as they did forty years ago.

> The arts, like the humanities, like the sciences, are part of the function of education and of learning. Artists are professionals. They have often received the same degree and intensity of professional training as the other professions. And yet . . . There are *very* few artists in this country who make a *living*. There are a few of what I would call superstars—a few musicians, a few composers, a few dancers, a few painters who actually have either national or international status and actually make a living at that point. But you must remember that all of them devoted ten, perhaps fifteen years to their art, living well below the poverty line, and had to teach and do a whole lot of other things in order to make a living. So, that's a very narrow group of artists. The bulk of artists make a living at everything else *but* their art.[593]

As for Ron, he never pursued anything other than music and never could—although one could quite convincingly argue that he enjoyed the freedom to fully commit to his passion as a musician and songwriter thanks in large part to the women who raised his kids. I remember him telling me once that the last "real" job he had ever held was gutting fish down by the harbour in Ferryland. "How old were you?" I asked him. "Twelve," he replied. As someone who has flitted from social work to education to academia, I'm well placed to appreciate this kind of single-minded commitment. I'm not sure I ever told him just how proud I was of him and just how much I admired what he had created and achieved, which saddens me. Yet, listening to warm remembrances and stories about him from his friends and colleagues gave me some solace—that he might continue to speak through their memories.

"He was just an incredibly generous performer and incredibly encouraging to young people," Anita Best told me.

593 Boak, (1984).

> I was amazed at his generosity of spirit when it came to other musicians. I know everyone thinks your dad had a big ego. He did in some ways, but it was more of a protective façade, I think, because he really had no ego when it came to welcoming other musicians to take part in the show. He just had no jealousies or anything of that nature on the go. And he was *always* writing songs. He was always writing down phrases that he'd hear people say. He'd write them on pieces of paper and tuck them into his pocket while we were on the bus.
>
> I never found him egocentric. I know he had a stage presence that sometimes could seem egotistic. At the same time, he was an extremely creative and generous individual, and I dearly loved him. He was one of the important people in my life.
>
> And another thing about him. He played no matter where it was. He played down at The Rose and Thistle. Any bar that would have him in there, he'd play. He didn't have that type of ego that you see in a lot of musicians now: "I'm only going to play in front of audiences of a thousand or more." He just played. That was his life and that was his heart and that was his talent.[594]

"He was *the* great Newfoundland songwriter," concurred Chris Brookes.

> He never got the recognition he deserved. He really didn't. But partly it was, I guess, you know, the personal battles he had with drugs. But there was an era when he came back home and he'd be performing every Friday and Saturday night downtown at The Rose and Thistle and cover was like five bucks or something. Jeez, you could go hear a major Canadian songwriter . . . Five bucks! In this tiny bar down on Water Street. It was crazy! It was wonderful. You know, but he should have been playing Massey Hall.[595]

---

594 Best, interview.
595 Brookes, interview.

Kent at the Rose, mid-2000s.[596]

I can't say if Ron really was the "man of a thousand songs," as he was known to have sometimes assured those who booked him, because he wrote a great many songs that were never recorded, some of which I only discovered for the first time during the course of this study. Moreover, Ron did virtually nothing in an organized fashion and that included songwriting. When inspiration struck him, he would end conversations in mid-sentence and reach immediately for the nearest writing implements, however flimsy or inappropriate to the task. Rebecca once found a napkin sitting on the back of the toilet tank in Ron's bathroom upon which was scrawled:

> *She's not going out in no blaze of glory,*
> *She's not wild anymore, she's just sorry.*

596 Photo by Kent Barrett.

"She's Not Wild Anymore" is a gorgeous song and Damhnait Doyle really made it her own when she sang it on *11:11*, an album Ron and Connie Hynes co-wrote and produced in 1997. It's one of Ron's lesser known songs, but one of my personal favourites despite the fact that I never once heard him sing it. I am very glad he finished it because I cannot imagine how many of his songs went unrecorded or unshared.

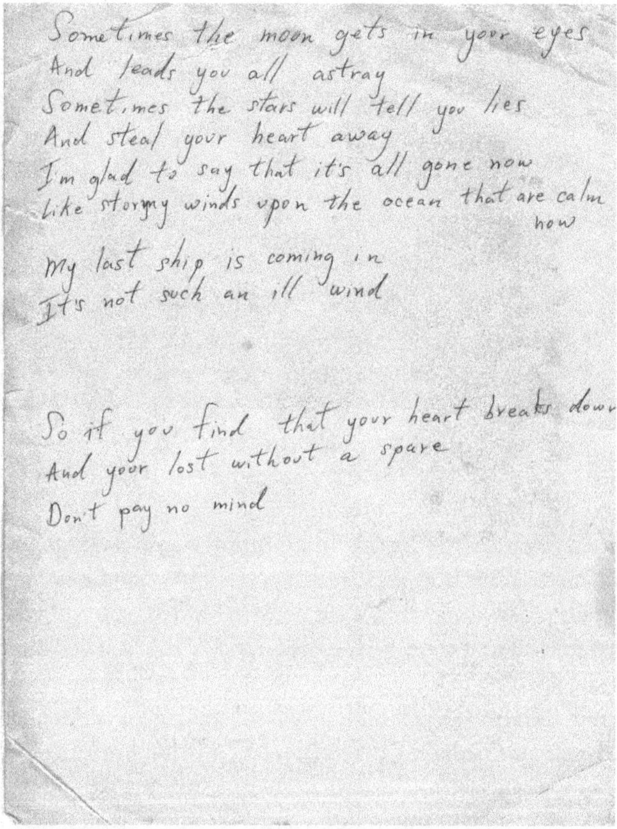
Sometimes the moon gets in your eyes
And leads you all astray
Sometimes the stars will tell you lies
And steal your heart away
I'm glad to say that it's all gone now
Like stormy winds upon the ocean that are calm
now
My last ship is coming in
It's not such an ill wind

So if you find that your heart breaks down
And your lost without a spare
Don't pay no mind

Half of the song lyrics for "Sometimes the Moon." [597]

---

597 Sometime between the summer of 1981 and the spring of 1983 (impossible to say when), Ron wrote the lyrics for the first half of "Sometimes the Moon," on the back of a theatre program from one of Jane's productions. Ron never recorded this song for release, to my knowledge, but a live version recorded at the LSPU Hall in 1992 is still extant, in which he performs it as a duet with Liz Solo (private collection).

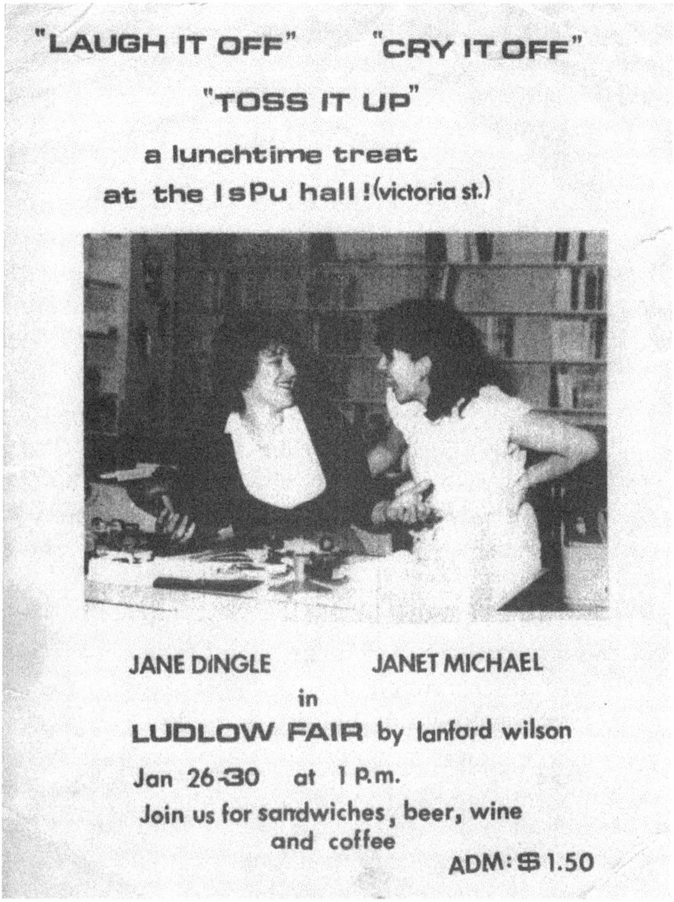

Lunchtime Theatre, *Ludlow Fair* theatrical program, 1981.[598]

598 During the late 1970s and early 1980s, the LSPU Hall managed to carve out more temporal and physical space to employ artists and enrich the cultural community with "Lunchtime Theatre," an initiative that recalls the lunchtime concerts at MUN's Little Theatre by the Philadelphia Cream Cheese Band in the late 1960s. Downtown residents and workers could bring their bagged lunch to the LSPU Hall on a weekday and see a short one-act play (Paddy Warrick, "Review of Ludlow Fair," *Evening Telegram*, January 28, 1981). Photo by Paul Dingle (private collection).

As for Ron's catalogue as a whole, I have a great many other favourites and would be hard-pressed to state one unequivocally, but "Atlantic Blue," his requiem for the eighty-four men who tragically perished in the 1982 *Ocean Ranger* disaster, probably comes closest. Next to "Sonny's Dream," it's probably Ron's most celebrated work and deservedly so. "'Sonny' was a gift," he used to say. "It just came to me on a bus one day while I was out on tour. I wrote it in about ten minutes and it was a year before I played it for anyone." The beauty of "Sonny," as with many folk songs that stand the test of time, is its simplicity and relatability. It has the feel of authentic experience, spontaneously and honestly expressed and it paints a very clear mental picture of a young man trapped by love and obligation. "Atlantic Blue" however, as music historian Stuart Pierson once wrote, is "poetry," a series of exquisitely phrased questions the answers to which speak silently yet eloquently of hopelessness, death, and cruel loss. The melody descends or "sinks," Pierson noted, "as the rig sank . . . as the hearts of the friends and relatives of the drowned sank."[599] The song's relatability and impact was in many ways greater in a regional context than "Sonny" could ever have been because "the intimacy and interconnectedness of lives" in Newfoundland and Labrador meant that a huge proportion of the province's people experienced personal loss as a result of the disaster.[600]

Both "Sonny's Dream" and "Atlantic Blue" represent a fundamental facet of Ron's gift as a songwriter—the ability to write from a perspective other than one's own, in this case, a woman's. Pierson observed that Ron's songwriting was rather unique among artists influenced by the country and Western musical tradition. "I think," Pierson wrote, "you may search the works of Hank Williams, Roy Orbison and 'the King' (despite his momma fixation) at length and in vain for so tiny and yet so momentous a leap of the imagination . . . to tell the story in a widow's voice.

> 'I hold my hurt at bay,
> I hold the lives of his children in my hands.'"[601]

---

599 Stuart Pierson, "Medieval Survivals: Reflections on Ron Hynes, *Cryer's Paradise*," *Newfoundland Studies* 13, no. 1 (1996): 53–55.

600 Stuart Pierson, 52.

601 Stuart Pierson, 56, 58.

Ron was a wonderful musician, an impressive guitarist with a great voice, and a dynamic stage presence. His facility with words and language was amazing, but his gift of writing in the voices of others, of inhabiting their personalities and realities, was his greatest achievement. No one earns the title of "bard" or "poet laureate" who has not learned to articulate an infinitely broader and more unifying cultural identity than your average regional folk singer/songwriter. It is most likely incorrect, at least partially, to refer to this quality as a "gift," however. It became clear to me as I progressed through this study that Ron spent many years cultivating this ability as a participant in the much broader cultural movement.

Chris Brookes realized just how interconnected and interdependent artists of his generation were in terms of their professional and creative development when he saw Ron play at a small private house show that was held in Torbay just a few days before Ron passed.

> At the end, because it was a tiny group, people were asking questions. Somebody asked him how it was that he came to put himself out there, to be able write about things outside of himself. Many other songwriters write about their own experiences . . . love, personal crises, but many of Ron's songs, most of his songs, were about other people. He said: "It started with working with the Mummers." We were doing shows about communities here, about unions and strikes and stuff. Ron was our in-house musician who had to write a song about the IWA strike or about the cop on the corner downtown. Not about him! We didn't need him to write about himself. I didn't realize that he saw that as a formative experience until he said so that night.[602]

Ron was and is much admired for his talent and his commitment to telling his people's stories, but his development and achievement did not happen in a vacuum. The collectivity and interdisciplinarity of the broader movement had an enormous impact on the growth of his artistic sensibilities and process, both in terms of his tendency toward collaborative songwriting and mentorship of other writers as well as the development of that outward-looking perspective. Not all artistic works,

602 Brookes, interview.

however, can be commissioned and produced in a few days or weeks. The songs Ron wrote for the various Mummers Troupe productions in which he appeared showcased his linguistic gifts and developing exterior perspective, but a song like "Atlantic Blue" could never have been written under such circumstances. Ron remarked that compared to the other songs on *Cryer's Paradise*, "Atlantic Blue" was "the real thing," a song that had taken years to complete and yet was offered, in contrast to the rest of a highly produced album, in a simple acoustic style with no backing tracks—just Ron singing and accompanying himself on guitar.[603] Brookes recalled reaching out to Ron in February of 1982, on the very day of the *Ocean Ranger* disaster.

> By that time, I was the producer of *The Afternoon Show* at CBC here. I had just gotten a real job for the first time in my *life* and the first day on the job, the *Ocean Ranger* went down. And I said, "Oh Jesus Christ, what do I do now?" That whole week I was running around and trying to do something special, something with poetry and music. I remember calling up Ron and saying: "Any chance you could try to write a song about the *Ranger* by Friday?" He called me back the next day and he said: "I really would like to, but I just can't. It's just too quick." And it was like four years later that he came up with "Atlantic Blue." It took that long to percolate after the *Ranger* went down. It was a brilliant song. But in that instance, I guess he didn't want to debase the thing. You know, to sell it cheap, the tragedy. He wanted it to be the best song he ever wrote and he didn't want to do that by Friday. He *couldn't* do it by Friday. Who could do that by *Friday*?[604]

Ron may have had a gift or talent, if you will, but I would argue that his mastery was equally due, if not more so, to the years of effort and commitment he made to his art. One can be passionate about music, theatre, literature, or the visual arts, but the courage to truly venture into the life of an artist is also something that has to be cultivated. An artist's job frequently involves having to cope with intense personal

---

603 Pierson, 53, 63.
604 Brookes, interview.

vulnerability, a natural response to constant appraisal and criticism. In addition, an artist needs to develop a creative process that helps them produce at their best and most prolific. "I thought that Ron was a good model that I could draw on for so many things," Bob Joy told me.

> Mostly his relationship with his creative impulse. I encountered this when I was in a play about Andy Warhol. What occurred to me is that the difference between an artist and a non-artist is that an artist has an idea and rolls with it and a non-artist has an idea and it just stays an idea. Ron was so good at it. He seemed to have an idea and before you knew it, it was a song. Andy Warhol would have an idea, and before you knew it, it was a print or an event. That impulse, the CODCO folks had it too. There was no respect for the empty page. There was no feeling that: "I better have it right before I put pen to paper." That's death. You have to desecrate the page right away. That idea occurred to me watching people like Ron. It didn't have to be a fully formed idea for them to start running with it. That became *so* important as an inspiration for the whole movement, the whole renaissance. You've got to run with the idea before you know where the idea's going.[605]

Joy described Ron's relationship with his creative impulse as seemingly "easy," but when viewed in this light, it suggests years of work—and faith that the idea one is running with is going to pan out. I am certain that Ron felt an increasing confidence in his own ability and artistry over the years. I didn't know that his first album existed until I was in my late teens. It was long out of print by then, but I knew Ron had a copy though he never played it for us. This struck me as strange coming from a man who always seemed happy to play you his newest song. He never said so, but my sister Rebecca believed he was embarrassed by *Discovery*. If such were the case, I wouldn't agree, but I can understand the impulse. I completed my master's thesis just a few short years ago and I'm already embarrassed by it. Yet, both projects represent markers on the road to becoming—a road that is apt to feel odd and bumpy for a while before direction and destination are revealed with more clarity.

---

605 Joy, interview.

I thought that *Discovery* featured a young man's beautiful poetry. The entirely acoustic style felt very Ron, but his tendency to sing precisely in the middle of his range throughout sounded strange to me considering the impressive tenor he later developed during the late 1970s and 1980s, or the decidedly country baritone he adopted as his voice began to age. I came away from *Discovery* feeling like it owed more to Neil Young or John Denver than to anyone Ron had ever claimed to be influenced by, like Johnny Cash or Buddy Holly. Ron used to say he was always thinking about *the next song*. Perhaps this was why he seemed to have stopped performing any of the songs from his first album by the late 1970s.

Articulation and Actualization

Finally, Ron's motivation came from an impulse to pursue his passion, but like his fellow artists, he was driven by a collective regional consciousness that sought to push back against the economic inequities and cultural colonialism that had remained seemingly unchanged since Newfoundland and Labrador's Confederation with Canada. "It was a time of trying to prove that we weren't who they thought we were," Mary Walsh reflected, "in this country that we were supposed to belong to, where we didn't fit in at all it seemed, and were just relegated to the country bumpkin fool."

> Goofy Newfies. There was a lot of standing up against that. We were a country, a whole country. We have a whole culture that existed before. That is the renaissance that we're talking about. We're talking about the 1949 complete eradication of Newfoundland as a Dominion, as its own Dominion, as the oldest colony of Great Britain, as a country in and of itself. Some people, even to this day, say: "Right over on the other side of the country," and they're not talking about BC, they're talking about Corner Brook. There was that sense and there was a lot of talk, mostly rum-fuelled talk, about seceding from Confederation. There was talk of there having been a conspiracy to get us in there. There was a lot of resentment and a lot of pride.

There was a feeling that there was something that we didn't want to let go of. We felt that it should be celebrated and that the Newfoundland way of seeing things was worth something, even though basically the entire world was telling us that it was worthless and should be burnt! Even our own Premier was saying that we should burn our boats. Joey always wanted us to come into the twentieth century and into industrialization and yet, some of us felt . . . I'm not sure we could've said, but we felt: "No, no. There's something really worthwhile here." I don't know what's going on with the young crowd these days, but that's where we were. Resentful, angry, and proud and falling in love with all the things that we had been ashamed of when we were growing up.

We were reclaiming ourselves, me and Ron and Greg . . . all of us. That was a very brave thing. I never fully committed to it. I always felt a little sense of shame. I tried not to let on, but inside I felt: "Oh my God, we're not as good as anybody." It's so great now when you see things like *Son of a Critch* on CBC. They're getting nine hundred [thousand] to a million viewers and nobody's getting that, except American shows. It's just great to see that carrying on. That time that we, still somewhat shamefacedly, stood up and said—your father and your mother being part of that—"No, no. What we have is worth celebrating, worth holding onto and worth reclaiming and we're going to write songs and plays about it and make fun of it as if everybody knows about it." We made fun of things that people didn't even know about. We were satirizing the way people saw Newfoundland when a lot of people didn't even *see* Newfoundland. We faked it till we made it.[606]

606 Mary Walsh, interview.

Conclusion: Bold Face Firmly in Place

"Art is not made alone."

- Pam Hall (2022)

"The function of the artist is to disturb. His duty is to arouse the sleeper, to shake the complacent pillars of the world. He reminds the world of its dark ancestry, and shows the world its present and points the way to its new birth. He is at once the product and preceptor of his times."

- Dr. Norman Bethune (1937)

The Newfoundland Renaissance: Evolution and Impact

Newfoundland and Labrador was confronted with enormous changes during the immediate post-Confederation decades. The push for industrialism and modernity that had begun in the earlier twentieth century had by then drastically eroded traditional modes of life, and a consumer and mass media-driven monoculture seemed to threaten regional cultural and historical memory with erasure. What has been called the "Newfoundland renaissance" constitutes a moment of impressive intellectual unity among an otherwise significantly divided mass of people. Academics, social and development workers, and artists of all disciplines coalesced into a loose network of individuals and groups all seemingly pursuing the same goals of uplift, reclamation, and collective self-actualization, albeit in different ways and via different means.

Together, this multi-generational, interdisciplinary movement began to articulate a common history, to claim and celebrate a shared cultural identity, and to envision and establish a common future for themselves. Previous and concurrent decolonization, independence, and nationalist movements throughout the Atlantic world, the artists who led them, and the international youth counterculture influenced this process and left their marks on the shape and ethos of the Newfoundland art that emerged during this period. Institutions played crucial roles in providing a baseline of opportunity and resources, which those in the cultural vanguard—a group heavily dominated by artists—then used to carve out, develop, and define a new industry.

Scholars and commentators have traditionally given much credit for the emergence of the renaissance to provincial and federal institutions, as well as to Brian Peckford's government for galvanizing and directing a strong sense of neo-nationalism in the province. Institutions and government did indeed play important roles, and the funding and resources they provided constituted necessary scaffolding to support the subsequent efforts of artists, but an examination of artists' experiences throughout the study period shows that their efforts and output far exceeded what could reasonably have been expected of them considering the rudimentary and sometimes nonexistent infrastructure and support they had to work with. Brian Peckford employed his impressive rhetorical skills and the power of his political position to amplify the nationalist elements of public discourse. Nonetheless, it must be acknowledged that Peckford's platform of regional nationalism was one that saw its emergence and crystallization throughout the previous one to two decades and was particularly well articulated within the artistic community. Peckford expressed outrage over outsider control of the province's resources and the "have not" status of Newfoundlanders compared to their fellow Canadians. He identified Newfoundland's outports as the primary repository for its unique culture and expressed his fears for the survival of both. In large part, it had been the artists in the vanguard of the cultural movement who had stimulated public dialogue about these ideas and shifted popular opinion and culture—a fact Peckford himself acknowledged in his writings.[607]

607 Gulliver, 276–81; A. Brian Peckford, *The Past in the Present: A Personal Perspective on Newfoundland's Future* (St. John's: Harry Cuff Publications Limited, 1983), v–vi.

The election of Brian Peckford saw the beginning of a new period of development in arts policy and infrastructure. In the years ahead, artists would continue to advocate for the support of their industry and professions. The talent pool in Newfoundland and Labrador only continued to increase as a new generation of young people grew up watching the *WGB* and *CODCO* TV shows, went to the Folk Festival with their families every year, and attended school with a curriculum that placed increasingly greater emphasis on the history and achievements of Newfoundlanders and Labradorians. Subsequent generations of artists have stood upon increasingly firmer ground than their predecessors and some commentators have noted a shift in the regional voice that might indicate some waning of the kind of overt nationalism that was featured prominently in many works conceived during the 1970s. Newfoundland artists still create works and tell stories about regional life, history, and culture, but also feel free to explore broader themes. Few seem to be opposed to welcoming and exploring non-regional themes and influences in art.[608]

Despite some common goals and perspectives, there were marked divisions within the arts community during the study period. These reflected historical, cultural, class-based, and generational divides within the broader society of the province. As we have observed, there were fundamental disagreements among artists, bureaucrats, and larger institutional bodies about just what "art" or "culture" are and what their purpose or place in the provincial landscape ought to be. There were struggles between the notions of "elite" or "high" culture and "popular" culture; between the goals of cultural refinement on one hand and authenticity and social action on the other; and between the promotion of the amateur and the development of the professional. Even the notions of collective vs. single-authored works seemed to signal political and generational divides during the 1970s. Finally, tensions existed between "colonial" imported works and "regional" art or cultural artifacts. If Shakespeare, classic opera, and American musicals were examples of sophisticated "good" art, what did that say about irreverent home-grown satire, political theatre, traditional folk music, or traditional crafts like quilting, knitting, or hand-carving? Because they were in a very real sense expressions of a nascent regional nationalist movement, even forms of art that were in no way political on the face of them became marked by political and class distinctions.

---

608 Devine, 382, 407; Butt, interview; Malone, STAGE Project, 17–21.

At the institutional level, the respective approaches to nourishing and supporting the arts by MUN Extension and the Division of Cultural Affairs came to signify perceived differences in political and class affiliation as well. These divisions were evident not only in the tensions between Perlin and the theatre community, but also in the 1973 struggle between Perlin and Memorial University staff and administrators over the provincial art gallery.[609] Perlin was not alone in his reservations regarding MUN Extension-backed programming. In a December 1975 editorial to the *Daily News*, a columnist writing under the pseudonym of "Anti-Arty Crafty" wrote of his experience attending a "fine production" at the St. John's Arts and Culture Centre but also of his "disgust" at "the mass confusion I was expected to wade through in order to reach the theatre."

> The upper concourse resembled the worst sort of Petticoat Lane, with long haired creeps, grannie-gowned females, the usual assortment of blue-jeaned freaks; the whole thing was billed as a sort of folk art display, which it was in more ways than one. I think it was appalling. I'd like to see any other Arts and Culture Centre in Canada so despoiled by such a collection of riff-raff.... No more of this please, Mr. Perlin.[610]

Clearly, differing perspectives on art and culture influenced not only interactions between institutions and artists, but also between artists and their audience. Pamela Morgan spoke thoughtfully about and with some regret that the Newfoundland folk music tradition that groups like Figgy Duff worked hard to resurrect and preserve did not seem to permeate the broader provincial music culture as much as the Irish Celtic tradition did.

> There's a part of me that's really sad that everything that we tried to do with the ballads and the Newfoundland music... It didn't seem to make as much of an impact as I would have liked to have seen. The Newfie-Irish thing is still very, very prevalent. I'm not saying there's anything wrong with it, I'm just saying there's more to Newfoundland music than

609 Gulliver, 51–53, 102, 115–116.

610 "Arts, Culture Centre despoiled," *Daily News*, December 12, 1975, quoted in Gulliver, 115–16.

> that—much, much more. And the beautiful, gorgeous ballads. There's only a handful of people perpetuating that and I would've loved to see a lot more. I mean, we played the jigs and the reels, we played them well. Everybody got excited and went: "Rah, rah, rah!" But then, we would play the most beautiful, ancient ballad with all this gorgeous language and this incredible melody in between. But nowadays, the norm is to play all the "rah, rah, rah!" stuff, and then in the middle of it, play "Nancy Spain" or some Irish song, do you know what I mean? That beautiful thing didn't seem to roll over us as much as I would've liked it to.[611]

Donna Butt expressed a somewhat similar sentiment regarding the works of theatre that were produced during the 1970s, which was echoed by Don Walsh and Sandy Morris as well. Not everyone who watched the renaissance unfold identified personally with the message artists were trying to convey, nor did everyone necessarily like how artists were portraying Newfoundland culture.[612]

> Some audiences didn't quite get it. It's not true that instantly Newfoundlanders all accepted the work of Newfoundland artists. That's a nonsense recollection. It wasn't really quite like that at all. Certain people embraced it, but not everybody by a very long shot. When we did *Daddy, What's a Train?*, which was our first show, some people liked it and other people thought: "Well, come on, Newfoundlanders don't talk or behave like that." There were really great divisions in Newfoundland society and St. John's society, I can tell you, at the time. A lot of different views about what we were doing and how we were all doing it.[613]

By the mid-1980s, some began to voice concern about the nature and function of the concept of "Newfoundland culture," Edythe Goodridge among them. She recalled the summers of her childhood and early

611 Morgan, interview.
612 Don Walsh interview; Morris, interview.
613 Butt, interview.

adolescence during which she had had the opportunity to visit almost every outport community along the provincial coast with her father—a railway worker on the coastal boats. By the time she began working with Extension roughly a decade later, it became clear to her that in the interim these communities had changed immeasurably and that the arts, which she identified as a major component of civic and cultural cohesion and of collective memory, had fallen by the wayside and been neglected in community development schemes. Much of Goodridge's work with Extension, as curator of the MUN art gallery and later as head of the visual arts section of the Canada Council, had been to establish a status for the artist, a base of support and infrastructure for artists as primary producers and major contributors to the economic and social life of their communities. In a 1984 interview, Goodridge recalled the romantic shape of her impressions of Newfoundland outports during the late 1940s and early 1950s, but expressed concern that even though many of these communities had evolved to be nearly unrecognizable compared to what they had been, artistic expressions continued to romanticize and sentimentalize the outport life, injecting it with a nostalgia that made it seem almost like propaganda. Goodridge also expressed concern that Newfoundland cultural perceptions were being distilled down to highly "simplistic notions of ourselves," predominantly those of the rural, White, English-speaking settler, a rather uniform cultural identity that masked much greater regional diversity.[614]

Others have echoed Goodridge's doubts and concerns around cultural authenticity in the years since, particularly as it applies to culture's commodification and entrenchment in the tourism industry,[615] as well as the issues arising from the frequent conflation of art with culture. In his speech at MUN's 1998 commencement, Shane O'Dea called for greater support for the province's artists, asserting that it was they who not only established a new "narrative" and "mindscape" for the province, but also stood against the reduction of regional art and culture to mere "entertainment and souvenir."[616] Donna Butt posed questions about the intersection between the "role of the arts in the economy," and the "role of the arts as artistic."

614 Boak, (1984).

615 Overton, "Coming Home," 97; O'Dea, "Oration honouring Edythe Ryan Goodridge," 5.

616 O'Dea, "Oration honouring Edythe Ryan Goodridge," 5.

> The arts started to become more widely accepted once somebody felt, including government, that there was an economic component. Art and culture, in this province, are very much thought about in the context of economic generators, and so then the question becomes: "How do you hold onto the other part of the art?" And I think that's the big question. What's the difference between art and culture? Because culture is something everybody owns—everybody believes they own—and what people express as their culture is not necessarily the same as what people are expressing artistically. How do you define that in a place like Newfoundland and Labrador where these words are interchanged very easily? I think the lines blur sometimes.[617]

Butt makes an excellent point. Newfoundland and Labrador has a dedicated government department—the Department of Tourism, Culture, Arts and Recreation—that not only institutionally conflates culture with art but ties both explicitly to the economic imperatives of tourism, entertainment, and capital. Artistic companies and individual artists in Newfoundland and Labrador have acclimatized themselves to an arts environment situated within the industrial capitalist model and have operated the best they could in recent decades while continuing to advocate for greater investment in their industry. In fact, it was in large part because artists began to explicitly identify their industry as a proven economic generator within the given model that more comprehensive infrastructure and support for the arts has been established since the 1980s. "It's really interesting too," Donna continued, "because people will say: 'Look, you're getting money from economic development areas or whatever and why should that be?' Well, it's because of economic impact."

> That doesn't mean that people don't think the arts aren't important; that the stories you're telling, or the songs you're singing, or the pictures you're painting aren't important. They do. But would they think the same if suddenly they were not having the same economic impact? I don't know. It's hard to say. I think it's probably always going to be in some degree

617 Butt, interview.

> incumbent upon the people who are in the arts to make sure that the art doesn't get lost. But you're under a lot of pressure too if you're running a company, for example, that's non-profit. You're trying to employ people, you're trying to make sure that people can stay in this province, so you've got a lot of forces coming at you.[618]

The perception of regional art as an economic generator has stimulated the growth over time of institutions, bodies, and programs to educate, fund, and support artists. The various campuses comprising Memorial University and the College of the North Atlantic have diverse arts education programs. Artist-run centres, cooperatives, and independent artistic companies have continued to appear across the province. Artist-focused bodies like ArtsNL, MusicNL, and the Newfoundland and Labrador Film Development Corporation are just a few institutional examples of the progress that has been made in a relatively brief span of time. These are all encouraging signs, but they all continue to depend on funding from within a given model—one that tends to distrust or disregard calls for investment in initiatives that cannot completely pay for themselves through profit alone. Cultural programming is a crucial part of community cohesion and public dialogue. It's certainly possible to cover all costs for, say, a theatre production through box office alone, but then the tickets will cost hundreds of dollars, defeating the purpose of cultural programming accessible to the public.

Looking Back, Looking Forward

When Sandra Gwyn first coined the term "Newfoundland renaissance," it seemed to suggest a resurrection of traditional regional artistic forms and indeed this was the case with regard to some disciplines like music, theatre traditions like mummering, as well as traditional crafts. In the years since, subsequent commentators have disagreed, referring to the artistic and cultural flowering that took place during the late 1960s,

618 Butt, interview.

1970s, and early 1980s as an "arrival" rather than a "revival."[619] There was indeed a distinctly fresh regional aesthetic in theatre, literature, visual art, and music during the 1970s, and it is also true that even revivals like traditional Newfoundland music were undertaken with a certain amount of innovation by artists. If the movement was not a true renaissance, then questions of cultural identity and authenticity once again become relevant. How can we conceptualize and understand the various incarnations of Newfoundland culture over time? If that which emerged in the 1970s did not really resemble the culture of the past, then what exactly was created? What was lost? What is Newfoundland culture now? And importantly, what will it become?

Both Pamela Morgan and Donna Butt had much to say on these issues. "The Newfoundland that I knew is pretty much gone," Morgan remarked. "I feel like an old fart, an old codger, a geezer," she said and laughed.

> It's different, it's just different. There was that lost generation when the fishery closed and everybody kind of . . . All of that pride and hope and wonderful feeling that had been generated kind of just went poof! The whole culture . . . the fabric of the place unravelled because everybody left. And then, you couple that with the advent of mass media and all those stations coming in from the United States, just the loss of community and community spirit, entertaining each other at home, those kinds of things. That all just kind of happened at once. There's a lot of trying to reclaim that, but it's almost like a caricature of what it was, just sort of a replica of who we were. It's not real. To my mind, it doesn't feel real. Now, it's real to the people who are doing it. I'm not saying people are being false or fake. They're just doing what they know. It's great to have pride in the place and if that's what you know, then that's the only thing you're equipped with in order to present it. But the Newfoundland that I knew, it's gone.
>
> There is one really great example that illustrates that for me. When I was learning songs from people, I used the oral

619 Bill, 96.

> tradition; I never used a tape recorder. I used to learn the songs. You'd have to go back a few times and you'd exchange songs and become friends. I didn't just want to take it and leave; I wasn't a collector. I was a student, a learner, and I learned that different songs belonged to different people. It was unspoken. It was just something that was known in the community, like "that song, oh that's Mary's song." Or "that's Jilly's song." Or "that's Peter's song." And it wasn't like an ownership thing per se, it was just something that evolved. Like, "The Girl Who Slighted Me" is definitely Gerald Campbell's song. And so, if you wanted to learn the song, then the person whose song it was would *give* you their song. Again, it was all unspoken and very informal, but nonetheless real for that. They would give you their song, if you asked for it. "I'd love to have that song. Would you teach it to me?" "Yes, I will." That passing of the song, it was like a gift from the singer to the person who wanted to learn it. That seems to have totally disappeared.
>
> I tried to explain that to some of the members of Great Big Sea at one point, and they had never heard tell of it. I mean, they were doing Newfoundland songs, but that part of the tradition had somehow escaped them and they didn't know about it. So that's one example of what I mean about the Newfoundland that I knew. It's different now. It changed. We lost a lot along the way. But now, of course, we've gained a lot as well, so you know, it's not as if: "Oh she's gone, b'y, she's gone." It's just different. Things change, they have to.[620]

Donna Butt concurred with Morgan, reflecting soberly on the marked change she has observed in Trinity since Rising Tide Theatre permanently re-established themselves out there thirty-odd years ago. For Butt, the outport Newfoundland of the mid-twentieth century is steadily fading into history. "Those voices, that way of life, is almost gone," she said.

620 Morgan, interview.

When I came to Trinity in 1993, there were a lot of those people and now the last of that generation is passing, right while we're talking today. One passed yesterday. Another one passed a week ago. Another one passed a month ago. With the last of that generation will go the last of a certain way of life, definitely, because no one is living that way of life again, the way my grandmother did, or my own mother, who's eighty-nine.

When we came here, there was a church women's group, the ACW. We used to rent the parish hall just across the way from the theatre here—there was no theatre here then. Almost every one of them now are gone, those women who used to go over to the church suppers when I came here. So yeah, I think some of the old Newfoundland has gone. What it will be replaced with, I don't know. How does my generation and how does our expression differ from the young people I work with now, who also have very strong ties to the place? The stories they're telling are different, or expressed in different ways. I think there's still an exploratory stage going on in terms of what those stories are going to ultimately be and how they're going to be told. What remains of the Newfoundland that *we* valued and fought for and loved and gave a lot to—many of us over the years—*I don't know.* Will any of what we created or wrote endure? I hope so.

We came to Trinity after the cod moratorium. The coast was decimated. Coming to a rural community and deciding to try to build this concept of telling the stories of people in the places where they had happened . . . Maybe something of that will last. I'm getting up to the end of the time when I'll be running it, for obvious reasons and so, I wonder, what will it be? If I'm still living in Trinity and come down over the hill and look, I wonder, what will still be here of everything that was built by these amazing people, too many of whom are already gone?

These communities have altered so much—just the number of people living in them. Constantly the effort is to try to

> get young people to come and live and raise their families, but these communities are not the places that they once were. This is not a place where everybody grew up here for generations and generations. The workforce is changing. The fishery has changed enormously. The two shipyards are gone. I also think about tourism and cultural tourism. What are those things? How are they going to be interpreted and explored moving forward? It's about those things too, and they're all great! The high-end B&Bs, the food, but it's all changing. The lifeblood of these communities is changing and a lot of these places are really not year round the way they need to be. I remember when we came out to Trinity, and someone who lived in Trinity Bight said to me: "You know, these places are not really communities if they only thrive in the summer."
>
> I wonder what the place we knew and fought for *is* and *will be*. I think about this a great deal. The Newfoundland of today is not the one of '49. It's not the one of '73, when we started in the theatre. It's not the one of '93, when we came to Trinity. There's all kinds of fabulous things happening in this province. I always believed: "Go forward. Keep finding a way to build and hold on. Change and cherish. Figure a way."[621]

As Newfoundland and Labrador's demography and modes of work and life continue to shift, so too will the people's sense of themselves and the question of just what the province's culture is will require examination, reflection, and redefinition. "The Newfoundland cultural renaissance constantly has to be examined and re-examined," Pam Hall remarked thoughtfully as our interview was coming to an end.

> Just in those three words. What do you mean by Newfoundland, White girl? What do you mean by cultural? Whose culture? Whose history? And what do you mean by using a term from Eurocentric White history like the Renaissance? Define Newfoundland, make history plural,

621 Butt, interview.

> and what do you mean by art? How can you talk about a single history? The thing I love about the cultural renaissance is that there are multiple histories in there and they haven't been written in yet. Some of them are being written in now: the immigrants, the newcomers, the refugees that have changed the food culture of St. John's overnight. Suddenly we're eating Korean pancakes and amazing African curries. When I came to Newfoundland in 1973, you couldn't get spinach in the supermarket, let alone a spinach salad in a restaurant. Every version of the word culture has constantly got to be revisited. My rule of thumb for thoughtful critical thinking is always put an "s" on the end, just to remind yourself of the plurality.[622]

It is this very plurality, an outgrowth of the concept of autonomous voice in place, which has increased in cultural importance in the decades since. During the post-Confederation years, many White settler Newfoundlanders viewed Confederation as a colonizing phenomenon with Canada simply replacing imperial Britain. Yet, Indigenous Newfoundlanders and Labradorians had virtually no voice in the process that made their traditional homeland part of Canada and were, in fact, not mentioned at all in the final draft of the Terms of Union.[623] Such facts did not begin to assume any importance in the provincial mindset until the latest stages of the cultural movement. The nourishment of the Newfoundland voice in place helped strengthen and legitimize calls to address broad marginalization in provincial Indigenous communities, and more besides.

As Newfoundland and Labrador steadily becomes a more diverse society and history studies in the province become increasingly connected to a broader Atlantic history, regional historians such as Afua Cooper, Sonja Boon, Xaiver Campbell, and Heather Barrett have in recent years begun to connect Newfoundland and Labrador to the "Black Atlantic," with examinations of enslaved fishermen and domestic servants, Black naval men, sailors, and pirates, and the many

622 Hall, interview.

623 David MacKenzie, "The Indian Act and the Aboriginal Peoples of Newfoundland at the Time of Confederation," 161–181; Hillier, 2024.

decades of Newfoundland's ties to Atlantic slavery.[624] Likewise, the "Red Atlantic" space has become much more fleshed out in Newfoundland and Labrador. Elders from Inuit, Innu, and Mi'kmaq nations across the province such as Mi'sel Joe, Louie Montague, and Paulus Maggo have published histories and memoirs in recent years, which have done a great deal to centre Indigenous voices in historical discourse.[625]

Within the arts community, the plurality that Hall discussed is a theme that Newfoundland artists of the last two or three decades have become more and more comfortable with. The artists who broke ground during the cultural movement placed marked emphasis on art of regional significance in order to counter what were perceived to be colonial cultural and economic influences. The generations of artists who followed them stood upon a firmer foundation and with perhaps a more definitive sense of themselves. Now that the urgency to carve out space for insiders is less urgent, artists have felt free to explore diverse themes in recent years. Explorations of the history, life, and culture of Newfoundland and Labrador are still very much a part of the artistic landscape, but the wariness for outside themes and influences, once so prominent in art during the 1970s, has lessened quite considerably. In a 2012 interview, Greg Malone, an enormously important figure in the vanguard of the cultural movement and the province's arts scene in general, spoke about his great enjoyment doing Shakespeare again in recent years and how much rich material there was to explore continually as an actor.[626] Fifty years ago, the lack of support for original art created by regional artists might have given such productions a colonial tinge—especially when performed by visiting professional companies. Today, there seems to be much less concern about outsider art drowning out the regional voice.

---

624 Sonja Boon, *What the Oceans Remember: Searching for Belonging and Home* (Waterloo: Wilfrid Laurier University Press, 2019); Heather Barrett and Xaiver Campbell, *Black Harbour: Slavery and the Forgotten Histories of Black People in Newfoundland and Labrador* (Portugal Cove-St. Philip's: Boulder Books, 2023); Rhea Rollman, "Newfoundland in the Black imaginary," *The Independent*, September 9, 2016. https://theindependent.ca/news/newfoundland-in-the-black-imaginary/.

625 Raoul R. Andersen and John K. Crellin (eds.), *Mi'sel Joe, An Aboriginal Chief's Journey* (St. John's: Flanker Press, 2009); Mi'sel Joe and Sheila O'Neill, *My Indian* (St. John's: Breakwater Books, 2021); Elizabeth Dawson (ed.), Louie Montague, *I Never Knowed it Was Hard: Memoirs of a Labrador Trapper* (St. John's: Memorial University Press, 2013); Carol Brice-Bennet (ed.), Paulus Maggo, *Remembering the Years of My Life: Journeys of a Labrador Inuit Hunter* (St. John's: Institute of Social and Economic Research, 1999).

626 Malone, STAGE Project, 17–21.

Writing around the turn of the twenty-first century, Shane O'Dea reflected that the Newfoundland novelists and playwrights of the late 1990s seemed to have gone beyond a fixation and re-litigation of the province's political and social history and, by writing largely about Newfoundland and Labrador's present, seemed to have "attained a confidence" as well as a forward-looking perspective.[627] In 2009, Michael Devine wrote that the archetype of the "Stranger" was still very prevalent in Newfoundland drama, but that a shift in voice among Newfoundland playwrights had significantly altered the position and treatment of such characters. Newfoundland and Labrador's history of community isolation, external control, exploitative resource extraction, and cultural denigration within larger colonial bodies has likely entrenched the Stranger figure permanently within the province's imagination. It is still, Devine notes, a crucial archetype against which many people continue to define themselves and as such, must still be "disarmed or demystified." However, within the work of more recent artists, Newfoundland and Labrador is a place where the wandering Stranger is not only more common and far less threatening, but quite integral to regional identity as a whole. In the works of some of the province's more recent playwrights, the Stranger does not seek to assimilate but simply acts as a member of the community under the assumption that they will eventually be accepted. For insiders who ultimately cannot extend inclusion and acceptance, the problem is their own, not the Stranger's.[628] Considering that Newfoundland and Labrador has been continually visited and peopled by numerous groups of wandering strangers throughout the many millennia of the region's history of human habitation, this perspective seems quite fitting.

***

The arts community of Newfoundland and Labrador is now broader, more diverse, and better supported than it has been in the past. The changes and improvements artists sought were hard-won and slow to

627 O'Dea, "Culture and Country," 385.
628 Devine, 382, 407, 411.

develop over the last four decades as political regimes continued to shift back and forth, yet direct support to individual artists remained modest. Policy papers published during the early 1990s advocated for greater support and the creation of a formal arts policy. One study estimated that only approximately fifteen per cent of the province's cultural budget actually supported artists and cultural workers, while the Arts and Culture Centres and other government-run cultural programs continued to receive the most generous share of annual funding. Most of the next two decades saw a deeper and further entrenchment of arts funding in the capital-oriented model with much development of the tourism and ecotourism sectors and the commissioning of artistic works geared largely toward the commemoration of historical milestones—also useful for promoting tourism.[629]

Despite the issues that can arise from arts investment primarily in the tourism potential of historical milestones, this strategy has brought some significant benefits to the province as a whole, if not to artists specifically. Milestone-oriented cultural events, because they anticipate the arrival of tourists, usually necessitate the building or improvement of public edifices and resources. These improvements not only prove attractive to visitors and returning expats, but also serve the individual communities in which they are built. The 1966 Come Home Year and Centennial Year celebrations provided an economic infusion that saw the establishment of recreation and community centres, ice rinks, libraries, and other welcome public spaces across the province.[630]

It was not until 2007 that policy-makers once again began to seriously consider the status of the artist. Unfortunately, this did not translate to a funding increase for the Newfoundland and Labrador Arts Council or increased direct support for artists.[631] Those particular agenda items remained on the back burner for more than a decade. In response to repeated campaigns by the local arts community, the annual budget for ArtsNL was increased three times between 2019 and 2023. During the 2022–23 funding year, individual artists in the province collectively received roughly two million dollars in individual grants

---

629 Rompkey, 275–78.

630 Gulliver, 50–51.

631 "Newfoundland and Labrador Arts Council, 2007–2008 Annual Report," Department of Tourism, Culture and Recreation, Government of Newfoundland and Labrador. https://www.assembly.nl.ca/business/electronicdocuments/NLArtsCouncilAnnualReport2007-08.pdf.

and seed money to create and launch their projects—an amount equivalent to the entire budget for the Newfoundland and Labrador Arts Council just five years before.[632] Artists continue to couch their bids for further policy development and support within the framework of broad economic benefit for Newfoundland and Labrador, a fact that is undeniable. The arts and culture industry produces hundreds of millions of dollars annually for the provincial coffers and creates thousands of local, well-paying, full-time jobs, all with a comparatively small investment of a few million dollars per year.[633] The music industry alone was estimated to be worth more than fifty million annually in 2018.[634] There is still more work to do. The 2022–23 annual report from ArtsNL called for a decolonization of artistic spaces and observed that Indigenous artists continue to be conspicuously underrepresented in provincial arts funding schemes.[635]

Indigenous visual artists have received increased recognition and opportunities for exhibiting and selling their work at the local and regional level in recent decades, but the incorporation of Indigenous works in more prominent national galleries and museums has been both less frequent—sporadic in fact—and troublingly problematic. Like the artists of Newfoundland and Labrador, Indigenous artists across North America have seen a great deal of the funding available to them in recent decades channelled into events of historical commemoration, such as the 1992 Columbus Quincentennial. Critics have referred to this practice of only incorporating Indigenous art for such milestones as opportunistic. The work of Indigenous artists exhibited at various North American institutions commemorating Columbus's landing reflected upon centuries of untold loss and long generational trauma.

---

632 "Arts and culture funding the focus of letter-writing campaign," *CBC News*, March 22, 2019. https://www.cbc.ca/news/canada/newfoundland-labrador/artsnl-funding-letter-campaign-1.5063927; "ArtsNL Annual Report 2022–23," Newfoundland and Labrador Arts Council, 19. https://www.gov.nl.ca/tcar/files/ArtsNL2022-23AnnualReport.pdf; "Newfoundland and Labrador Arts Council Annual Report, 2018–19," Department of Tourism, Culture, Industry and Innovation, 14. https://www.gov.nl.ca/tcar/files/AR2018-19-NLAC.pdf.

633 Andie Bulman, "NL Election 2021: The Arts as Renewable Resource," *The Independent*, February 10, 2021. https://theindependent.ca/news/arts/nl-election-2021-the-arts-as-renewable-resource/.

634 "Music Industry Study & Economic Impact Assessment," MusicNL, Atlantic Canada Opportunities Agency (May 2018): 1. https://musicnl.ca/wp-content/uploads/2021/01/MusicNL-Industry-Study-and-Economic-Impact-V2.pdf.

635 "ArtsNL Annual Report 2022–23," 8.

Quite disturbingly, these exhibitions were situated in the context of a liberal intellectual framework of recognition, inclusion, and integration, while simultaneously commemorating the voyages of the man who launched the first of many acts of exploitation, dispossession, and genocide upon Indigenous peoples in the Americas. Re-examinations of such historical issues as Columbus's legacy or the myths surrounding the first Thanksgiving permeated public discourse in the 1990s. The Native American Graves Protection and Repatriation Act saw its passage by the United States Congress the same year as the Quincentennial. Just two years prior in 1990, Canadians had followed the development of the Oka Crisis in which Indigenous activists maintained a months-long armed standoff against Quebec police and Canadian military forces to prevent the expansion of a golf course onto a Mohawk burial ground.[636]

In the years since, scholars and artists alike have begun to question whether all aspects of the liberal framework are still useful, considering that inclusion and integration within fundamentally colonial contexts does nothing to disrupt the still-potent forces of colonialism and capitalism—the very forces that have historically sublimated Indigenous nations. Some have instead begun to advocate for an indigenization of artistic and cultural spaces in which the stories told and the manner in which they are told originate within the Indigenous community and are similarly curated and exhibited.[637] As an artist and a scholar interested in helping to amplify Indigenous voices in the provincial arts community, Pam Hall spoke candidly and frankly on this point.

> I think that Fine Art, as in capital "F" and capital "A" . . . is just one small tip of one small iceberg . . . Humans have been creating meaning for centuries across cultures and across difference. So, I don't really buy into the one that we call Western art history or European art history, because it's so colonial, it's totally patriarchal, and it's capitalist, and I don't believe in any of those things. I don't really want to sit in conversation with that stuff. I want to sit in resistance to that stuff, which is a place where I think art has a *huge* role to play.[638]

---

636 Ash-Milby and Phillips, 11–13.

637 André Dudemaine, Gabrielle Marcoux, and Isabelle St-Amand, "Indigenous Cinema and Media in the Americas," *Canadian Journal of Film Studies* 29, no. 1 (Spring 2020): 30.

638 Hall, interview.

***

In the context of Canada as a whole, artists continue to face challenges that have endured for decades, largely related to persistently low incomes, which can fluctuate wildly from year to year. In a 2022 study surveying the responses of 4,747 Canadian artists, less than half of them reported working full-time in their artistic disciplines and nearly two-thirds worked only part-time in their fields, deriving their main income from other sources, such as additional part-time or full-time jobs either within the arts or in other industries. Many continue to rely on family members for financial or housing support. Sixty-four per cent are self-employed, limiting their access to programs like Employment Insurance, which for self-employed persons is complicated, difficult to qualify for, and often not worth nearly as much support as regular EI benefits. As of 2019, the average Canadian artist made less than forty thousand dollars annually and only the top eight per cent made eighty thousand dollars a year or more (to a maximum of one hundred and fifty thousand dollars per year). Predictably, the COVID-19 pandemic dramatically disrupted the lives and incomes of performing artists, roughly eighty per cent of whom reported significant losses in income during lockdowns and long-term closure of public performance spaces. More than half of the artists surveyed were forced to apply for federal emergency benefit programs during the pandemic.[639]

As a group, Canadian artists are still struggling as the cost of living continues to rise across the country and the resources available to them fail to keep pace. Artists in Newfoundland and Labrador likewise continue to face the same challenges, but this province stands out as a region that places marked importance on the arts. Regardless of shifts in political leadership, the artistic community continues to work with the existing regime to make greater provision for artistic producers. It is also noteworthy that actual artists can often be found holding top infrastructure or policy jobs in arts administration. Newfoundlanders and Labradorians as a group seem to have always valued their unique

639 "Canadian Artists and Content Creators Economic Survey Report, 2022," Canadian Heritage, 6, 7, 10. https://www.canada.ca/en/canadian-heritage/services/copyright-policy-publications/results-survey-artist-content-creators.html#a4.

cultures and artistic community. Despite differences in politics, social class or the ways in which they defined art or culture specifically, they were united in that one principle.

After half a century of advocacy, the notion of the arts as a key economic generator and a worthy investment for both its tangible and intangible benefits is now ubiquitous in provincial policy discussions, whether they take place among Conservatives, Liberals, or the NDP.[640] The increasingly welcoming environment for artists Newfoundland and Labrador has cultivated in recent years has continued to attract quite a few artists from larger Canadian centres, who not only appreciate the incredible natural landscape and comparatively lower cost of living, but also the bulwark of resources built by both institutions and artists themselves.[641] Going forward, the real challenge may not lie so much in continuing these improvements, but in keeping and maintaining the ground they have thus far gained. All this being said, if I've learned anything during the course of pursuing this study, it's that this province is still a true community in many ways, and if any province's people have the ability to come together and support one another, it's Newfoundland and Labrador. Innumerable people who have at various times called this place home were of immeasurable help to me all throughout my research process. People were as interested in what I was doing and as eager to help as the Newfoundlanders of half a century ago that Dudley Cox described, who always "had time to listen."[642]

***

The CBC continues to employ Canada's artists in accordance with their mandate, but the CBC is not the same experimental public broadcaster that it once was during the 1960s, 1970s, and 1980s. The CBC's approach to

---

640 Bill, 91; Bulman, (2021); Robert Chafe, "If you want to know about arts funding, think of the tiniest slice of pie you've ever seen," *CBC News*, May 10, 2019. https://www.cbc.ca/news/canada/newfoundland-labrador/pov-robert-chafe-arts-nl-funding-1.5102253.

641 Jon Younger, "How Canada's Newfoundland and Labrador Builds an Amazing Creative Community," *Forbes*, April 17, 2022. https://www.forbes.com/sites/jonyounger/2022/04/17/how-canadas-newfoundland-and-labrador-builds-an-amazing-creative-community/?sh=5f13436255e4.

642 Cox, interview.

programming since the 1990s seems to have been more producer-driven than artist-driven. As a result, the opportunities for regional or local artists to obtain employment or exposure with the CBC diminished. During the 1960s, 1970s, and 1980s, the CBC frequently showed openness to experimental local programming, as a public broadcaster arguably should. If a theatre production or musical group became popular locally or received good reviews, the CBC would often show an openness to collaborating with them on original programming. CBC Newfoundland in the 1980s, like most provincial arts infrastructure or policy jobs at the time, was staffed by artists who had been in the thick of the cultural movement. Producers and creators like Glen Tilley and Mac Furlong did impressive work at the CBC during the 1980s. "Those two guys were amazing," Pam Hall recalled.

> The CBC in the eighties was making a larger contribution to cultural practice and creation in this place than the Newfoundland and Labrador Arts Council, than the Canada Council, than anybody else. I think in 1980, they spent over $685,000 commissioning plays, paying musicians, paying writers. I was on the committee that helped push the government to make an arts council, so I've been watching what they've been doing with meagre resources. We have overabundant talent in this place.[643]

It remains to be seen to what extent the CBC will pick up this paradigm again and index more consistently on developing artist-driven content as it exists—and exists quite organically within Canada's cultural community—and collaborate directly with Canadian artists to produce regional or national programming, as a public broadcaster should.

***

Newfoundland and Labrador has long been cognizant of both the tangible and intangible value its arts community contributes to the province, even if its government took quite a while to show its appreciation

643 Hall, interview.

for that fact in a more concrete way. I would encourage both elected and appointed officers of the federal government to take note of what Newfoundlanders and Labradorians already know: Artists add hundreds of millions more dollars to the Canadian economy than it costs to support them. The return on investment is more than generous and what's more, much of that return constitutes money that stays in Canada, nourishes existing businesses, and creates many more jobs. When Chris Brookes canvassed Newfoundland and Labrador's MHAs for support for the artistic community in 1978–79, he warned them of the talent drain that would result from the ongoing exodus of artists and performers to mainland Canada.[644]

For decades now, American movie theatres and television screens have been graced by some of the greatest actors, comedians, and musicians ever to come out of Canada. If we continue as a country to force artists into a choice between poverty or abandoning their vocations, we're going to lose even more talent to markets where they can actually work in the arts. Their work will then nourish and enrich other economies while our arts community continues to decline and some of our officials, eager to cut public programs in favour of private enterprise, will grow even firmer and bolder in their contention that public funding of the arts is a pointless hole to pour money into. We should rather be building up our arts industry as a valuable resource so we can instead address equally challenging concerns facing working Canadian artists today, such as securing more export markets, navigating recent technological developments impacting the arts across disciplines, or addressing the decline of royalties in the face of an almost total corporate takeover of media.

Beyond these more bread and butter issues, I firmly believe that a more intangible but no less important goal—the cultivation of a cohesive healthy society—lies in securing infrastructure and support for the arts and humanities. During the 1960s and 1970s, Memorial University's English, Folklore, and Music departments were well funded and heavily staffed by artists whose academic and artistic efforts were integral to the cultural movement. With its provincial outreach arm of Extension, this institution encouraged experimentation, autonomy, intergenerational partnership, interdisciplinarity, and community development. The loss of Extension in the midst of the bleak economic climate of the

644 Brookes, *A Public Nuisance*, 207–209.

early 1990s seemed to signal a decline in the emphasis on community development as part of the university's mandate and the arts community bitterly resisted it.[645] The 2015 Reid Theatre History Project sought to persuade Memorial University's administration to allow the theatre to operate as both a teaching and learning resource for the university *and* a community resource for the arts as Extension had once done, but unfortunately they did not succeed.[646] As matters currently stand at the time of this writing, the cost of renovating the Reid Theatre for *any* purpose seems to be prohibitive. There has also been talk of turning the old Capitol Theatre in St. John's into a new theatre space of comparable size to the old Little Theatre, which had the advantage of four times the capacity of the Basement Theatre or other small venues, yet half the capacity of the Arts and Culture Centre, which seats a thousand—hardly ideal for smaller and less generously funded productions.[647] This would certainly answer the needs of arts infrastructure, but it does nothing to renew the links and partnership between university and community that the Little Theatre always preserved throughout the years of Extension.

University administrators may not perceive such a responsibility for community partnership as being equal to their mandate of teaching and learning—few universities in North America do these days. In most places, a university is a lofty silo of self-improvement where scholars come to kneel at the altar of knowledge and mastery. These days, they're also heavily corporatized places in which tuition continues to rise out of all affordability, students are nickeled and dimed at every turn and most professors are underpaid with little job security, earning a fifth of what the administrators earn. MUN began and operated for many years as an institution that reached out to the people, fostered closer community, and made everyone partners in their collective development. It only remains to ask what kind of institution both the university and the community would like it to be moving forward.

---

645 Webb, "The Rise and Fall of Memorial University's Extension Service," 84–5, 106–110.

646 Hall, "Report on the Reid Theatre History Project," 1–2.

647 Hall, "Report on the Reid Theatre History Project," 1–2; "Gutted Reid Theatre has a vision, but no funds to make it work," *CBC News*, March 23, 2019. https://www.cbc.ca/news/canada/newfoundland-labrador/mun-theatre-vision-danielle-irvine-1.5068519; "To build, or rebuild—that is the question: Promise of a new mid-sized theatre in St. John's has resurrected talk about MUN's shuttered Reid Theatre," *Saltwire*, May 9, 2023. https://www.saltwire.com/atlantic-canada/news/to-build-or-rebuild-that-is-the-question-promise-of-a-new-mid-sized-theatre-in-st-johns-has-resurrected-talk-about-muns-shuttered-reid-theatre-100851490/.

***

Those in the vanguard of the Newfoundland and Labrador cultural movement articulated a new artistic aesthetic, a national ethos, the beginnings of a common cultural identity, and a vision for the region's future. They helped stimulate and shift public dialogue and perspectives on numerous political, economic, and social issues. The value of artists' contributions to society is undeniable and cannot be encouraged or nurtured without support and emphasis on the arts and humanities, which, in recent years, have been lagging badly in funding, as well as perceived importance and usefulness compared to STEM fields at all levels of education across North America.

As a former history and English teacher, as well as a perennial theatre kid inside, allow me a mere moment to pontificate on the crucial nature of the arts and humanities. They teach us how to imagine and envision, how to think, how to reason, how to argue, how to compromise, and how to reach consensus. They teach us to reflect, to organize perspectives logically and in a manner that is consistent with a given philosophy. More importantly, they give us the ability to definitively challenge enduring philosophical and intellectual frameworks that may no longer be suited to the times, conditions, or cultures in which we exist. Without public investment in the arts and the humanities, who controls our dialogue as a society? Without the impetus to an active, engaged public forum that the arts and humanities provide, do we not place ourselves even more at the mercy of manipulation by political elites and ridiculously overmighty corporate entities?

Tell Your Stories

I can easily forgive you, dear reader, if you've found my tone throughout this volume a bit confused or divided. I have attempted to balance two aspects of my voice in this text: that of the disciplined historian and researcher, as well as that of Ron and Jane's daughter. If I have done my job well, then you can be in no doubt as to why I alternated between these two vantage points. First, I am a historian—at least I'm trying to be. I don't have a PhD. I don't currently work for an academic institution. I've transitioned out of public education and I'm not sure I'll ever go back. I have largely been writing freelance since the onset of the COVID-19 pandemic and doing my own independent research, which I hope to have published. Where, one might ask, does such a person get off calling themselves a historian? I've made precious little income thus far with these efforts, which seems to be the only worthy validation of professional achievement in a capitalist society. Yet, when my insecurity creeps in on me, I seem to hear countless voices of those who came before me with passions of their own saying: "F--k that. Do it with a bold face!" Where did *they* get off calling themselves actors, musicians, writers, directors? With minimal infrastructure to support the arts or to educate or train artists, they nonetheless dared to desecrate the blank page, to stand up, smile, and strut arrogantly across the boards, to alternately inform, inspire, entertain, or good-naturedly berate their audiences, and to tell their stories. As a historian, I hope that I have been disciplined and measured enough to help tell a small piece of that story as fairly and accurately as possible. Yet, I am also Ron and Jane's daughter and trying to write this book with no acknowledgement or exploration of how that influences my perspective felt like an exercise in denial.

As I progressed through this project, I found that I simply could not divorce my own experience from the period and people under analysis. What they created together during the late 1960s and 1970s not only shaped the experiences of the province's artists and the province in general in the decades to follow, but profoundly shaped my own life as well, though I did not know or understand to what extent until recently. The vanguard of that cultural flowering left their marks on me and did a great deal to shape the lens through which I see the world.

At the bottom of my drive to complete this project was a desire to *understand*. To investigate. It involved asking one of the most fundamental questions for any historically minded person: *Why is my life, my world, the way it is?* This question is one I would encourage everyone to ponder as deeply as they're able, and on all levels—the individual, family, community, and broader social level. The benefits of exploring this question extend from individual fulfillment to much broader social utility. A person who understands their own history stands on firmer ground, has a sense of their own identity and place in the world, as well as an indispensable sense of perspective—a cumulative and coherent picture of a span of time and way of life that extends far beyond the individual's own living memory. Such a perspective not only encourages personal actualization, but also perhaps nourishes a sense of purpose, giving individuals the determination to pursue goals as disparate as preservation or change, or simply the desire to do better. A family, community, or broader social unit who understands their own history will invariably function more cohesively thanks to the notion of their shared past, than one with no notion of just what binds them to any of their neighbours.

***

The life of an artist is hard. I certainly wouldn't be the first child of artists to feel that somehow life might have been easier for all of us if Mom and Dad had been dentists or claims adjusters. Growing up watching them struggle to achieve their ambitions or simply to make enough income to support us all was enough to warn me away from pursuing the arts myself in any but the most amateur way. I've paid a high price for this personally because I love few things in life as much as music—singing particularly. I've always loved to sing more than almost anything. My wariness at the thought of a life as an artist, however, does not prevent me from being interested and engaged with the arts nor does it serve to obscure their obvious value.

Historically, artists have invariably been sustained by the seemingly arbitrary whims of rich patrons. Those who lacked the advantages of such paternalistic arrangements had either to freeze and starve or abandon their artistic pursuits. Despite the progress we have made in building up resources for the cultivation and support of art and artists, I'm not sure we yet know how to properly support or reward the majority of our artists for what they actually contribute. In a new, ever-burgeoning and historic age of labour, as workers in many industries all struggle to meet a cost of living that has risen out of all proportion to wages, artists are just one among many professional groups whose workers feel undervalued for the service they provide. Yet still, I would raise my voice particularly loudly in their favour. The labour of artists mirrors and communicates our successes and failures as a society, spurs us into action, changes our discourse and our historical trajectory, and reminds us of the endless beauty and pain alike, which emerge from the life of this world. I believe with all my heart that art changes all the matter it touches. Art moves the world and simultaneously makes it worth living in. Many of us weep and experience genuine grief when a beloved artist dies whose work has touched us, comforted us in difficult moments, or shifted our consciousness. Perhaps we could do more for those struggling artists still living. As Pam Hall so astutely observed: "Art is not made alone."

***

I am very grateful to the narrators who gave generously of their time and their memories by contributing to this book. I am glad that I reached out to them, met them and had the opportunity to listen to their stories when I did. I was deeply saddened to learn, mere months after first meeting them and interviewing them, of the passing of Dudley Cox in December 2022 and Chris Brookes in March 2023. Newfoundland has lost several major figures of the renaissance period in the last couple of years. In October of 2022, John Perlin was laid to rest in his hometown of St. John's. Bryan Hennessey passed just the year before, Kevin Noble just one month after Dudley, and we lost White, Rick Boland, and Denis Parker all in just the first few months of 2024. Talk to your families and the members of your community. Encourage them to tell their stories, and tell your own. Despite the vast ocean of time that a nourished historical perspective implies, individually, we don't really have all that much time. Life is short, but historical memory is long if carefully and lovingly cultivated.

EPILOGUE

"We have to show people themselves,
before they forget who they are."
– Chris Brookes (1976)

Family Reunion

I came home to St. John's again during the spring of 2023 to conduct further archival research. Between visits to the MUN library, the provincial archives, and the homes of various relatives, I dashed off an email to my cousin Heather, letting her know that I was in town for a few weeks and would she like to have lunch? She came back with an extraordinary offer. There was an afternoon party planned at the Delta Hotel that very week for my great-aunt Rita's 103rd birthday, she wrote. Would I come by? I had only met Aunt Rita once before, at Dad's funeral, and I so rarely get the chance to spend time with my Hynes relatives and extended family. "Absolutely!" I replied. "I'll be there!"

My aunts recognized me first, voices instantly rising to the level of shrill as they hugged me. I made my way through a room packed with Hyneses, related cousins and in-laws, meeting several dozen people for the first time. I reconnected with Dad's brothers and sister as well, who invited me along on a day-trip up the Southern Shore to Long Beach, along the very same route I had traced with my sisters six years before to scatter Dad's ashes. Uncle Keith good-naturedly bristled at the fact that I hadn't interviewed him for my book, to which I replied with a sheepish smile, which begged his indulgence: "But it's not really a biography!" By the end of the next day's excursion, however, I assured him that I would not fail to chronicle our day in my epilogue.

The Hynes contingent picked me up at my Airbnb the next morning around eleven o'clock and we started out. I told them all about my odyssey with Rebecca and Lori to find Long Beach and admitted rather shamefacedly that I wasn't sure we'd put the old man in the right river. "Jeez, where'd you put him?" Keith asked me.

"I'll show you," I assured him. "Where's Gordon, by the way?"

"Already down at Long Beach," Keith replied. "Sure, he'll be fishing all day till we get there. He was probably out there by eight o'clock."

We didn't actually get to Long Beach until four-thirty in the afternoon. It turned into a wonderfully slow day. There was construction on the highway, so the drive to reach the Ferryland area took nearly an hour longer than usual. Evelyn and Keith were full of stories in the car, however, and my face and jaw were sore from laughing by the time we all trooped into Aunt Dolores's kitchen. There were hugs and chatter, moose stew, fish and brewis, and blueberry cake. The waistband on my slightly-too-small leggings seemed to be hanging on for dear life. Aunt Evelyn brought out a photo album, opening it to reveal a black-and-white photo of a large family. "That's your great-grandmother, Matilda O'Neill, and her children. That's Mary, your grandmother, the eldest of eight. They were all born in the house at Long Beach." I gazed at all the faces as she named each of Nanny Hynes's brothers and sisters.

Promising we'd stop in again on the way back up the shore, we continued on toward Long Beach. We stopped at the cemetery in Ferryland to pay our respects to Nanny and Papa Hynes. I stood awhile before their shared plot in the cool sunshine, feeling that odd longing and disconnected sorrow I feel every time I visit Ferryland. Truthfully, I only met my father's parents on three or four occasions in my entire life. My uncles led me away to show me the graves of older Hynes ancestors going back to the mid-nineteenth century, which I had never seen before on any previous visit. They moved away, chatting in low voices. I breathed of the enduringly quiet peace of the cemetery, eyes closed for a moment, and the icebergs spread out before me on the vast expanse of ocean blurred a little when I opened them.

As we departed the cemetery, our little caravan split. Half of us headed back to Aunt Dolores's kitchen, while the other half continued south along the highway. When we arrived in Portugal Cove South, my visual memory immediately clicked into gear. *There* was that ridiculously rocky road my poor rental car had resisted so valiantly! There had been no signs posted there in 2017, but there was one quite prominently posted in 2023, which identified the road as a hiking trail. Thank God my folly had known some bounds. As we approached the road that runs along the southern coast, I was surprised to note that what had been a narrow gravel path six years before was now a solidly paved road. As we continued along, I marvelled to Keith at just how much of it had been paved since I had been there last. "Yeah," he responded in a more serious tone of voice than I'd heard him use all day. "More and more tourists and people looking to build cabins are coming out here all the time. Your Uncle Gordon is probably up ahead smashing up the pavement with a shovel as we speak," he added and chuckled, giving me a sideways grin from the driver's seat that reminded me immediately of Dad.

"There!" I exclaimed as we came in sight of the unmistakable little bridge with the river running underneath. "That's where we scattered his ashes." I looked across the road, realizing that sometime in the last six years, someone had posted a sign that read "Bristol Cove." "Oh, you put him in Bristy Cove!" Keith exclaimed in a slightly confused tone. "Yeah, I guess," I replied and explained that our plan to hike north from here had been impeded at the time by a yawning hellscape of brambles and bog. "Long Beach is east of here," he said blankly, "not north." Well, shit. The maps I'd consulted were fairly old, and they in no way lined up with what Google Maps had presented at the time. Lori, Rebecca, and I would only have had to continue along the gravel path another fifteen or twenty minutes to reach Long Beach. Yet, even if we had done so, it seems unlikely we would have been able to confirm for certain that we'd found it. There's a sign posted there now, but I'm quite certain it wouldn't have been there in 2017.

"I feel terrible," I confessed tearfully to Keith. "We put him in the wrong frigging river! I really wanted more than anything to do right by him."

"Oh, I'm sure he wouldn't have minded," he said comfortingly. "Your dad used to catch salmon in that river—quite illegally," Keith added and snorted.

Finally, our car topped a rise and there was Long Beach, spread out below us. With the exception of two or three dispersed cabins, the landscape was spare, rugged, and gorgeous. The grass was long, a tangly mass of green and beige. The wind blew continuously, singing past my ears with a sound somewhere between a whistle and a whisper. The ground was squelchy beneath my feet as I got out of the car and my flimsy little canvas sneakers sank and moistened immediately where I stood. I hardly noticed. The sky was cloudy and impossibly broad and the ocean crashing against the rocks to the south was dull bluish grey. The river that my sisters and I had sought lay several yards west of the foundations that once supported the O'Neill family home. As we approached, we saw Gordon walking towards us from the direction of the river. He greeted us with an upward tilt of his chin.

"How'd you do?" Keith asked him. "Catch anything?"

"Not a thing," Gordon replied with morose disgust and shook his head. He nodded toward me and added, "if your dad were here, he would've caught ten trout by now. He was always lucky like that."

They showed me around the property, pointing out the still-discernible outlines in the grass of Matilda O'Neill's kitchen garden, the outline of an old hayfield. I wandered over to the river and crouched at the edge, trying to see down through the gurgling mass of water running at full spate. The river was a lovely warm brown colour with a wonderfully fresh smell emanating from it. There was no sign among the rocks beneath the surface of the silvery-greenish trout that had stubbornly eluded poor Uncle Gordon all day. I reached down and dipped my fingers into the cold swirling current for a moment.

"Well Dad, I'm here," I said quietly. "I made it. I hope you're resting easy." Only the wind answered and I felt that sting in my nasal passage as I resisted the sudden tears. As I went to rejoin my uncles, I tried not to hear the joyful shouts of children now grown and gone as they splashed and cavorted in the summer sunshine.

Nostalgia, Longing, and the Folk Process

Nostalgia is perhaps far more than a wistful feeling of sentimentality toward the past. Some scholars have theorized that it represents a desperate hope to somehow recapture a world and a life that either no longer exists, or never really existed in the first place. Those unable to reconcile themselves to what can never be realized or redeemed may seek belonging and the recovery of an identity to temper the feeling of rootlessness and loss.[648] I may be guilty of some or all of these (mis)conceptions. The Newfoundland that I perceive continues to challenge me intellectually and emotionally because I know it's not the place that I and others think it is. Of course not all Newfoundlanders are friendly; some are downright unpleasant. The winters last nearly half the year and the climate and landscapes can be harsh and forbidding despite their beauty and grandeur. It's still one of the toughest places in Canada to find a job. Food and energy prices remain among the most prohibitively expensive in the country and housing prices have shot up alarmingly in recent years, especially in St. John's. Fewer and fewer outports are thriving today, or at all resemble what they were during the early- to mid-twentieth century, yet the close-knit working-class culture of the outports in years past seems to have become the official cultural face of Newfoundland—at least as far as the tourism industry with its thriving souvenir trade goes. Following my first attempted excursion to Long Beach, I had woven for myself this narrative of memory and meaning, while ultimately I ended up scattering the old man's ashes in the wrong damned river and later learned from my uncles that those little red foxes, like the one that charmed my sisters and I so much, are as common as dirt down there.

Nonetheless, I seem unable to change my perception of Newfoundland as a fundamentally magical place. As I get older, I feel a deep indefinable pull to spend as much time there as I can and eventually, to "come home" for good. It's hard to verbalize how being there makes me feel, which likely indicates it's not rational and more akin to nostalgia than I'm probably aware. The landscape alone has always struck something nearly atavistic in me. Newfoundland feels utterly eternal, a perennial watcher of the ages and nowhere else on Earth can I summon the belief that there is any kind of continuing consciousness beyond this life.

* * *

I have a few dim memories of my early childhood before we left Newfoundland and of the few years immediately following when we went home a bit more often than we did later in life. These memories

648 Gulliver, 23; Svetlana Boym, *The Future of Nostalgia* (New York: Basic Books, 2001), xiii–xv.

are impossibly rosy: being held in Nanny Mélanie's arms; watching Papa Dixie make bread; going out with Nanny and Rebecca to tend the goats; playing outdoors in snow deep enough to drown in.

Being with Dad during those years was wonderful too; Ron was always great with little kids. They just loved being around him. He was always joking around, getting up and dancing, making up silly songs. He once randomly came into my room while I was on the phone with someone, sat down and without any preamble began playing and singing an off-the-cuff blues song about a guy who buries all of his money with his recently deceased dog to hide it from the government.

I'll never forget our trip to Rainbow Valley in Prince Edward Island. Because it was so hot, we spent most of the day in the waterpark area. I was five years old—exactly the wrong age to do anything there that was at all fun since pretty much all the water slides were for kids six and older, or for kids four or younger. After a few hours of watching me sit on a stone bench in the hot sun while my stepmom Connie, bless her, kept me company and while Rebecca and Lily played in the water, Dad had gotten pissed off enough to start confronting park staff. "She's four!" he began insisting to everyone who tried to bar my entrance to a water slide or pool. "But Dad," I said with artless naivety, "I'm five." He nudged me gently, silently willing me to shut up. "She tells everyone she's five," he said exasperatedly. "She's four!"

It's odd, the tiny and seemingly insignificant things that help you feel warm and loved years later, but looking back, I remember how happy I was when I finally got the chance to play in the water too and how determined Dad was that I should have fun. I held fast to these memories in the years to come. Ron used to record cartoons on VHS tapes from cable TV for us, and we watched them over and over—*Bugs Bunny, Small Fry, The Family Dog*, some of the earliest episodes of *The Simpsons*. I remember how he used to sing virtually every second he was awake, and how no song—whether he had written it or not—was safe from his absurdly hilarious alternate lyrics. I had a sense that good-natured teasing or being teased was one of the highest expressions of affection for Dad, and he could take it as good as he gave. Thus, it never offended or hurt me when he called me "turkey brains," "horse's arse," "donkey's arse," "stunned arse," or "stunned as me hole," whatever combination of animal posteriors and suggestions of idiocy he happened to employ. It was simply hilarious. No one else has ever said my name quite like Dad did either: "Ee-*lay*-na," with a little exhalation of air from between his tongue and right molar on the "L," and a teasing sideways look in his eye.

I hugged these memories to myself for many years, storing them up against the hard years when our relationship became infinitely more distant, difficult, and painful. I won't delve into his years of drug addiction. Ron collaborated with filmmaker William McGillivray and made a whole documentary about it and there was plenty of talk in public forums after Ron's death—the topic is well-covered as far as I'm concerned. Suffice it to say, the drugs dramatically altered his personality and his relationships and not for the better. Throughout roughly a decade and a half, I felt like we were strangers. We did eventually find our way back to a better relationship, but it was far from perfect, as anyone with parents would undoubtedly understand. Dad and I were separated almost from my birth and I was lucky if I saw him once or twice a year and so, weirdly, I knew exactly what Pam Hall had meant when she said she "connected to him more through his music than through any personal encounters."[649] For years, I did too. I could be angry at him, resentful, in a state of non-communication even, but still feel connected to him through his songs.

When I learned to play piano and ukulele, Dad's songs were among the first ones I learned. My admiration for what he did, what he created, served to help me intellectually and emotionally balance the complicated nature of my relationship with him. One of the best days I ever spent with Dad was the day I finally shared that fact with him. It was just a few years before he died, in 2012 or 2013, I think. We hung out all afternoon, drank endless cups of chai tea and just jammed, me on ukulele and he on guitar. I found the courage to explain how I'd managed to continue feeling connected to him all the years we'd been apart with recriminations between us, and I played for him every song of his that I had learned on my own. "Sonny's Dream" "Man of a Thousand Songs," "St. John's Waltz," "30 for 60," "Roy Orbison Came On," "Atlantic Blue," "Away." It didn't take him long to pick up his guitar and join in. We must have played "Piccadilly Sand Farewell" for a solid half an hour. He just kept changing the key at the end of the second verse and then we'd go right back into the first, with Dad changing and enhancing his harmony with each iteration. "That was fabulous, we should do that again," he said as I was putting on my shoes and getting ready to head out. "I

649 Hall, interview.

didn't know you could sing." This statement absolutely blew my mind and I realized that he had known me about as well as I had known him.

It may be that I'm afflicted with both personal and professional nostalgia, casting around blindly and trying to shape the past into some kind of coherent and authentic configuration, trying to invent some sort of reconciliation arc between Dad and I that was never, in fact, so clearly defined. This history I've written, and the narrative of personal experience that I've constructed, may be no more authentic than the "traditional Newfoundland culture" trotted out for summer tourists, a matter of perception and emotion rather than reality. But perhaps the strictest notions of authenticity don't matter so much when it comes to culture, art, or in some cases history, for that matter, since the passage of such artifacts as songs and stories nearly always somehow involves mutation in what Ron once referred to as "the folk process."

The boys in the Wonderful Grand Band learned a great deal of music from Émile Benoît, some of whose fiddle tunes, both original and traditional, were recorded on the band's first album. Ron, Sandy Morris, and Kelly Russell had learned, among several others, two fiddle tunes from Émile, "Piccadilly Sand" and "Farewell's Reel." After recording both tunes, they played the recordings for Émile. "He told us we had them reversed," Sandy remembered. "The song that we thought was 'Piccadilly Sand' was actually 'Farewell's Reel.'" What's more, Ron had written lyrics for the song he thought was "Piccadilly Sand," depicting the sad and inevitable separation of two lovers, and called it "Piccadilly Sand Farewell," while the "Farewell's Reel" actually pertained to a family for whom the song was named—the Farewells.[650]

In the documentary film *Ron Hynes: The Irish Tour*, Ron addressed another example of this "folk process." The Portuguese version of "Sonny's Dream," he said, literally translates to "The Day is Ending." The Portuguese translation had interpreted "Sonny" not as a young man's name, but as the sun. "Sonny don't go away" then became a wish for the sun to remain and forestall the dark of night.[651] Apparently, Rosemary House, the documentary's director had heard this version

650 Morris, interview.

651 *Ron Hynes: The Irish Tour*, directed by Rosemary House, produced by Mary Sexton, Rink Rat Productions, 2000; Joan Sullivan, "Newfoundland musician Ron Hynes was a man of a thousand songs," *The Globe and Mail*, November 23, 2015. https://www.theglobeandmail.com/arts/music/newfoundland-musician-ron-hynes-was-a-man-of-a-thousand-songs/article27445834/.

from a random cab driver who had no idea where Newfoundland was, yet knew the song. Ron said that, through the folk process, "something is lost and something is gained."[652] Whatever is lost, it cannot erase the meaning that is created in the mind of the person who hears the song for the first time and immediately identifies with it. It becomes part of their soul, something to be handed down once again to others in the fullness of time—perhaps a little altered but no less beautiful for being handled by reverent and loving hands.

I claim my own history: I emerged from an exciting and vibrant community of people with a purpose, in a time and place positively pregnant with possibilities. Most of us are who we are because of the experiences of those who birthed us, who came before us. Wherever I belong and whoever I may be, I'm sure it has a good deal to do with what Ron and Jane and their numerous fellow artists created together at the beginning of that blaze of collective self-actualization in Newfoundland and Labrador between 1967 and 1982.

---

652 *Ron Hynes: The Irish Tour*, 2000.

Acknowledgements

Many thanks to all the staff at Breakwater Books for their support, and most especially to my editor, Eva Crocker, for her kindness, hard work, and constructive advice.

I owe a significant debt of gratitude to Archives and Special Collections at Memorial University of Newfoundland's Queen Elizabeth II Library, particularly Colleen Quigley, who gave me access to the unpublished Mummers Troupe and Rising Tide Theatre scripts in their collection, and importantly, twenty-one oral history interviews from the STAGE Project, a massive oral history collection effect spanning roughly three decades thus far under the direction of Dr. Denyse Lynde.

In addition to the STAGE Project, I was also given access to sixteen interviews from the 2015 Reid Theatre History Project,[653] for which I am deeply grateful to Pam Hall—who not only agreed to be interviewed for this study but also generously offered to read and give me feedback on my manuscript.

I am also grateful to Paula French at the City of St. John's Archives for kindly helping me to navigate their collection. The insurance maps and local business directories held by the Archives for the years 1968 through 1979 not only painted a comprehensive picture of existing infrastructure, community resources, and daily life, but were also particularly helpful in tracking the growth of hospitality and service venues, which provided an unintended and de facto infrastructure that supported the local music industry.[654]

I would like to acknowledge the kindness and mentorship of the late Dudley Cox, who was the first narrator I interviewed for this project. Until his passing just six months after our initial interview, Dudley continued to email me with little remembrances about the 1960s and 1970s in Newfoundland and sent me articles he thought I should read. He was also generous enough to give me a copy of his in-progress memoir, "The Rise and Fall of the Newfoundland Travelling Theatre Company: A Stage Too Far." This beautifully written gem of a manuscript remains unpublished and I have therefore directly referenced it as little as possible in this study. However, Dudley's memoir was extraordinarily helpful in confirming the timing and sequence of events, and developments

653 Hall, "Report on the Reid Theatre History Project," 1–51.

654 See Appendix 6.

discussed in other sources. Moreover, it is chock-full of wonderfully funny and charming anecdotes from the period under examination. I sincerely hope that some scholar, biographer, or writer will take up Cox's unfinished manuscript at some point and fittingly amplify the voice of a person who was a true mentor and committed supporter of numerous young Newfoundland artists during the cultural movement.

Many of the photographs in this book were taken and developed by my uncle, Paul Dingle, another incredibly talented and interdisciplinary artist, a concert pianist, and music professor who was also active in Newfoundland's arts community. Paul photographed almost every production in which his sister Jane, my mother, appeared in with the Newfoundland Travelling Theatre Company. His pictures are beautiful artifacts of those productions, and I am very appreciative that he allowed me to use them in this book.

I also wish to express thanks and appreciation to photographers Ron Fitzgerald and Manfred (Mannie) Buchheit. Fitzgerald kindly allowed me to use a few of the photographs he took of Jane Dingle, Beni Malone, and Kent Barrett for their 1975 production of *The Madman's Cabaret*. Buchheit took the gorgeous photograph that appears on the cover of this volume during a promotional shoot for the Wonderful Grand Band in Bauline in 1978. I wish to express to both Fitzgerald and Buchheit my thanks for their permission to use their photos, and my admiration for their long and impressive careers as photographers and artists in Newfoundland and Labrador. Their work mirrors the many changes and developments the province has seen throughout the last half-century.

I would like to express my deep gratitude to the family of the late Kent Barrett. A brilliant photographer and media artist, Kent's work throughout the Newfoundland renaissance managed to capture a great many individuals and moments both significant and memorable. A large proportion of the photographs used to illustrate this history were taken and developed by Kent, whose family very generously permitted me to use them. Kent, a Toronto native, came to Newfoundland in 1974. His own artistic practice throughout his subsequent years in Newfoundland helped chronicle and depict the cultural flowering taking place all around him. It was also a movement in which he himself was deeply involved—not only as a photographer but also as a visual artist—and from time to time, as an actor and writer. I loved Kent very much and have fond memories of him babysitting and playing with my sister and me during our early years in Toronto. I am thus glad and proud to be able to acknowledge and memorialize his work and contributions to the Newfoundland arts community in this volume.

Finally, I want to thank my wonderful family and friends who all encouraged me throughout my journey to become a published historian, especially my beloved husband Richard, without whose support and calm faith in me I could never have completed this book.

Bibliography

Primary Sources:

Boak, Cathryn Jean (Host). "Pathways: Edythe Goodridge." Memorial University of Newfoundland Educational Television Centre, 1984. CITL-MUN Archive Video Collection. Accessed May 17, 2023. https://collections.mun.ca/digital/collection/extension/id/871/rec/1.

Brookes, Chris. *A Public Nuisance: A History of the Mummers Troupe*. St. John's: Institute of Social and Economic Research, 1988.

Carter, Peter, dir. *The Rowdyman*. Starring Gordon Pinsent. Crawley Films, 1972.

CODCO, Series 1, Episode 3: "The Beothucks." CBC Television, 1988.

Companies and Deeds Online (CADO). Government of Newfoundland and Labrador. https://cado.eservices.gov.nl.ca/.

Cox, Dudley. "The Rise and Fall of the Newfoundland Travelling Theatre Company: A Stage Too Far." Unpublished manuscript. 2022.

"Cultural Affairs Division, Department of Culture, Recreation and Youth present Rising Tide Theatre's Production of *So Oft it Chances (The Bond Years: 1898–1919)* by Tom Cahill." May 10–12, 1984. Memorial University of Newfoundland Digital Archives Initiative. https://collections.mun.ca/digital/collection/a_posters/id/421/rec/5.

Dingle, Jane. Interview by Author. Seattle/St. Johns. September 5, 2022 (private collection).

Douglas, Kristen. "Divorce Law in Canada." Publications Canada: Law and Government Division. Revised March 27, 2001. https://publications.gc.ca/Collection-R/LoPBdP/CIR/963-e.htm.

Henderson's St. John's Newfoundland City Directory, 1968, including Mount Pearl. Winnipeg: Henderson Directories Ltd., 1968.

Henderson's St. John's Newfoundland City Directory, 1969, including Mount Pearl. Winnipeg: Henderson Directories Ltd., 1969.

Henderson's St. John's Newfoundland City Directory, 1970, including Mount Pearl. Winnipeg: Henderson Directories Ltd., 1970.

Henderson's St. John's Newfoundland City Directory, 1973, including Mount Pearl. Winnipeg: Henderson Directories Ltd., 1973.

Henderson's St. John's Newfoundland City Directory, 1975, including Mount Pearl. Winnipeg: Henderson Directories Ltd., 1975.

Henderson's St. John's Newfoundland City Directory, 1977, including Mount Pearl. Winnipeg: Henderson Directories Ltd., 1977.

Henderson's St. John's Newfoundland City Directory, 1978–79, including Mount Pearl. Winnipeg: Henderson Directories Ltd., 1978–79.

House, Rosemary, dir. *Ron Hynes: The Irish Tour.* Produced by Mary Sexton. Rink Rat Productions, 2000.

Hynes, Ron. "Back Home on the Island." Originally written for *What's That Got to Do With the Price of Fish?* The Mummers Troupe, 1976.

Hynes, Ron. *Discovery.* Halifax: Audat, 1972. LP.

Hynes, Ron. "The Final Breath." Track 9 on Face to the Gale. EMI Music, 1992.

Insurance Plan of the City of St. John's, Nfld. October 1967, partially revised September 1968. Canadian Underwriters' Association (PDF). City of St. John's Archives. https://www.stjohns.ca/media/bw1fkobw/1967-1969-insurance-map.pdf.

Jones, Michael, dir. *Secret Nation.* Starring Cathy Jones. National Film Board, 1993.

Jones, Michael and Andy, dir. *The Adventure of Faustus Bidgood.* Starring Andy Jones. Faustus Bidgood Productions in association with Newfoundland Independent Filmmakers Cooperative, 1986.

Kellum, Jack, prod. *Ryan's Fancy.* CBC St. Johns. Original airdate: June 5, 1979.

Letter to Jane Dingle from Chris Brookes. December, 1976 (private collection).

"Music, Romance, Wanderlust, and 'a time' for all in Rising Tide Theatre's *Newfoundlanders Away.*" Original theatrical advertisement (private collection).

Pennebaker, D.A., dir. *Monterey Pop.* Leacock-Pennebaker, 1968.

Pittman, Ken, dir. *Finding Mary March.* Starring Andrée Pelletier. Red Ochre Productions in association with CBC, 1988.

R. v. Morgentaler. 1988. Supreme Court of Canada (SCC), 1 SCR 30.

"Rising Tide Theatre Presents: Arthur Miller's 'The Price.'" Original theatrical program (private collection).

Snider, Jamie. "In Pursuit of the Wild Bologna." Track 1 on *In Pursuit of the Wild Bologna.* Quay Records, 1978. LP.

"Stars in the Sky Morning." Presented by Molly Grub Productions, 1978. Original theatrical program (private collection).

"Sun Theatre Presents A Madman's Cabaret." Eastport, July 1–August 15, 1976. Original theatrical program (private collection).

The Bard of Prescott Street. Directed by Chris Brookes. Original theatre script. Memorial University Libraries, Archives and Special Collections, Collection 126, 4.02.

"The Newfoundland Travelling Theatre Company Presents, *See How They Run*, A Comedy by Philip King, Directed by Dudley Cox." Original theatrical program, 1972 (private collection).

Wonderful Grand Band. *Wonderful Grand Band.* Stephenville: Clode Sound, 1978. LP.

Secondary Sources: Books

Bailyn, Bernard. *Atlantic History: Concept and Contours* (e-book version). Cambridge: Harvard University Press, 2005.

Blake, Raymond B. *Canadians at Last: Canada Integrates Newfoundland as a Province.* Toronto: University of Toronto Press, 1994.

Cadigan, Sean. *Newfoundland and Labrador: A History.* Toronto: University of Toronto Press, 2009.

Erlmann, Veit. *Nightsong: Performance, Power, and Practice in South Africa.* Chicago: University of Chicago Press, 1996.

Feldstein, Ruth. *How It Feels to Be Free: Black Women Entertainers and the Civil Rights Movement.* Cambridge: Oxford University Press, 2013.

Filewod, Alan. *Collective Encounters: Documentary Theatre in English Canada.* Toronto: University of Toronto Press, 1987.

Graham, Laura and H. Glenn Penny (eds). *Performing Indigeneity: Global Histories and Contemporary Experiences.* Lincoln: University of Nebraska Press, 2014.

Hegarty, Neil. *Frost – That Was the Life That Was: The Authorised Biography.* London: Random House, 2016.

Iverson, Noel and Ralph Matthews. *Communities in Decline: An Examination of Household Resettlement in Newfoundland.* St. John's: Institute of Social and Economic Research, 1968.

Kealey, Linda (ed). *Pursuing Equality: Historical Perspectives on Women in Newfoundland and Labrador.* St. John's: Institute of Social and Economic Research, 1993.

MacLeod, Roderick. *Montreal: The History of a North American City.* Montreal/Kingston: McGill-Queen's University Press, 2017.

MacKenzie, David. *Inside the Atlantic Triangle: Canada and the Entrance of Newfoundland into Confederation, 1939–1949.* Toronto: University of Toronto Press, 1986.

Malone, Greg. *Don't Tell the Newfoundlanders: The True Story of Newfoundland's Confederation with Canada.* Toronto: Knopf Canada, 2012.

Neary, Peter. *Newfoundland in the North Atlantic World, 1929–1949*. Montreal/Kingston: McGill-Queen's University Press, 1988.

Neary, Peter. *The Political Economy of Newfoundland*. Toronto: Copp Clark, 1973.

Noel, S.J.R. *Politics in Newfoundland*. Toronto: University of Toronto Press, 1971.

Overton, James. *Making a World of Difference: Essays on Tourism, Culture and Development in Newfoundland*. St. John's: Institute of Social and Economic Research, 1996.

Peckford, A. Brian. *The Past in the Present: A Personal Perspective on Newfoundland's Future*. St. John's: Harry Cuff Publications Limited, 1983.

Peters, Helen (ed.) *The Plays of CODCO*. New York: Peter Lang Publishing, 1992.

Pittman, Al. *West Moon*. St. John's: Breakwater Books, 1995.

Rose, Clyde (ed). *Baffles of Wind and Tide*. Portugal Cove, Newfoundland: Breakwater Books, 1973.

Story, G.M., W.J. Kirwin and J.D.A. Widdowson (eds.) *Dictionary of Newfoundland English*. Toronto: University of Toronto Press, 1982.

White, Marian Frances. *The Finest Kind: Voices of Newfoundland and Labrador Women*. St. John's: Creative Publishers, 1992.

Secondary Sources: Articles, Theses, Reports, and Media

"AGNL: Peter Bell." Bibliothèque et Archives Canada. https://epe.lac-bac.gc.ca/100/205/301/ic/cdc/agnl/bell.html.

"Arts and culture funding the focus of letter-writing campaign." *CBC News*. March 22, 2019. https://www.cbc.ca/news/canada/newfoundland-labrador/artsnl-funding-letter-campaign-1.5063927.

"ArtsNL Annual Report 2022–23." Newfoundland and Labrador Arts Council. https://www.gov.nl.ca/tcar/files/ArtsNL2022-23AnnualReport.pdf.

Ash-Milby, Kathleen and Ruth B. Phillips. "Inclusivity or Sovereignty? Native American Arts in the Gallery and the Museum since 1992." *Art Journal* 76, no. 2 (Summer 2017): 10–38.

Bannister, Jerry. "Making History: Cultural Memory in Twentieth-Century Newfoundland." *Newfoundland and Labrador Studies* 18, no. 2 (2002): 175–194.

Bannister, Jerry. "The Politics of Cultural Memory: Themes in the History of Newfoundland and Labrador in Canada, 1972–2003." Royal Commission on Renewing and Strengthening Our Place in Canada (March 2003): 119–165.

Best, Kelly. "Making Cool Things Hot Again: Blackface and Newfoundland Mummering." *Ethnologies* 30, no. 2 (2008): 215–48.

"Bigger than Elvis: Rick Mercer praises Wonderful Grand Band in q interview." *CBC News*. January 15, 2017. https://www.cbc.ca/news/canada/newfoundland-labrador/rick-mercer-tom-power-radio-q-1.3934950.

Bill, Roger. "Culture vs. Policy vs. Culture: The Evolution of Cultural Policy in Newfoundland and Labrador, 1967–2007." *Newfoundland and Labrador Studies* 24, no. 1 (2009): 91–109.

Blake, Raymond B. "The Resettlement of Pushthrough, Newfoundland, in 1969." *Newfoundland and Labrador Studies* 30, no. 2 (2015): 220–245.

Bradbury, Tara. "CDs of '60s Songs." *The Telegram*. March 22, 2017.

Bulman, Andie. "NL Election 2021: The Arts as Renewable Resource." *The Independent*. February 10, 2021. https://theindependent.ca/news/arts/nl-election-2021-the-arts-as-renewable-resource/.

Campbell, Horace G. "Coral Gardens 1963: The Rastafari and Jamaican Independence." *Social and Economic Studies* 63, no. 1 (March 2014): 197–214.

"Canadian Artists and Content Creators Economic Survey Report, 2022." Canadian Heritage. https://www.canada.ca/en/canadian-heritage/services/copyright-policy-publications/results-survey-artist-content-creators.html#a4.

City of St. John's Archives: Streets, Areas, Monuments and Plaques (PDF). July 5, 2021. https://www.stjohns.ca/media/bc5jieoc/city-archives-streets-areas-monuments-and-plaques-2021.pdf.

Cooke, Ryan. "25 years after Harvey Road inferno, St. John's is still nervous about fire." *CBC News*. December 22, 2017. https://www.cbc.ca/news/canada/newfoundland-labrador/harvey-road-fire-25-year-anniversary-downtown-st-johns-1.4461522.

Chafe, Robert. "If you want to know about arts funding, think of the tiniest slice of pie you've ever seen." *CBC News*. May 10, 2019. https://www.cbc.ca/news/canada/newfoundland-labrador/pov-robert-chafe-arts-nl-funding-1.5102253.

Chaulk, Amy. "How Them Days Magazine Has Kept Labrador History Alive." *Inuit Art Quarterly* (June 19, 2024). https://www.inuitartfoundation.org/inuit-art-quarterly/iaq-online/how-them-days-magazine-has-kept-labrador-history-alive.

Clark, Annette. "Newfoundland: Downtown Views." *Canadian Theatre Review* (1984): 116–119.

Devine, Michael. "Necessary Evils: Strangers, Outsiders, and Outports in Newfoundland Drama" (unpublished PhD thesis). University of Toronto, 2006.

"Don Walsh Fonds." Memorial University of Newfoundland Digital Archives Initiative. https://dai.mun.ca/digital/donwalsh/.

Dudemaine, André, Gabrielle Marcoux and Isabelle St-Amand. "Indigenous Cinema and Media in the Americas." *Canadian Journal of Film Studies* 29, no. 1 (Spring 2020): 27–51.

Duncan, Russell. "The Summer of Love and Protest: Transatlantic Counterculture in the 1960s." In *The Transatlantic Sixties: Europe and the United States in the Counterculture Decade*, edited by Grzegorz Kosc, Clara Juncker, Sharon Monteith and Britta Waldschmidt-Nelson. Transcript Verlag, 2013.

Erlewine, Stephen Thomas. "15 Essential Robbie Robertson Songs." *LA Times*. August 9, 2023. https://www.latimes.com/entertainment-arts/music/story/2023-08-09/15-essential-robbie-robertson-band-songs.

Ferry, David. "The Development of Professional Theatre in St. John's, 1967–1982: A Personal Perspective." Revised extracts from a presentation delivered at the conference, 'Shifting Tides: Atlantic Canadian Theatre Yesterday, Today, and Tomorrow,' March 26, 2004.

"Figgy Duff receives small, but enthusiastic response." *The Western Star*. Wednesday April 29, 1981, p. 5. Memorial University of Newfoundland Digital Archives Initiative. https://collections.mun.ca/digital/collection/westernstar/id/171683/rec/2.

Filewod, Alan. "The Mummers Troupe, the Canada Council, and the Production of Theatre History." *Theatre Research in Canada* 19, no. 1 (Fall 1998): 3–34. https://journals.lib.unb.ca/index.php/tric/article/view/7116/8175.

Finlayson, Kenneth. "The 1960s: A Decade of Revolution." *Veritas* 4, no. 4 (2008). https://arsof-history.org/articles/v4n4_1960s_page_1.html.

Fitzgerald, John. "Newfoundland Politics and Confederation Revisited." *Newfoundland Studies* 9, no. 1 (1993): 103–124.

Fitzgerald, John. "'The Difficult Little Island' That 'Must Be Taken In': Canadian Interests in Newfoundland During World War Two." *Newfoundland Quarterly* (Spring 2001): 21–8.

Fox, Margalit. "Amiri Baraka, Polarizing Poet and Playwright, Dies at 79." *The New York Times*. January 9, 2014. https://www.nytimes.com/2014/01/10/arts/amiri-baraka-polarizing-poet-and-playwright-dies-at-79.html.

Genzlinger, Neil. "Myrna Lamb, Feminist Playwright in an Unwelcoming Era, Dies at 87." *The New York Times*. September 22, 2017. https://www.nytimes.com/2017/09/22/theater/myrna-lamb-feminist-playwright-dead-at-87.html.

Graesser, Mark. "Who voted for Confederation? An analysis of voting patterns in the 1948 National Referendum." Presented to the Newfoundland Historical Society Symposium "Encounters with the Wolf," March 20, 1999.

Gulliver, Mekaela. "Preserving the Best: Newfoundland's Cultural Movement, 1965–1983" (unpublished PhD thesis). Memorial University of Newfoundland, 2014.

"Gutted Reid Theatre has a vision, but no funds to make it work." *CBC News*. March 23, 2019. https://www.cbc.ca/news/canada/newfoundland-labrador/mun-theatre-vision-danielle-irvine-1.5068519.

Gwyn, Sandra. "The Newfoundland Renaissance." *Saturday Night* 91, no. 2 (1976). Reprinted in *The Newfoundland Quarterly* 103, no. 3 (Winter 2010/11): 39-54.

Hale, Charles R. "Cultural Politics of Identity in Latin America." *Annual Review of Anthropology* 26 (1997): 567–90.

Hall, Pamela. "Report on the Reid Theatre History Project." Submitted to the Dean of Arts, Memorial University (April 2016): 1–51.

Hartman, Ian C. "Violence, Culture and Resistance: New Directions in the Study of Settler Colonialism and Indigeneity," *American Studies* 55, no. 1 (2016): 133–143.

Higgins, Jenny, writer/ed. "Resettlement." Documentary Video Series (English). Heritage: Newfoundland and Labrador. https://www.youtube.com/watch?v=39SsGU1ooJI.

Hiller, Harry H. "Dependence and independence: Emergent nationalism in Newfoundland." *Ethnic and Racial Studies* 10, no. 3 (1987): 257–275.

Hillier, Bernice. "Confederation anniversary is no cause to celebrate, says Mi'kmaw elder." *CBC News*, April 1, 2024. https://www.cbc.ca/news/canada/newfoundland-labrador/mi-kmaq-confederation-anniversary-newfoundland-1.7158585.

Historical Statistics of Newfoundland and Labrador. Newfoundland Statistics Agency (November 1994). https://www.stats.gov.nl.ca/publications/Historical/PDF/Historical_Statistics_of_Newfoundland_and_Labrador_V2_N7_1994.pdf.

Historical Statistics of Newfoundland and Labrador, Vol II (1). Newfoundland Statistics Agency (July 1977). https://www.stats.gov.nl.ca/publications/Historical/PDF/Historical_Statistics_of_Newfoundland_and_Labrador_V2_N1_1977.pdf.

Historical Statistics of Newfoundland and Labrador, Volume II (3). Newfoundland Statistics Agency (July 1981). https://www.stats.gov.nl.ca/publications/Historical/PDF/Historical_Statistics_of_Newfoundland_and_Labrador_V2_N3_1981.pdf.

"How filmmakers and fishers saved Fogo Island." CBC Radio. Original airdate: December 14, 2017. Posted: July 25, 2018. https://www.cbc.ca/radio/ideas/how-filmmakers-and-fishers-saved-fogo-island-1.4447208.

Igloliorte, Heather, Julie Nagam and Carla Taunton. "Back to the Future: What Nunatsiavut Art History Reveals About Inuit Art in the 21st Century." In *Future Possible: An Art History of Newfoundland and Labrador.* Goose Lane: 2021.

Independent Appointments Commission of Newfoundland and Labrador. Newfoundland and Labrador Arts Council. Department of Tourism, Culture, Arts and Recreation. https://www.exec-abc.gov.nl.ca/public/agency/detail/?id=566&.

"Intangible Cultural Heritage: Mummering & Janneying." Memorial University of Newfoundland. https://www.mun.ca/ich/search-ich-collections/hearts-content/christmas-traditions/mummering-and-janneying/.

Irele, Abiola. "Négritude or Black Cultural Nationalism." *The Journal of Modern African Studies* 3, no. 3 (October 1965): 321–348.

Jackson, Peter, Local Journalism Initiative, PNI Atlantic, "To build, or rebuild—that is the question: Promise of a new mid-sized theatre in St. John's has resurrected talk about MUN's shuttered Reid Theatre." *Saltwire*, May 9, 2023. https://www.saltwire.com/atlantic-canada/news/to-build-or-rebuild-that-is-the-question-promise-of-a-new-mid-sized-theatre-in-st-johns-has-resurrected-talk-about-muns-shuttered-reid-theatre-100851490/.

Jones, Andy. "LSPU Hall—There's nobody can touch us!" *Showtime* 1, no. 1 (Spring 1981): 2.

Kennedy, Alex. "Alan Doyle shares the struggles of pandemic life and his connection to a Ron Hynes classic." *CBC News*. May 11, 2021. https://www.cbc.ca/news/canada/newfoundland-labrador/alan-doyle-back-to-the-harbour-first-listen-1.6017777.

Keough, Sara Beth. "Canada's Cultural Media Policy and Newfoundland Music on the Radio: Local Identities and Global Implications." Unpublished PhD dissertation. University of Tennessee (2007).

Keough, Willeen. "'Good Looks Don't Boil the Pot': Irish-Newfoundland Women as Fish (-Producing) Wives." *Signs* 37, no. 3 (Spring 2012): 536–544.

Langhorst, Caroline. "Grannies From Hell, Daring Bicycle Repairment, Upper-Class Twits and 'Make Tea Not Love': Mony Python's Flying Circus and 1960s British (Popular) Culture." In Kate Egan and Jeffrey Andrew Weinstock (eds.) *And Now for Something Completely Different: Critical Approaches to Monty Python.* Edinburgh University Press, 2020.

Langston, Donna Hightower. "American Indian Women's Activism in the 1960s and 1970s." *Hypatia* 18, no. 2 (Spring, 2003): 114–132.

Ledgard, Chris, prod. "Doctor Who – The Lost Episodes." *Archive on 4,* hosted by Shaun Ley. BBC Radio 4. December 26, 2009. https://www.bbc.co.uk/sounds/play/boopjoy2.

Lemonius, Michele. "'Deviously Ingenious': British Colonialism in Jamaica." *Peace Research* 49, no. 2 (2017): 79–103.

Leo, Geoff, Roxanna Woloshyn and Linda Guerriero. "Who is the real Buffy Sainte-Marie?" *CBC News*. October 27, 2023. https://www.cbc.ca/newsinteractives/features/buffy-sainte-marie.

Liu, Kimberley E. and William A. Fisher. "Canadian physicians' role in contraception from the 19th century to now." *Journal of Obstetrics and Gynaecology Canada* 24, no. 3 (March 2002): 239–244.

Llosa, Mario Vargas. "Latin America from the Inside Out." *Salmagundi* 153/154 (Winter–Spring 2007): 32–41.

MacDonald, David B. and Graham Hudson. "The Genocide Question and Indian Residential Schools in Canada." *Canadian Journal of Political Science* 45, no. 2 (June 2012): 427–449.

MacKenzie, David. "The Indian Act and the Aboriginal Peoples of Newfoundland at the Time of Confederation." *Newfoundland and Labrador Studies* 25, no. 2 (2010): 161–181.

Martin, Cynthia. "Donna Butt: 'That sense of wanting to belong to something is universal.'" *The Globe and Mail*. October 23, 2017. https://www.theglobeandmail.com/report-on-business/careers/management/donna-butt-that-sense-of-wanting-to-belong-to-something-is-universal/article36676794/.

Matthews, Keith. "Historical Fence Building." *The Newfoundland Quarterly* 9, no. 3 (1978): 21–30.

McCann, Phillip. "British Policy and Confederation." *Newfoundland Studies* 14, no. 2 (1998): 155–168.

McLaughlin, Noel and Martin McLoone. "Hybridity and National Musics: The Case of Irish Rock Music." *Popular Music* 19, no. 2 (Apr. 2000): 181–199.

Morgan, Bernice. "The Culture of Place." *Newfoundland Studies* 19, no. 2 (2003): 373–377.

"Music Industry Study & Economic Impact Assessment." MusicNL. Atlantic Canada Opportunities Agency. May 2018. https://musicnl.ca/wp-content/uploads/2021/01/Music-NL-Industry-Study-and-Economic-Impact-V2.pdf.

"Newfoundland and Labrador Arts Council, 2007–2008 Annual Report." Department of Tourism, Culture and Recreation. Government of Newfoundland and Labrador. https://www.assembly.nl.ca/business/electronicdocuments/NLArtsCouncilAnnualReport2007-08.pdf.

"Newfoundland and Labrador Arts Council Annual Report, 2018–19." Department of Tourism, Culture, Industry and Innovation. https://www.gov.nl.ca/tcar/files/AR2018-19-NLAC.pdf.

Newfoundland and Labrador, Department of Finance. Population Projections—Demographic Overview. "Net Migration, Newfoundland and Labrador 1972–2043" (October 2023). https://www.gov.nl.ca/fin/economics/pop-overview/#mig.

Newhook, Susan. "Six Degrees of Film, Social, and Cultural History: The Fogo Island Film Project of 1967 and 'Newfoundland Renaissance.'" *Acadiensis* 39, no. 2 (Summer/Autumn, 2010): 48–69.

O'Dea, Shane. "Culture and Country: The Role of the Arts and Heritage in the Nationalist Revival in Newfoundland." *Newfoundland Studies* 19, no. 2 (2003): 378–386.

O'Dea, Shane. "Oration honouring Edythe Ryan Goodridge." Memorial University of Newfoundland. *Gazette* 31, no. 6 (October 29, 1998): 5. https://dai.mun.ca/PDFs/mun_gazette/MUNGaz_V31No6.pdf.

O'Flaherty, Patrick. "Drawing Conclusions: The Report of the Arts Policy Committee." St. John's: Department of Municipal and Provincial Affairs, 1990.

Overton, James. "A Newfoundland Culture?" *Journal of Canadian Studies* 23, nos. 1 & 2 (Spring/Summer 1988): 5–22.

Overton, James. "Coming Home: Nostalgia and Tourism in Newfoundland." *Acadiensis* 14, no. 1 (Autumn 1984): 84–97.

Overton, James. "Sparking a Cultural Revolution: Joey Smallwood, Farley Mowat, Harold Horwood and Newfoundland's Cultural Renaissance." *Newfoundland Studies* 16, no. 2 (2000): 166–204.

Palmer, Craig T. "Mummers and Real Strangers: The Effect of Diminished Isolation of Newfoundland Christmas House Visiting." *Newfoundland Studies* 8, no. 2 (1992): 125–134.

Peacock, Kenneth. "The Native Songs of Newfoundland." *National Museum of Canada Bulletin* 190 (Ottawa, 1965) and "Songs of the Newfoundland Outports." Vol. 1–3. *National Museum of Man Bulletin* 197 (Ottawa, 1965). *The Canadian Encyclopedia*. https://www.thecanadianencyclopedia.ca/en/article/kenneth-peacock-emc.

Pierson, Stuart. "Medieval Survivals: Reflections on Ron Hynes, *Cryer's Paradise*." *Newfoundland Studies* 13, no. 1 (1996): 30–78.

Pocius, Gerald. "The Mummers Song in Newfoundland: Intellectuals, Revivalists and Cultural Nativism." *Newfoundland Studies* 4, no. 1 (1988): 57-85.

Pope, Sharon Gray and Jane Burnham. "Change Within and Without: The Modern Women's Movement in Newfoundland and Labrador." In Kealey (ed). *Pursuing Equality: Historical Perspectives on Women in Newfoundland and Labrador*. St. John's: Institute of Social and Economic Research, 1993, 163–221.

"Profile: Actress Jane Dingle keeps active with stage, film, television work." *The Newfoundland Herald TV Week*. November 1, 1978, pp. 4–5.

"Release: ArtsNL announces temporary changes to Professional Project Grants Program funding for all 2023." ArtsNL: Newfoundland and Labrador Arts Council, September 13, 2023. https://artsnl.ca/release-artsnl-announces-temporary-changes-to-professional-project-grants-program-funding-for-fall-2023/.

"Return to the Babylon Mall! Mark Critch featured in remake of Wonderful Grand classic." *CBC News*. December 7, 2017. https://www.cbc.ca/news/canada/newfoundland-labrador/babylon-mall-covered-for-avalon-s-50th-s-1.4437039.

Rielly, Terry. "Musical Notes." *Showtime* 1, no. 1 (Spring 1981).

Rompkey, Ronald. "The Idea of Newfoundland and Arts Policy Since Confederation." *Newfoundland Studies* 14, no. 2 (1998): 266–281.

Sullivan, Joan. "Newfoundland musician Ron Hynes was a man of a thousand songs." *The Globe and Mail*. November 23, 2015. https://www.theglobeandmail.com/arts/music/newfoundland-musician-ron-hynes-was-a-man-of-a-thousand-songs/article27445834/.

Suri, Jeremi. "The Rise and Fall of an International Counterculture, 1960–1975." *The American Historical Review* 114, no. 1 (Feb. 2009): 45–68.

Sweers, Britta. "Contemporary British Music Traditions." *The World of Music* 46, no. 1 (2004): 5–10.

"The Canada Council: 21st Annual Report, 1977–78." https://canadacouncil.ca/about/governance/corporate-reports.

"The Canada Council: 22nd Annual Report, 1978–1979." https://canadacouncil.ca/about/governance/corporate-reports.

"The Canada Council: 23rd Annual Report, 1979–1980." https://canadacouncil.ca/about/governance/corporate-reports.

"The Canada Council: 24th Annual Report, 1980–1981." https://canadacouncil.ca/about/governance/corporate-reports.

"The Canada Council: 25th Annual Report, 1981–1982." https://canadacouncil.ca/about/governance/corporate-reports.

"The NFB and Fogo Island, Newfoundland: A Continuing Story." https://www.nfb.ca/film/films-of-fogo-island/.

Tunney, Catharine. "CBC/Radio-Canada to cut 10 per cent of workforce, end some programming as it faces $125M budget shortfall." *CBC News*. December 4, 2023. https://www.cbc.ca/news/politics/cbc-radio-canada-layoffs-budget-1.7048530.

"Two Legendary NL Recording Studios Receive MusicNL Honorary Awards for Industry Builder of the Year." MusicNL Press Release, February 4, 2021. https://musicnl.ca/two-legendary-nl-recording-studios-receive-musicnl-honorary-awards-for-industry-builder-of-he-year/.

Tye, Diane. "At Home and Away: Newfoundland Mummers and the Transformation of Difference." *Material Culture Review* 68 (Fall 2008): 48–57.

Warren, Nagueyalti. "Pan-African Cultural Movements: From Baraka to Karenga." *The Journal of Negro History* 75, no. 1 (Winter–Spring, 1990): 16–28.

Warrick, Paddy. "Review of Ludlow Fair." *Evening Telegram*. January 28, 1981.

Webb, Jeff. "Collapse of Responsible Government, 1929–1934." Politics and Government Bibliography. Heritage: Newfoundland and Labrador (2001). https://www.heritage.nf.ca/articles/politics/collapse-responsible-government.php.

Webb, Jeff. "Confederation, Conspiracy and Choice: A Discussion." *Newfoundland Studies* 14, no. 2 (1998): 169–187.

Webb, Jeff. "The Rise and Fall of Memorial University's Extension Service, 1959–1991." *Newfoundland and Labrador Studies* 29, no. 1 (Spring 2014): 84–116.

Weir, Gail and Colleen Quigley. "John Holmes Papers." Collection 127 (finding aid), Archives and Special Collections. Queen Elizabeth II Library, Memorial University of Newfoundland, 1999.

"What is STAGE?" Memorial University Libraries. https://www.library.mun.ca/stage/.

Widdowson, J.D.A. "Chasing Shadows: Retrieving the Text and Context of the Change Islands, Newfoundland, Mummers' Play." Folk Drama Studies Today, International Traditional Drama Conference (2002): 243–253. https://folkplay.info/files/papers/200207/Widdowson2002.pdf.

Windover, Michael and Hilary Grant. "Chapter Nine: Tuning in to Radio Heritage in Newfoundland." In Tuuli Lähdesmäki, Suzie Thomas and Yujie Zhu (eds.) *Politics of Scale: New Directions in Critical Heritage Studies*. New York: Berghahn Books, 2019.

Younger, Jon. "How Canada's Newfoundland and Labrador Builds an Amazing Creative Community." *Forbes*. April 17, 2022. https://www.forbes.com/sites/jon-younger/2022/04/17/how-canadas-newfoundland-and-labrador-builds-an-amazing-creative-community/?sh=5f13436255e4.

Zwicker, Barrie. "Rochdale: The Ultimate Freedom." *Change in Higher Education* 1, no. 6 (Nov–Dec, 1969): 37–43.

APPENDIX 1:
Oral History Interviews Project (OHI1)

(chronologically by date)

	Code	Narrator	Location	Date
1	OHI1A	Dudley Cox	Seattle, WA/ Vancouver Island, BC	July 21, 2022
2	OHI1B	Chris Brookes	Seattle, WA/ St. John's, NL	July 23, 2022
3	OHI1C	Don Walsh	St. John's, NL	July 27, 2022
4	OHI1D	Pamela Morgan	St. John's, NL	August 3, 2022
5	OHI1E	Shifra Zisman	St. John's, NL/ Toronto, ON	August 4, 2022
6	OHI1F	Andy Jones	St. John's, NL	August 8, 2022
7	OHI1G	Pamela Hall	St. John's, NL	August 9, 2022
8	OHI1H	Kelly Russell	St. John's, NL	August 12, 2022
9	OHI1I	Sandy Morris	St. John's, NL	August 12, 2022
10	OHI1J	Mary Barry	St. John's, NL	August 15, 2022
11	OHI1K	Greg Malone and (Mary) White	St. John's, NL	August 16, 2022
12	OHI1L	Jane Dingle	St. John's, NL	August 23, 2022
13	OHI1M	Bob Joy	Seattle, WA/ New York, NY	September 3, 2022
14	OHI1N	Mary Walsh	Seattle, WA/ St. John's, NL	September 13, 2022
15	OHI1O	Anita Best	Seattle, WA/ Norris Point, NL	December 4, 2022
16	OHI1P	Donna Butt	Seattle, WA/Trinity, NL	December 20, 2022

Note: All interviews conducted, recorded, and transcribed by author. Edited transcripts and accompanying recordings pending donation to the performing arts collection at Memorial University of Newfoundland's Queen Elizabeth II Library, Archives and Special Collections.

APPENDIX 2:
STAGE Project Interview Transcripts

(alphabetically by last name)

	Narrator	Interviewer	Location	Date
1	Anita Best	Mark Callanan	St. John's, NL	August 23, 1999
2	Rick Boland	Craig Stowe	St. John's, NL	Part 1: October 1, 1997 Part 2: October 8, 1997
3	Chris Brookes	Kim Frail	St. John's, NL	Part 1: July 21, 1997 Part 2: August 18, 1997
4	Diane Butt	Kim Frail	Corner Brook, NL	Part 1: February 22, 1995 Part 2: March 15, 1995
5	Donna Butt	Charlie O'Keefe	Trinity, NL	August 20, 2000
6	Dudley Cox	Gail Weir	Port Coquitlam, BC	April 13, 1995
7	Jane Dingle	Alicia Hartley	St. John's, NL	November 16, 2012
8	Bryan Hennessey	Craig Stowe	St. John's, NL	February 2, 1998
9	Andy Jones	Winifred Mellor	St. John's, NL	Part 1: July 5, 1995 Part 2: July 11, 1995 Part 3: July 15, 1995
10	Andy Jones	Alicia Hartley	St. John's, NL	Part 1: October 13, 2011 Part 2: October 18, 2011
11	Robert Joy	Unknown	Unknown	Unknown
12	Ruth Lawrence	Joaquin Gai	St. John's, NL	November 13, 2012
13	Beni Malone	Unknown	St. John's, NL	November 1, 2011
14	Greg Malone	Liam O'Keefe	St. John's, NL	March 20, 2012
15	Rick Mercer	Unknown	St. John's, NL	July 19, 2012
16	Janet Michael	Mark Callanan	St. John's, NL	Part 1: September 28, 1999 Part 2: April 29, 2000
17	Sandy Morris	Unknown	Unknown	June 20, 2013
18	Rhonda Payne	Winifred Mellor	St. John's, NL	Part 1: September 13, 1995 Part 2: September 14, 1995
19	Des Walsh	Liam O'Keefe	St. John's, NL	June 24, 2011
20	Mary Walsh	Lois Brown	St. John's, NL	1988-1991
21	(Mary) White	Danine Farquharson	St. John's, NL	Part 1: August 14, 1996 Part 2: September 23, 1996

Note: All original transcripts are housed at Memorial University of Newfoundland's Queen Elizabeth II Library, Archives and Special Collections.

APPENDIX 3: Reid Theatre History Project Transcripts

(alphabetically by last name)

	Narrator(s)	Interviewer	Location	Date
1	Anita Best	Jacquey Ryan	St. John's, NL	November 9, 2015
2	Sharon Buehler, Tony Chadwick, John Moyes, Magda Moyes and Pat Wright	Jacquey Ryan	St. John's, NL	October 20, 2015
3	Tony Chadwick	Jacquey Ryan	St. John's, NL	October 13, 2015
4	Don Cook	Jacquey Ryan	St. John's, NL	November 25, 2015
5	Danielle Irvine and Gordon Jones	Jacquey Ryan	St. John's, NL	November 27, 2015
6	Andy Jones	Jacquey Ryan	St. John's, NL	October 13, 2015
7	Bob Joy	Jacquey Ryan	St. John's, NL	October 25, 2015
8	Bob Joy and Mary Walsh	Jacquey Ryan	St. John's, NL	October 25, 2015
9	Jillian Keiley	Jacquey Ryan	St. John's, NL	November 9, 2015
10	Denyse Lynde	Jacquey Ryan	St. John's, NL	October 28, 2015
11	Beni Malone	Jacquey Ryan	St. John's, NL	October 16, 2015
12	Greg Malone	Jacquey Ryan	Avondale, NL	October 14, 2015
13	Janet Michael	Jacquey Ryan	St. John's, NL	November 13, 2015
14	Shane O'Dea	Jacquey Ryan	St. John's, NL	October 28, 2015
15	Bob Petrie	Jacquey Ryan	St. John's, NL	October 16, 2015
16	Linda Rimsay	Jacquey Ryan	St. John's, NL	October 19, 2015
17	Jamie Skidmore	Jacquey Ryan	St. John's, NL	November 20, 2015

APPENDIX 4: Oral History Interviews Project 1 (OHI1): Analysis of 17 Narrator Responses

While there was some variation in the interview questions across interviews in Oral History Interviews Project 1, all narrators were asked to discuss the following with regard to the period of study:

- General experiences in the arts community and industry
- Nature and quality of interactions with institutions and bodies (Memorial University, MUN Extension, Canada Council for the Arts, Division of Cultural Affairs, etc.)
- Economic conditions for artists and their ability to make a living

Interview questions were fairly broad and relatively few, but some notable similarities emerged across multiple interviews in the project nonetheless.

More than half stated a motivation, or simply an awareness of such a motivation in others, to specifically pursue cultural reclamation or assert regional pride among Canadian counterparts. Narrators also aligned heavily over the importance of institutions in providing a foundation for their artistic and cultural efforts, yet most also acknowledged the challenges still posed by lack of educational and professional resources for artists at the time. Almost all narrators reported significant difficulties making stable income as artists throughout the study period. More than half reported engaging in collective and interdisciplinary or multidisciplinary professional experiences during the study period.

Narrators' Connection to Newfoundland and Labrador:

Born/raised in rural or outport NL	Born/raised in urban NL	Emigrated to NL (as children)	Emigrated to NL (as adults)
4	8	2	3

Extent of Association with Memorial University or MUN Extension:

Studied at Memorial	Did not study at Memorial	Reported benefiting as artists from resources or assistance from Memorial or MUN Extension
8	9	14

Role of Institutions and Funding Bodies:

Reported receiving grants or seed money	Identified significant problems or insufficiencies with funding/granting bodies	Identified institutional figures and contacts by name, spoke about their impact on the arts (positive or negative)
17	9	12

Economic Experiences:

Referred to difficult economic conditions for artists in general	Reported personal challenges meeting the cost of living as an artist
16	8

Consciousness of a Broader Movement:

Referred specifically to a broad movement characterized by regional pride or cultural reclamation
14

Collective and Multidisciplinary Experiences:

Reported working on collective projects	Reported engaging with more than one artistic discipline professionally
12	12

APPENDIX 5
Oral History Interviews Project 1 (OHI1), STAGE Project, and Reid Theatre History Project: Analysis of Combined Narrator Responses

Consciousness of a Broader Movement (OHI1 and STAGE):

26 Narrator Responses

Referred specifically to a broad movement characterized by regional pride or cultural reclamation
18

Collective and Multidisciplinary Experiences (OHI1 and STAGE):

26 Narrator Responses

Reported working on collective projects	Reported engaging with more than one artistic discipline professionally
19	20

Narrators' Connection to Newfoundland and Labrador (all three projects):

40 Narrator Responses

Born/raised in rural or outport NL[655]	Born/raised in urban NL[656]	Emigrated to NL (as children)	Emigrated to NL (as adults)
13	15	2	11

Association with Memorial University or MUN Extension (all three projects):

40 Narrator Responses

Studied at Memorial	Did not study at Memorial	Reported benefits to artists from resources or assistance from Memorial or MUN Extension
16	24	29

655 This figure includes those who were born in outports/rural areas who later moved to urban areas. As a result, some respondents fall into both categories.

656 Some respondents fall into both categories.

APPENDIX 6
Arts Infrastructure Maps, 1967–1979

Sources and methodology:

The maps in this section were created using a variety of both primary and secondary sources, including academic journal articles, memoirs, and oral history narratives. The construction of the maps depicting Downtown St. John's, St. John's East, and St. John's West/Mount Pearl were heavily reliant on records, directories, and other documents housed in the City of St. John's Archives. These sources include the city's 1968 insurance map, published business and service directories spanning the years 1968 through 1979, and a working document that tracks building and development in St. John's over time through a combination of extant and locally crowd-sourced records and artifacts. The Companies and Deeds Online (CADO) database was also extremely helpful for confirming the existence of sites that were discussed in oral history sources, but were absent from published directories. Please note, these maps are not to scale, nor are they fully complete representations of mid-twentieth-century St. John's. Since the purpose of these maps is to identify and highlight the presence and development of both planned and de facto arts infrastructure, some predominantly residential sections of the city that existed at the time are not depicted, including Pleasantville and the residential streets around Wishing Well Road.

Discussion:

The sites indicated in red on the following four maps represent planned arts infrastructure such as the Arts and Culture Centres, the CBC, artist-run centres, or the sites of annual arts festivals. The sites indicated in green represent de facto arts infrastructure, primarily hospitality and service venues that employed and provided performance space to artists. Each map site is marked with a number that corresponds to an entry in the inventories below.

The *Henderson's* St. John's city directories for the years 1968, 1969, 1973, 1975, 1977, and 1978/79 listed a total of sixty-seven potential live music or other performance venues under the headings "Hotels," "Clubs," "Cocktail Lounges," "Restaurants," and "Taverns." Occasionally, a venue might be listed under a different classification in subsequent years, but their business names and addresses rarely changed, with a few exceptions. Nineteen of these venues were no longer listed in directories by 1978/79. Roughly half of these disappeared from directories between 1975 and 1977, leaving a total of forty-eight such establishments in the St. John's/Mount Pearl area. However, an important consideration is that these directories would have only listed businesses that voluntarily provided their information for listing and paid the required fees. Thus, it seems very likely that there were numerous other similar venues in operation throughout the period.

Oral history narratives and digitized business records were helpful in providing additional insight beyond published business directories. Some oral history sources from OHI1 and from the STAGE Project identified additional venues not listed in directories, the existence of some of which I was able to confirm using the CADO database. With the addition of nine such unlisted establishments, this brings the total number of de facto arts infrastructure venues to fifty-seven. Again, it is very likely that there were any number of others operating in the area, but even if there were not, this final figure seems a generous one for both patrons and potential artists in a city that still had a population of less than 100,000 people by 1979.[657]

Interestingly, Ron Hynes's broadside ballad, "Who Burned All the Bars?" written for *The Bard of Prescott Street*, was also a useful source. Most of the bars Hynes mentioned as having burned down in the song disappeared from business directories between 1975 and 1977 including the "Circle," the "Belmont," the "Pic," and the "Tudor." In fact, the majority of hospitality venue closures seem to have occurred between 1975 and 1977—ten of them. Was this a sign of an increasingly tight

657 "Historical Statistics of Newfoundland and Labrador," Vol II (VII), November 1994: 16. https://www.stats.gov.nl.ca/publications/Historical/PDF/Historical_Statistics_of_Newfoundland_and_Labrador_V2_N7_1994.pdf.

economic climate or did some of these bars burn too? Hynes's song also mentioned "The Dory" and "Donovan's Country Club," both of which were unlisted in directories but confirmed in the CADO database. Unfortunately, we do not know the addresses for several of these unlisted venues because digital CADO records listed only incorporation dates for some entries.

Map Inventories

Map 1: Newfoundland and Labrador, 1967–1982[658]

Red sites:

1) Corner Brook Arts and Culture Centre
2) Clode Sound (Stephenville)
3) Eastport Theatre Festival
4) Gander Arts and Culture Centre
5) Grand Falls Arts and Culture Centre
6) Newfoundland and Labrador Arts Council
7) Stephenville Arts and Culture Centre
8) St. Michael's Printshop

Map 2: Downtown St. John's, 1967–1979

Red sites:

1) 77 Bond St.
2) Annual Folk Festival (St. John's Folk Arts Council) —Bannerman Park
3) Bishop Feild Auditorium—44 Bond St.
4) Canadian Broadcasting Corporation (CBC Radio) —324 Duckworth St.
5) Echo Music—Long's Hill

658 Please note, the annual Dominion Drama Festival is omitted because it was hosted in a different city each year.

6) Holy Heart Theatre—55 Bonaventure Ave.
7) LSPU Hall—3 Victoria St.
8) NIFCO (Newfoundland Independent Filmmakers Co-op) —40 King's Rd.
9) Pitts Memorial Hall—20 Long's Hill

Green sites:

10) Belmont Tavern—162 New Gower St.[659]
11) Bridgett's Club—29 Cookstown Rd.
12) Campenn Inn Tavern / Sting Lounge—203 Duckworth St.[660]
13) Capitol Lounge—302 Water St.
14) Capitol Cocktail Lounge—184 Water St.
15) City Club—189 Water St.[661]
16) City Tavern—5 Queen St.
17) Cochrane Hotel—47 Cochrane St.
18) Continental Lounge / Horse Shoe Club—373 Duckworth St.[662]
19) Corner Club—82 Hayward Ave.
20) Cottage Gardens Ltd.—34 Freshwater Rd.
21) Dirty Dick's / The Ship Inn—265 Duckworth St.[663]
22) Donovan's Country Club—address unknown[664]

---

659 First listed in 1968 directory and no longer listed as of 1977. Also mentioned in "Who Burned All the Bars?" and thus presumably burned down during the 1975/1976 period.

660 Campenn Inn Tavern listed in 1968, but disappears in 1975 directory, at which time, Sting Lounge is first listed at this address.

661 Listed in 1968 directory. No longer listed as of 1977.

662 Horse Shoe Club listed in 1968. Continental Lounge listed at this address as of 1975 and Horse Shoe Club no longer listed as of 1977.

663 While this venue is unlisted, Rhonda Payne mentioned it in her first STAGE Project interview. Payne recalled that she had seen Ron Hynes and Peter Narváez play at Dick's many times when it was still a rock 'n' roll bar. She also recalled that it had burned down in 1974 and that The Ship Inn had risen in its place. Additionally, Ron's song, "Who Burned All the Bars?" seems to reference it although he places the burnings in "the winter of '75." "Some say 'twas the owners, an insurance trick, or a great dirty scheme that toked up at Dick's."

664 Mentioned in the song "Who Burned All the Bars?" Also listed on the CADO database with no address and no "dissolved" date, but an incorporation date of 1974. Presumably, it burned down the following year.

23) East End Club / Jim's Tavern—110 Water St.[665]

24) El Tico Nite Club / Embassy Dining Room and Lounge —208 Water St.[666]

25) Esquire Lounge—392 Water St.

26) Finnegan's Pub—53 Harvey Rd.

27) Fogo-A-Go-Go / Seabreeze Lounge—Baird's Cove[667]

28) Freddie Michael's—51 Cochrane St.[668]

29) Georgetown Realty Co.—80 Hayward Ave.[669]

30) Gosse's Tavern—53 New Gower St.

31) Hamilton Inn—16 Hamilton Ave.

32) Happy Jack's—address unknown[670]

33) Harbour Inn Tavern—69 Duckworth St.

34) Hillview Inn Club—148 Duckworth St.

35) Irish Club—48 Queen's Rd.

36) Key Club—446 Water St.

37) Killick Lounge—Cavendish Sq.

38) Laurier Club / Press Club / Meadow Acres Lounge —301 Hamilton Ave.[671]

39) Moondust Club—2 Bates Hill[672]

---

665 Jim's Tavern listed in 1968 directory and no longer listed in 1970, when East End Club first appears at this address.

666 El Tico Nite Club listed in all directories consulted from 1968 through 1979, yet Embassy Dining Room and Lounge also appears at the same address in the 1973 directory—a shared building perhaps? Embassy no longer listed as of 1977.

667 Directory first lists Fogo-A-Go-Go in 1975, but lists Seabreeze Lounge at this address by 1977. CADO database confirms that company name was changed from Fogo-A-Go-Go Limited in 1975.

668 Unlisted in any directories or business records, but mentioned in Don Walsh's interview for OHI1 as well as in Rhonda Payne's first STAGE Project interview. Payne knew the address because she lived above the bar in 1974, next door to actor Rick Boland who, at the time, lived above the Royalton at 49 Cochrane St.

669 Listed in 1968 directory. No longer listed as of 1975.

670 Unlisted, but mentioned in Dudley Cox's memoir as having been located on Duckworth Street, "near the war memorial."

671 Laurier Club listed in 1969 directory and no longer listed as of 1978/79. Press Club appears at this address in the 1977 directory and Meadow Acres Lounge appears at the same address in 1978/79. Did the latter two share a building perhaps? Or did Press Club simply close down?

672 Listed in 1970. No longer listed as of 1977.

40) Paddy's Inn / Porthole Lounge—456 Water St.[673]
41) Park View Tavern—643 Water St.
42) Pillar Lounge / Upper Deck Lounge—208 Water St.[674]
43) Ringside Tavern—125 Queen's Rd.
44) Riviera Tavern—448 Water St.
45) Royalton Club—49 Cochrane St.
46) Stardust Lounge—96 Water St.[675]
47) Starrigan Club—address unknown[676]
48) Sterling Tavern—Holdsworth St.
49) Strand Lounge—Atlantic Place[677]
50) Tai Mee Club—5 Bates Hill[678]
51) The Dory—address unknown[679]
52) The Void—Harvey Rd.[680]
53) Terra Nova Lounge—260 Duckworth St.
54) Tudor Inn—King's Beach[681]
55) Waterfront Club / King's Head Club—161 Water St.[682]
56) West End Tavern—719 Water St.
57) United Nail and Foundry (U.N.F.) Employees Club—151 Pleasant St.[683]

---

673 Porthole Lounge listed in 1968 directory and no longer listed as of 1973. Paddy's Inn is listed at this address in the 1975 directory.

674 Both the Pillar Lounge and the Upper Deck Lounge were first listed in the 1978/79 directory at the same address—a shared building perhaps? Note also that El Tico Nite Club (or variously El Tico Lounge) is also still listed at this address in 1978/79.

675 Listed in 1969 directory. No longer listed as of 1978/79.

676 Location unknown but likely a downtown venue. Mentioned in White's second STAGE Project interview and also listed on CADO database—incorporated 1979.

677 One of three Strand Lounges that appeared in St. John's during this period.

678 Listed in 1968 directory. No longer listed as of 1977.

679 Mentioned in Ron's song "Who Burned All the Bars." Also listed on CADO database but with no address, only an incorporation date of 1974—presumably burned down the following year.

680 Confirmed in the oral history interviews of Don Walsh, Sandy Morris, and Mary Barry (OHI1), all of whom stated that it was located in an alley between the C.L.B. Armoury and a Dominion Supermarket on Harvey Rd.

681 Listed in 1968 directory. No longer listed as of 1977. Mentioned in "Who Burned All the Bars?"

682 Waterfront Club listed in 1970 directory. No longer listed as of 1978/79, at which point the King's Head Club is listed at this address.

683 Listed in 1968 directory and no longer listed as of 1977. Also mentioned in Dudley Cox's memoir as a bar open to any and all patrons, not just U.N.F. employees.

Map 3: St. John's West/Mount Pearl, 1968–1979

Red sites:

1) Breakwater Books—1 Stamp's Lane[684]

Green sites:

2) Centennial Lounge—38 Bannister St.[685]
3) Jerry's Hi-Way Club—Topsail Rd.
4) New Piccadilly Club—Topsail Rd.[686]
5) Old Mill Nite Club—Brookfield Rd.[687]
6) Strand Lounge—Village Mall[688]
7) The Limit—Topsail Rd.[689]
8) The Zodiac—Topsail Rd.[690]

Map 4: St. John's East, 1968–1979

Red sites:

1) Canadian Broadcasting Corporation (CBC Television) St. John's —Prince Philip Dr. (at Westerland Rd.)
2) MUN Little Theatre—230 Elizabeth Ave.
3) St. John's Arts and Culture Centre (also housed the Basement Theatre and the Memorial University Art Gallery) —95 Allandale Rd.

684 Established 1973.

685 First listed in 1977.

686 Listed in 1973 and no longer listed as of 1977. I believe that Ron Hynes's mention of "The Pic" in "Who Burned All the Bars?" refers to this establishment.

687 Listed in 1968 directory. No longer listed as of 1977.

688 There are two other Strand Lounges listed in the directory (Avalon Mall and Atlantic Place). This location is unlisted, but mentioned in Don Walsh's interview (OHI1).

689 First listed in 1978/79.

690 Listed in 1977, but no longer listed as of 1978/79. It's possible "The Limit" replaced "The Zodiac."

Green sites:

4) Café Y (housed in YMCA)—New Cove Rd. (at King's Bridge Rd.)[691]
5) Circle Lounge—13 Rowan St.[692]
6) Club Commodore—Torbay Rd.
7) Four Aces Lounge—Torbay Rd.
8) Golden Stein Lounge—Airport Rd.
9) Old Colony Club—64 Portugal Cove Rd.
10) Runway Lounge—Airport Rd.
11) Schooner Lounge—Torbay Rd.
12) Strand Lounge—Avalon Mall
13) The Hideaway—Airport Rd.

691 Unlisted in any documentary sources but mentioned in Malone and White's interview (OHI1) as being housed in the YMCA, which, according the 1968 Henderson's directory, was located at the corner of New Cove Rd. and King's Bridge Rd.

692 First listed in 1970. No longer listed as of 1977. Mentioned in the song "Who Burned All the Bars?" as having burned down.

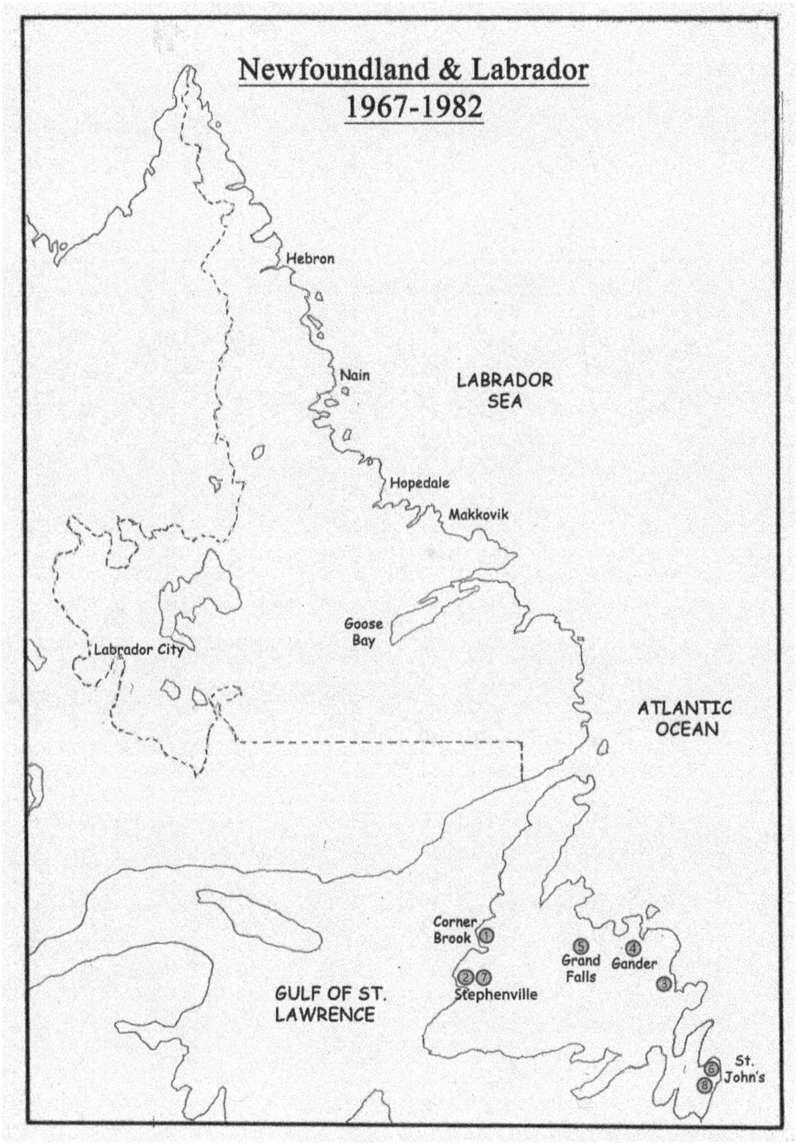

Map I.[693]

693 Map by E.G. Hynes, 2023–2024.

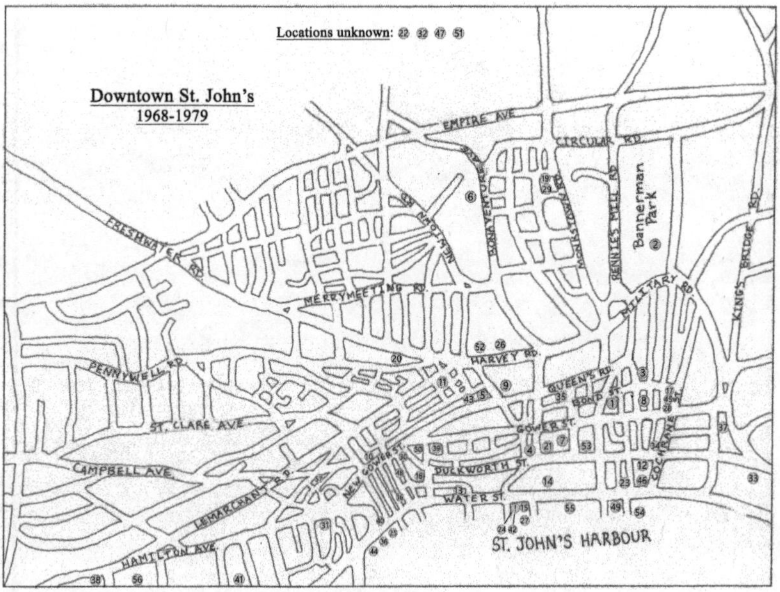

Map II.[694]

694 Map by E.G. Hynes, 2023–2024.

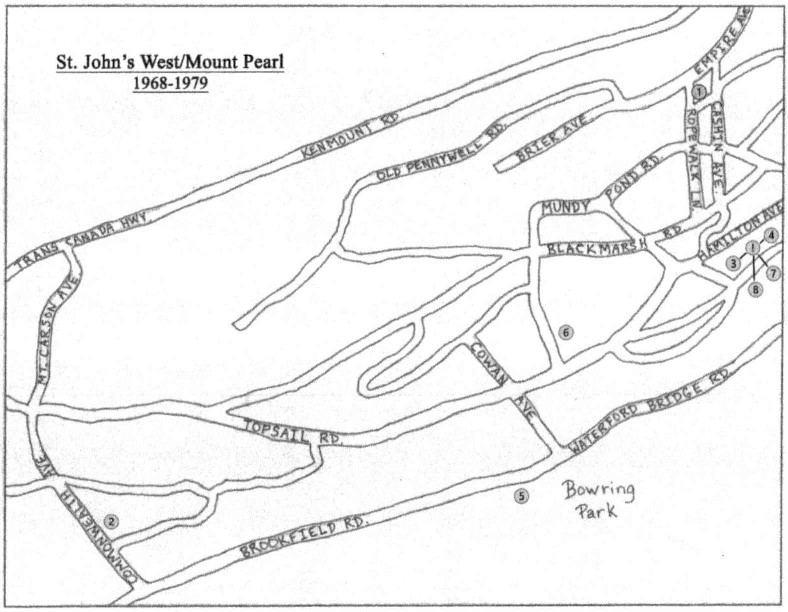

Map III.[695]

695 Map by E.G. Hynes, 2023–2024.

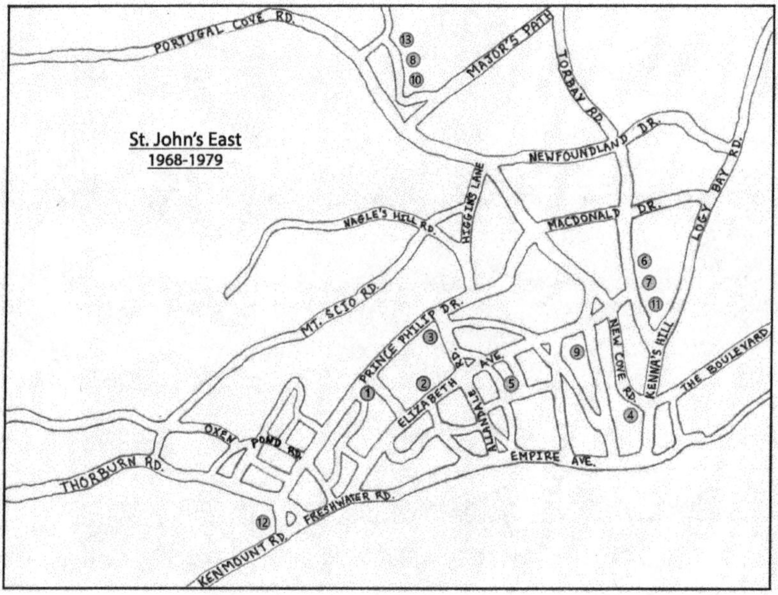

Map IV.[696]

696 Map by E.G. Hynes, 2023-2024.